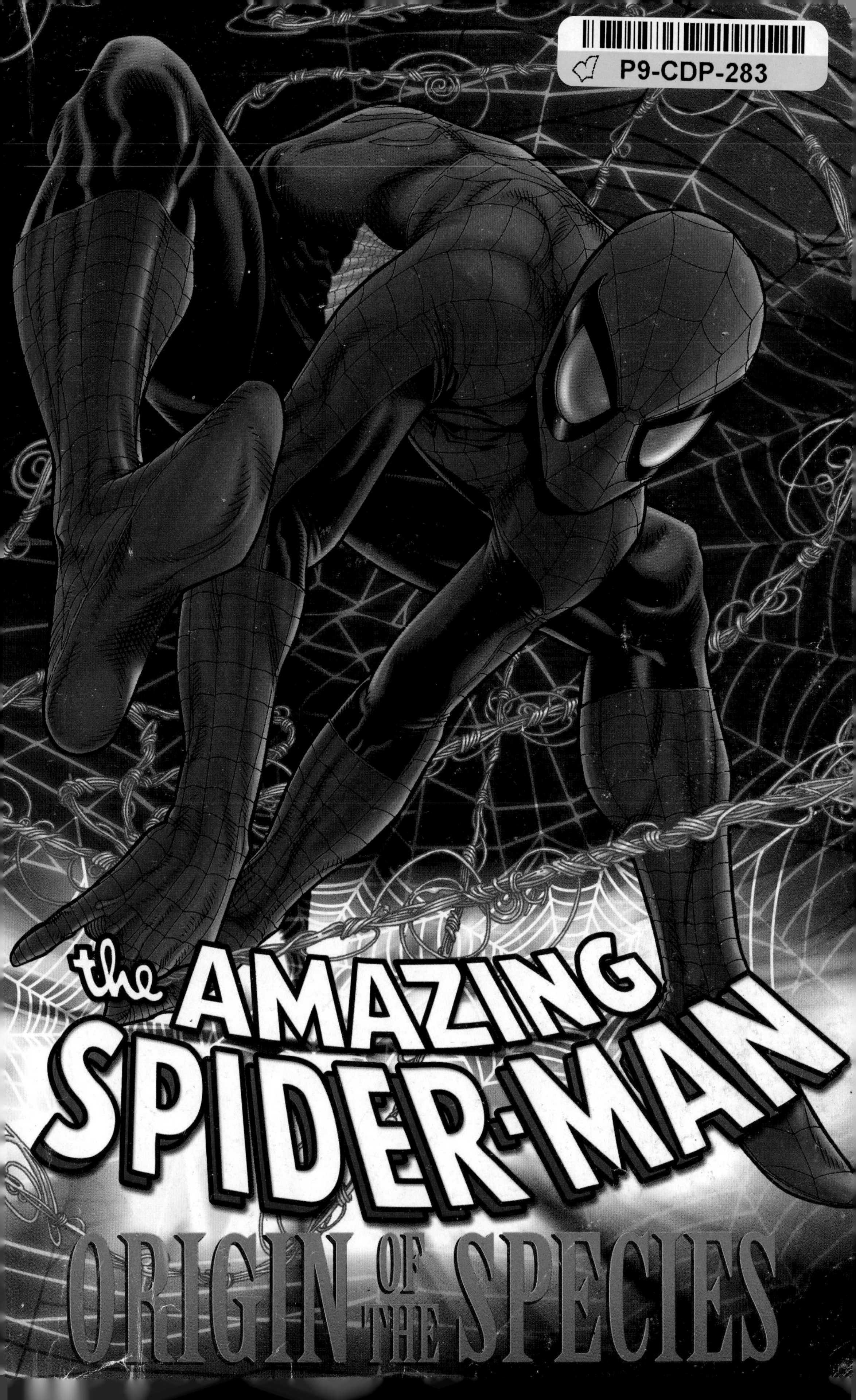
the AMAZING
SPIDER-MAN
ORIGIN OF THE SPECIES

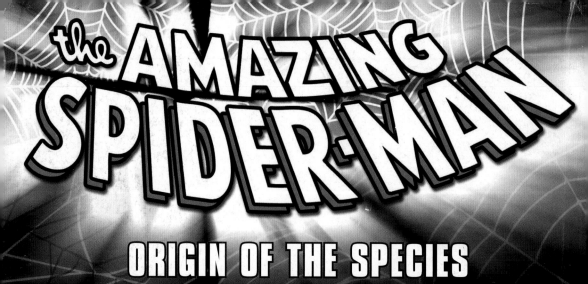

the AMAZING SPIDER-MAN

ORIGIN OF THE SPECIES

ISSUES #642-646
Writer: **MARK WAID**
Artist: **PAUL AZACETA** WITH **MATTHEW SOUTHWORTH** (ISSUES #645-646)
Colorist: **JAVIER RODRIGUEZ**
Letterer: **VC'S JOE CARAMAGNA**
Cover Art: **MARKO DJURDJEVIC**

"ARMS AGAINST A SEA OF TROUBLES"
Writer: **ROGER STERN**
Artist: **PHILIPPE BRIONES**
Colorist: **CHRIS SOTOMAYOR**
Letterer: **DAVE SHARPE**
Cover Art: **JELENA KEVIC DJURDJEVIC**

ISSUE #647
Writers: **FRED VAN LENTE, ZEB WELLS, BOB GALE, JOE KELLY,
MARK WAID, MARC GUGGENHEIM & DAN SLOTT**
Artists: **MAX FIUMARA, MICHAEL DEL MUNDO, KARL KESEL,
J.M. KEN NIIMURA, PAUL AZACETA, GRAHAM NOLAN &
MARK PENNINGTON** AND **ADAM ARCHER**
Colorists: **MORRY HOLLOWELL, MICHAEL DEL MUNDO, ANTONIA FABELA &
J.M. KEN NIIMURA**
Letterers: **VC'S JOE CARAMAGNA & J.M. KEN NIIMURA**
Cover Art: **MARKO DJURDJEVIC**

Web-Heads: **BOB GALE, JOE KELLY, DAN SLOTT, FRED VAN LENTE, MARK WAID & ZEB WELLS**
Assistant Editor: **THOMAS BRENNAN** • Editor: **STEPHEN WACKER** • Executive Editor: **TOM BREVOORT**

Collection Editor: **JENNIFER GRÜNWALD** • Editorial Assistants: **JAMES EMMETT & JOE HOCHSTEIN**
Assistant Editors: **ALEX STARBUCK & NELSON RIBEIRO** • Editor, Special Projects: **MARK D. BEAZLEY**
Senior Editor, Special Projects: **JEFF YOUNGQUIST** • Senior Vice President of Sales: **DAVID GABRIEL**

Editor in Chief: **JOE QUESADA** • Publisher: **DAN BUCKLEY** • Executive Producer: **ALAN FINE**

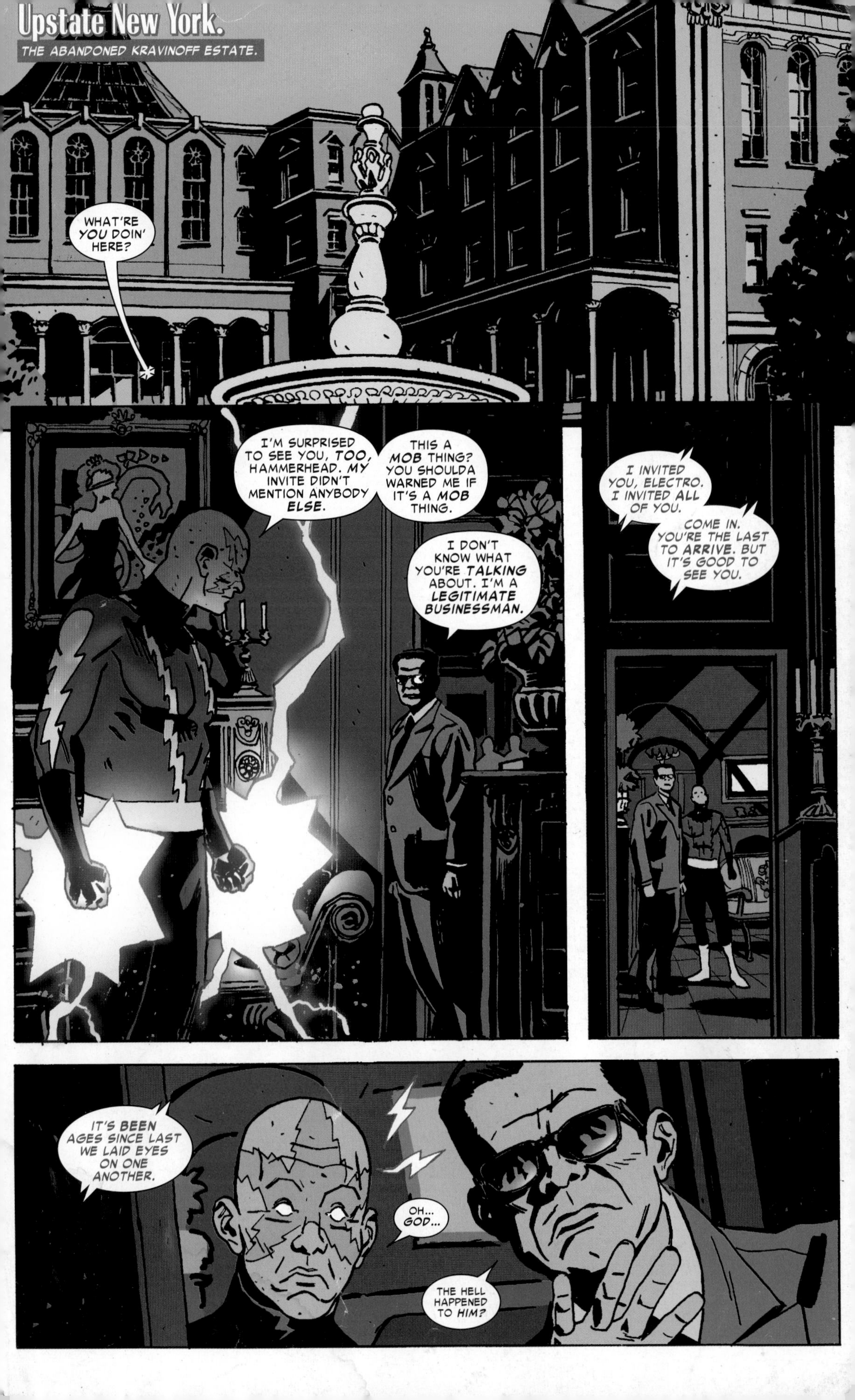
Upstate New York.
THE ABANDONED KRAVINOFF ESTATE.
WHAT'RE YOU DOIN' HERE?
I'M SURPRISED TO SEE YOU, TOO, HAMMERHEAD. MY INVITE DIDN'T MENTION ANYBODY ELSE.
THIS A MOB THING? YOU SHOULDA WARNED ME IF IT'S A MOB THING.
I DON'T KNOW WHAT YOU'RE TALKING ABOUT. I'M A LEGITIMATE BUSINESSMAN.
I INVITED YOU, ELECTRO. I INVITED ALL OF YOU.
COME IN. YOU'RE THE LAST TO ARRIVE. BUT IT'S GOOD TO SEE YOU.
IT'S BEEN AGES SINCE LAST WE LAID EYES ON ONE ANOTHER.
OH... GOD...
THE HELL HAPPENED TO HIM?

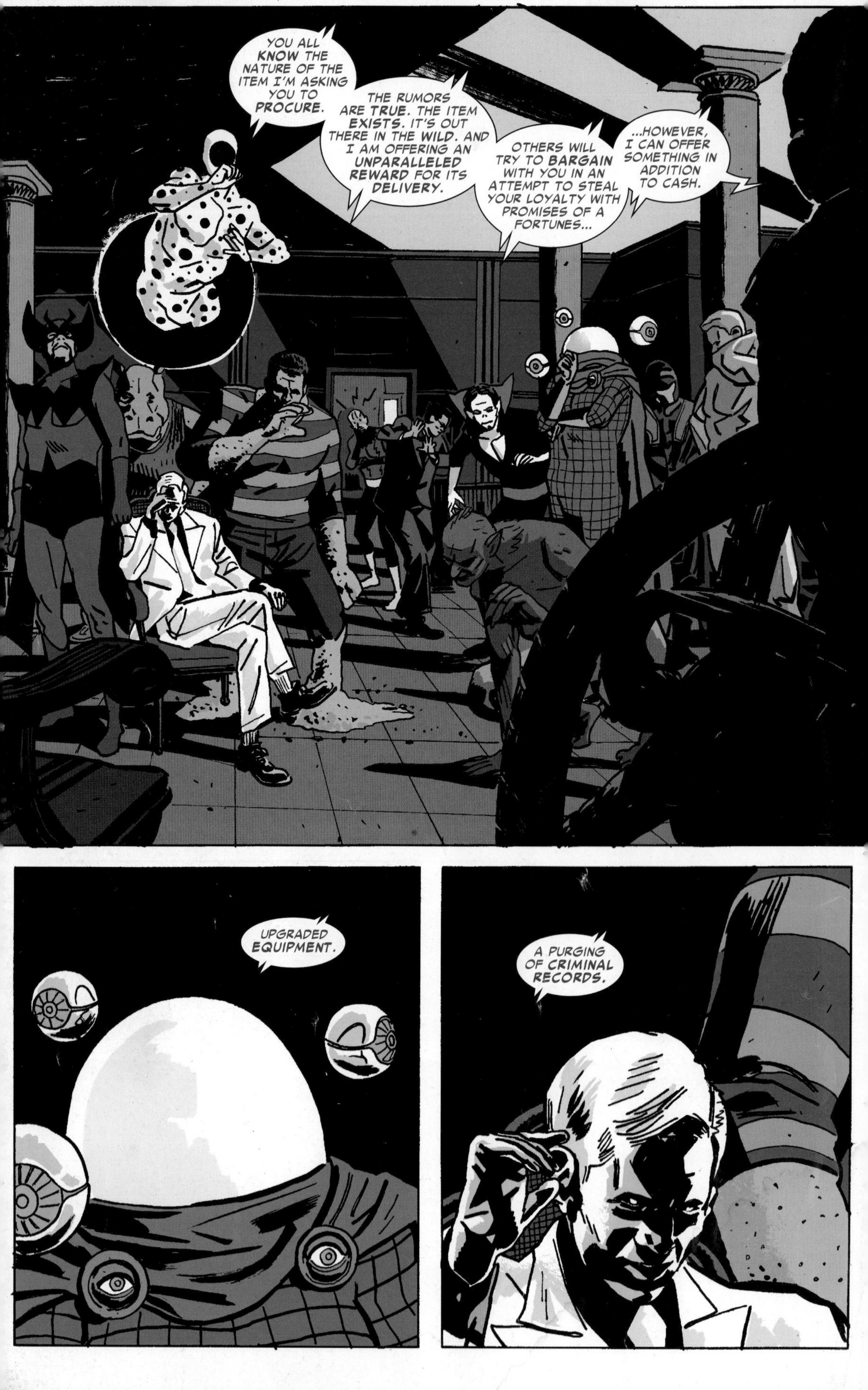
YOU ALL KNOW THE NATURE OF THE ITEM I'M ASKING YOU TO PROCURE.
THE RUMORS ARE TRUE. THE ITEM EXISTS. IT'S OUT THERE IN THE WILD. AND I AM OFFERING AN UNPARALLELED REWARD FOR ITS DELIVERY.
OTHERS WILL TRY TO BARGAIN WITH YOU IN AN ATTEMPT TO STEAL YOUR LOYALTY WITH PROMISES OF A FORTUNES...
...HOWEVER, I CAN OFFER SOMETHING IN ADDITION TO CASH.
UPGRADED EQUIPMENT.
A PURGING OF CRIMINAL RECORDS.

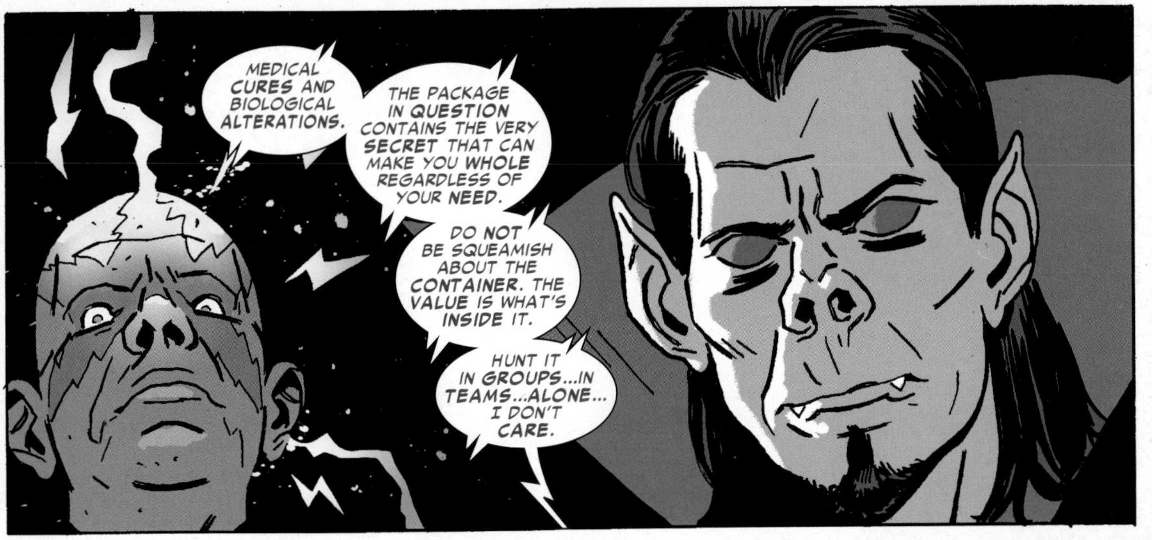
MEDICAL CURES AND BIOLOGICAL ALTERATIONS.
THE PACKAGE IN QUESTION CONTAINS THE VERY SECRET THAT CAN MAKE YOU WHOLE REGARDLESS OF YOUR NEED.
DO NOT BE SQUEAMISH ABOUT THE CONTAINER. THE VALUE IS WHAT'S INSIDE IT.
HUNT IT IN GROUPS...IN TEAMS...ALONE... I DON'T CARE.

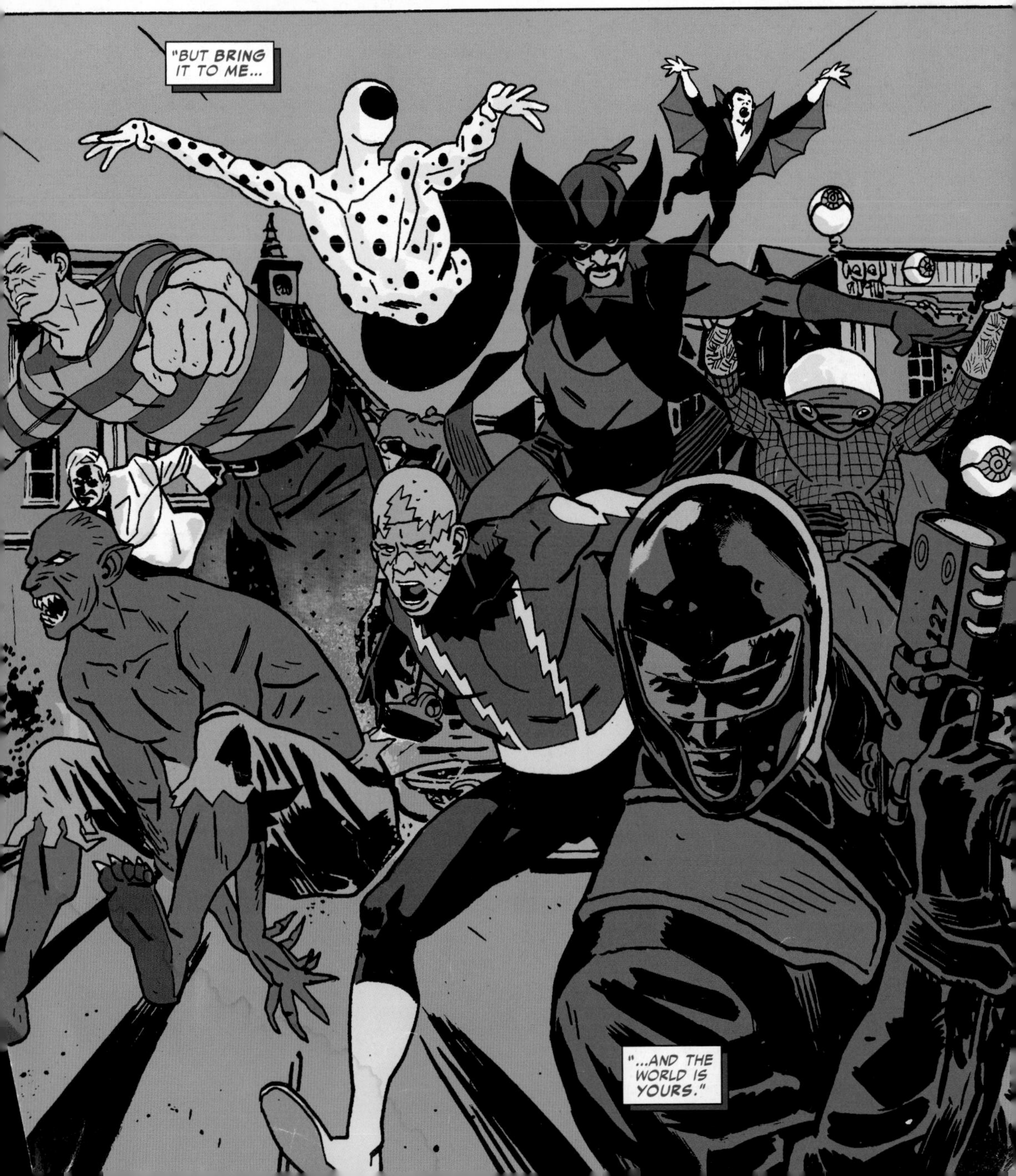
"BUT BRING IT TO ME...
"...AND THE WORLD IS YOURS."

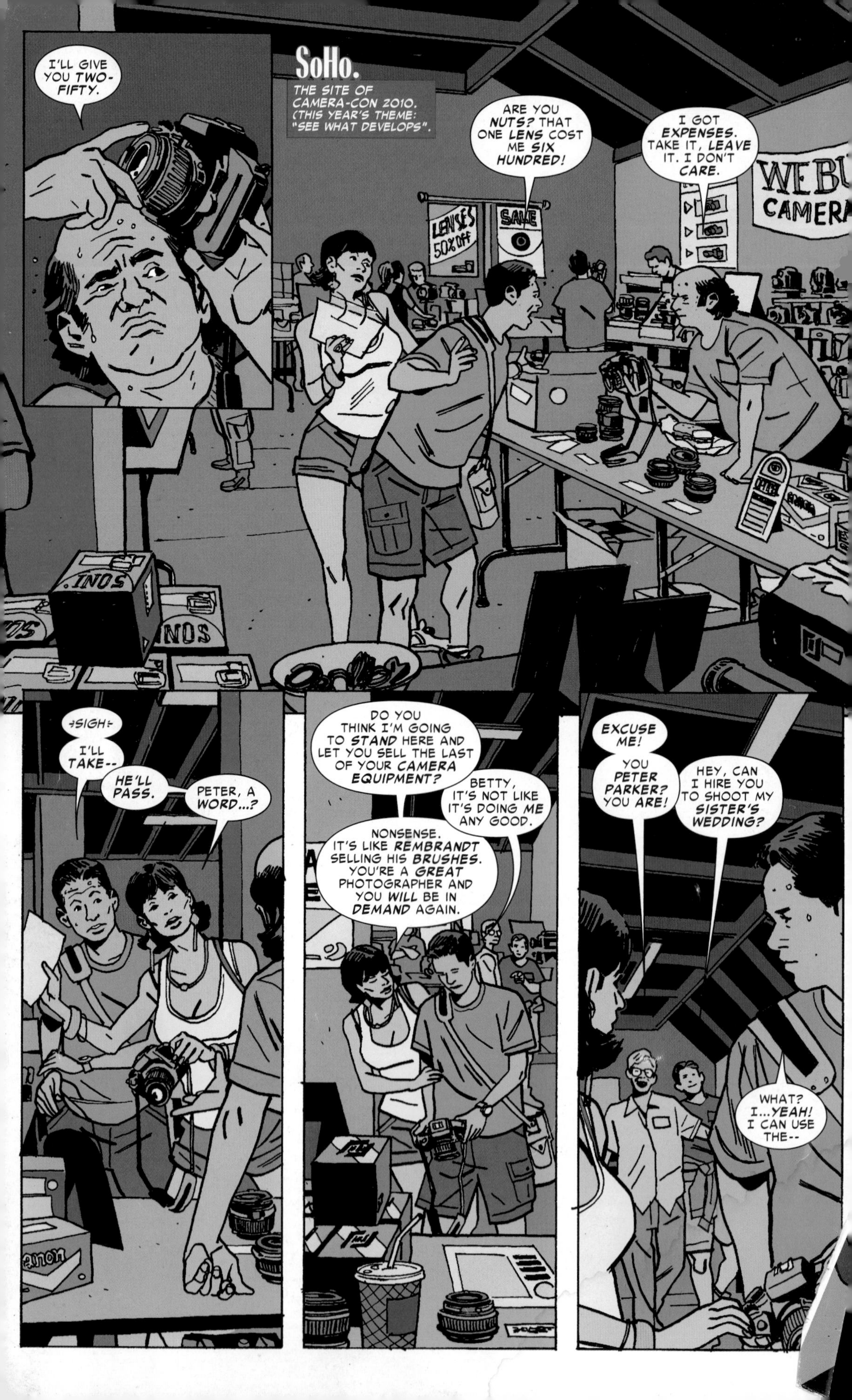
I'LL GIVE YOU TWO-FIFTY.
SoHo.
THE SITE OF CAMERA-CON 2010. (THIS YEAR'S THEME: "SEE WHAT DEVELOPS".
ARE YOU NUTS? THAT ONE LENS COST ME SIX HUNDRED!
I GOT EXPENSES. TAKE IT, LEAVE IT. I DON'T CARE.
WE BU
CAMERA
LENSES 50% OFF
SALE
SONI
SONI
SIGH
I'LL TAKE--
HE'LL PASS.
PETER, A WORD...?
DO YOU THINK I'M GOING TO STAND HERE AND LET YOU SELL THE LAST OF YOUR CAMERA EQUIPMENT?
BETTY, IT'S NOT LIKE IT'S DOING ME ANY GOOD.
NONSENSE. IT'S LIKE REMBRANDT SELLING HIS BRUSHES. YOU'RE A GREAT PHOTOGRAPHER AND YOU WILL BE IN DEMAND AGAIN.
EXCUSE ME!
YOU PETER PARKER? YOU ARE!
HEY, CAN I HIRE YOU TO SHOOT MY SISTER'S WEDDING?
WHAT? I...YEAH! I CAN USE THE--

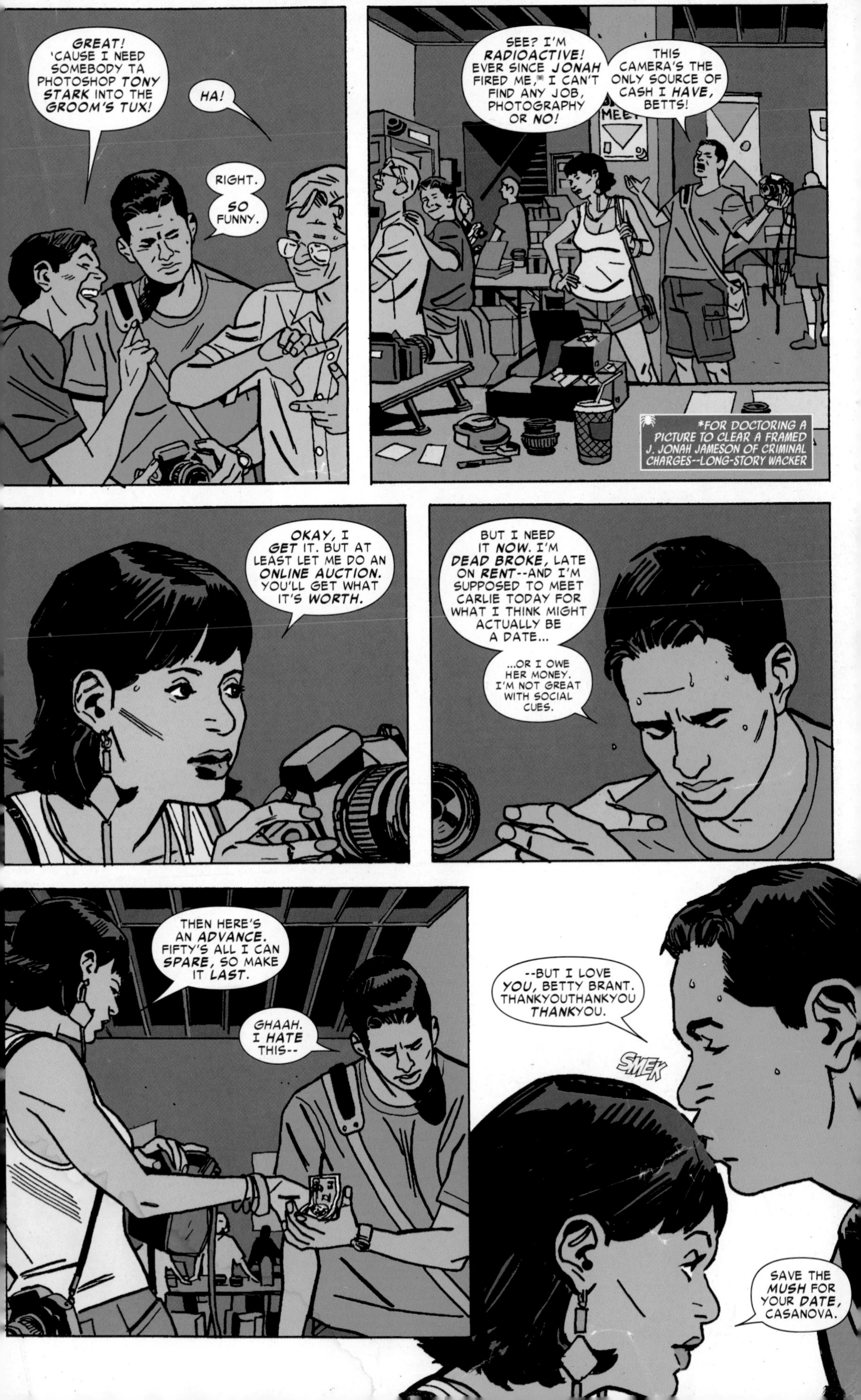
GREAT! 'CAUSE I NEED SOMEBODY TA PHOTOSHOP TONY STARK INTO THE GROOM'S TUX!
HA!
RIGHT.
SO FUNNY.
SEE? I'M RADIOACTIVE! EVER SINCE JONAH FIRED ME,* I CAN'T FIND ANY JOB, PHOTOGRAPHY OR NO!
THIS CAMERA'S THE ONLY SOURCE OF CASH I HAVE, BETTS!
*FOR DOCTORING A PICTURE TO CLEAR A FRAMED J. JONAH JAMESON OF CRIMINAL CHARGES--LONG-STORY WACKER
OKAY, I GET IT. BUT AT LEAST LET ME DO AN ONLINE AUCTION. YOU'LL GET WHAT IT'S WORTH.
BUT I NEED IT NOW. I'M DEAD BROKE, LATE ON RENT--AND I'M SUPPOSED TO MEET CARLIE TODAY FOR WHAT I THINK MIGHT ACTUALLY BE A DATE...
...OR I OWE HER MONEY. I'M NOT GREAT WITH SOCIAL CUES.
THEN HERE'S AN ADVANCE. FIFTY'S ALL I CAN SPARE, SO MAKE IT LAST.
GHAAH. I HATE THIS--
--BUT I LOVE YOU, BETTY BRANT. THANKYOUTHANKYOU THANKYOU.
SMEK
SAVE THE MUSH FOR YOUR DATE, CASANOVA.

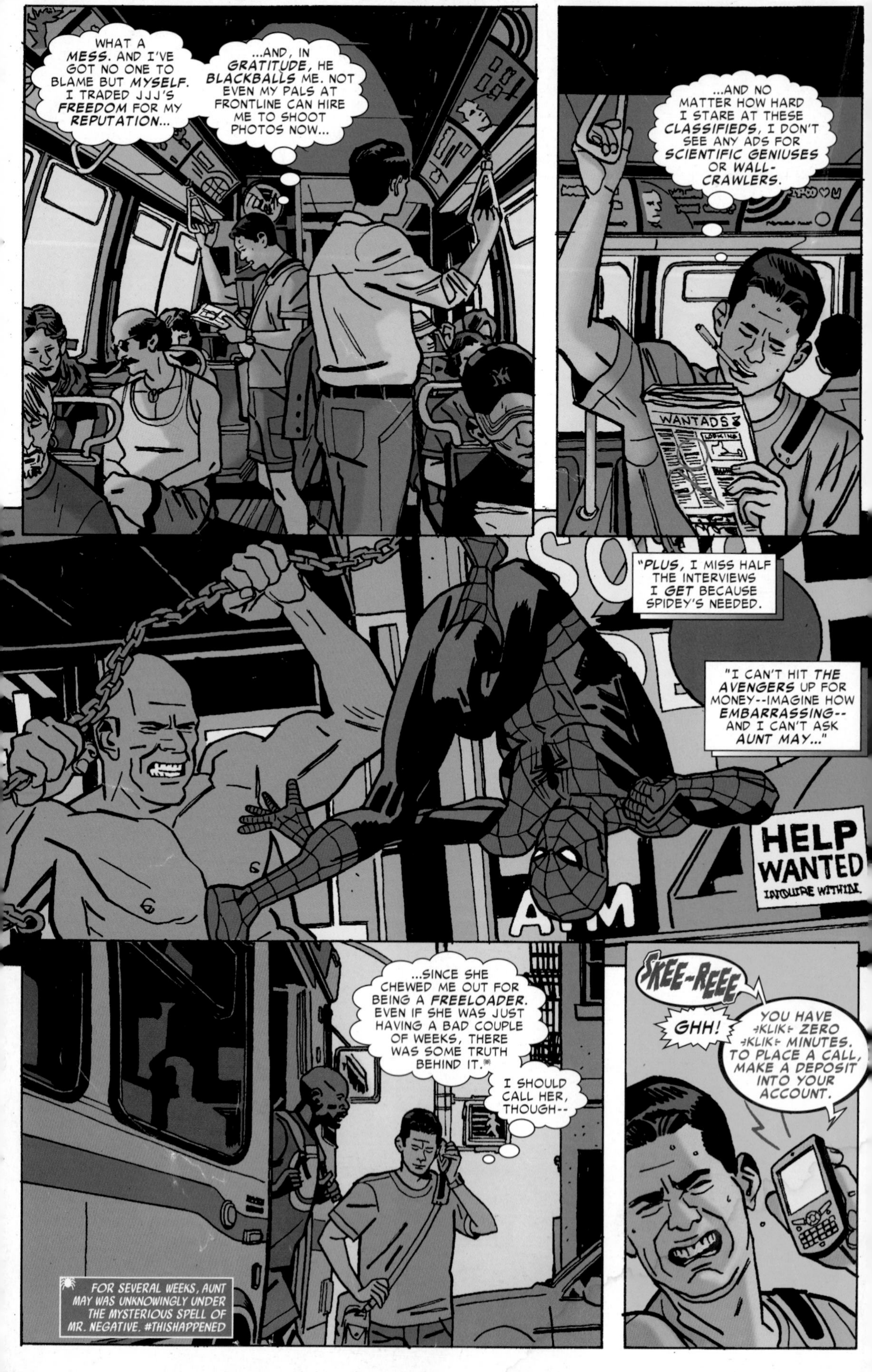
WHAT A MESS. AND I'VE GOT NO ONE TO BLAME BUT MYSELF. I TRADED JJJ'S FREEDOM FOR MY REPUTATION...
...AND, IN GRATITUDE, HE BLACKBALLS ME. NOT EVEN MY PALS AT FRONTLINE CAN HIRE ME TO SHOOT PHOTOS NOW...
...AND NO MATTER HOW HARD I STARE AT THESE CLASSIFIEDS, I DON'T SEE ANY ADS FOR SCIENTIFIC GENIUSES OR WALL-CRAWLERS.
WANTADS
"PLUS, I MISS HALF THE INTERVIEWS I GET BECAUSE SPIDEY'S NEEDED.
"I CAN'T HIT THE AVENGERS UP FOR MONEY--IMAGINE HOW EMBARRASSING--AND I CAN'T ASK AUNT MAY..."
HELP WANTED
INQUIRE WITHIN.
ATM
...SINCE SHE CHEWED ME OUT FOR BEING A FREELOADER. EVEN IF SHE WAS JUST HAVING A BAD COUPLE OF WEEKS, THERE WAS SOME TRUTH BEHIND IT.(*)
I SHOULD CALL HER, THOUGH--
FOR SEVERAL WEEKS, AUNT MAY WAS UNKNOWINGLY UNDER THE MYSTERIOUS SPELL OF MR. NEGATIVE. #THISHAPPENED
SKEE-REEE
GHH!
YOU HAVE -KLIK- ZERO -KLIK- MINUTES. TO PLACE A CALL, MAKE A DEPOSIT INTO YOUR ACCOUNT.

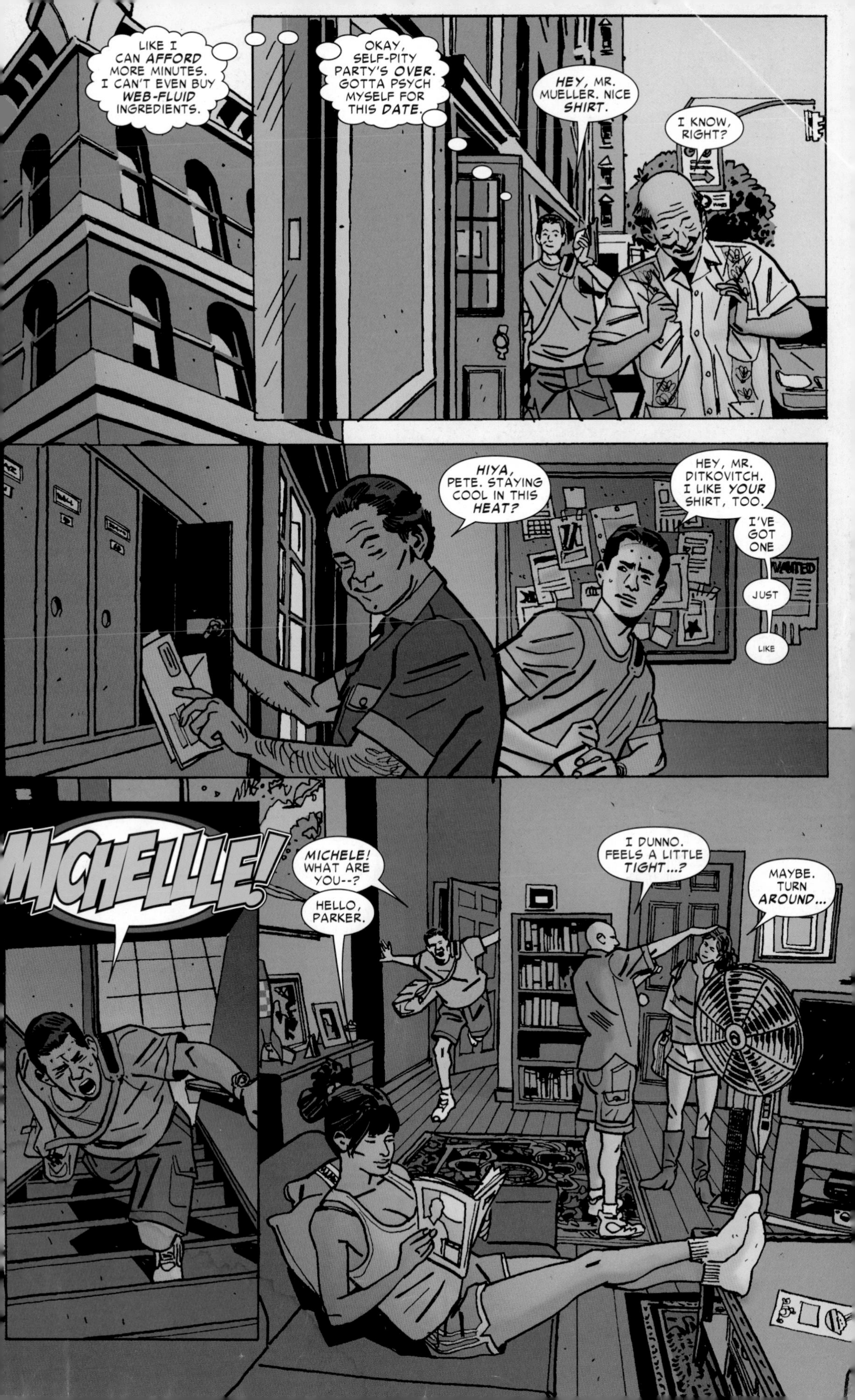
LIKE I CAN AFFORD MORE MINUTES. I CAN'T EVEN BUY WEB-FLUID INGREDIENTS.
OKAY, SELF-PITY PARTY'S OVER. GOTTA PSYCH MYSELF FOR THIS DATE.
HEY, MR. MUELLER. NICE SHIRT.
I KNOW, RIGHT?
HIYA, PETE. STAYING COOL IN THIS HEAT?
HEY, MR. DITKOVITCH. I LIKE YOUR SHIRT, TOO.
I'VE GOT ONE
JUST
LIKE
MICHELLE!
MICHELE! WHAT ARE YOU--?
HELLO, PARKER.
I DUNNO. FEELS A LITTLE TIGHT...?
MAYBE. TURN AROUND...

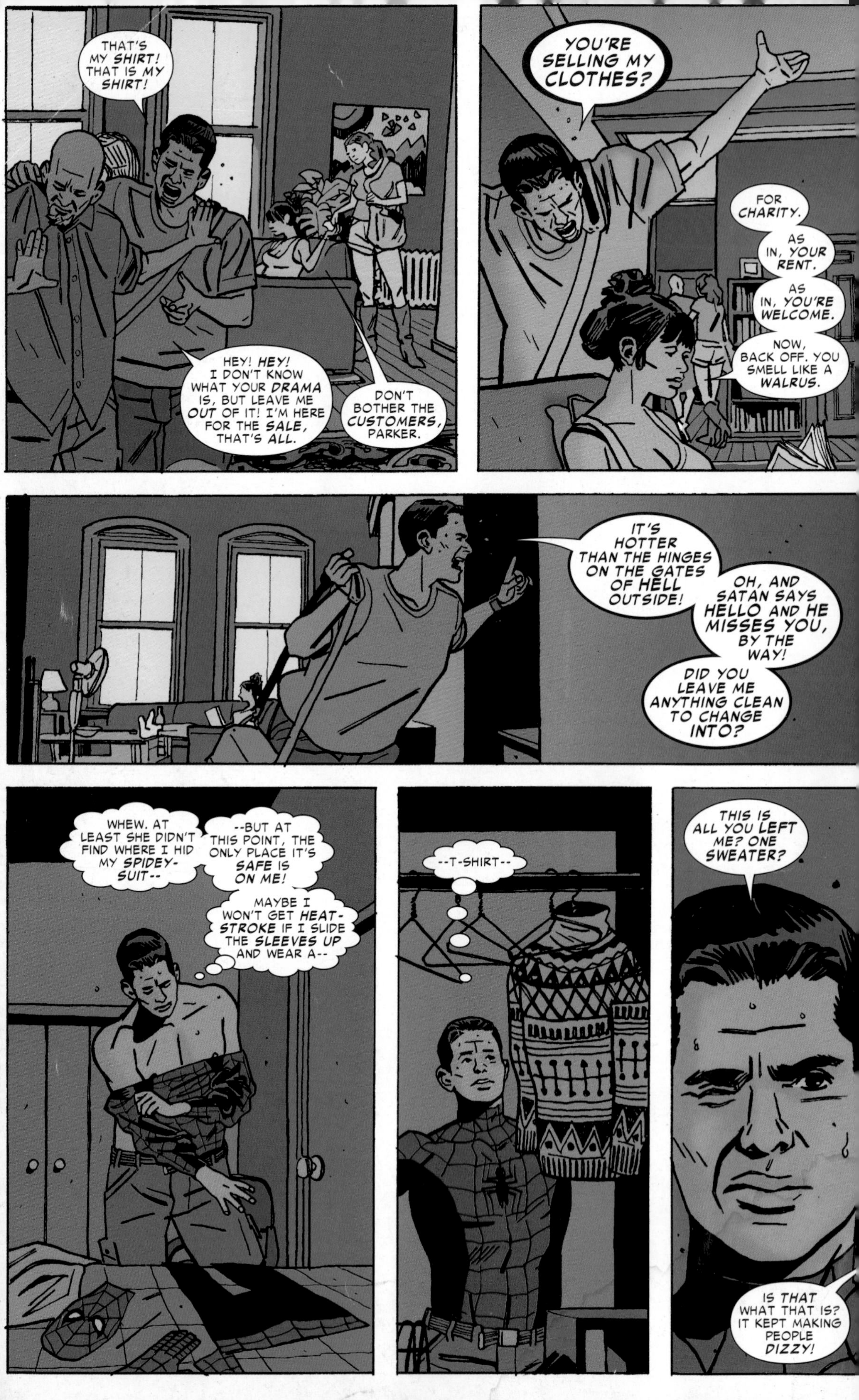
THAT'S MY SHIRT! THAT IS MY SHIRT!
HEY! HEY! I DON'T KNOW WHAT YOUR DRAMA IS, BUT LEAVE ME OUT OF IT! I'M HERE FOR THE SALE, THAT'S ALL.
DON'T BOTHER THE CUSTOMERS, PARKER.
YOU'RE SELLING MY CLOTHES?
FOR CHARITY.
AS IN, YOUR RENT.
AS IN, YOU'RE WELCOME.
NOW, BACK OFF. YOU SMELL LIKE A WALRUS.
IT'S HOTTER THAN THE HINGES ON THE GATES OF HELL OUTSIDE!
OH, AND SATAN SAYS HELLO AND HE MISSES YOU, BY THE WAY!
DID YOU LEAVE ME ANYTHING CLEAN TO CHANGE INTO?
WHEW. AT LEAST SHE DIDN'T FIND WHERE I HID MY SPIDEY-SUIT--
--BUT AT THIS POINT, THE ONLY PLACE IT'S SAFE IS ON ME!
MAYBE I WON'T GET HEAT-STROKE IF I SLIDE THE SLEEVES UP AND WEAR A--
--T-SHIRT--
THIS IS ALL YOU LEFT ME? ONE SWEATER?
IS THAT WHAT THAT IS? IT KEPT MAKING PEOPLE DIZZY!

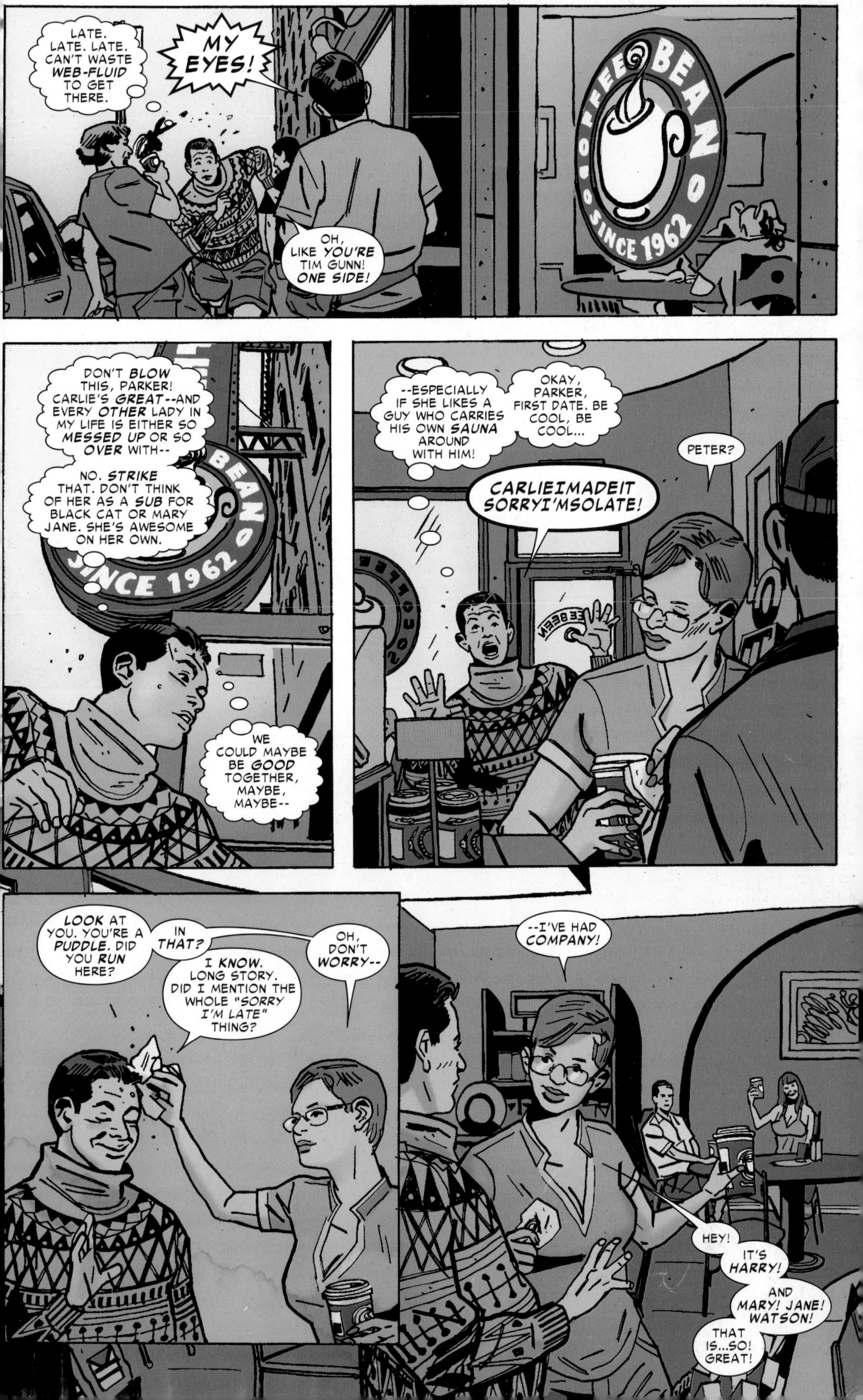
LATE. LATE. LATE. CAN'T WASTE WEB-FLUID TO GET THERE.
MY EYES!
OH, LIKE YOU'RE TIM GUNN! ONE SIDE!
COFFEE BEAN SINCE 1962
DON'T BLOW THIS, PARKER! CARLIE'S GREAT--AND EVERY OTHER LADY IN MY LIFE IS EITHER SO MESSED UP OR SO OVER WITH--
NO. STRIKE THAT. DON'T THINK OF HER AS A SUB FOR BLACK CAT OR MARY JANE. SHE'S AWESOME ON HER OWN.
WE COULD MAYBE BE GOOD TOGETHER, MAYBE, MAYBE--
OKAY, PARKER, FIRST DATE. BE COOL, BE COOL...
--ESPECIALLY IF SHE LIKES A GUY WHO CARRIES HIS OWN SAUNA AROUND WITH HIM!
PETER?
CARLIEIMADEIT SORRYI'MSOLATE!
LOOK AT YOU. YOU'RE A PUDDLE. DID YOU RUN HERE?
IN THAT?
I KNOW. LONG STORY. DID I MENTION THE WHOLE "SORRY I'M LATE" THING?
OH, DON'T WORRY--
--I'VE HAD COMPANY!
HEY!
IT'S HARRY!
AND MARY! JANE! WATSON!
THAT IS...SO! GREAT!

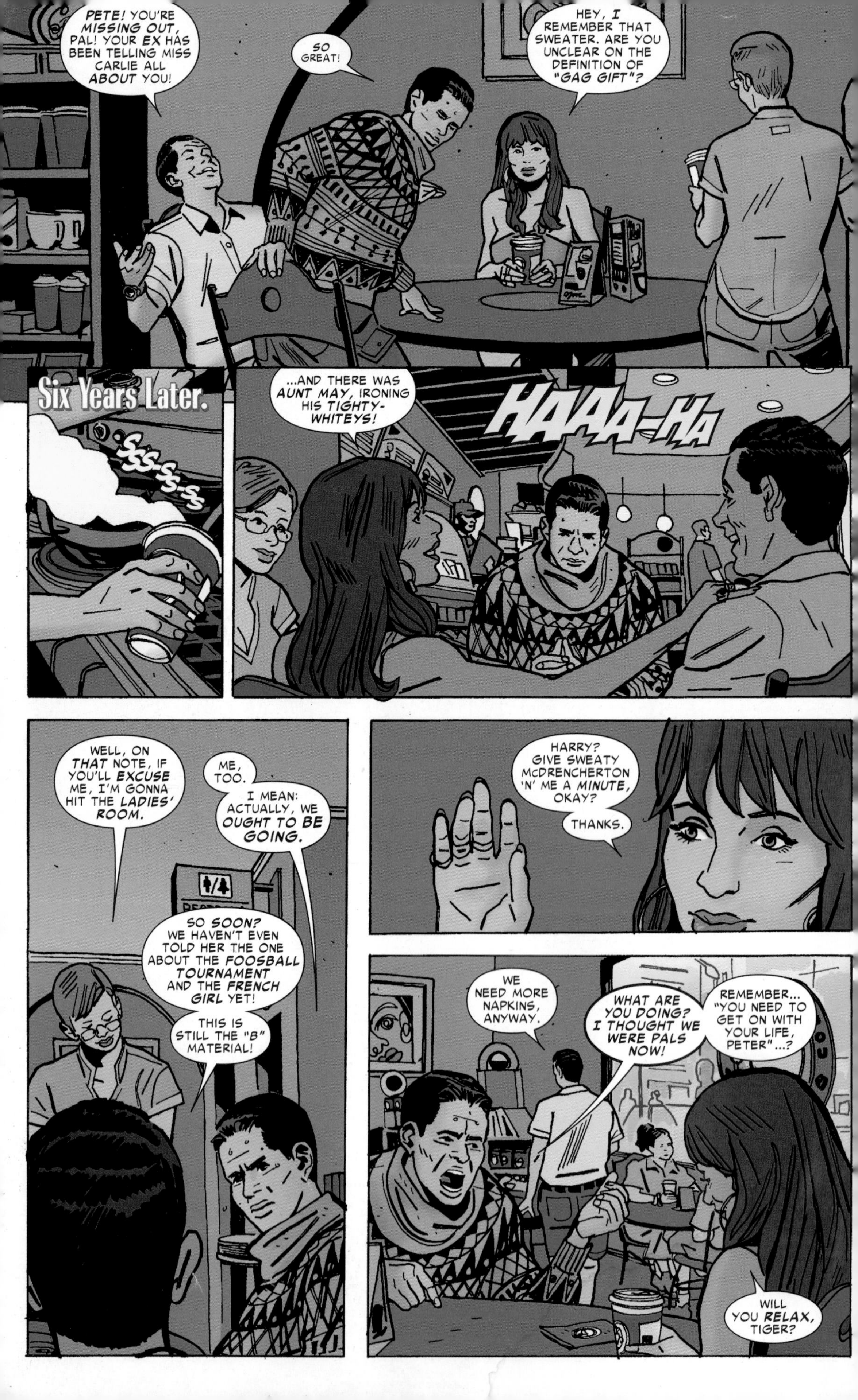
PETE! YOU'RE MISSING OUT, PAL! YOUR EX HAS BEEN TELLING MISS CARLIE ALL ABOUT YOU!
SO GREAT!
HEY, I REMEMBER THAT SWEATER. ARE YOU UNCLEAR ON THE DEFINITION OF "GAG GIFT"?
Six Years Later.
SSS-SS-SS
...AND THERE WAS AUNT MAY, IRONING HIS TIGHTY-WHITEYS!
HAAA-HA
WELL, ON THAT NOTE, IF YOU'LL EXCUSE ME, I'M GONNA HIT THE LADIES' ROOM.
ME, TOO.
I MEAN: ACTUALLY, WE OUGHT TO BE GOING.
SO SOON? WE HAVEN'T EVEN TOLD HER THE ONE ABOUT THE FOOSBALL TOURNAMENT AND THE FRENCH GIRL YET!
THIS IS STILL THE "B" MATERIAL!
HARRY? GIVE SWEATY McDRENCHERTON 'N' ME A MINUTE, OKAY?
THANKS.
WE NEED MORE NAPKINS, ANYWAY.
WHAT ARE YOU DOING? I THOUGHT WE WERE PALS NOW!
REMEMBER... "YOU NEED TO GET ON WITH YOUR LIFE, PETER"...?
WILL YOU RELAX, TIGER?

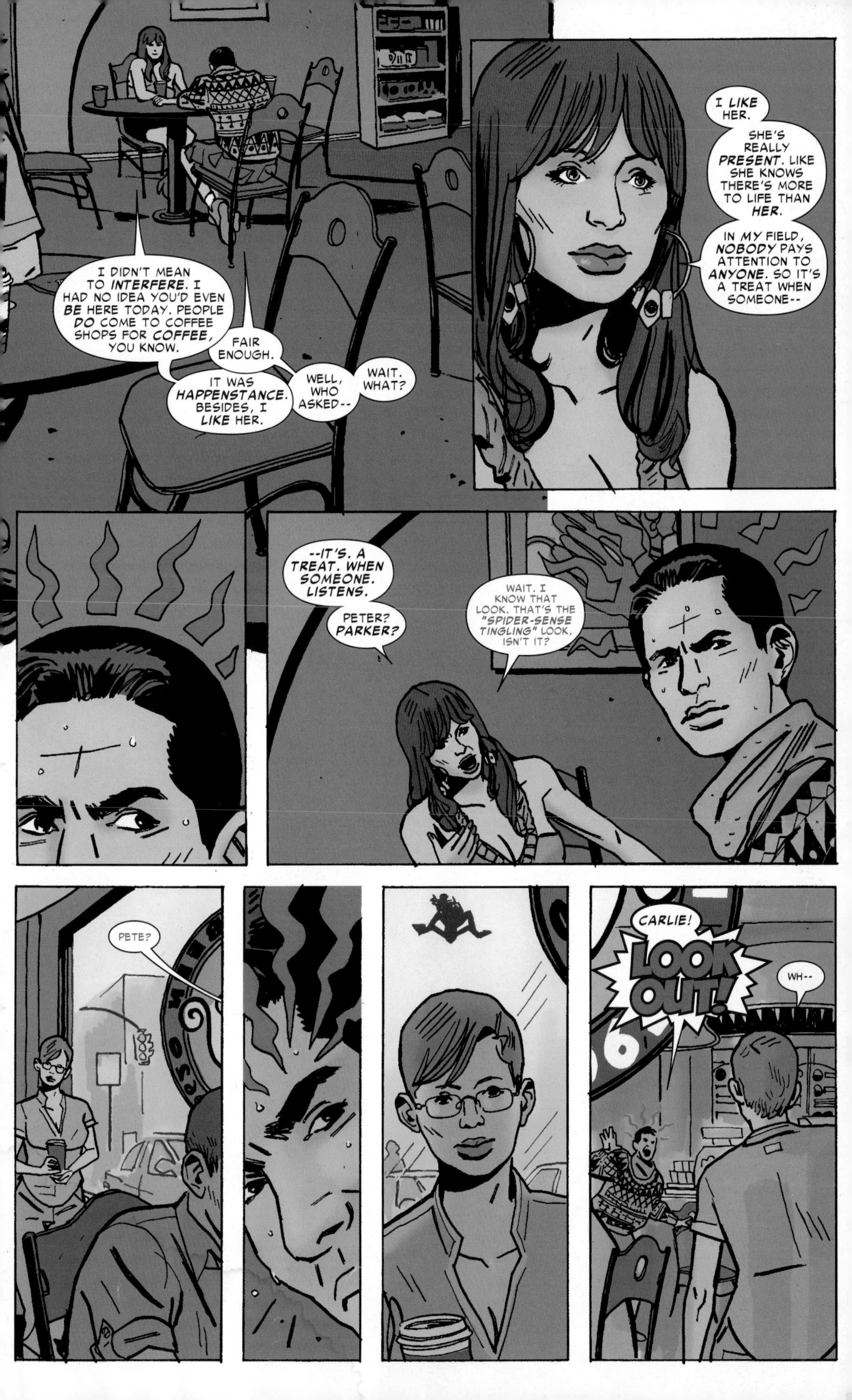
I DIDN'T MEAN TO INTERFERE. I HAD NO IDEA YOU'D EVEN BE HERE TODAY. PEOPLE DO COME TO COFFEE SHOPS FOR COFFEE, YOU KNOW.
FAIR ENOUGH.
IT WAS HAPPENSTANCE. BESIDES, I LIKE HER.
WELL, WHO ASKED--
WAIT. WHAT?
I LIKE HER.
SHE'S REALLY PRESENT. LIKE SHE KNOWS THERE'S MORE TO LIFE THAN HER.
IN MY FIELD, NOBODY PAYS ATTENTION TO ANYONE. SO IT'S A TREAT WHEN SOMEONE--
--IT'S. A TREAT. WHEN SOMEONE. LISTENS.
PETER? PARKER?
WAIT. I KNOW THAT LOOK. THAT'S THE "SPIDER-SENSE TINGLING" LOOK, ISN'T IT?
PETE?
CARLIE!
LOOK OUT!
WH--

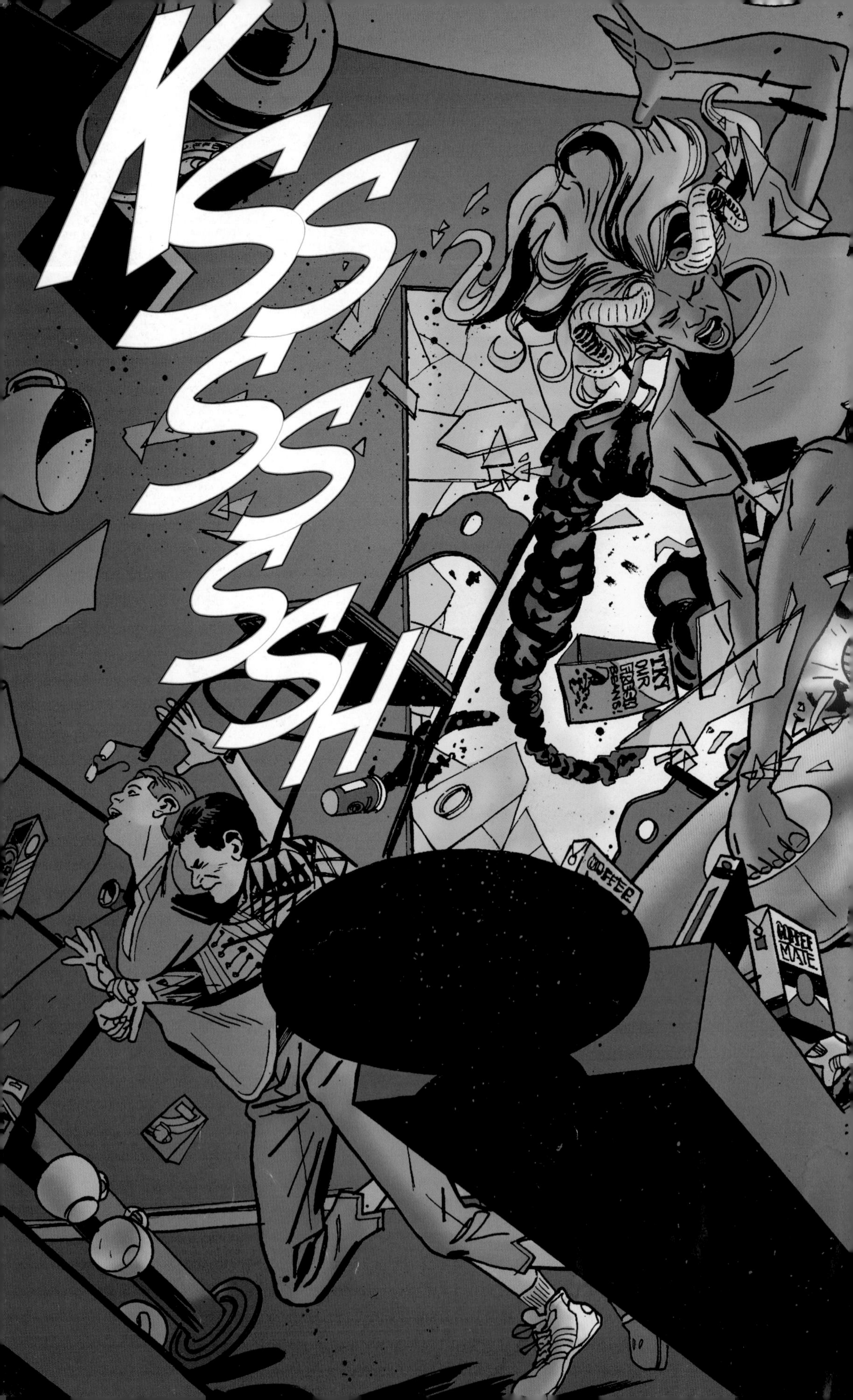
KSSSSSSH
COFFEE MATE

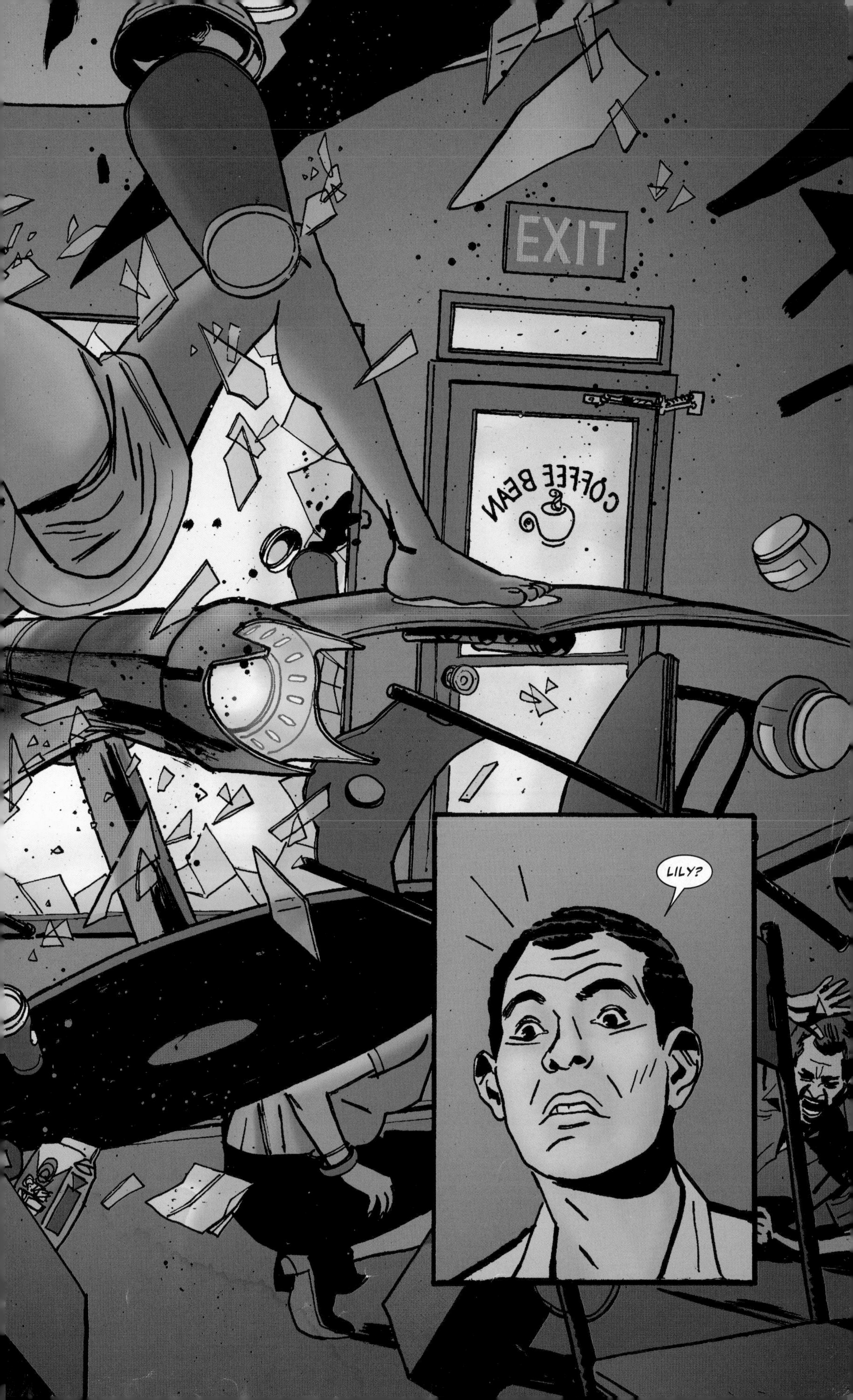
EXIT
LILY?

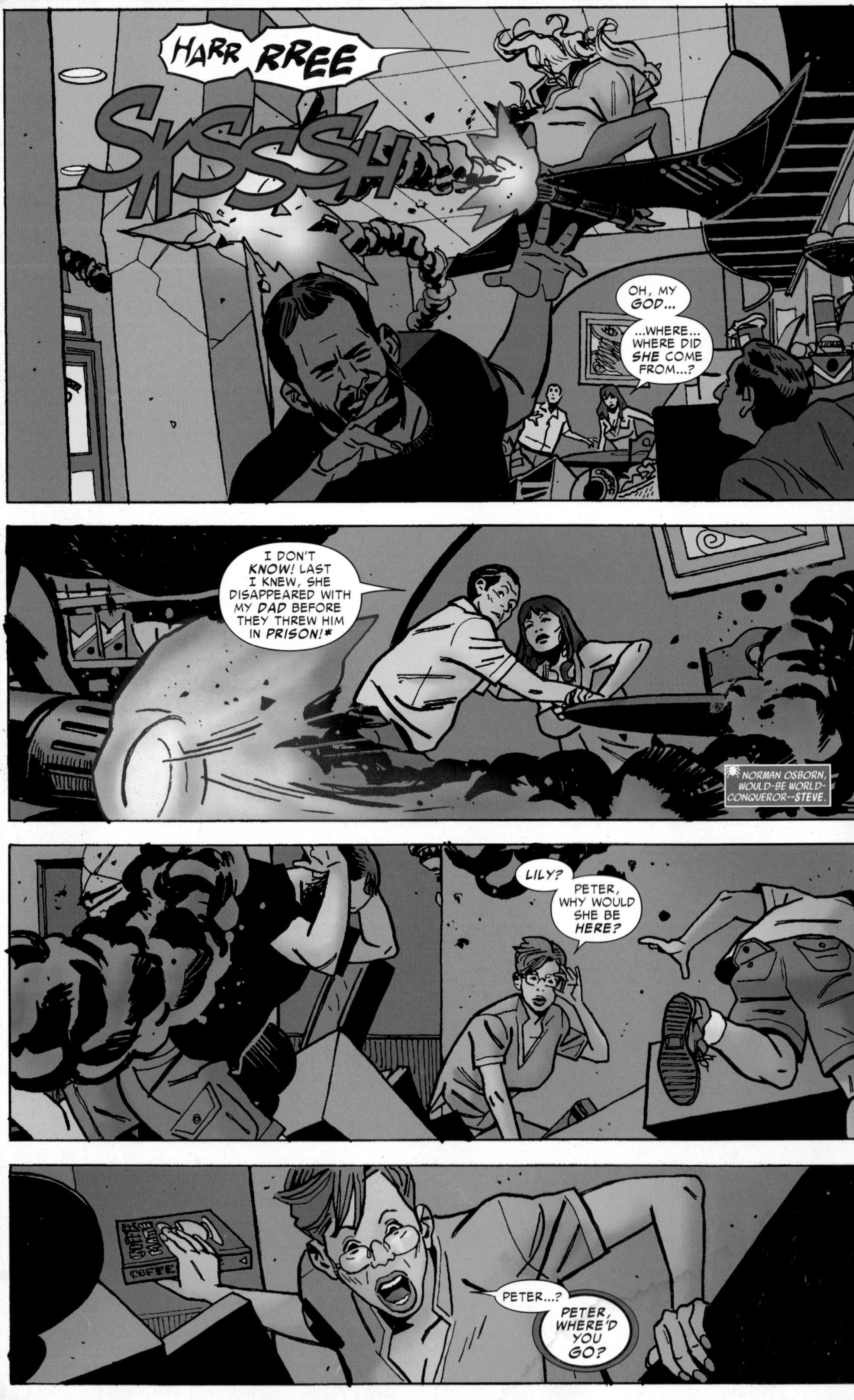
HARR RREE
SKSSSH
OH, MY GOD...
...WHERE... WHERE DID SHE COME FROM...?
I DON'T KNOW! LAST I KNEW, SHE DISAPPEARED WITH MY DAD BEFORE THEY THREW HIM IN PRISON!*
*NORMAN OSBORN, WOULD-BE WORLD-CONQUEROR--STEVE.
LILY?
PETER, WHY WOULD SHE BE HERE?
PETER...?
PETER, WHERE'D YOU GO?

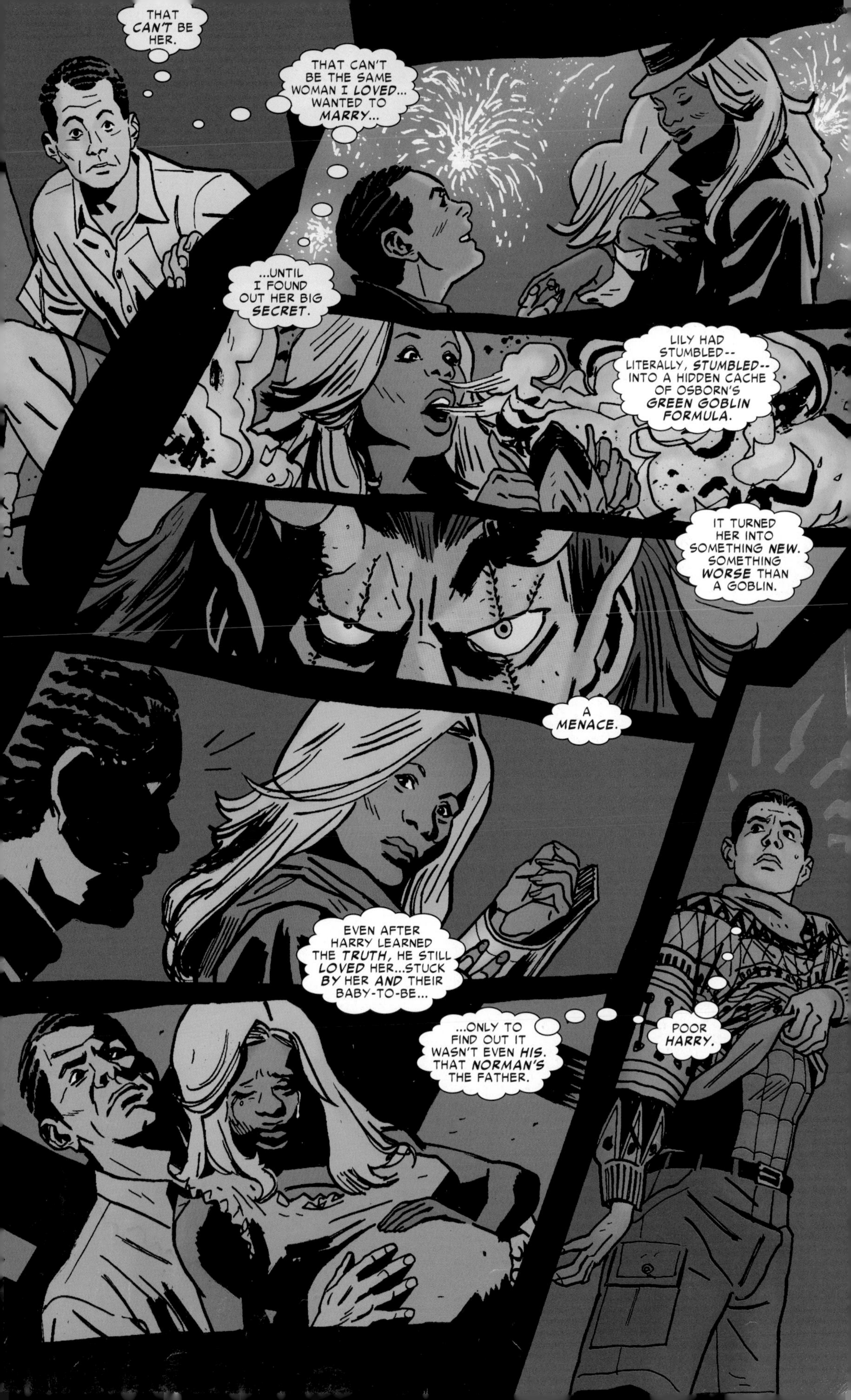
THAT CAN'T BE HER.
THAT CAN'T BE THE SAME WOMAN I LOVED... WANTED TO MARRY...
...UNTIL I FOUND OUT HER BIG SECRET.
LILY HAD STUMBLED-- LITERALLY, STUMBLED-- INTO A HIDDEN CACHE OF OSBORN'S GREEN GOBLIN FORMULA.
IT TURNED HER INTO SOMETHING NEW. SOMETHING WORSE THAN A GOBLIN.
A MENACE.
EVEN AFTER HARRY LEARNED THE TRUTH, HE STILL LOVED HER...STUCK BY HER AND THEIR BABY-TO-BE...
...ONLY TO FIND OUT IT WASN'T EVEN HIS. THAT NORMAN'S THE FATHER.
POOR HARRY.

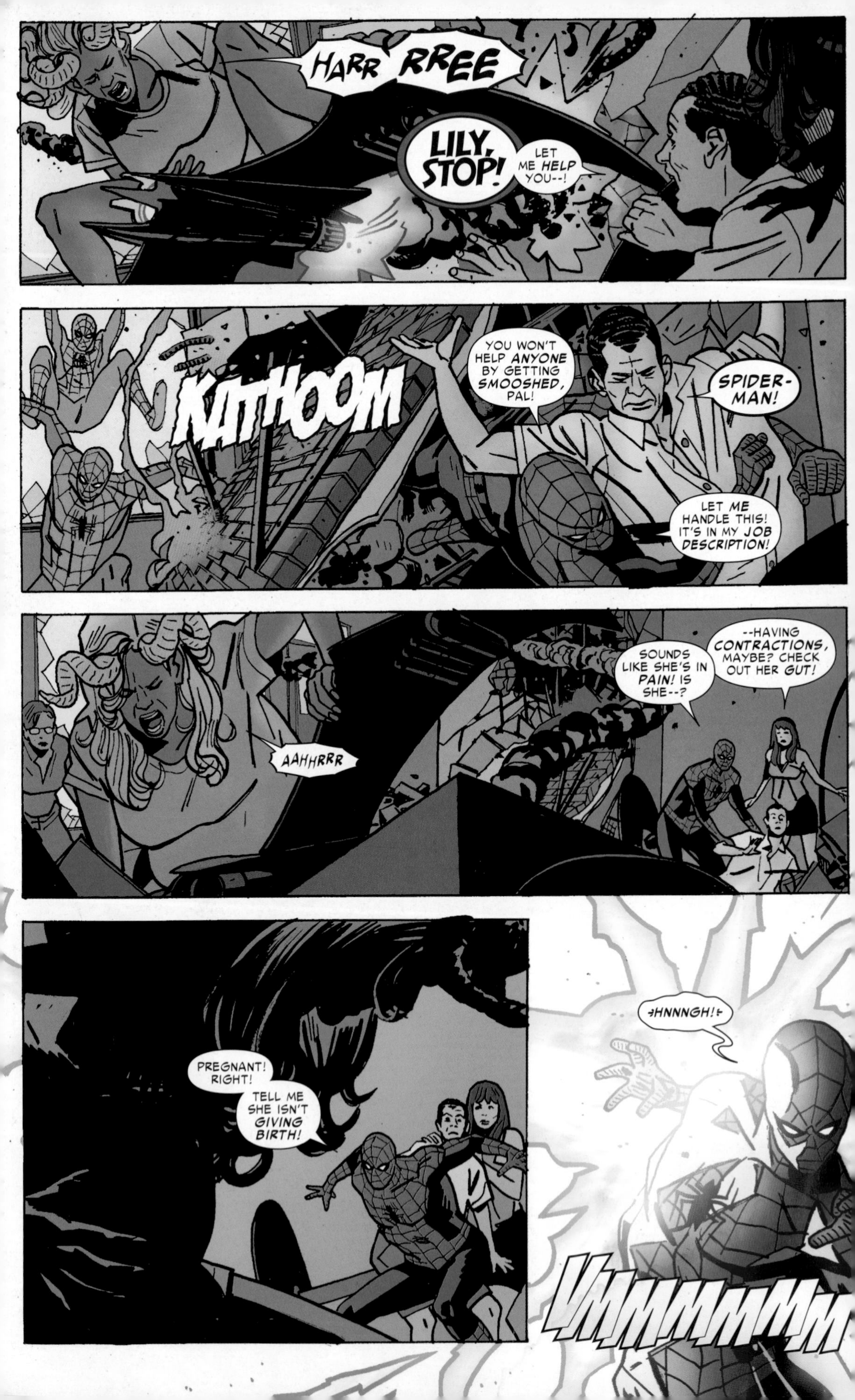
HARR RREE
LILY, STOP!
LET ME HELP YOU--!
KATHOOM
YOU WON'T HELP ANYONE BY GETTING SMOOSHED, PAL!
SPIDER-MAN!
LET ME HANDLE THIS! IT'S IN MY JOB DESCRIPTION!
AAHHRRR
SOUNDS LIKE SHE'S IN PAIN! IS SHE--?
--HAVING CONTRACTIONS, MAYBE? CHECK OUT HER GUT!
PREGNANT! RIGHT!
TELL ME SHE ISN'T GIVING BIRTH!
HNNNGH!
VMMMMMMMM

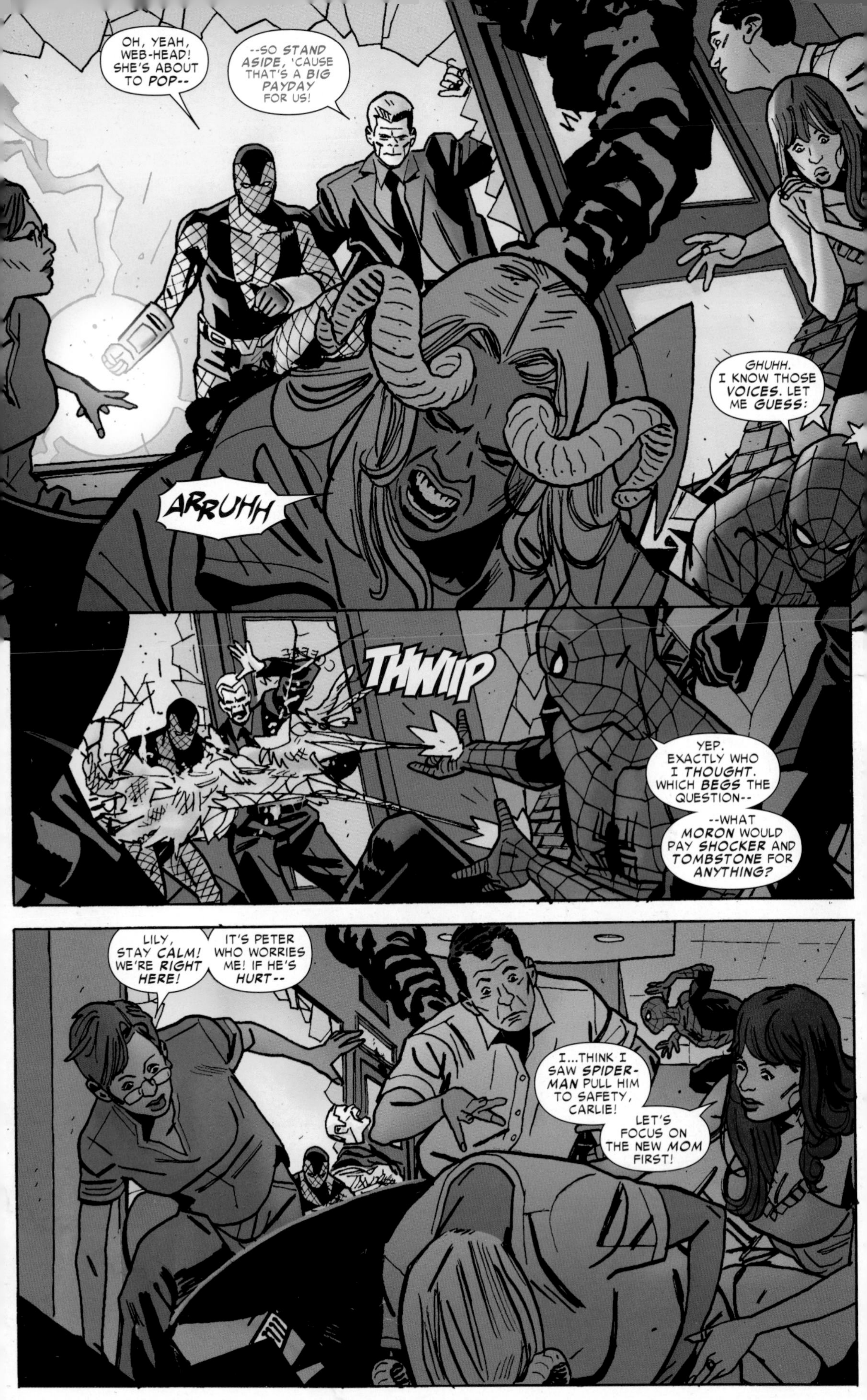
OH, YEAH, WEB-HEAD! SHE'S ABOUT TO POP--
--SO STAND ASIDE, 'CAUSE THAT'S A BIG PAYDAY FOR US!
GHUHH. I KNOW THOSE VOICES. LET ME GUESS:
ARRUHH
THWIIP
YEP. EXACTLY WHO I THOUGHT. WHICH BEGS THE QUESTION--
--WHAT MORON WOULD PAY SHOCKER AND TOMBSTONE FOR ANYTHING?
LILY, STAY CALM! WE'RE RIGHT HERE!
IT'S PETER WHO WORRIES ME! IF HE'S HURT--
I...THINK I SAW SPIDER-MAN PULL HIM TO SAFETY, CARLIE!
LET'S FOCUS ON THE NEW MOM FIRST!

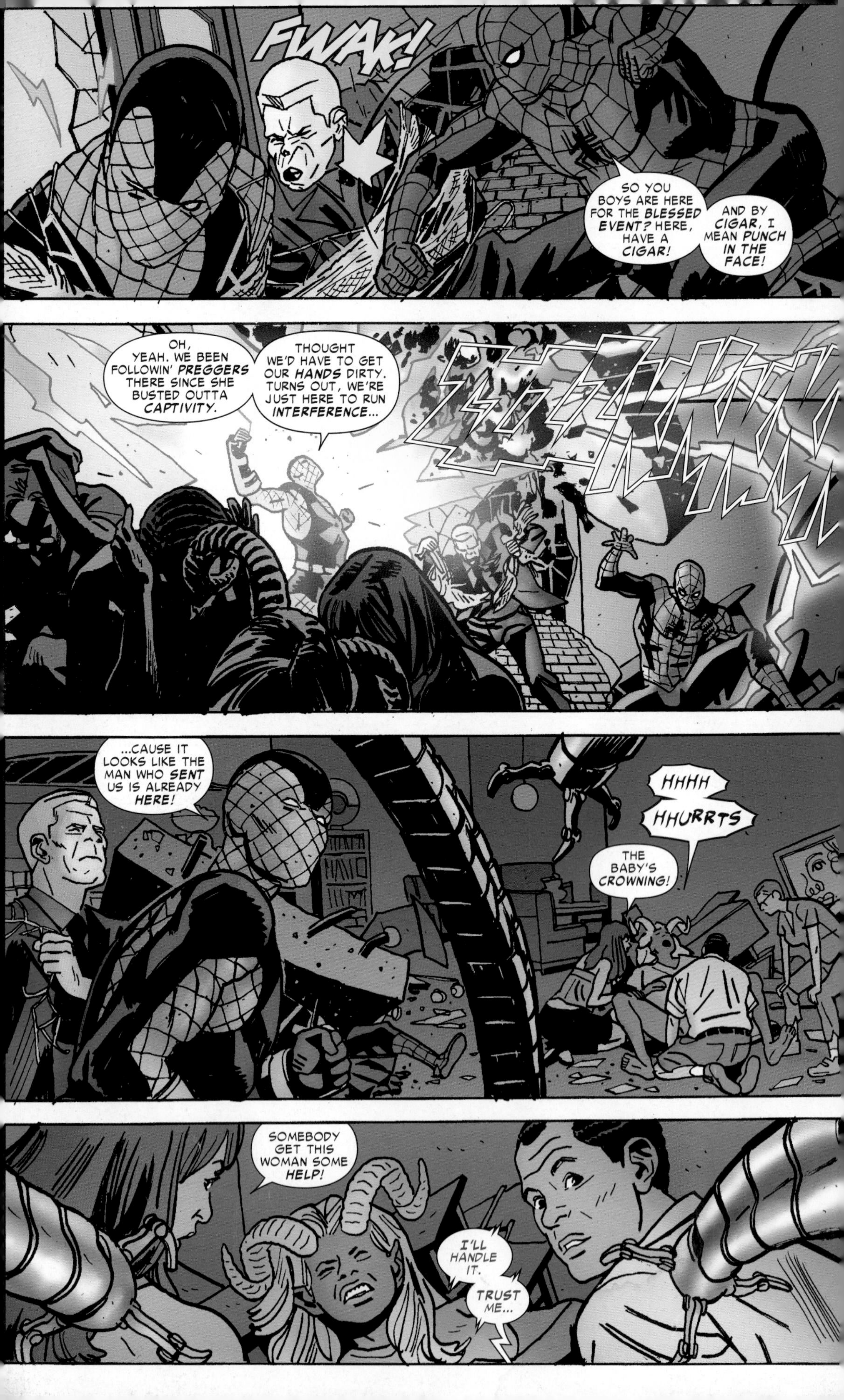
FWAK!
SO YOU BOYS ARE HERE FOR THE BLESSED EVENT? HERE, HAVE A CIGAR!
AND BY CIGAR, I MEAN PUNCH IN THE FACE!
OH, YEAH. WE BEEN FOLLOWIN' PREGGERS THERE SINCE SHE BUSTED OUTTA CAPTIVITY.
THOUGHT WE'D HAVE TO GET OUR HANDS DIRTY. TURNS OUT, WE'RE JUST HERE TO RUN INTERFERENCE...
...CAUSE IT LOOKS LIKE THE MAN WHO SENT US IS ALREADY HERE!
HHHH
HHURRRTS
THE BABY'S CROWNING!
SOMEBODY GET THIS WOMAN SOME HELP!
I'LL HANDLE IT.
TRUST ME...

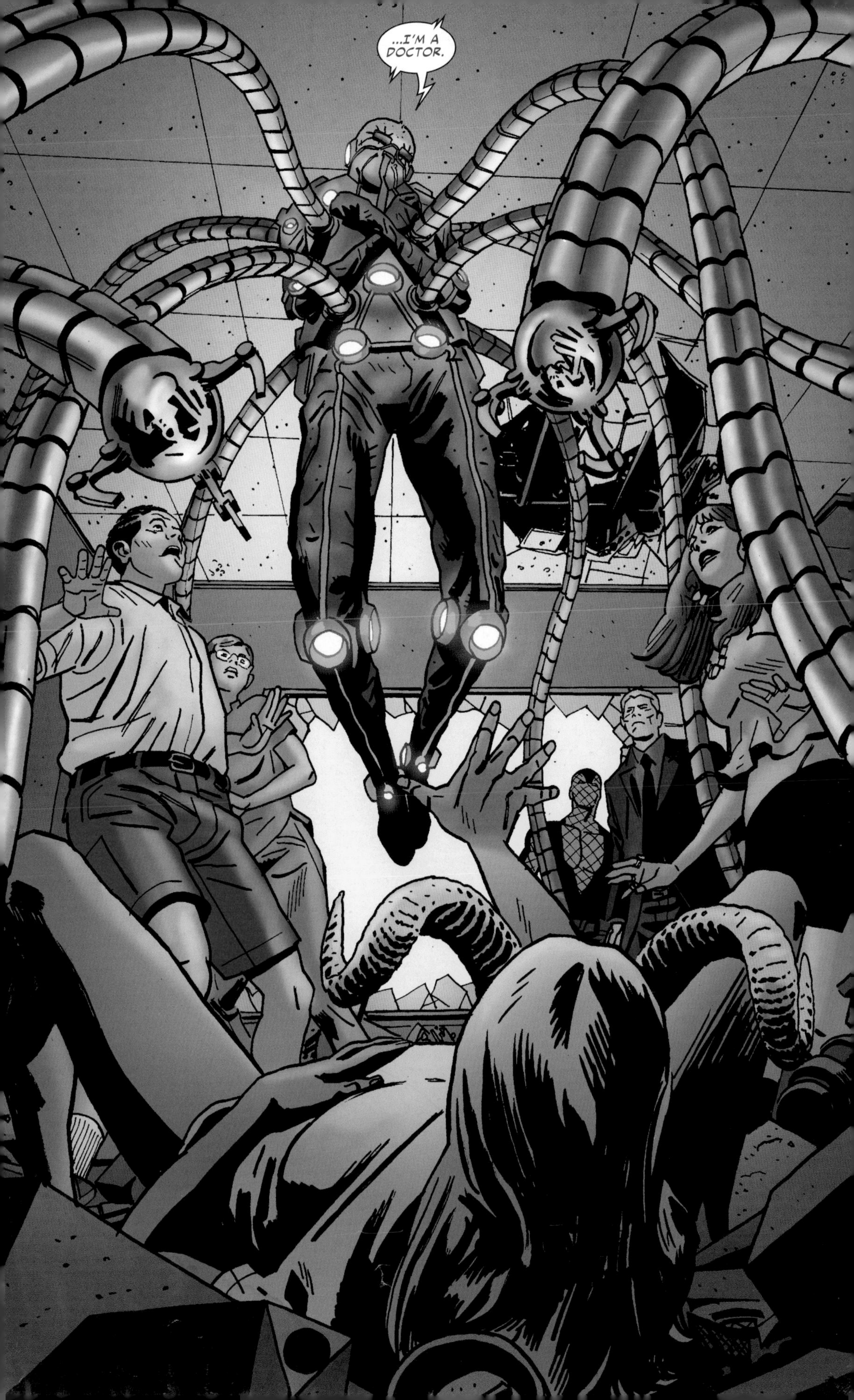
...I'M A DOCTOR.

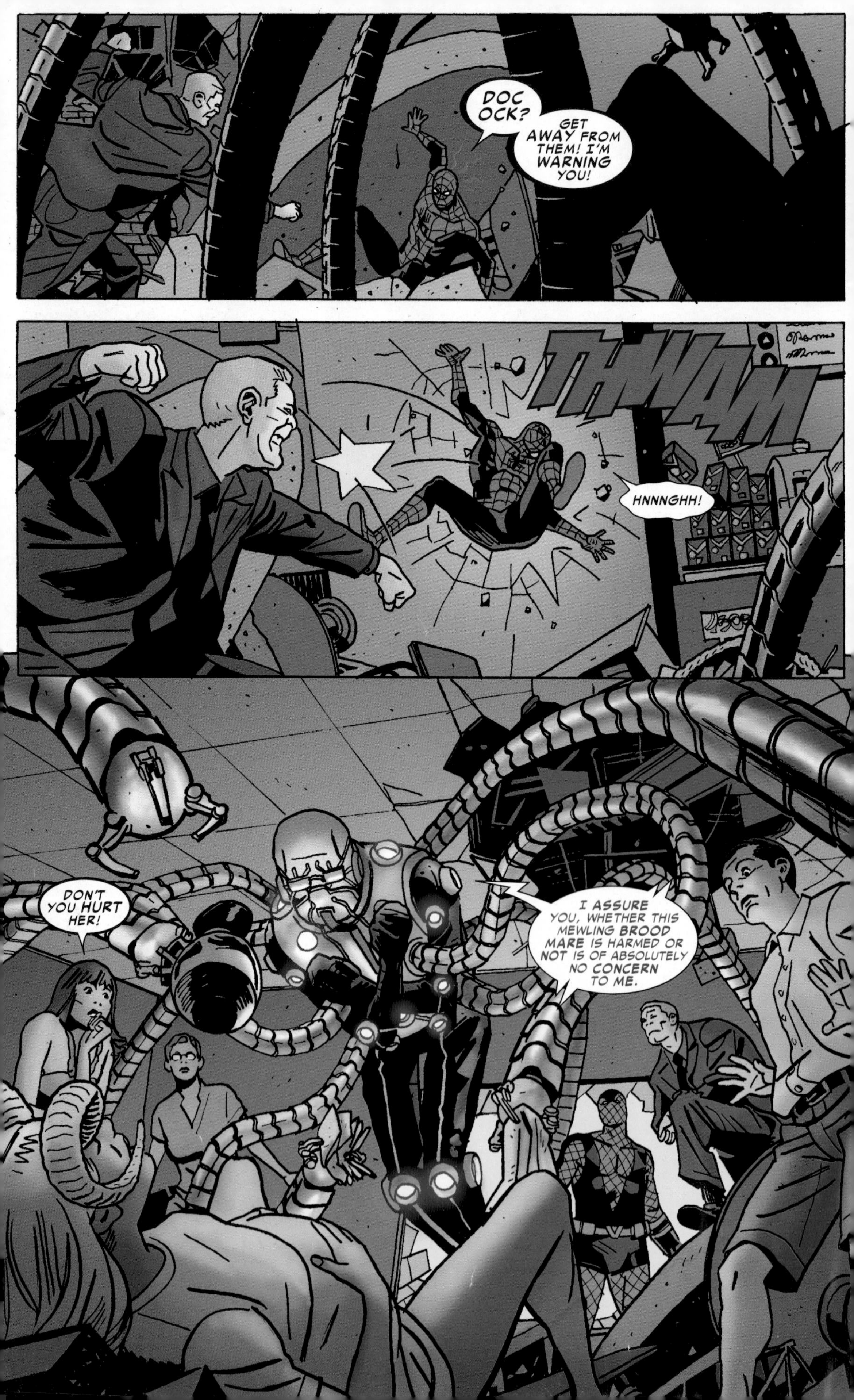
DOC OCK?
GET AWAY FROM THEM! I'M WARNING YOU!
THWAM
HNNNGHH!
DON'T YOU HURT HER!
I ASSURE YOU, WHETHER THIS MEWLING BROOD MARE IS HARMED OR NOT IS OF ABSOLUTELY NO CONCERN TO ME.

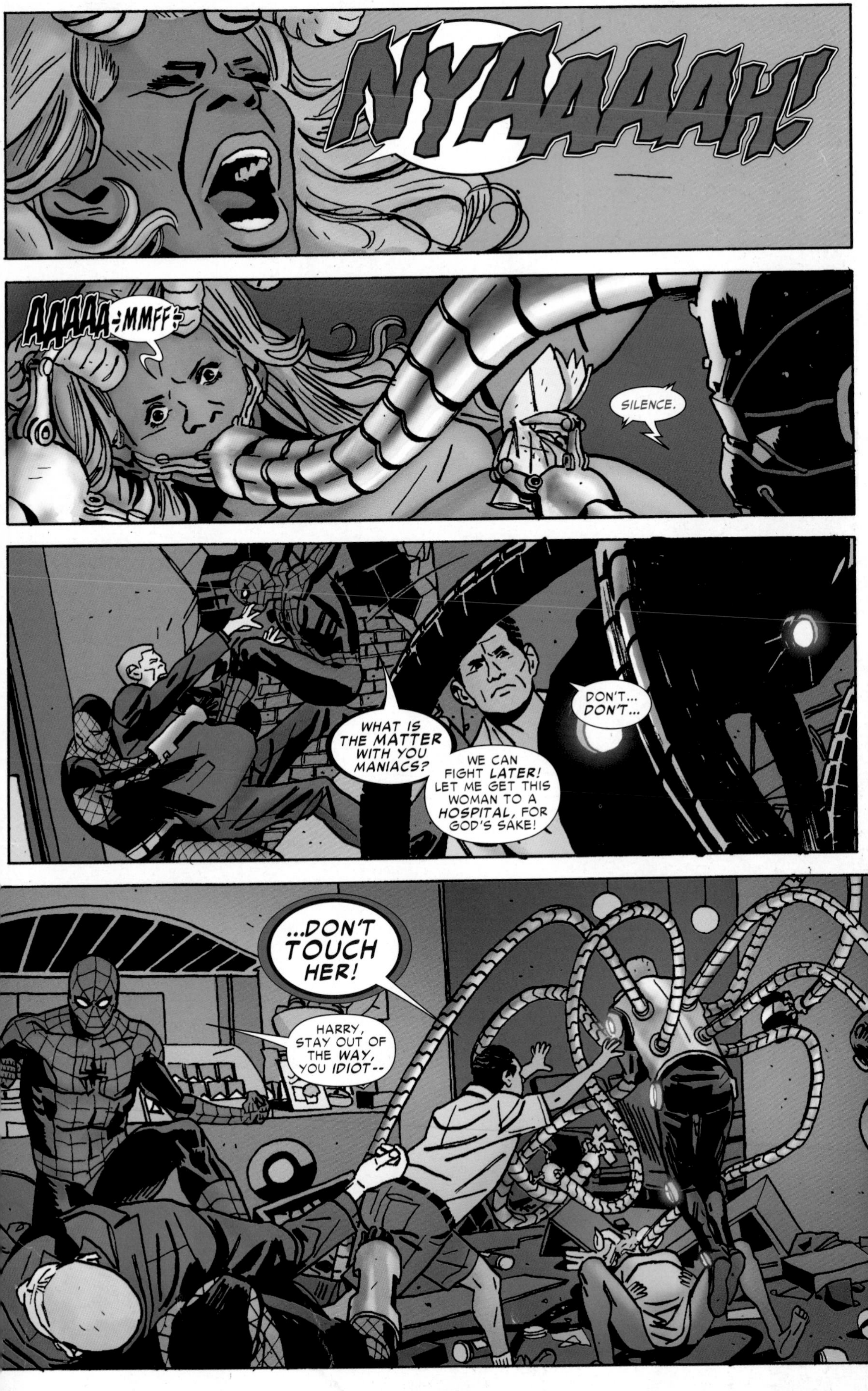

NYAAAAH!
AAAAA-MMFF-
SILENCE.
WHAT IS THE MATTER WITH YOU MANIACS?
WE CAN FIGHT LATER! LET ME GET THIS WOMAN TO A HOSPITAL, FOR GOD'S SAKE!
DON'T... DON'T...
...DON'T TOUCH HER!
HARRY, STAY OUT OF THE WAY, YOU IDIOT--

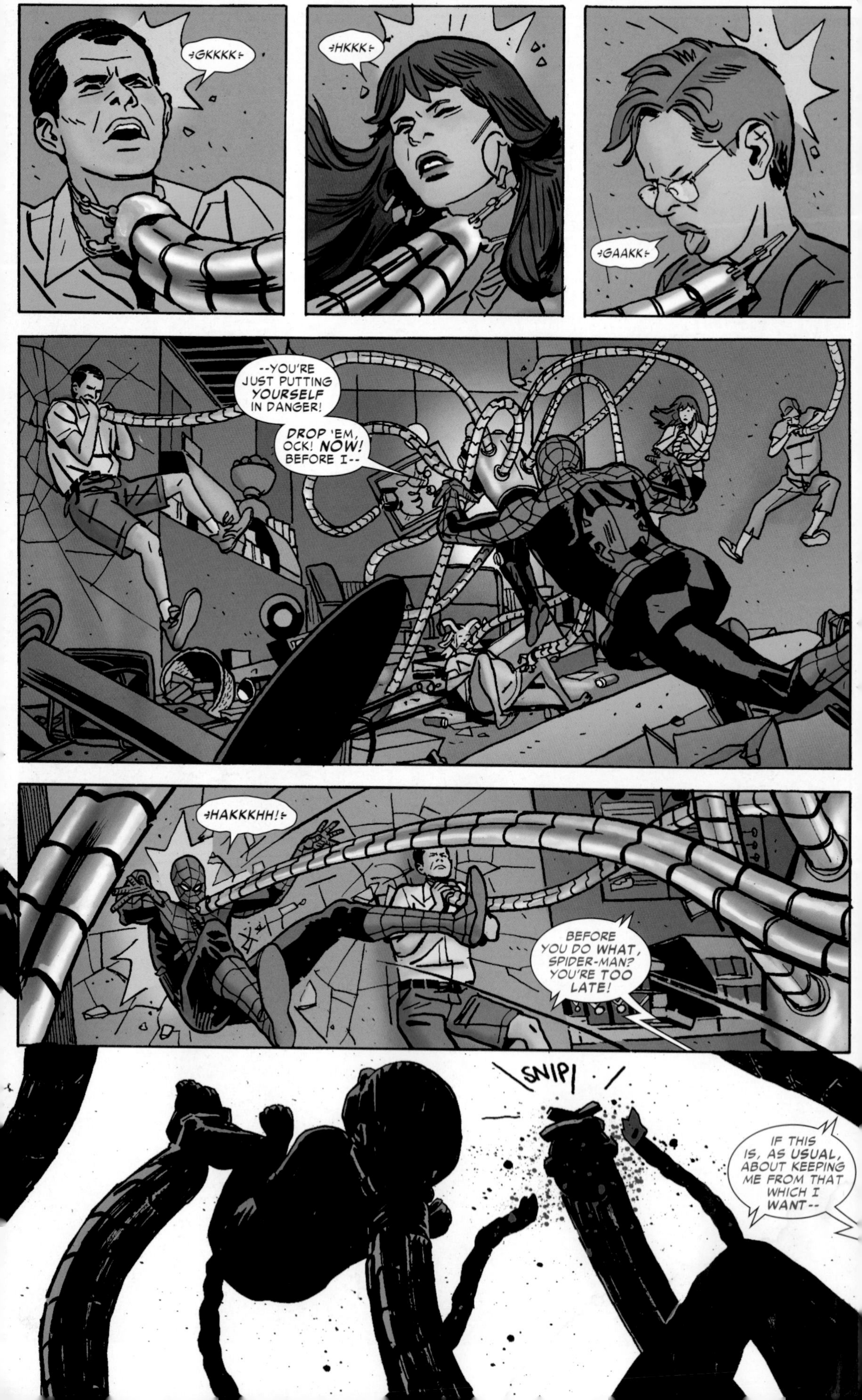
GKKKK
HKKK
GAAKK
--YOU'RE JUST PUTTING YOURSELF IN DANGER!
DROP 'EM, OCK! NOW! BEFORE I--
HAKKKHH!
BEFORE YOU DO WHAT, SPIDER-MAN? YOU'RE TOO LATE!
SNIP!
IF THIS IS, AS USUAL, ABOUT KEEPING ME FROM THAT WHICH I WANT--

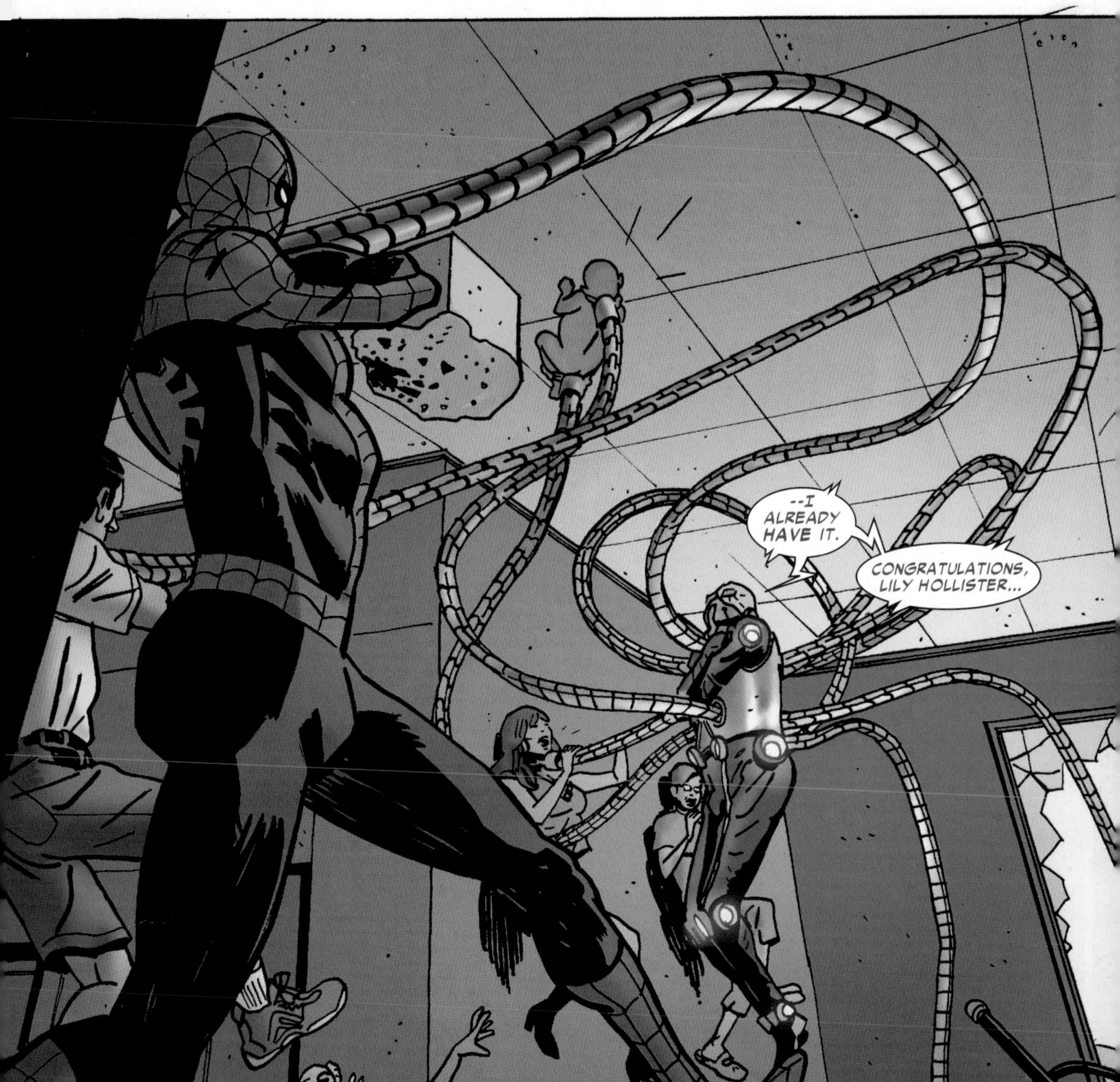
--I ALREADY HAVE IT.
CONGRATULATIONS, LILY HOLLISTER...

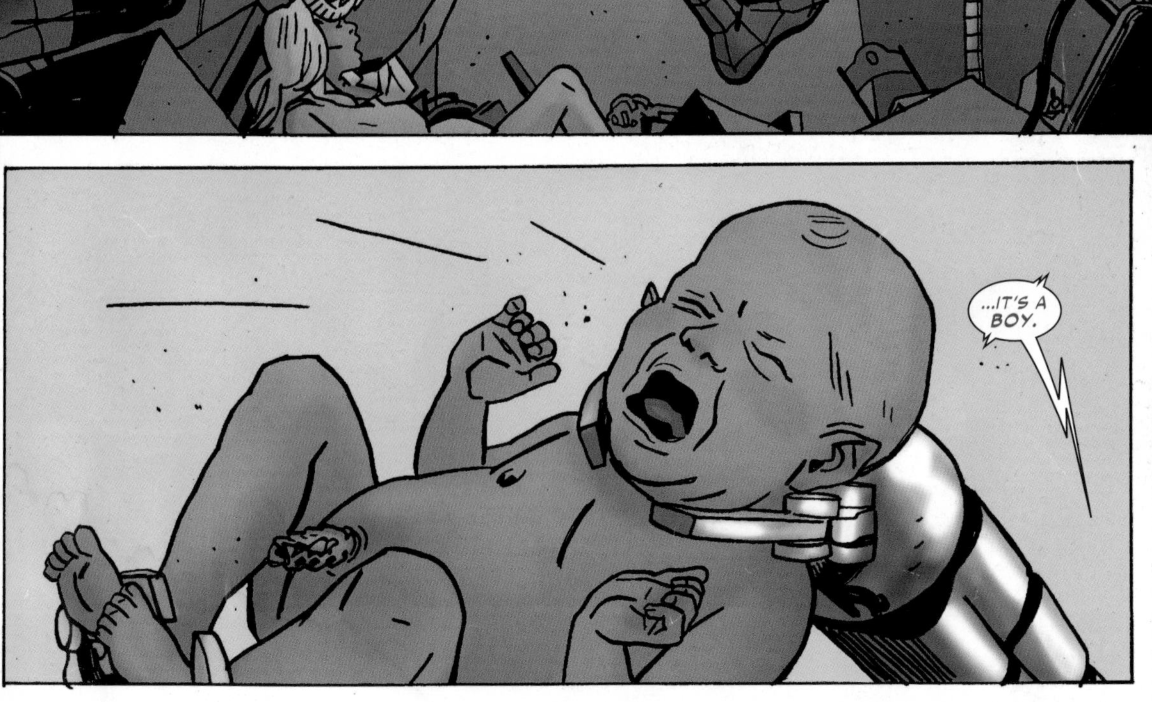
...IT'S A BOY.

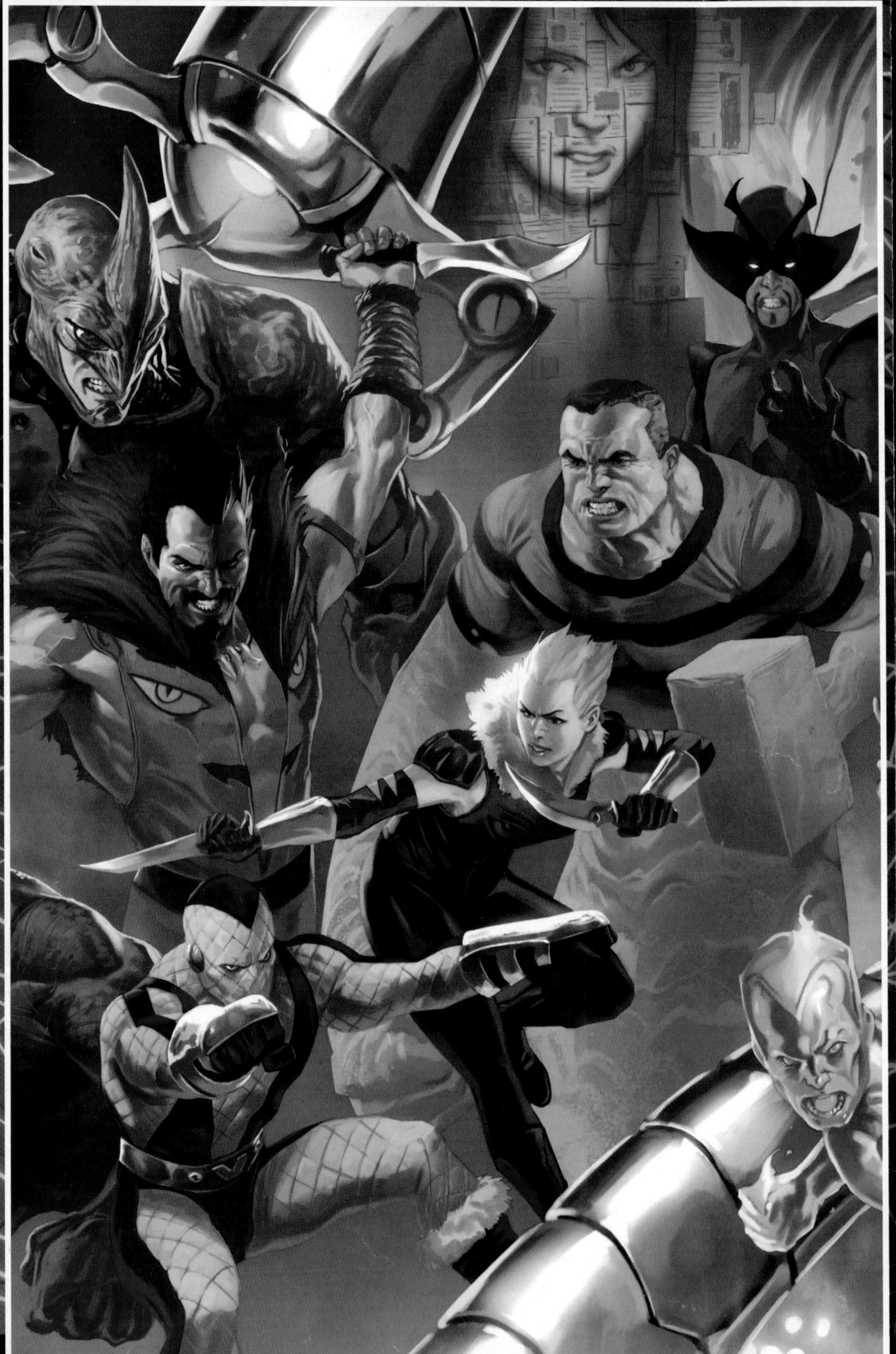

AMAZING SPIDER-MAN #643
COVER BY MARKO DJURDJEVIC

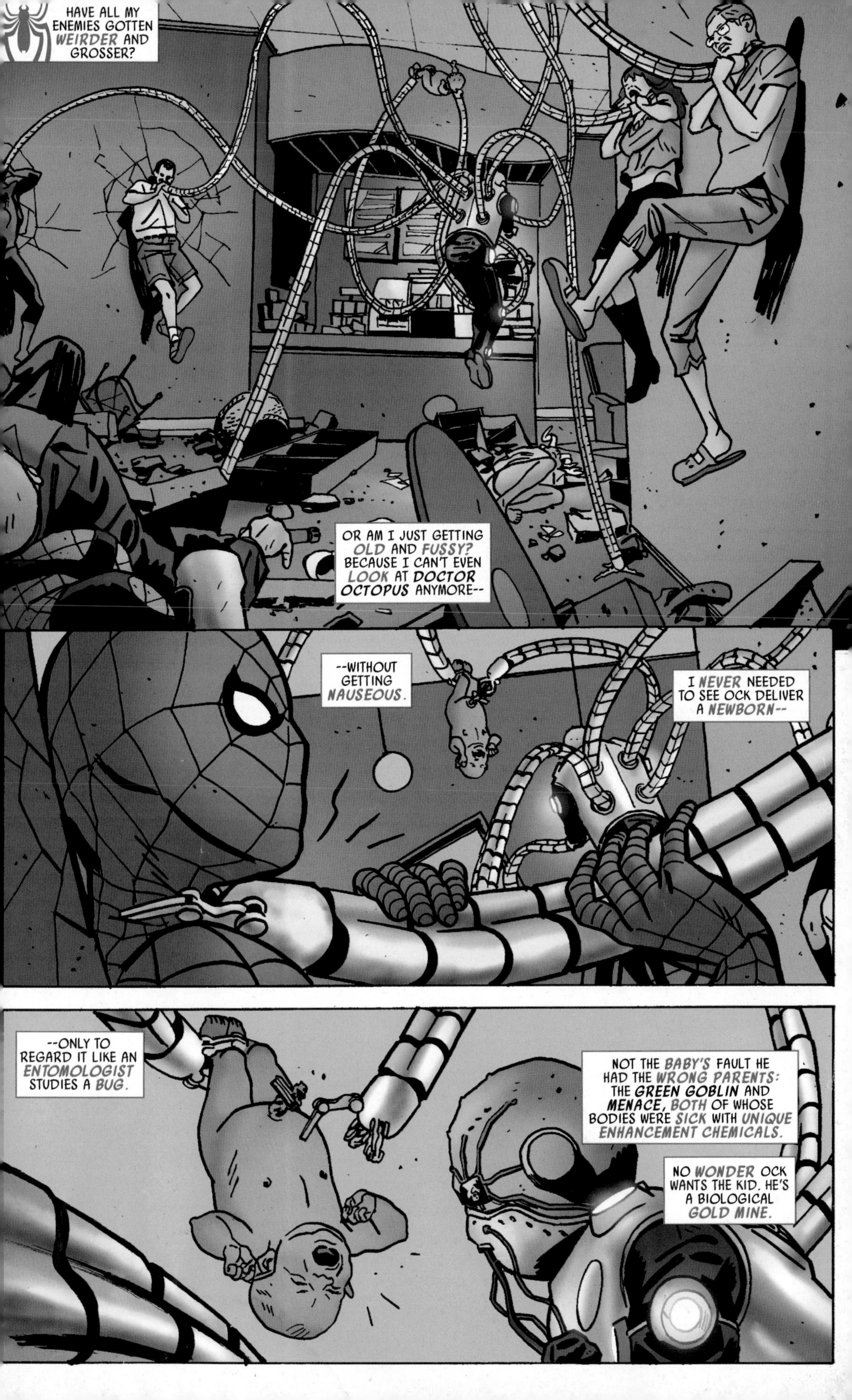
HAVE ALL MY ENEMIES GOTTEN WEIRDER AND GROSSER?
OR AM I JUST GETTING OLD AND FUSSY? BECAUSE I CAN'T EVEN LOOK AT DOCTOR OCTOPUS ANYMORE--
--WITHOUT GETTING NAUSEOUS.
I NEVER NEEDED TO SEE OCK DELIVER A NEWBORN--
--ONLY TO REGARD IT LIKE AN ENTOMOLOGIST STUDIES A BUG.
NOT THE BABY'S FAULT HE HAD THE WRONG PARENTS: THE GREEN GOBLIN AND MENACE, BOTH OF WHOSE BODIES WERE SICK WITH UNIQUE ENHANCEMENT CHEMICALS.
NO WONDER OCK WANTS THE KID. HE'S A BIOLOGICAL GOLD MINE.

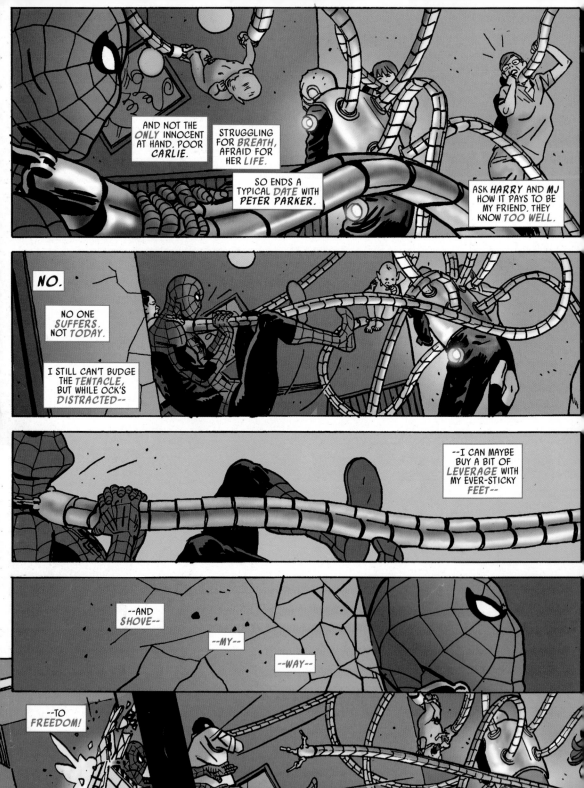

AND NOT THE *ONLY* INNOCENT AT HAND. POOR *CARLIE.*

STRUGGLING FOR *BREATH,* AFRAID FOR HER *LIFE.*

SO ENDS A TYPICAL *DATE* WITH PETER PARKER.

ASK *HARRY* AND *MJ* HOW IT PAYS TO BE MY FRIEND. THEY KNOW *TOO WELL.*

NO.

NO ONE *SUFFERS.* NOT *TODAY.*

I STILL CAN'T BUDGE THE *TENTACLE,* BUT WHILE OCK'S *DISTRACTED*--

--I CAN MAYBE BUY A BIT OF *LEVERAGE* WITH MY EVER-STICKY *FEET*--

--AND *SHOVE*--

--*MY*--

--*WAY*--

--TO *FREEDOM!*

SKRAAAAK!

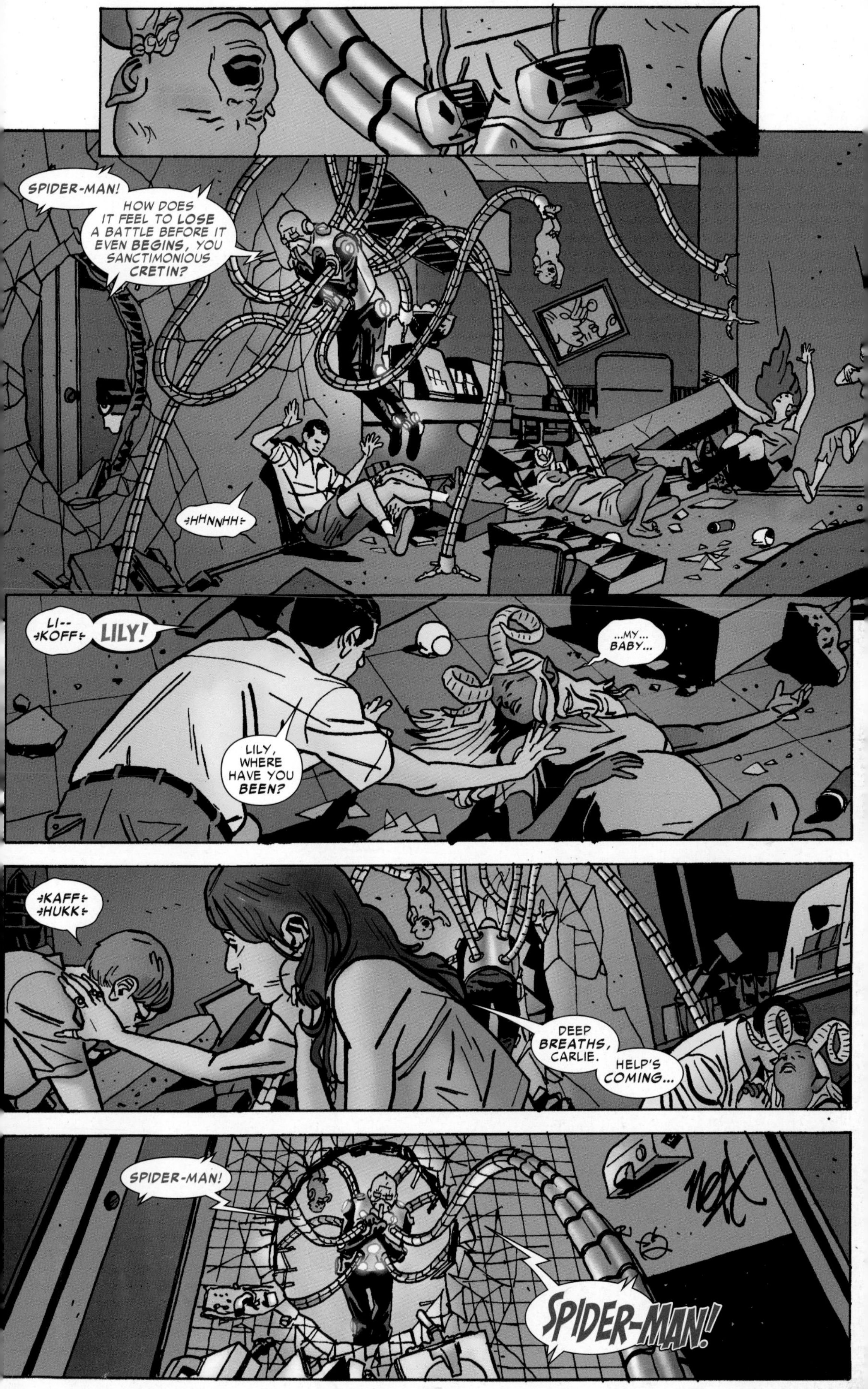
SPIDER-MAN!
HOW DOES IT FEEL TO LOSE A BATTLE BEFORE IT EVEN BEGINS, YOU SANCTIMONIOUS CRETIN?
HHNNHH
LI-- KOFF LILY!
...MY... BABY...
LILY, WHERE HAVE YOU BEEN?
KAFF HUKK
DEEP BREATHS, CARLIE.
HELP'S COMING...
SPIDER-MAN!
SPIDER-MAN!

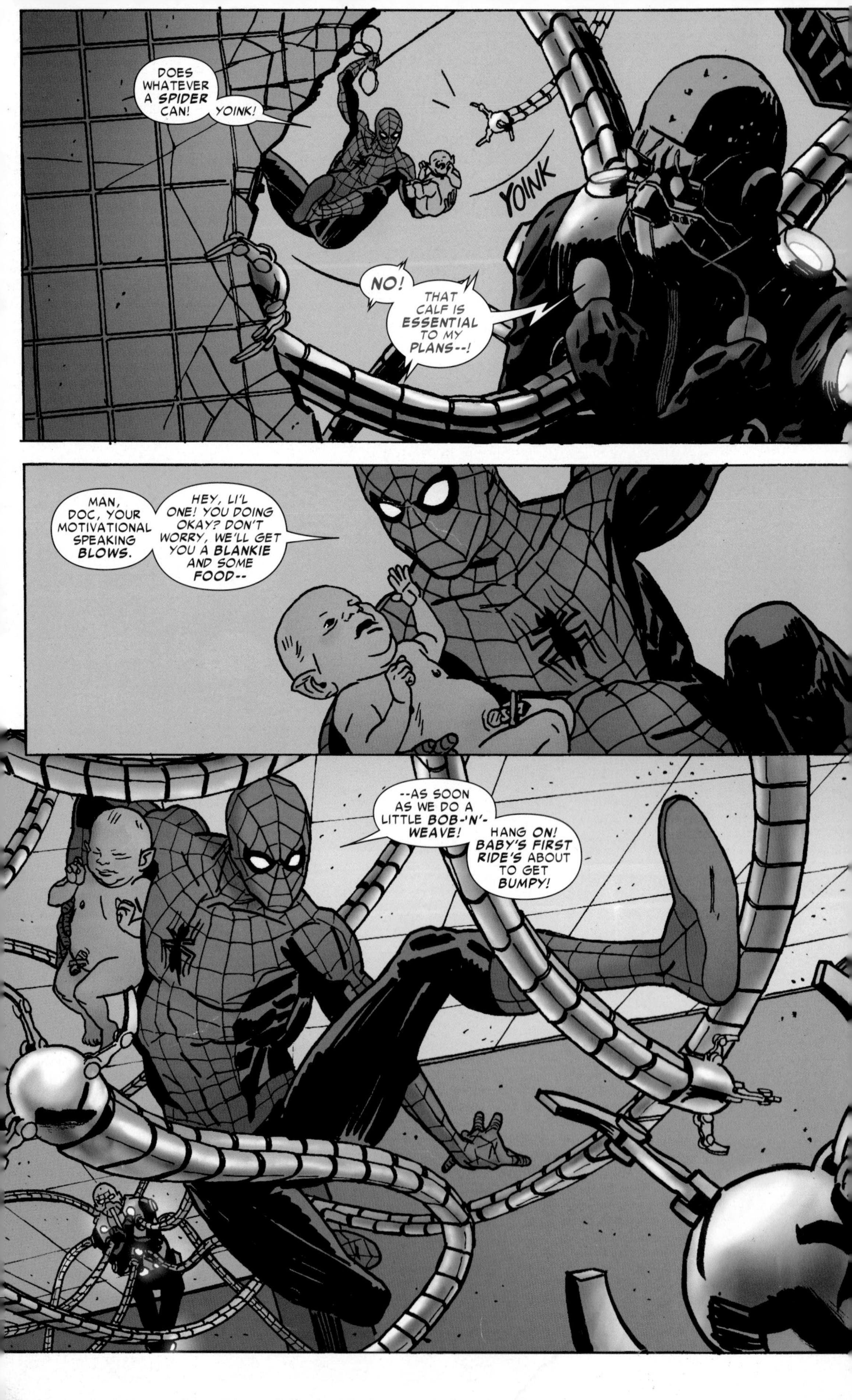
DOES WHATEVER A SPIDER CAN!
YOINK!
YOINK
NO!
THAT CALF IS ESSENTIAL TO MY PLANS--!
MAN, DOC, YOUR MOTIVATIONAL SPEAKING BLOWS.
HEY, LI'L ONE! YOU DOING OKAY? DON'T WORRY, WE'LL GET YOU A BLANKIE AND SOME FOOD--
--AS SOON AS WE DO A LITTLE BOB-'N'-WEAVE!
HANG ON! BABY'S FIRST RIDE'S ABOUT TO GET BUMPY!

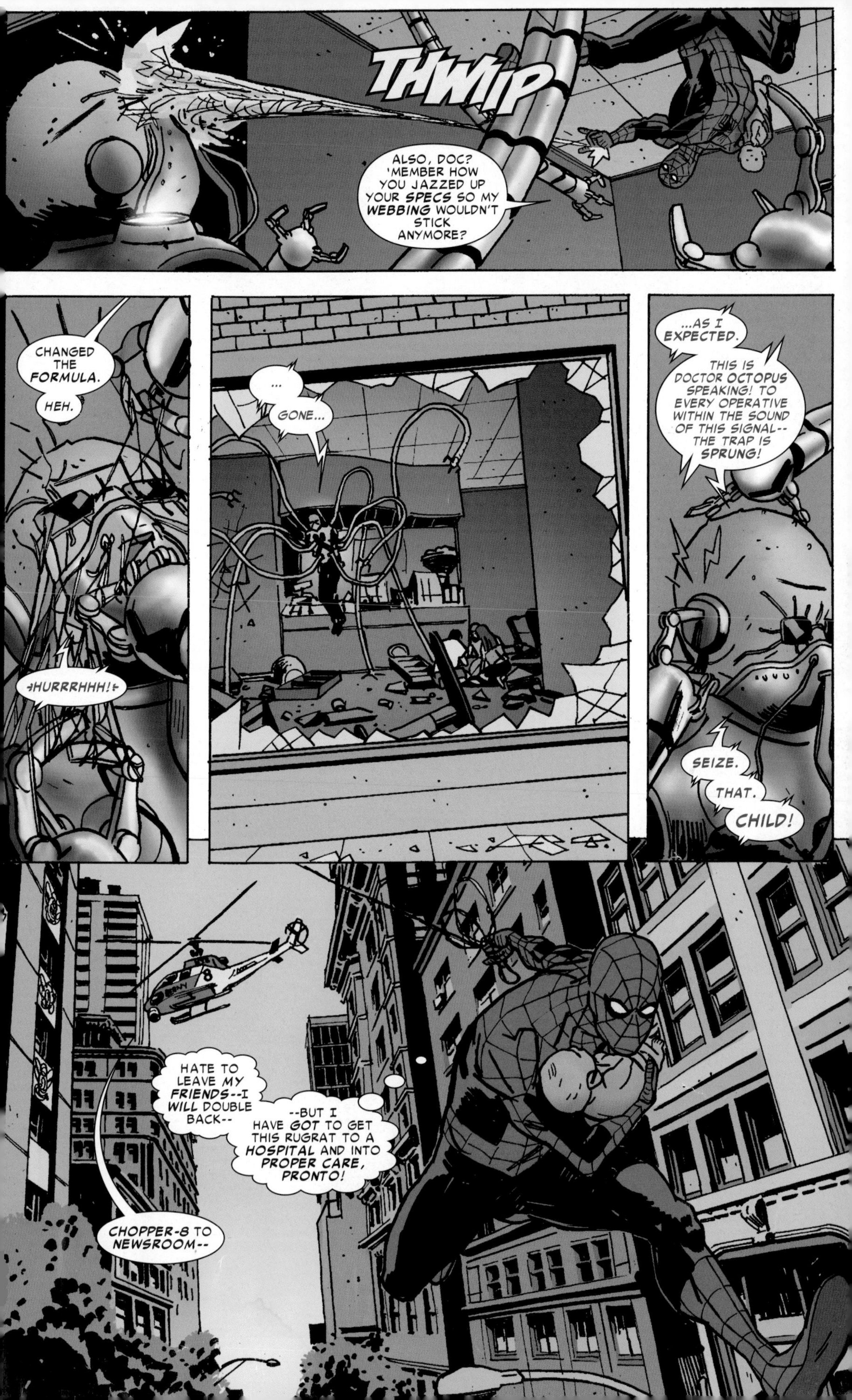
THWIP
ALSO, DOC? 'MEMBER HOW YOU JAZZED UP YOUR SPECS SO MY WEBBING WOULDN'T STICK ANYMORE?
CHANGED THE FORMULA.
HEH.
HURRRHHH!
...
GONE...
...AS I EXPECTED.
THIS IS DOCTOR OCTOPUS SPEAKING! TO EVERY OPERATIVE WITHIN THE SOUND OF THIS SIGNAL-- THE TRAP IS SPRUNG!
SEIZE.
THAT.
CHILD!
HATE TO LEAVE MY FRIENDS--I WILL DOUBLE BACK--
--BUT I HAVE GOT TO GET THIS RUGRAT TO A HOSPITAL AND INTO PROPER CARE, PRONTO!
CHOPPER-8 TO NEWSROOM--

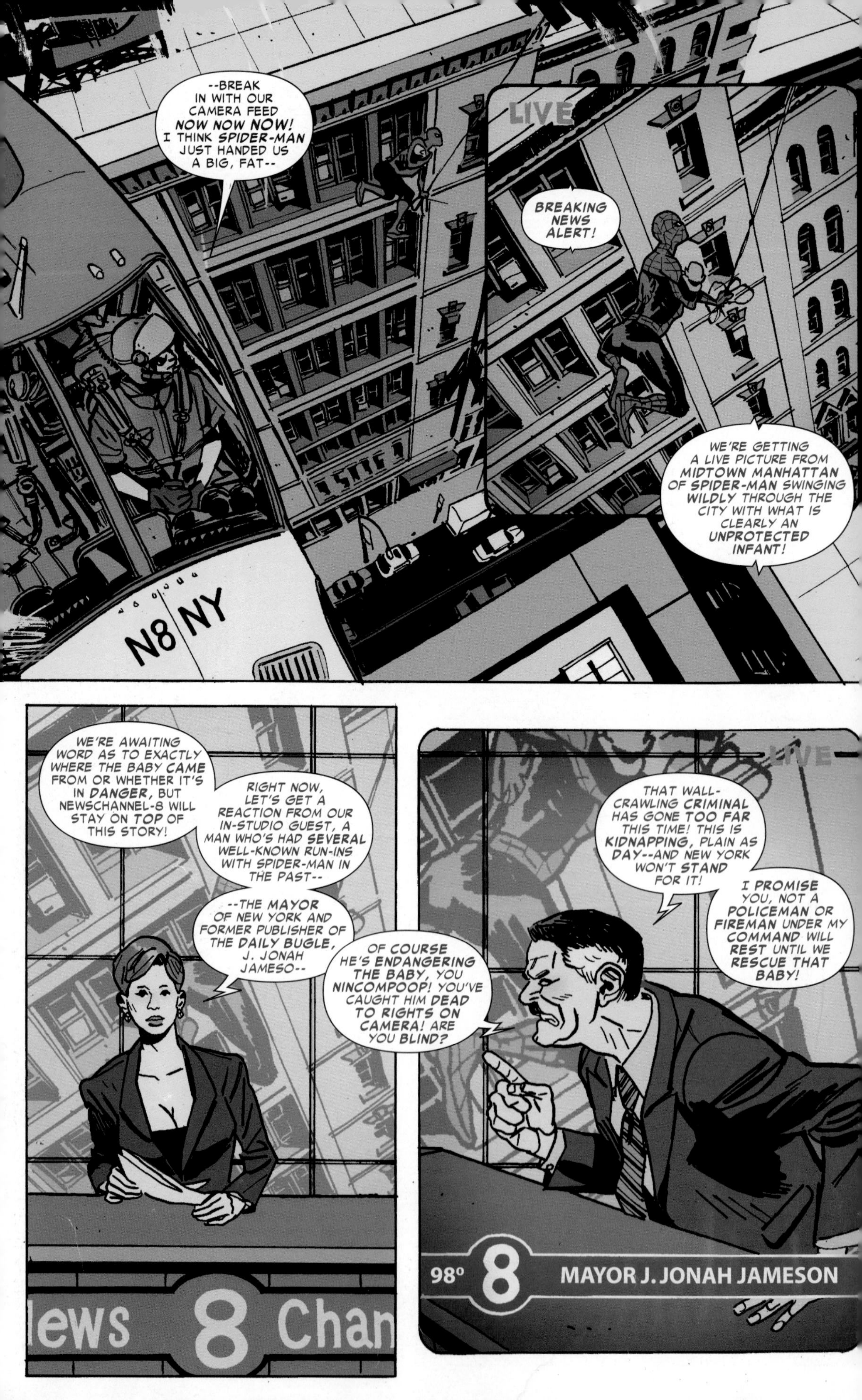
--BREAK IN WITH OUR CAMERA FEED NOW NOW NOW! I THINK SPIDER-MAN JUST HANDED US A BIG, FAT--
N8 NY
LIVE
BREAKING NEWS ALERT!
WE'RE GETTING A LIVE PICTURE FROM MIDTOWN MANHATTAN OF SPIDER-MAN SWINGING WILDLY THROUGH THE CITY WITH WHAT IS CLEARLY AN UNPROTECTED INFANT!
WE'RE AWAITING WORD AS TO EXACTLY WHERE THE BABY CAME FROM OR WHETHER IT'S IN DANGER, BUT NEWSCHANNEL-8 WILL STAY ON TOP OF THIS STORY!
RIGHT NOW, LET'S GET A REACTION FROM OUR IN-STUDIO GUEST, A MAN WHO'S HAD SEVERAL WELL-KNOWN RUN-INS WITH SPIDER-MAN IN THE PAST--
--THE MAYOR OF NEW YORK AND FORMER PUBLISHER OF THE DAILY BUGLE, J. JONAH JAMESO--
OF COURSE HE'S ENDANGERING THE BABY, YOU NINCOMPOOP! YOU'VE CAUGHT HIM DEAD TO RIGHTS ON CAMERA! ARE YOU BLIND?
lews 8 Chan
LIVE
THAT WALL-CRAWLING CRIMINAL HAS GONE TOO FAR THIS TIME! THIS IS KIDNAPPING, PLAIN AS DAY--AND NEW YORK WON'T STAND FOR IT!
I PROMISE YOU, NOT A POLICEMAN OR FIREMAN UNDER MY COMMAND WILL REST UNTIL WE RESCUE THAT BABY!
98º 8 MAYOR J. JONAH JAMESON

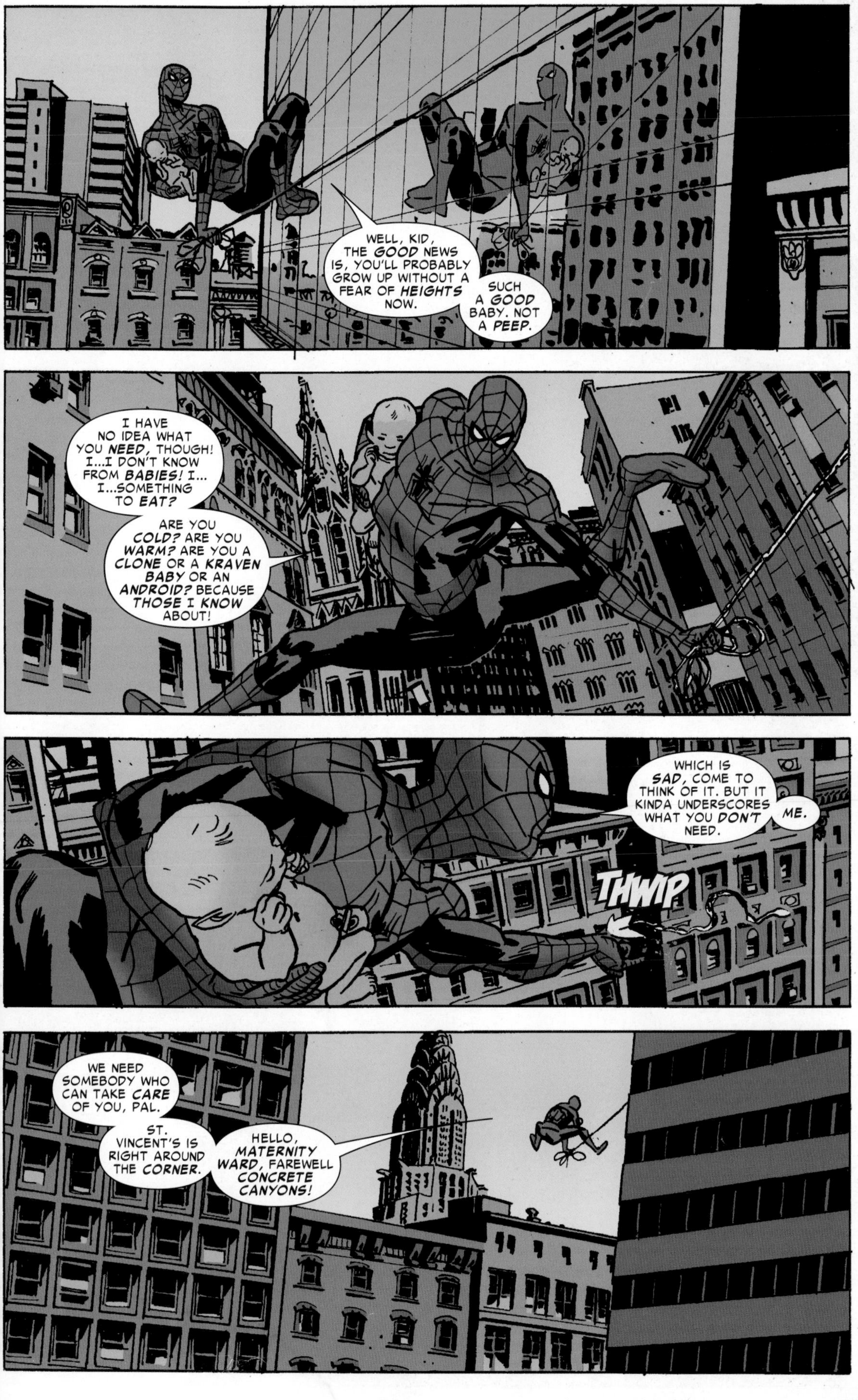

WELL, KID, THE GOOD NEWS IS, YOU'LL PROBABLY GROW UP WITHOUT A FEAR OF HEIGHTS NOW.
SUCH A GOOD BABY. NOT A PEEP.
I HAVE NO IDEA WHAT YOU NEED, THOUGH! I...I DON'T KNOW FROM BABIES! I... I...SOMETHING TO EAT?
ARE YOU COLD? ARE YOU WARM? ARE YOU A CLONE OR A KRAVEN BABY OR AN ANDROID? BECAUSE THOSE I KNOW ABOUT!
WHICH IS SAD, COME TO THINK OF IT. BUT IT KINDA UNDERSCORES WHAT YOU DON'T NEED.
ME.
THWIP
WE NEED SOMEBODY WHO CAN TAKE CARE OF YOU, PAL.
ST. VINCENT'S IS RIGHT AROUND THE CORNER.
HELLO, MATERNITY WARD, FAREWELL CONCRETE CANYONS!

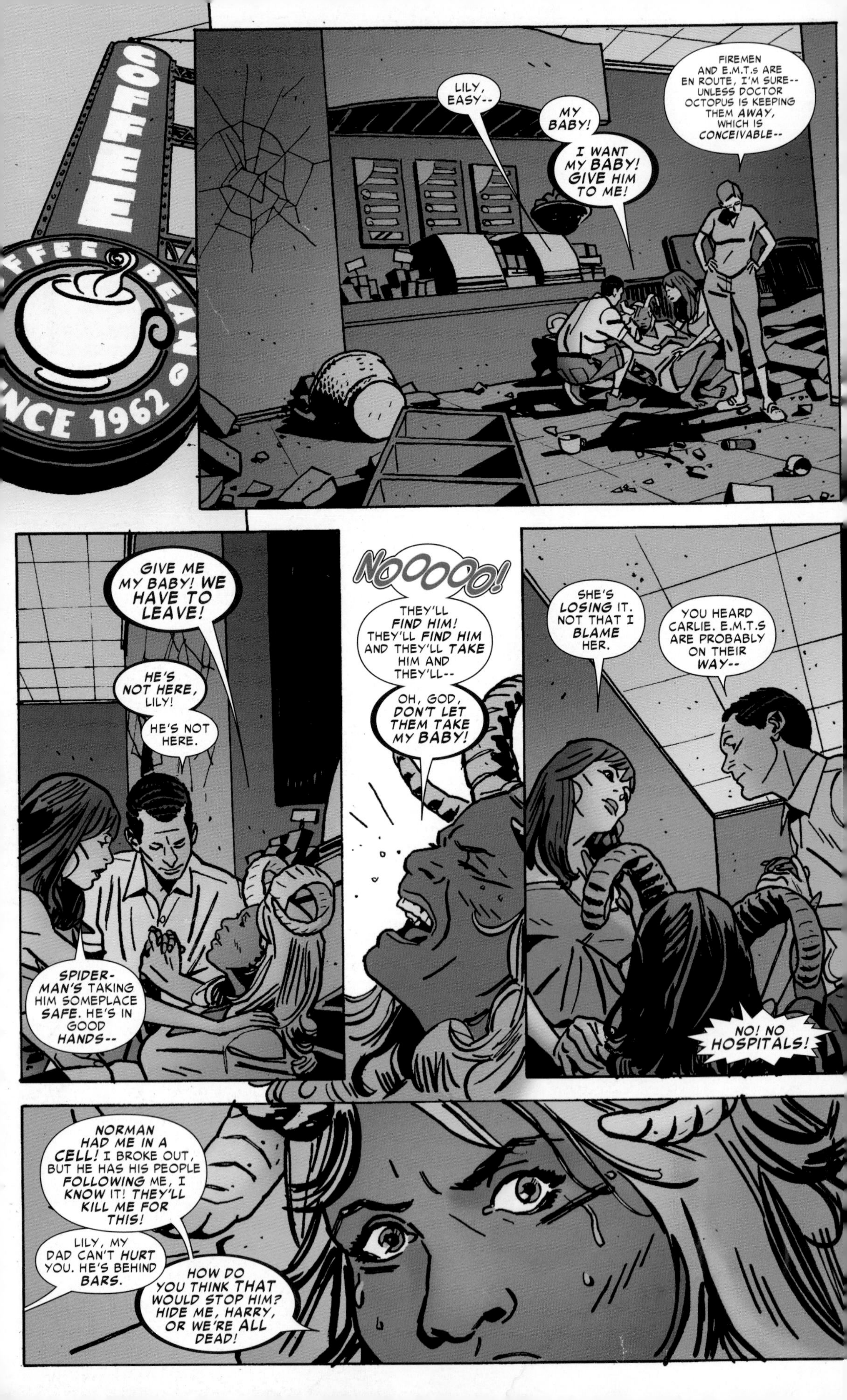
COFFEE
FFEE BEAN
NCE 1962
LILY, EASY--
MY BABY!
I WANT MY BABY! GIVE HIM TO ME!
FIREMEN AND E.M.T.s ARE EN ROUTE, I'M SURE-- UNLESS DOCTOR OCTOPUS IS KEEPING THEM AWAY, WHICH IS CONCEIVABLE--
GIVE ME MY BABY! WE HAVE TO LEAVE!
HE'S NOT HERE, LILY!
HE'S NOT HERE.
SPIDER-MAN'S TAKING HIM SOMEPLACE SAFE. HE'S IN GOOD HANDS--
NOOOOO!
THEY'LL FIND HIM! THEY'LL FIND HIM AND THEY'LL TAKE HIM AND THEY'LL--
OH, GOD, DON'T LET THEM TAKE MY BABY!
SHE'S LOSING IT. NOT THAT I BLAME HER.
YOU HEARD CARLIE. E.M.T.S ARE PROBABLY ON THEIR WAY--
NO! NO HOSPITALS!
NORMAN HAD ME IN A CELL! I BROKE OUT, BUT HE HAS HIS PEOPLE FOLLOWING ME, I KNOW IT! THEY'LL KILL ME FOR THIS!
LILY, MY DAD CAN'T HURT YOU. HE'S BEHIND BARS.
HOW DO YOU THINK THAT WOULD STOP HIM? HIDE ME, HARRY, OR WE'RE ALL DEAD!

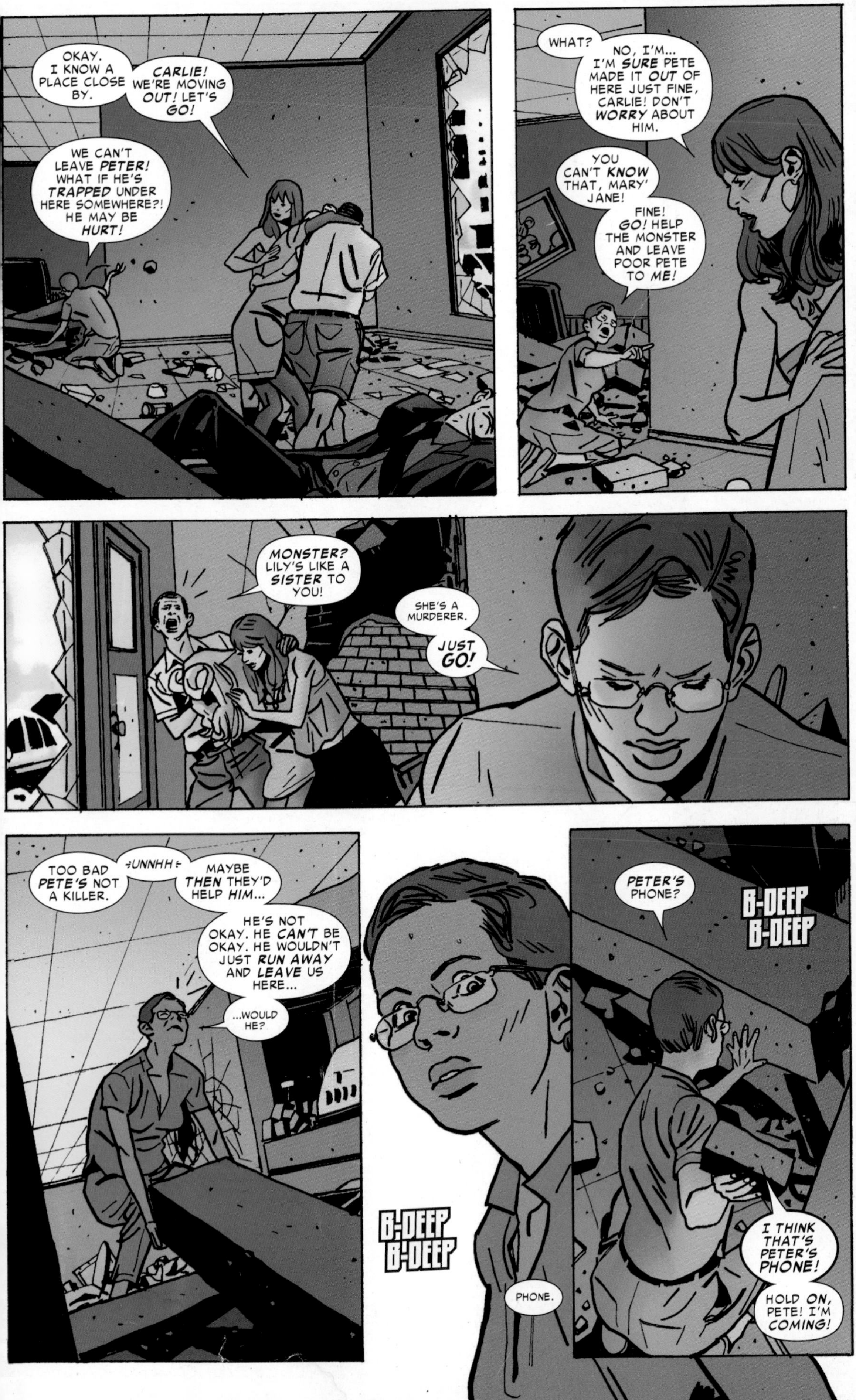
OKAY. I KNOW A PLACE CLOSE BY.
CARLIE! WE'RE MOVING OUT! LET'S GO!
WE CAN'T LEAVE PETER! WHAT IF HE'S TRAPPED UNDER HERE SOMEWHERE?! HE MAY BE HURT!
WHAT?
NO, I'M... I'M SURE PETE MADE IT OUT OF HERE JUST FINE, CARLIE! DON'T WORRY ABOUT HIM.
YOU CAN'T KNOW THAT, MARY JANE!
FINE! GO! HELP THE MONSTER AND LEAVE POOR PETE TO ME!
MONSTER? LILY'S LIKE A SISTER TO YOU!
SHE'S A MURDERER.
JUST GO!
TOO BAD PETE'S NOT A KILLER.
UNNHH
MAYBE THEN THEY'D HELP HIM...
HE'S NOT OKAY. HE CAN'T BE OKAY. HE WOULDN'T JUST RUN AWAY AND LEAVE US HERE...
...WOULD HE?
B-DEEP B-DEEP
PHONE.
PETER'S PHONE?
B-DEEP B-DEEP
I THINK THAT'S PETER'S PHONE!
HOLD ON, PETE! I'M COMING!

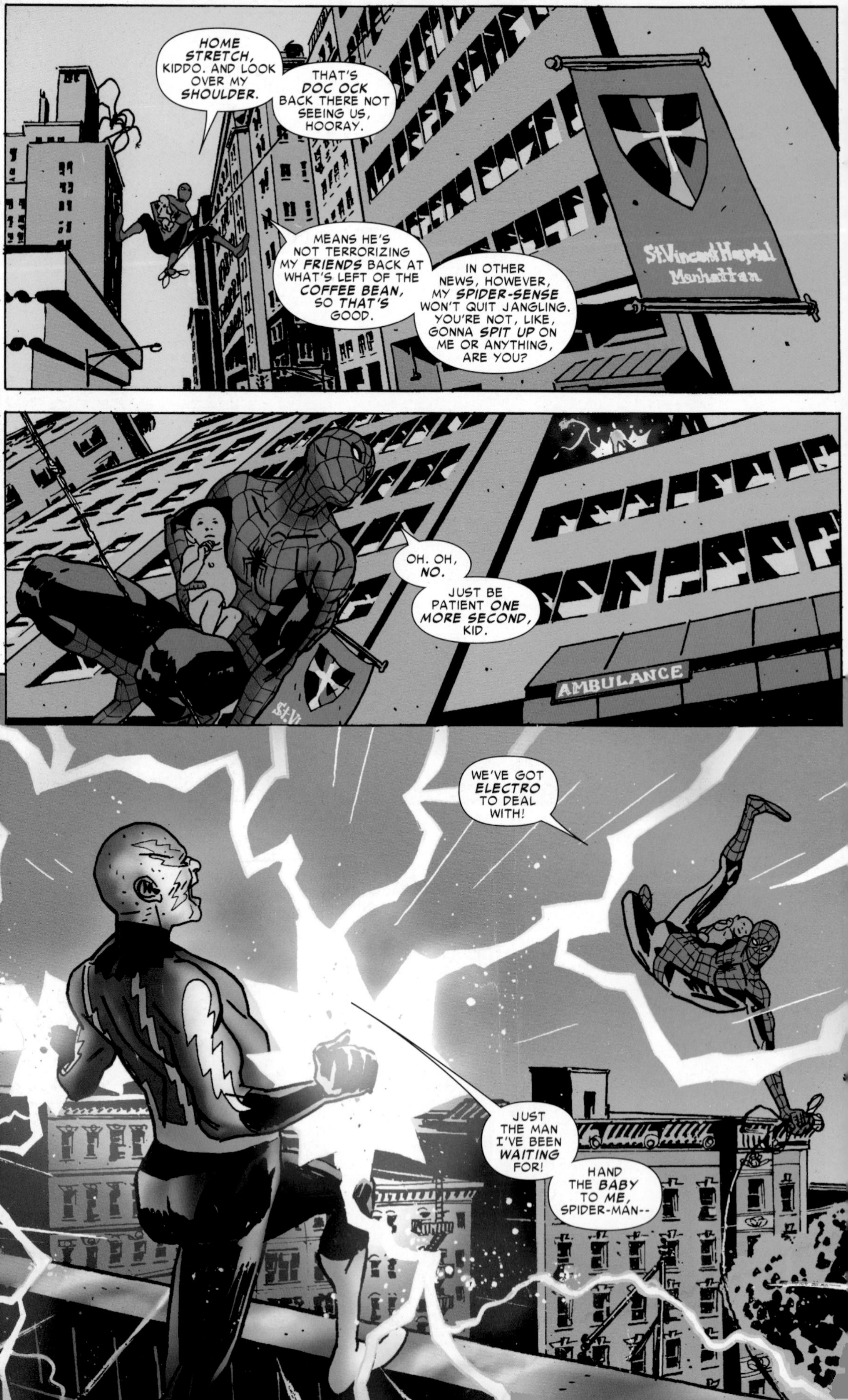
HOME STRETCH, KIDDO. AND LOOK OVER MY SHOULDER.
THAT'S DOC OCK BACK THERE NOT SEEING US, HOORAY.
St. Vincent's Hospital Manhattan
MEANS HE'S NOT TERRORIZING MY FRIENDS BACK AT WHAT'S LEFT OF THE COFFEE BEAN, SO THAT'S GOOD.
IN OTHER NEWS, HOWEVER, MY SPIDER-SENSE WON'T QUIT JANGLING. YOU'RE NOT, LIKE, GONNA SPIT UP ON ME OR ANYTHING, ARE YOU?
OH. OH, NO.
JUST BE PATIENT ONE MORE SECOND, KID.
AMBULANCE
WE'VE GOT ELECTRO TO DEAL WITH!
JUST THE MAN I'VE BEEN WAITING FOR!
HAND THE BABY TO ME, SPIDER-MAN--

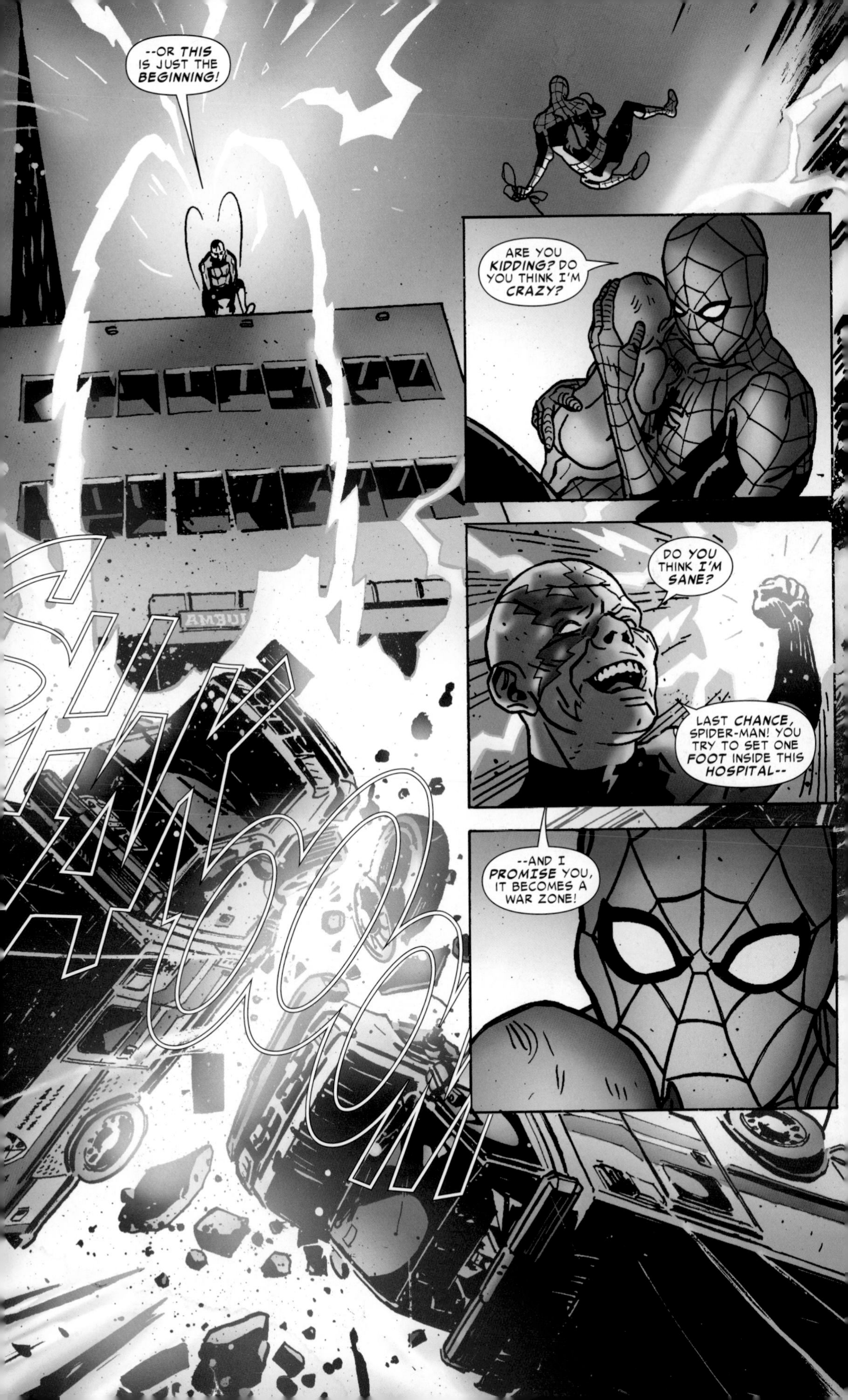
--OR THIS IS JUST THE BEGINNING!
ARE YOU KIDDING? DO YOU THINK I'M CRAZY?
DO YOU THINK I'M SANE?
LAST CHANCE, SPIDER-MAN! YOU TRY TO SET ONE FOOT INSIDE THIS HOSPITAL--
--AND I PROMISE YOU, IT BECOMES A WAR ZONE!
AMBU

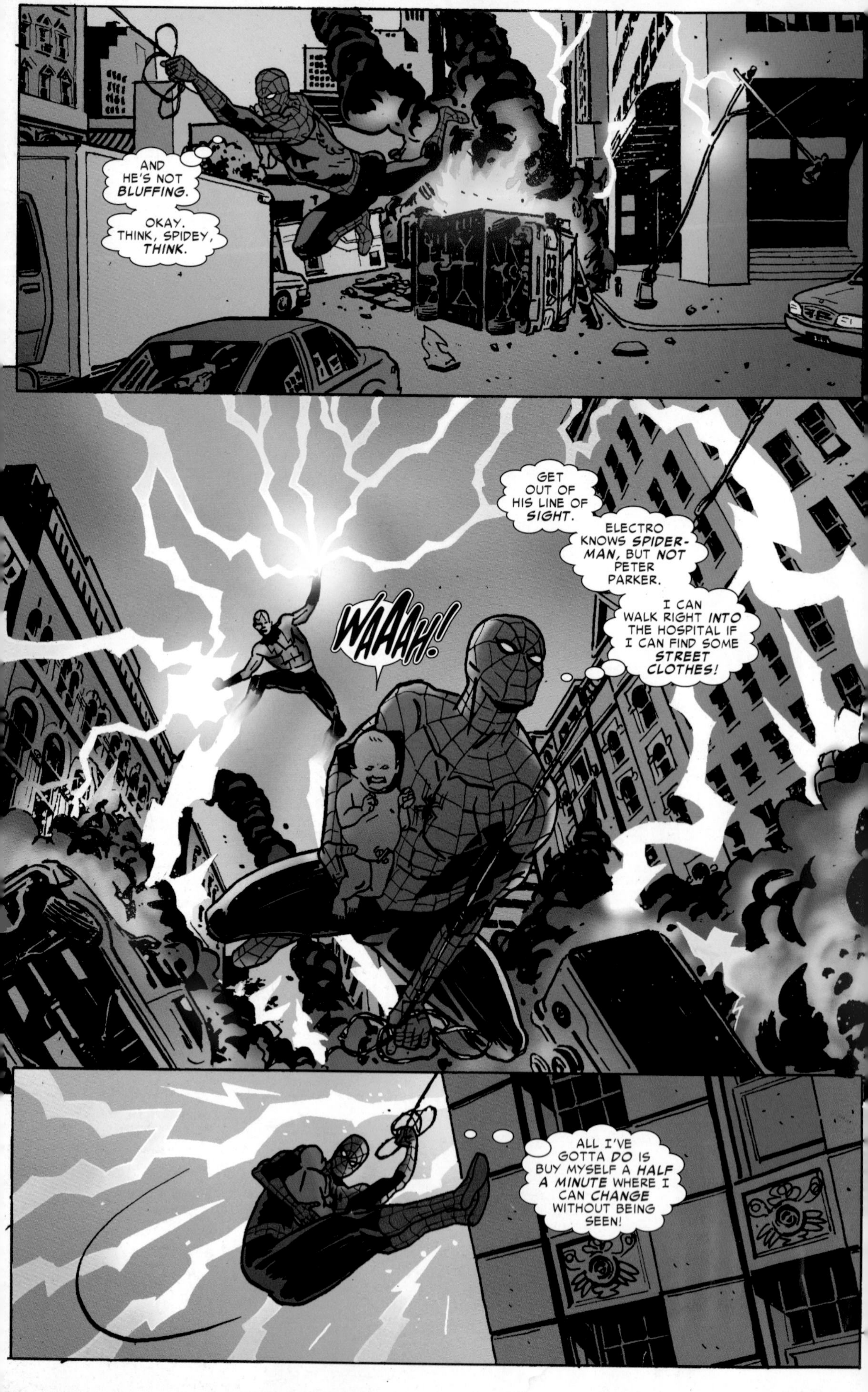
AND HE'S NOT BLUFFING.
OKAY. THINK, SPIDEY, THINK.
GET OUT OF HIS LINE OF SIGHT.
ELECTRO KNOWS SPIDER-MAN, BUT NOT PETER PARKER.
I CAN WALK RIGHT INTO THE HOSPITAL IF I CAN FIND SOME STREET CLOTHES!
WAAAH!
ALL I'VE GOTTA DO IS BUY MYSELF A HALF A MINUTE WHERE I CAN CHANGE WITHOUT BEING SEEN!

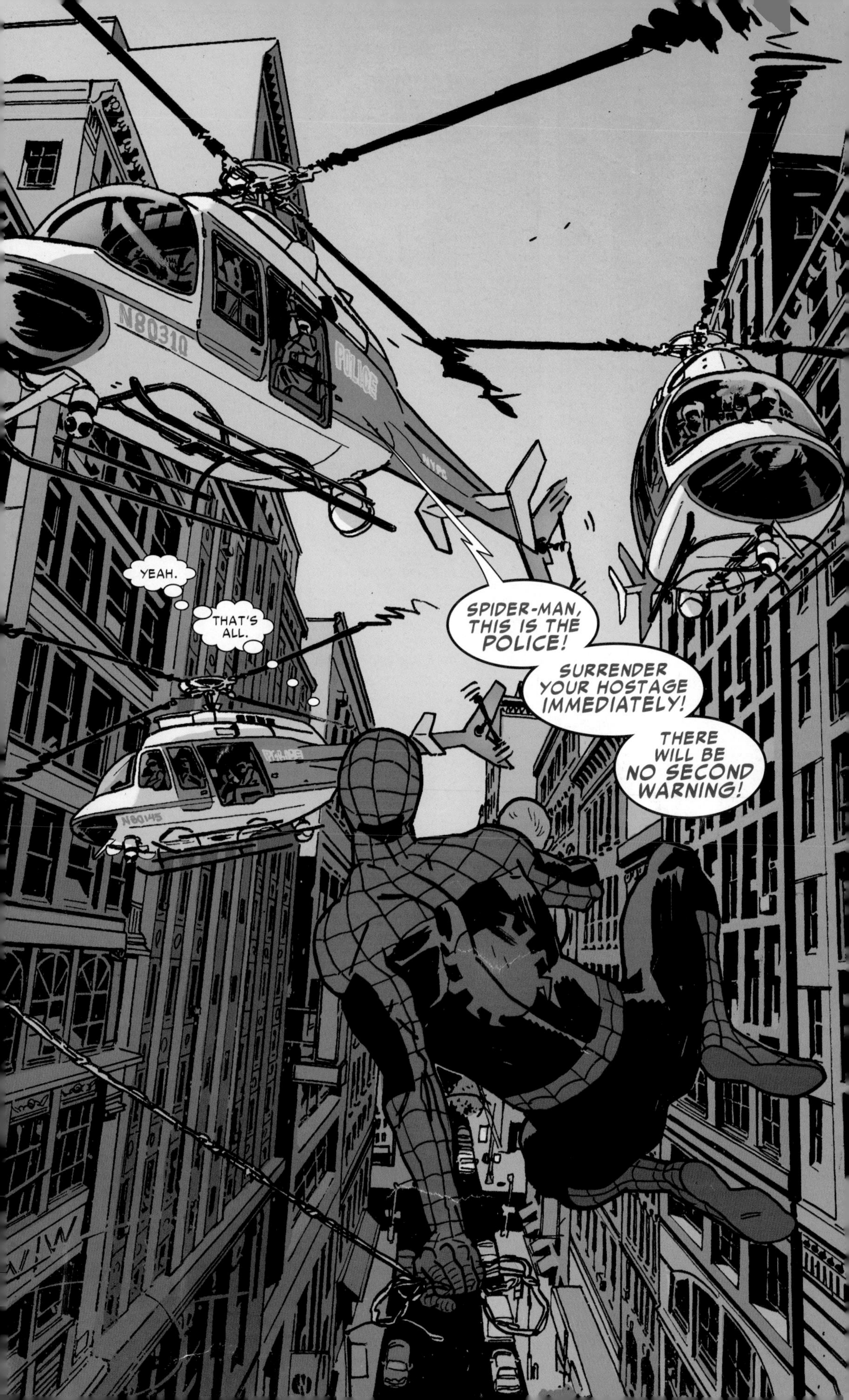
YEAH.
THAT'S ALL.
SPIDER-MAN, THIS IS THE POLICE!
SURRENDER YOUR HOSTAGE IMMEDIATELY!
THERE WILL BE NO SECOND WARNING!

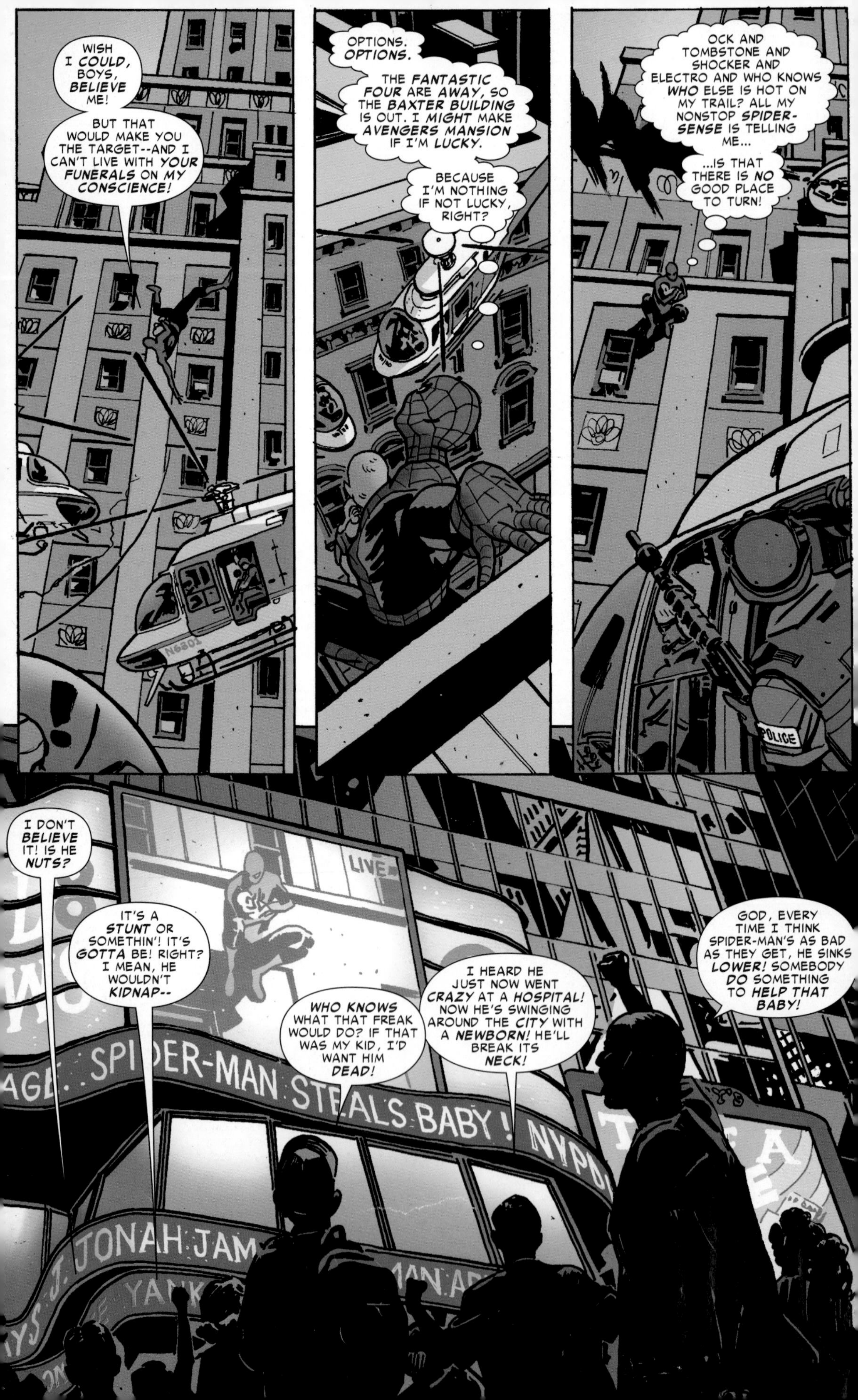
WISH I COULD, BOYS, BELIEVE ME!
BUT THAT WOULD MAKE YOU THE TARGET--AND I CAN'T LIVE WITH YOUR FUNERALS ON MY CONSCIENCE!
N6301
OPTIONS. OPTIONS.
THE FANTASTIC FOUR ARE AWAY, SO THE BAXTER BUILDING IS OUT. I MIGHT MAKE AVENGERS MANSION IF I'M LUCKY.
BECAUSE I'M NOTHING IF NOT LUCKY, RIGHT?
OCK AND TOMBSTONE AND SHOCKER AND ELECTRO AND WHO KNOWS WHO ELSE IS HOT ON MY TRAIL? ALL MY NONSTOP SPIDER-SENSE IS TELLING ME...
...IS THAT THERE IS NO GOOD PLACE TO TURN!
POLICE
I DON'T BELIEVE IT! IS HE NUTS?
IT'S A STUNT OR SOMETHIN'! IT'S GOTTA BE! RIGHT? I MEAN, HE WOULDN'T KIDNAP--
WHO KNOWS WHAT THAT FREAK WOULD DO? IF THAT WAS MY KID, I'D WANT HIM DEAD!
I HEARD HE JUST NOW WENT CRAZY AT A HOSPITAL! NOW HE'S SWINGING AROUND THE CITY WITH A NEWBORN! HE'LL BREAK ITS NECK!
GOD, EVERY TIME I THINK SPIDER-MAN'S AS BAD AS THEY GET, HE SINKS LOWER! SOMEBODY DO SOMETHING TO HELP THAT BABY!
LIVE
AGE.. SPIDER-MAN STEALS BABY! NYPD
J. JONAH JAM

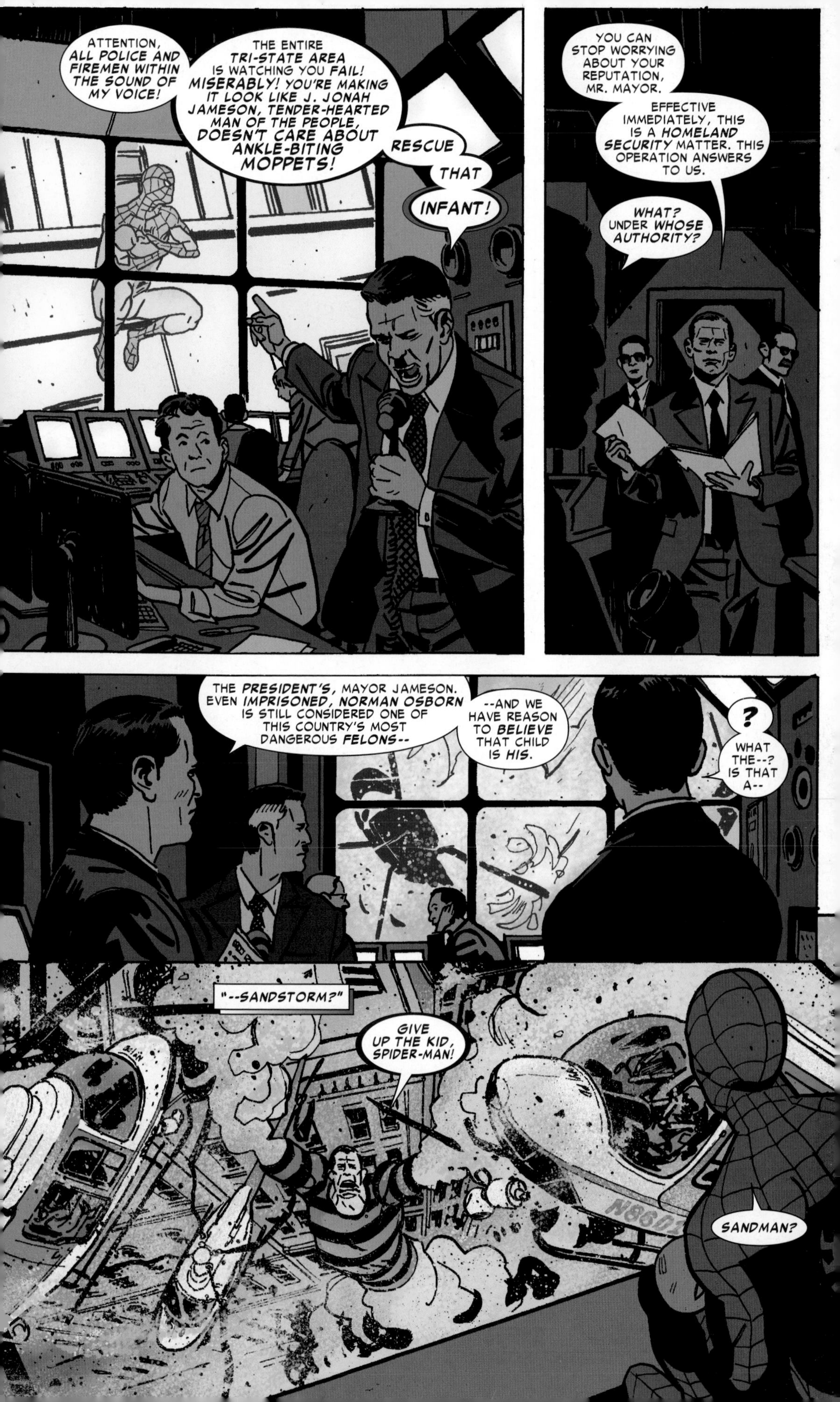

ATTENTION, ALL POLICE AND FIREMEN WITHIN THE SOUND OF MY VOICE!
THE ENTIRE TRI-STATE AREA IS WATCHING YOU FAIL! MISERABLY! YOU'RE MAKING IT LOOK LIKE J. JONAH JAMESON, TENDER-HEARTED MAN OF THE PEOPLE, DOESN'T CARE ABOUT ANKLE-BITING MOPPETS!
RESCUE
THAT
INFANT!
YOU CAN STOP WORRYING ABOUT YOUR REPUTATION, MR. MAYOR.
EFFECTIVE IMMEDIATELY, THIS IS A HOMELAND SECURITY MATTER. THIS OPERATION ANSWERS TO US.
WHAT? UNDER WHOSE AUTHORITY?
THE PRESIDENT'S, MAYOR JAMESON. EVEN IMPRISONED, NORMAN OSBORN IS STILL CONSIDERED ONE OF THIS COUNTRY'S MOST DANGEROUS FELONS--
--AND WE HAVE REASON TO BELIEVE THAT CHILD IS HIS.
?
WHAT THE--? IS THAT A--
"--SANDSTORM?"
GIVE UP THE KID, SPIDER-MAN!
SANDMAN?

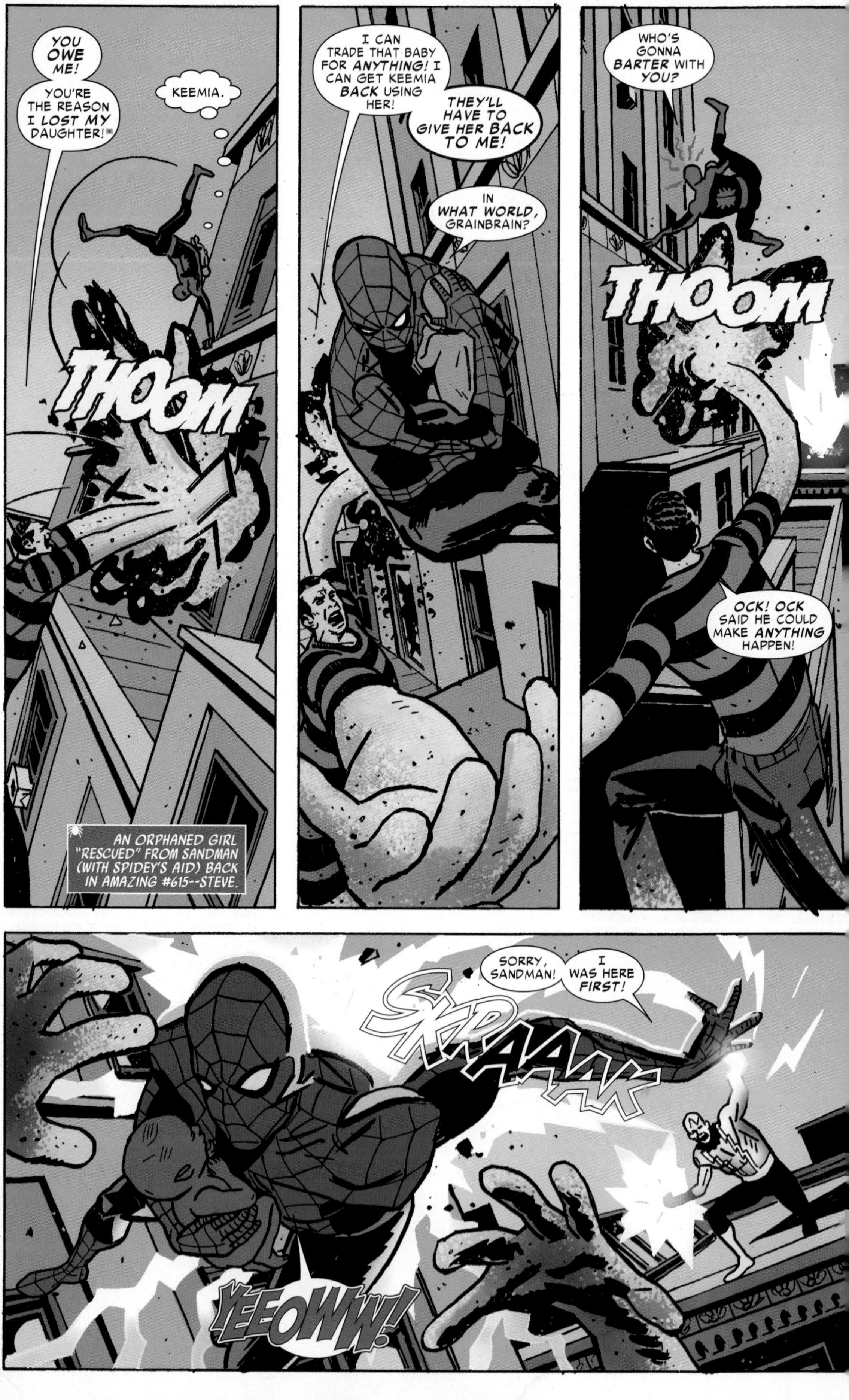

YOU OWE ME!
YOU'RE THE REASON I LOST MY DAUGHTER!*
KEEMIA.
THOOM
AN ORPHANED GIRL "RESCUED" FROM SANDMAN (WITH SPIDEY'S AID) BACK IN AMAZING #615--STEVE.
I CAN TRADE THAT BABY FOR ANYTHING! I CAN GET KEEMIA BACK USING HER!
THEY'LL HAVE TO GIVE HER BACK TO ME!
IN WHAT WORLD, GRAINBRAIN?
WHO'S GONNA BARTER WITH YOU?
THOOM
OCK! OCK SAID HE COULD MAKE ANYTHING HAPPEN!
SORRY, SANDMAN!
I WAS HERE FIRST!
SKRAAAK
YEEOWW!

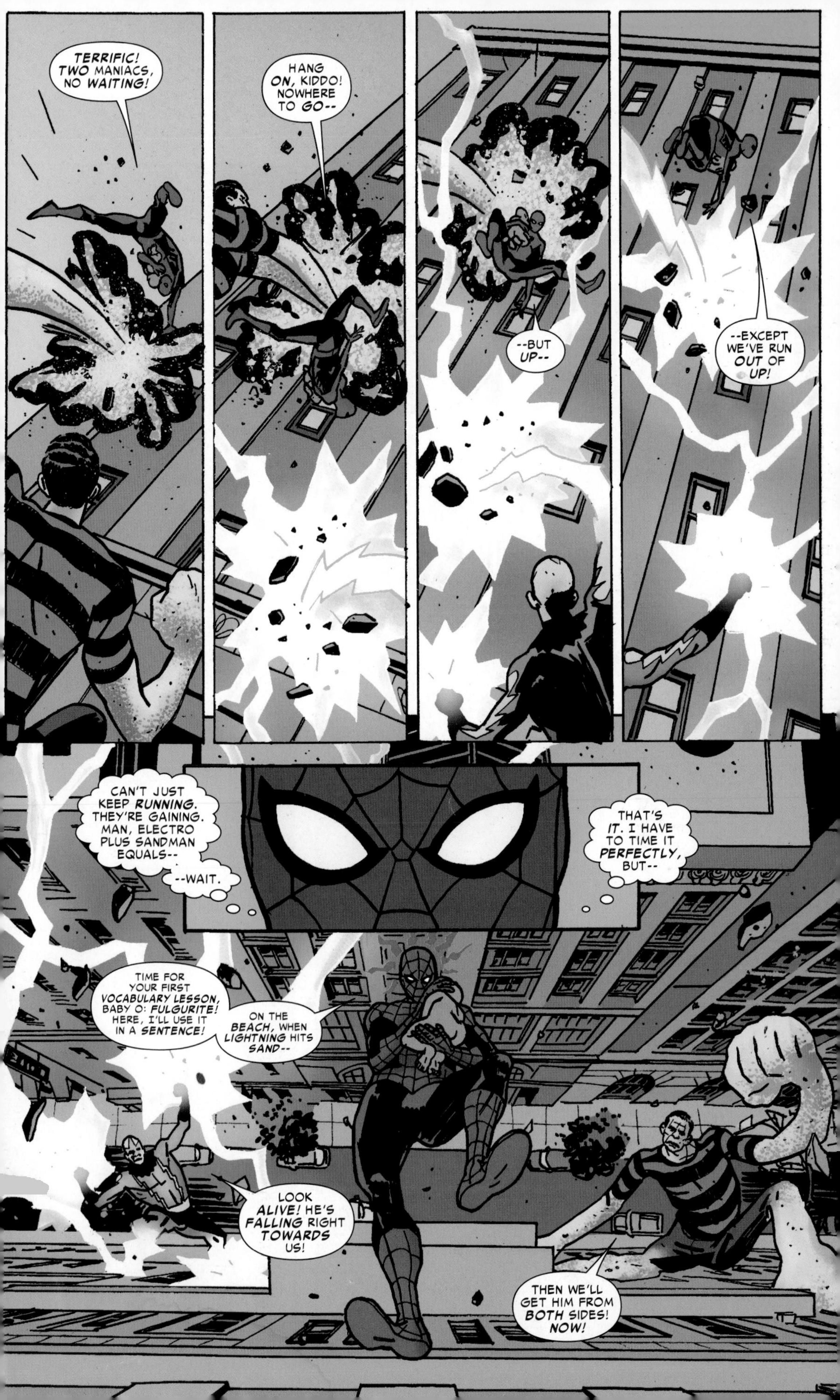

TERRIFIC! TWO MANIACS, NO WAITING!
HANG ON, KIDDO! NOWHERE TO GO--
--BUT UP--
--EXCEPT WE'VE RUN OUT OF UP!
CAN'T JUST KEEP RUNNING. THEY'RE GAINING. MAN, ELECTRO PLUS SANDMAN EQUALS--
--WAIT.
THAT'S IT. I HAVE TO TIME IT PERFECTLY, BUT--
TIME FOR YOUR FIRST VOCABULARY LESSON, BABY O: FULGURITE! HERE, I'LL USE IT IN A SENTENCE!
ON THE BEACH, WHEN LIGHTNING HITS SAND--
LOOK ALIVE! HE'S FALLING RIGHT TOWARDS US!
THEN WE'LL GET HIM FROM BOTH SIDES! NOW!

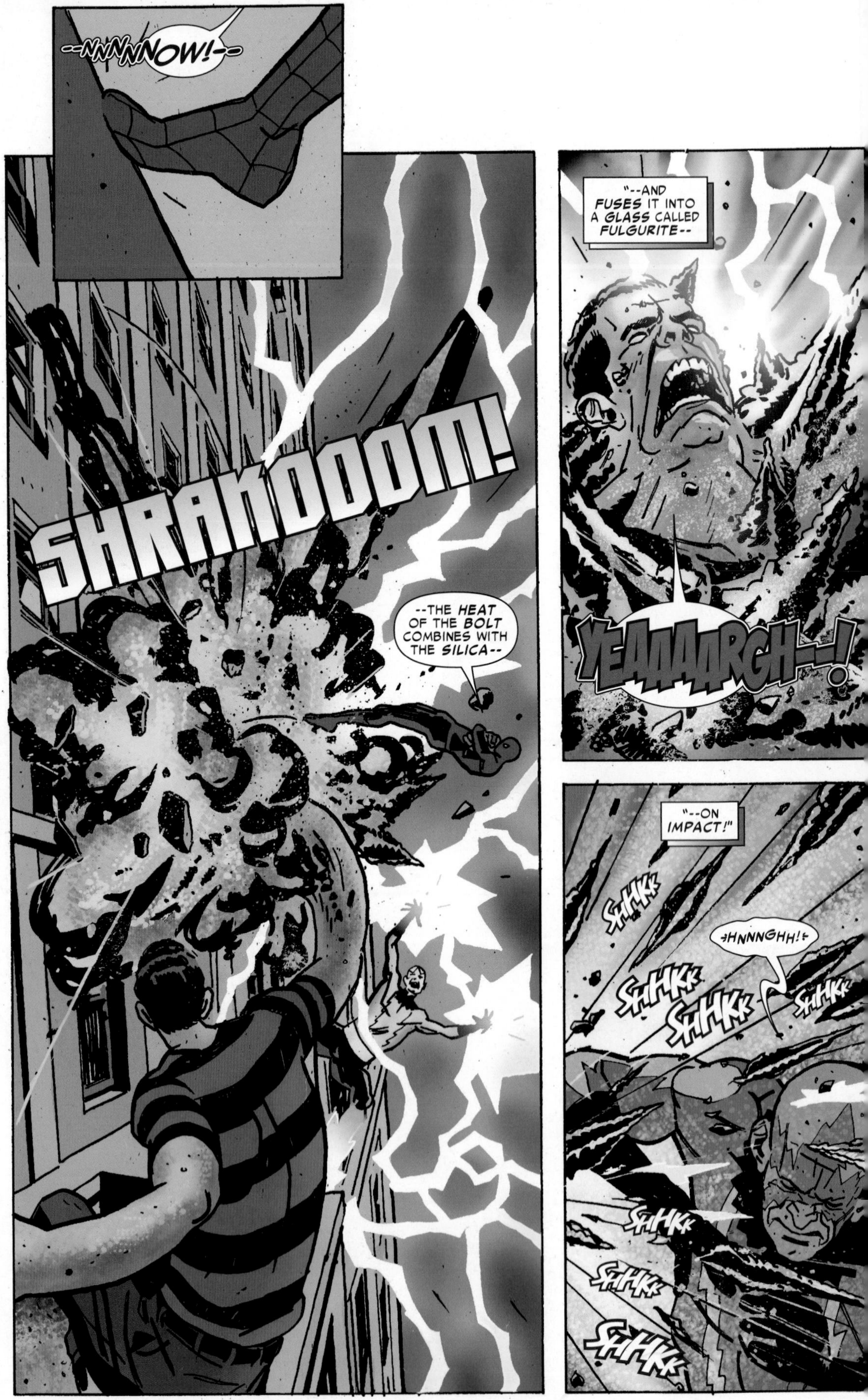
--NNNNNOW!--
SHRAKOOOM!
--THE HEAT OF THE BOLT COMBINES WITH THE SILICA--
"--AND FUSES IT INTO A GLASS CALLED FULGURITE--
YEAAAARGH--!
"--ON IMPACT!"
SHHKK
-HNNNGHH!-
SHHKK
SHHKK
SHHKK
SHHKK
SHHKK
SHHKK

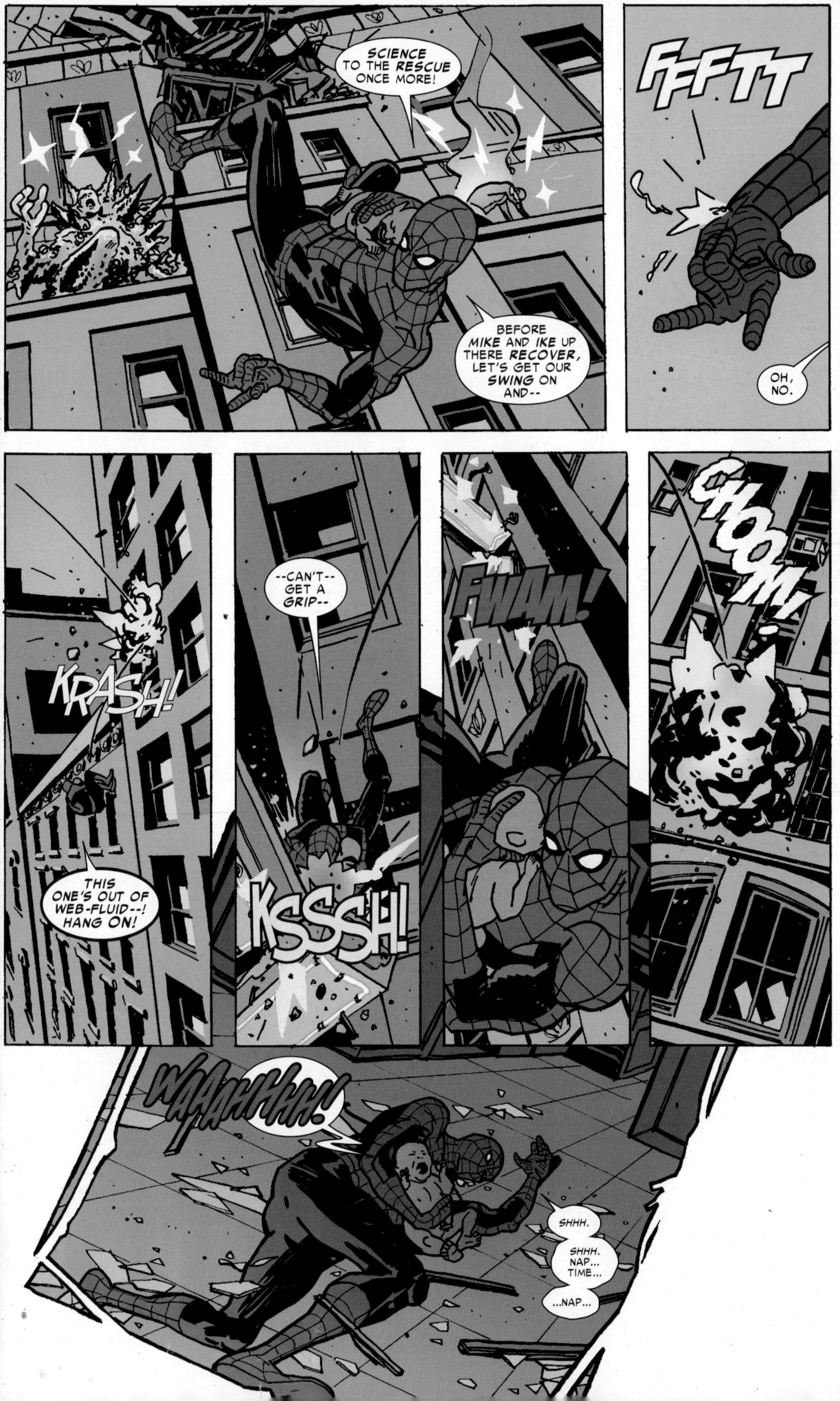

SCIENCE TO THE RESCUE ONCE MORE!
BEFORE MIKE AND IKE UP THERE RECOVER, LET'S GET OUR SWING ON AND--
FFFTTT
OH, NO.
KRASH!
THIS ONE'S OUT OF WEB-FLUID--! HANG ON!
--CAN'T-- GET A GRIP--
KSSSH!
FWAM!
CHOOM!
WAAAHHHH!
SHHH.
SHHH. NAP... TIME...
...NAP...

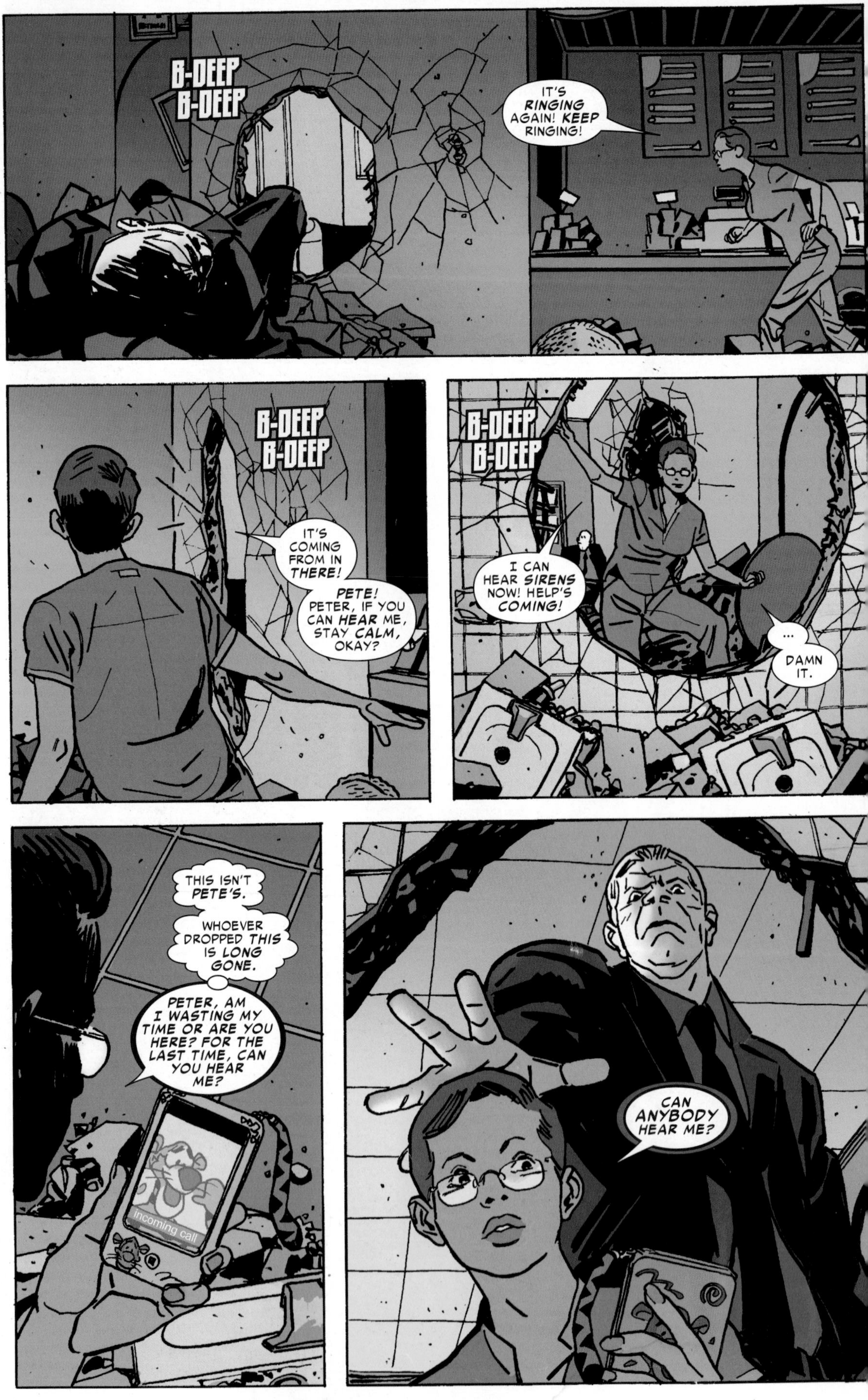
B-DEEP B-DEEP
IT'S RINGING AGAIN! KEEP RINGING!
B-DEEP B-DEEP
IT'S COMING FROM IN THERE!
PETE! PETER, IF YOU CAN HEAR ME, STAY CALM, OKAY?
B-DEEP B-DEEP
I CAN HEAR SIRENS NOW! HELP'S COMING!
...
DAMN IT.
THIS ISN'T PETE'S.
WHOEVER DROPPED THIS IS LONG GONE.
PETER, AM I WASTING MY TIME OR ARE YOU HERE? FOR THE LAST TIME, CAN YOU HEAR ME?
incoming call
CAN ANYBODY HEAR ME?

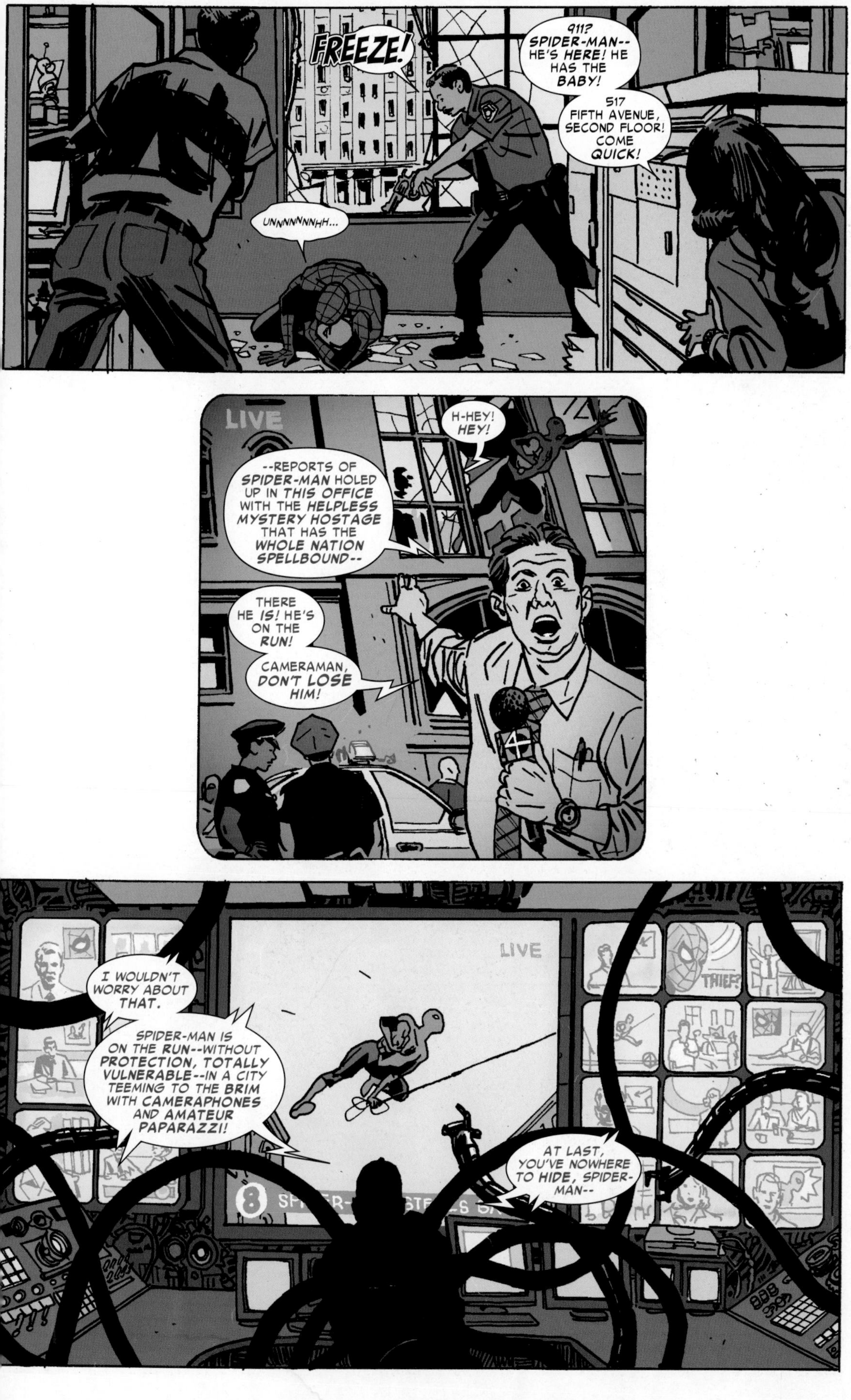

FREEZE!
911? SPIDER-MAN-- HE'S HERE! HE HAS THE BABY!
517 FIFTH AVENUE, SECOND FLOOR! COME QUICK!
UNNNNNNNHH...
LIVE
H-HEY! HEY!
--REPORTS OF SPIDER-MAN HOLED UP IN THIS OFFICE WITH THE HELPLESS MYSTERY HOSTAGE THAT HAS THE WHOLE NATION SPELLBOUND--
THERE HE IS! HE'S ON THE RUN!
CAMERAMAN, DON'T LOSE HIM!
LIVE
THIEF?
I WOULDN'T WORRY ABOUT THAT.
SPIDER-MAN IS ON THE RUN--WITHOUT PROTECTION, TOTALLY VULNERABLE--IN A CITY TEEMING TO THE BRIM WITH CAMERAPHONES AND AMATEUR PAPARAZZI!
AT LAST, YOU'VE NOWHERE TO HIDE, SPIDER-MAN--

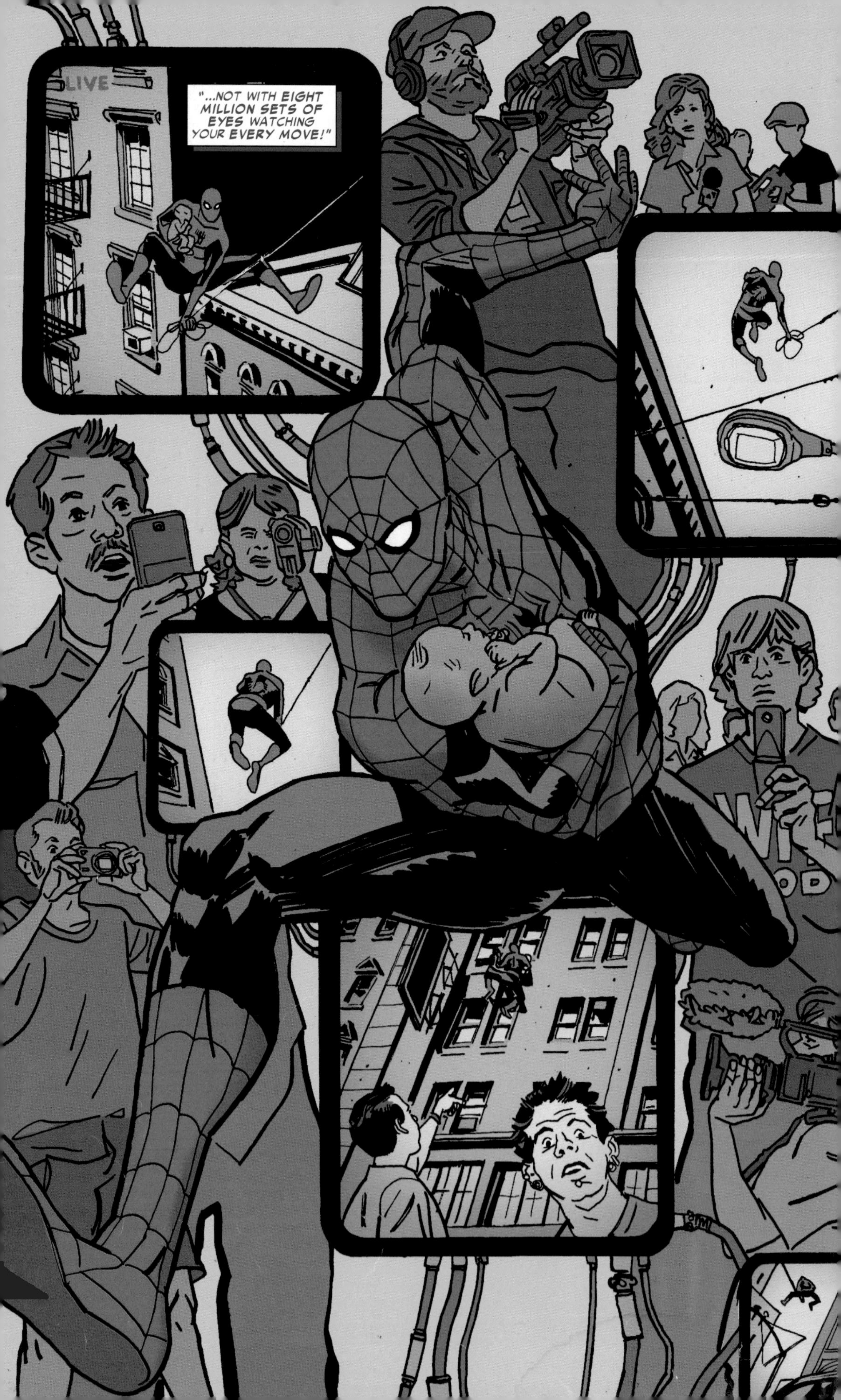
LIVE
"...NOT WITH EIGHT MILLION SETS OF EYES WATCHING YOUR EVERY MOVE!"

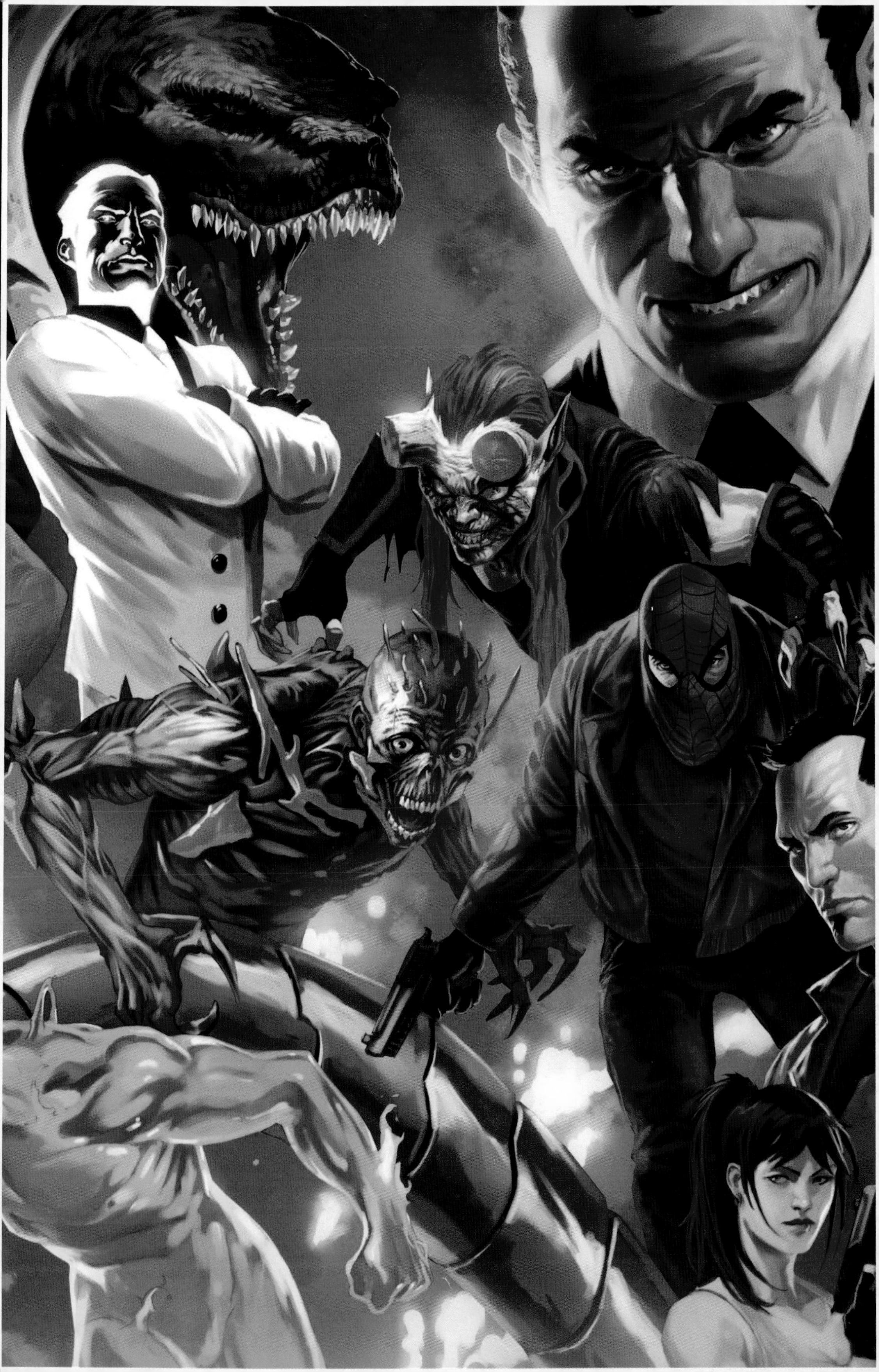

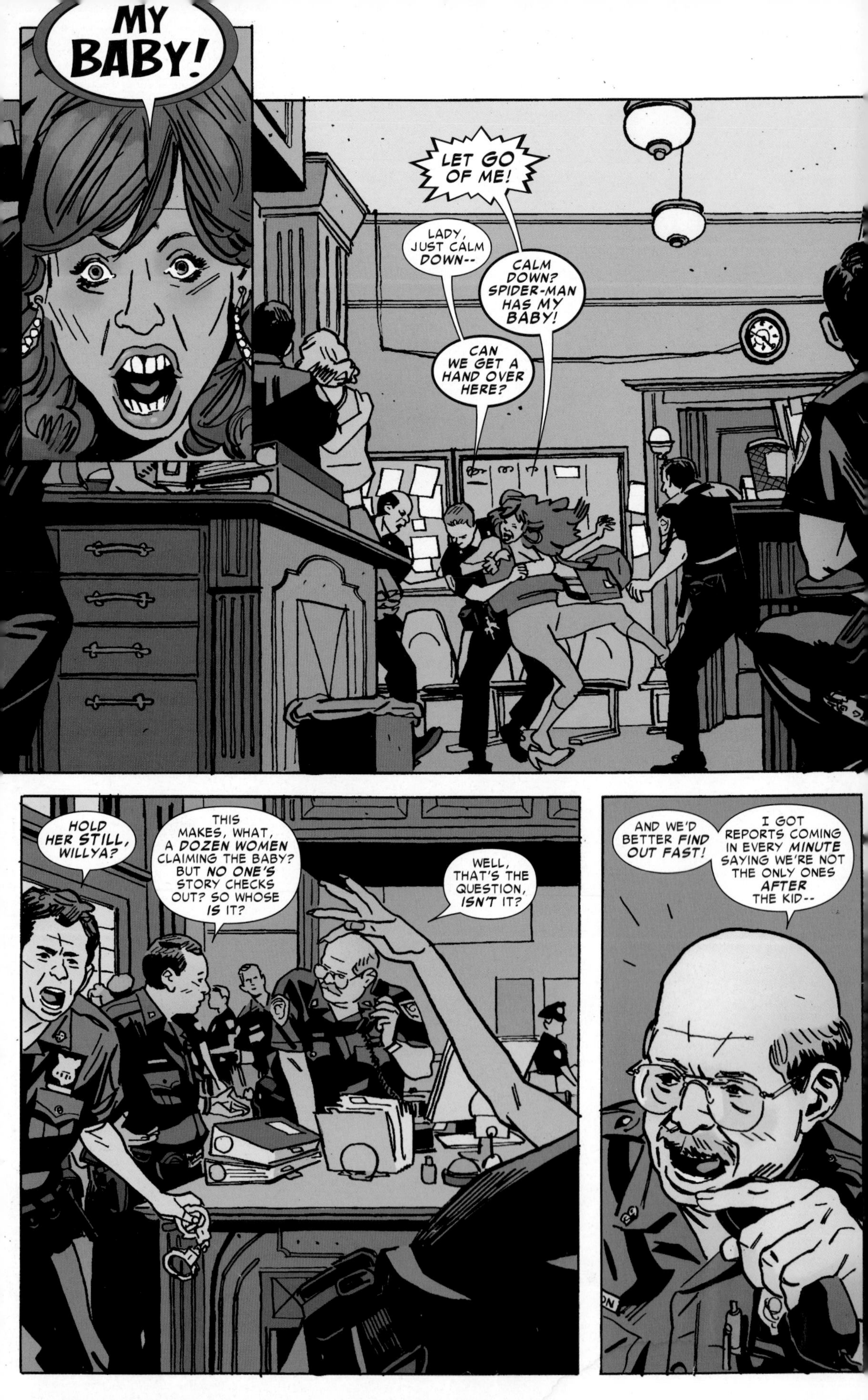
MY BABY!
LET GO OF ME!
LADY, JUST CALM DOWN--
CALM DOWN? SPIDER-MAN HAS MY BABY!
CAN WE GET A HAND OVER HERE?
HOLD HER STILL, WILLYA?
THIS MAKES, WHAT, A DOZEN WOMEN CLAIMING THE BABY? BUT NO ONE'S STORY CHECKS OUT? SO WHOSE IS IT?
WELL, THAT'S THE QUESTION, ISN'T IT?
AND WE'D BETTER FIND OUT FAST!
I GOT REPORTS COMING IN EVERY MINUTE SAYING WE'RE NOT THE ONLY ONES AFTER THE KID--

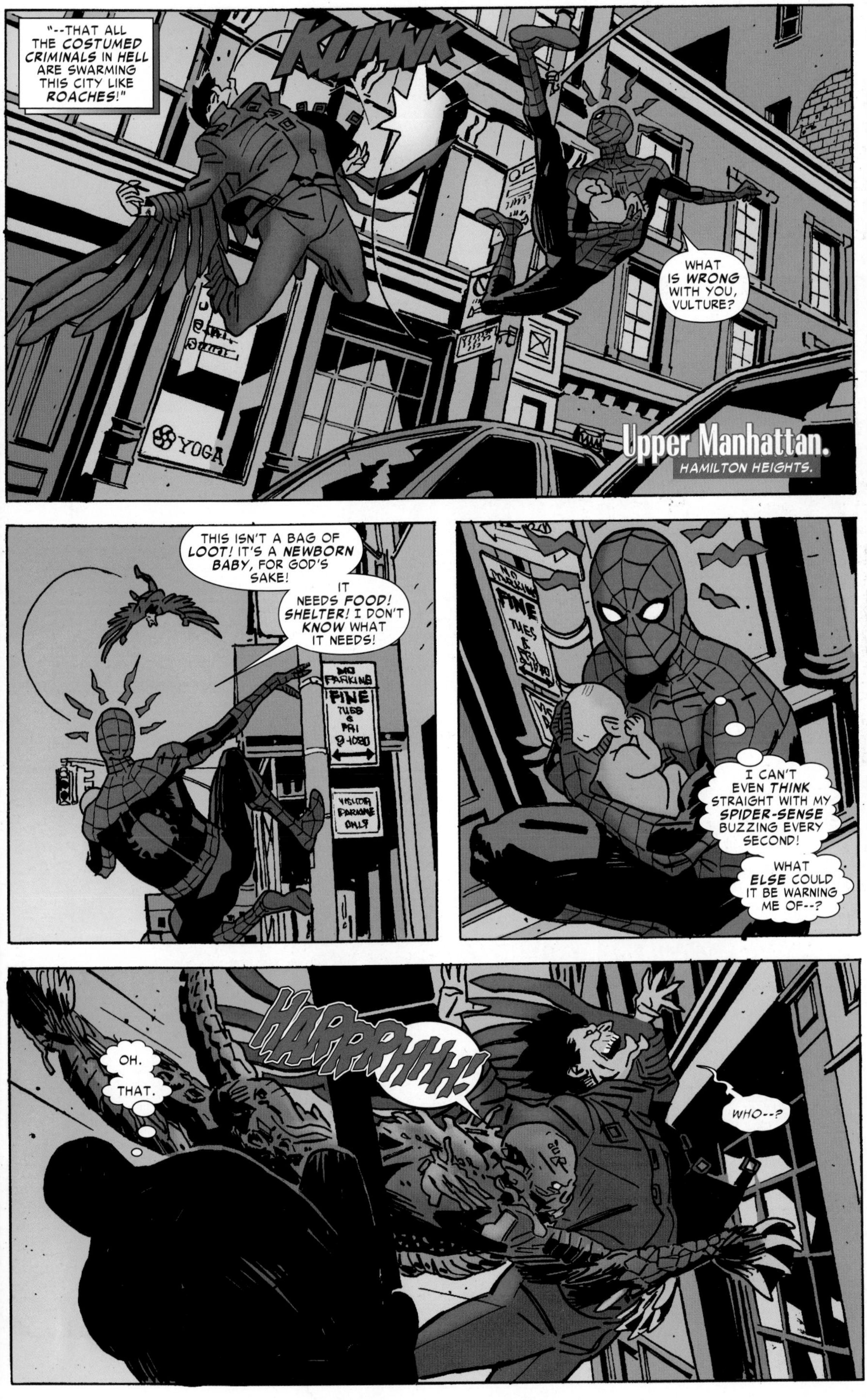
"--THAT ALL THE COSTUMED CRIMINALS IN HELL ARE SWARMING THIS CITY LIKE ROACHES!"
KUNNK
WHAT IS WRONG WITH YOU, VULTURE?
YOGA
Upper Manhattan.
HAMILTON HEIGHTS.
THIS ISN'T A BAG OF LOOT! IT'S A NEWBORN BABY, FOR GOD'S SAKE!
IT NEEDS FOOD! SHELTER! I DON'T KNOW WHAT IT NEEDS!
FINE
I CAN'T EVEN THINK STRAIGHT WITH MY SPIDER-SENSE BUZZING EVERY SECOND!
WHAT ELSE COULD IT BE WARNING ME OF--?
HARRRPHHH!
OH.
THAT.
WHO--?

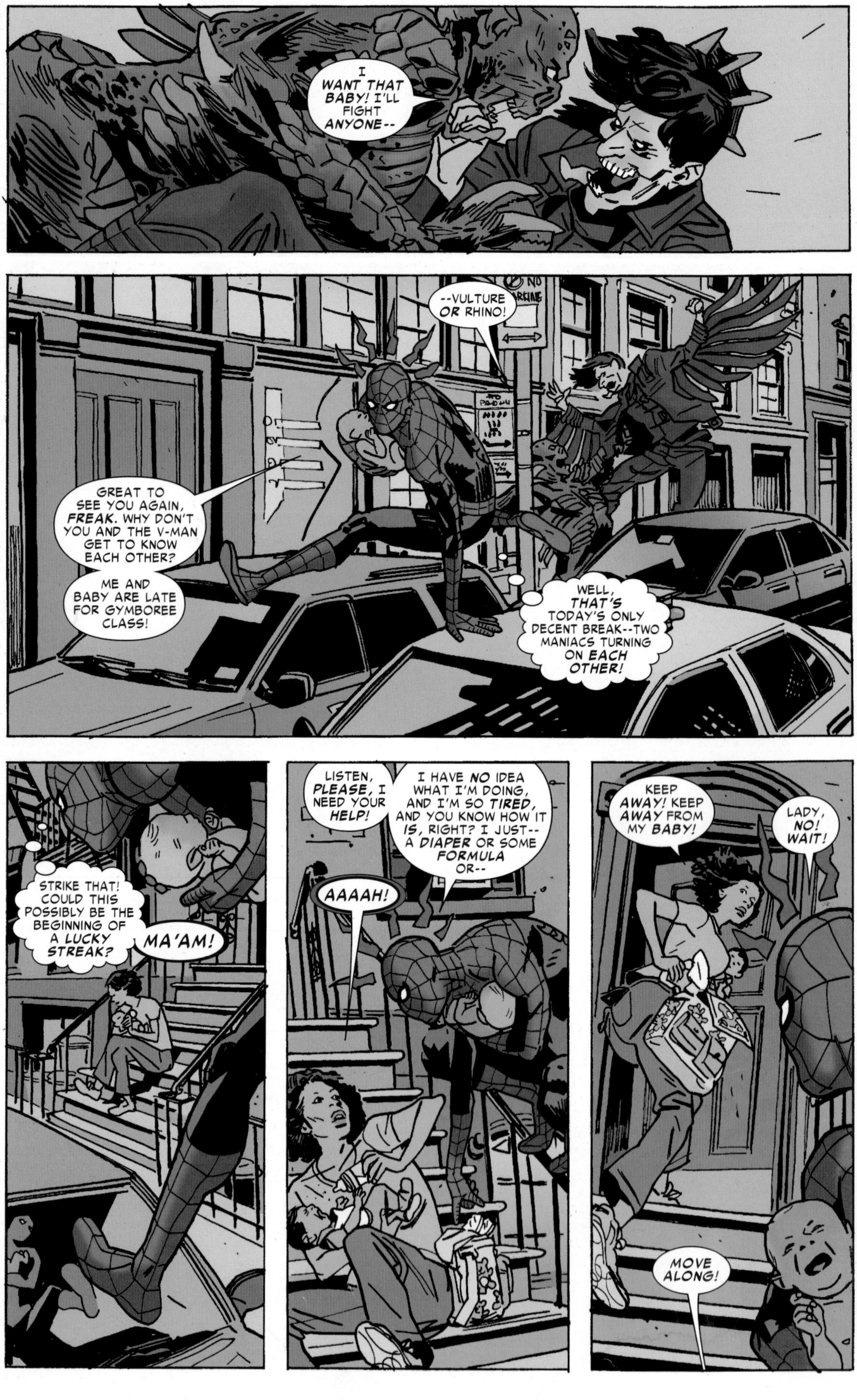
I WANT THAT BABY! I'LL FIGHT ANYONE--
--VULTURE OR RHINO!
GREAT TO SEE YOU AGAIN, FREAK. WHY DON'T YOU AND THE V-MAN GET TO KNOW EACH OTHER?
ME AND BABY ARE LATE FOR GYMBOREE CLASS!
WELL, THAT'S TODAY'S ONLY DECENT BREAK--TWO MANIACS TURNING ON EACH OTHER!
STRIKE THAT! COULD THIS POSSIBLY BE THE BEGINNING OF A LUCKY STREAK?
MA'AM!
LISTEN, PLEASE, I NEED YOUR HELP!
I HAVE NO IDEA WHAT I'M DOING, AND I'M SO TIRED, AND YOU KNOW HOW IT IS, RIGHT? I JUST-- A DIAPER OR SOME FORMULA OR--
AAAAH!
KEEP AWAY! KEEP AWAY FROM MY BABY!
LADY, NO! WAIT!
MOVE ALONG!

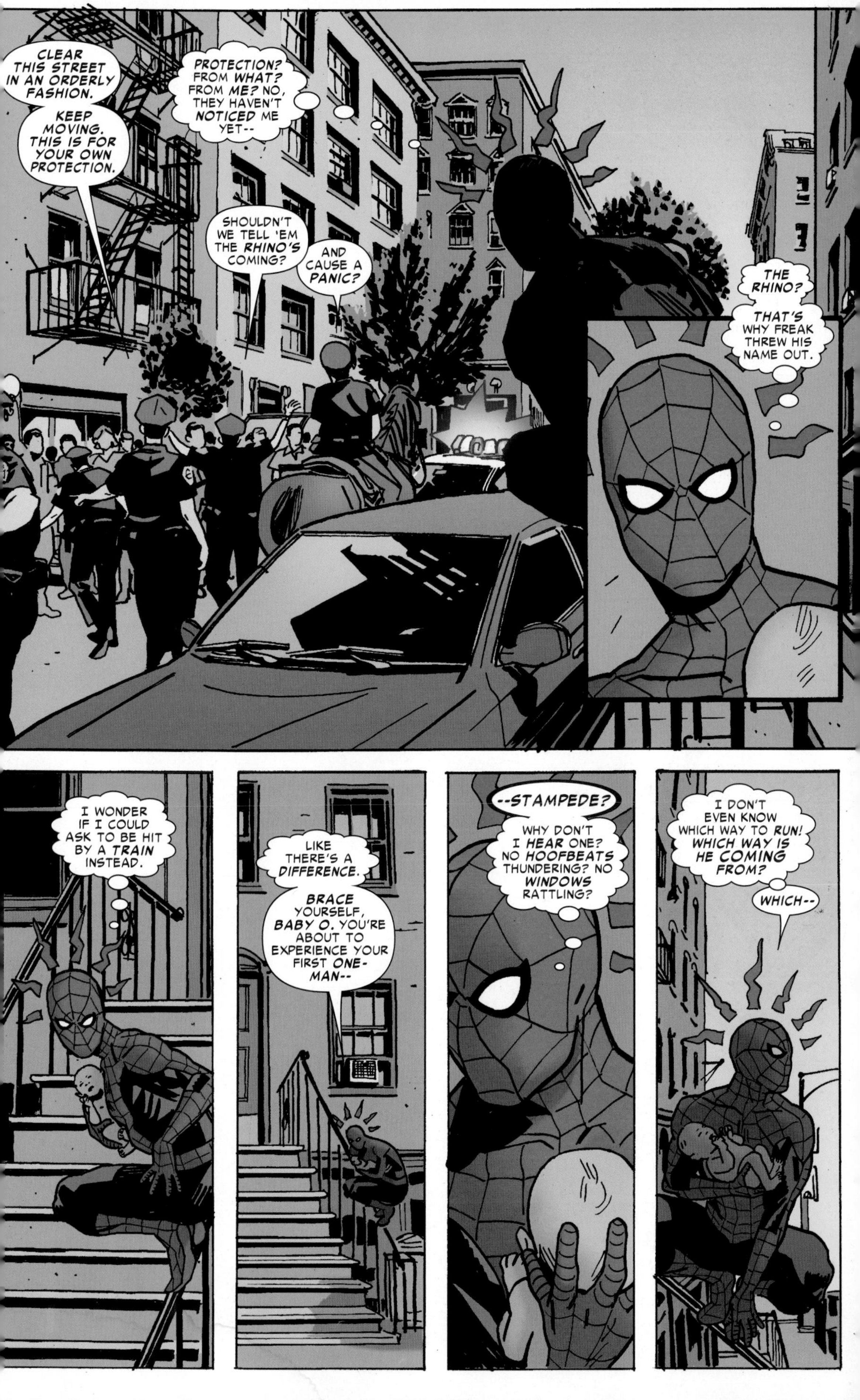

CLEAR THIS STREET IN AN ORDERLY FASHION.
KEEP MOVING. THIS IS FOR YOUR OWN PROTECTION.
PROTECTION? FROM WHAT? FROM ME? NO, THEY HAVEN'T NOTICED ME YET--
SHOULDN'T WE TELL 'EM THE RHINO'S COMING?
AND CAUSE A PANIC?
THE RHINO?
THAT'S WHY FREAK THREW HIS NAME OUT.
I WONDER IF I COULD ASK TO BE HIT BY A TRAIN INSTEAD.
LIKE THERE'S A DIFFERENCE.
BRACE YOURSELF, BABY O. YOU'RE ABOUT TO EXPERIENCE YOUR FIRST ONE-MAN--
--STAMPEDE?
WHY DON'T I HEAR ONE? NO HOOFBEATS THUNDERING? NO WINDOWS RATTLING?
I DON'T EVEN KNOW WHICH WAY TO RUN! WHICH WAY IS HE COMING FROM?
WHICH--

WHAROOOM!

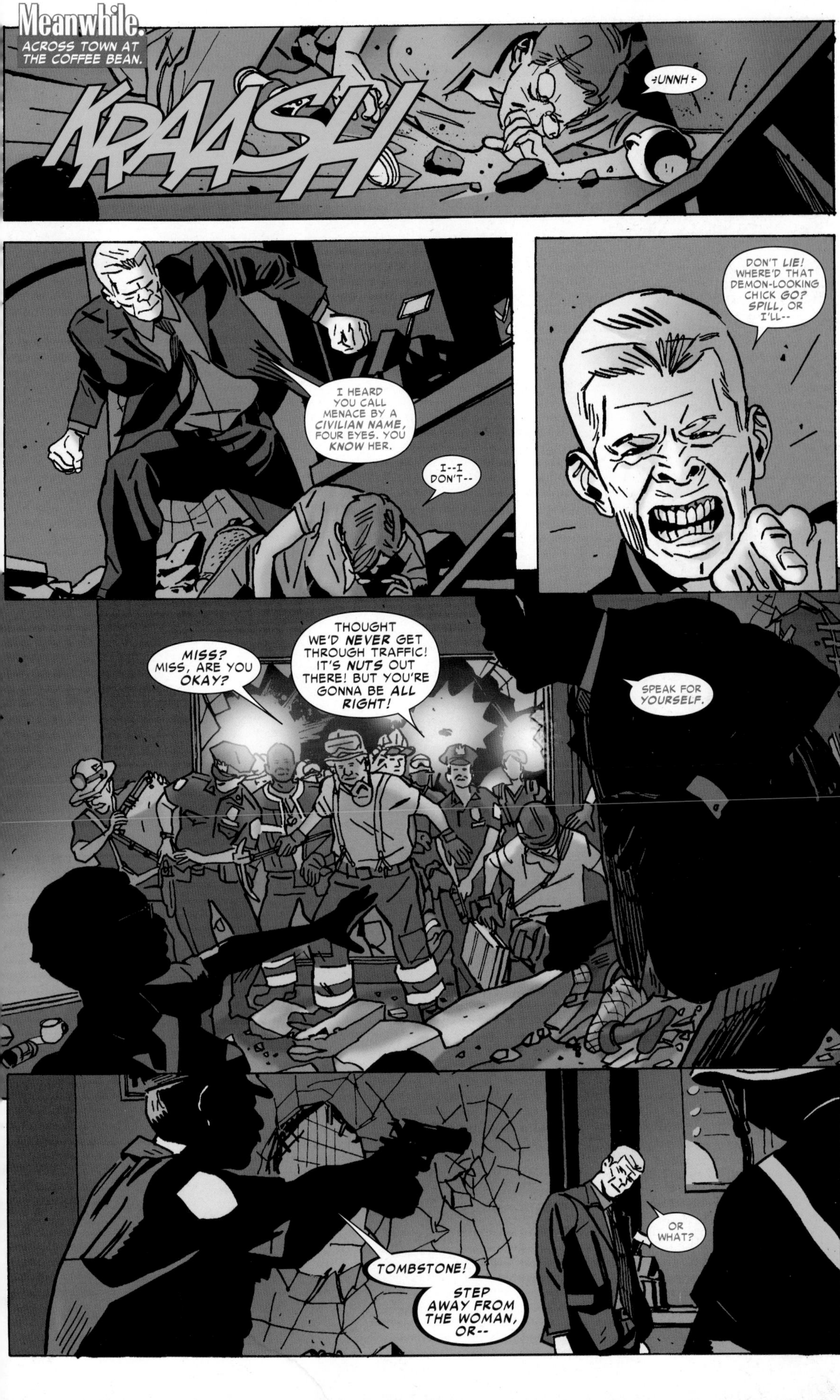
Meanwhile.
ACROSS TOWN AT THE COFFEE BEAN.
KRAASH
UNNH
I HEARD YOU CALL MENACE BY A CIVILIAN NAME, FOUR EYES. YOU KNOW HER.
I--I DON'T--
DON'T LIE! WHERE'D THAT DEMON-LOOKING CHICK GO? SPILL, OR I'LL--
MISS? MISS, ARE YOU OKAY?
THOUGHT WE'D NEVER GET THROUGH TRAFFIC! IT'S NUTS OUT THERE! BUT YOU'RE GONNA BE ALL RIGHT!
SPEAK FOR YOURSELF.
TOMBSTONE!
STEP AWAY FROM THE WOMAN, OR--
OR WHAT?

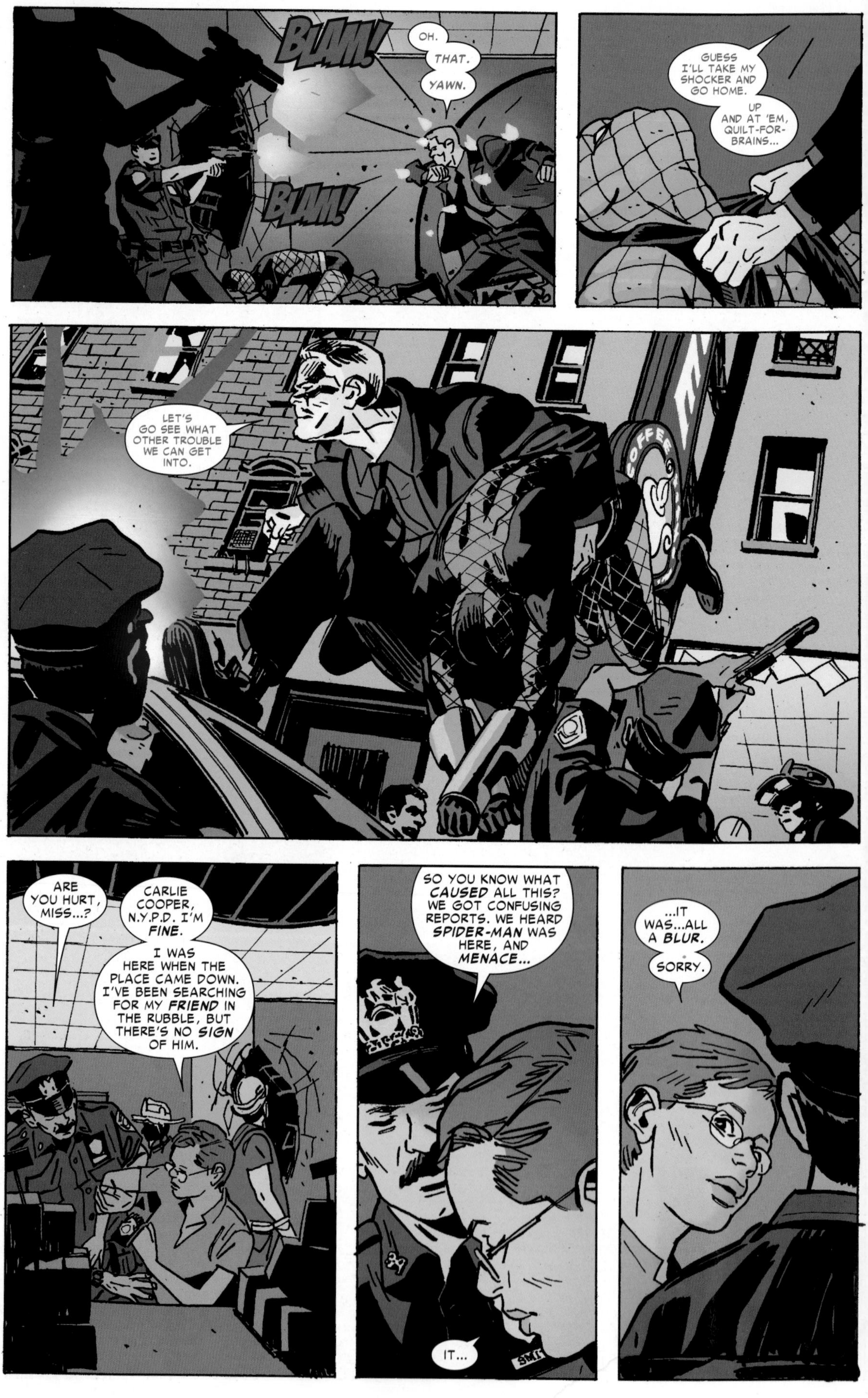
BLAM!
OH.
THAT.
YAWN.
BLAM!
GUESS I'LL TAKE MY SHOCKER AND GO HOME.
UP AND AT 'EM, QUILT-FOR-BRAINS...
LET'S GO SEE WHAT OTHER TROUBLE WE CAN GET INTO.
ARE YOU HURT, MISS...?
CARLIE COOPER, N.Y.P.D. I'M FINE.
I WAS HERE WHEN THE PLACE CAME DOWN. I'VE BEEN SEARCHING FOR MY FRIEND IN THE RUBBLE, BUT THERE'S NO SIGN OF HIM.
SO YOU KNOW WHAT CAUSED ALL THIS? WE GOT CONFUSING REPORTS. WE HEARD SPIDER-MAN WAS HERE, AND MENACE...
IT...
...IT WAS...ALL A BLUR.
SORRY.

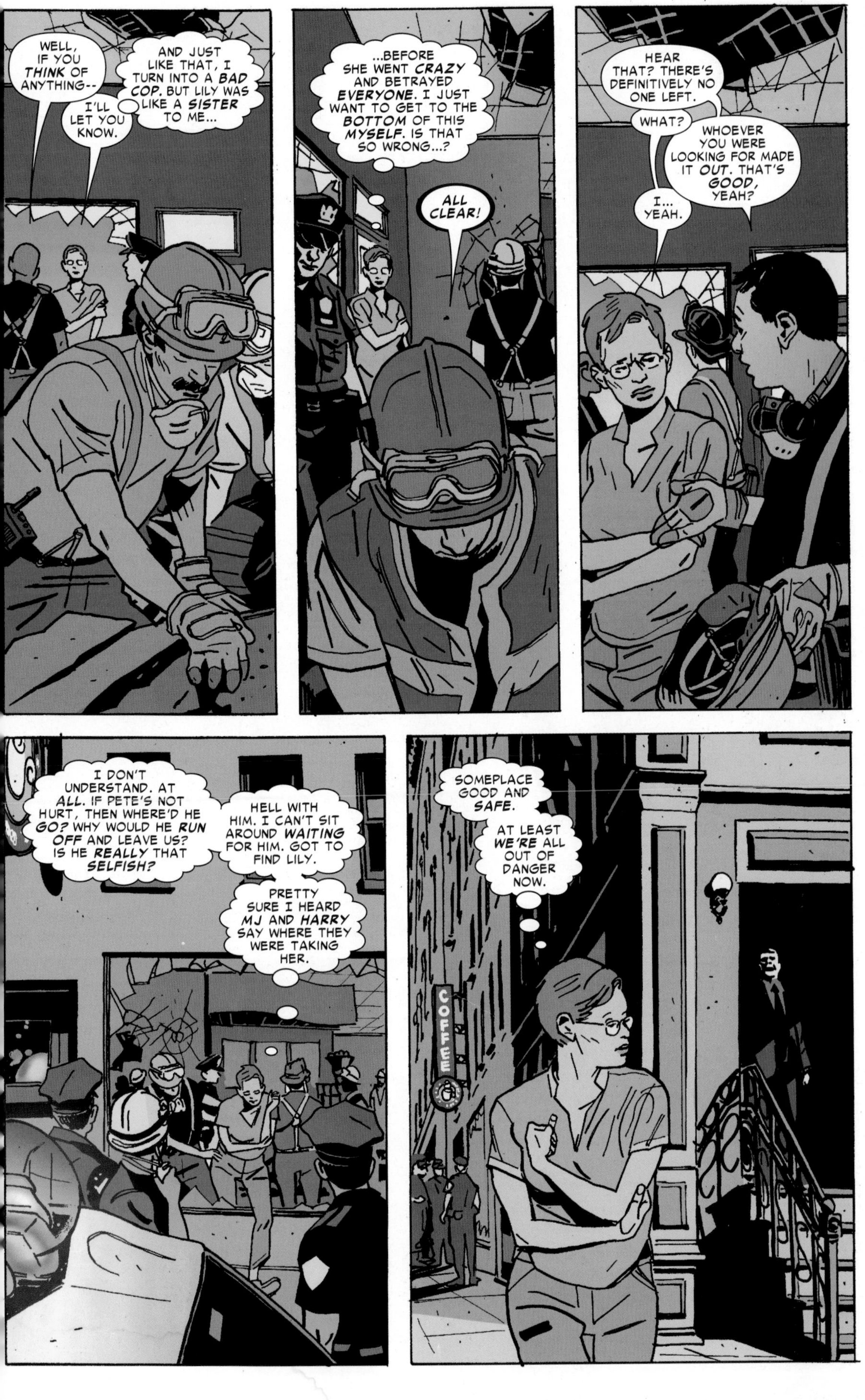
WELL, IF YOU THINK OF ANYTHING--
I'LL LET YOU KNOW.
AND JUST LIKE THAT, I TURN INTO A BAD COP. BUT LILY WAS LIKE A SISTER TO ME...
...BEFORE SHE WENT CRAZY AND BETRAYED EVERYONE. I JUST WANT TO GET TO THE BOTTOM OF THIS MYSELF. IS THAT SO WRONG...?
ALL CLEAR!
HEAR THAT? THERE'S DEFINITIVELY NO ONE LEFT.
WHAT?
WHOEVER YOU WERE LOOKING FOR MADE IT OUT. THAT'S GOOD, YEAH?
I... YEAH.
I DON'T UNDERSTAND. AT ALL. IF PETE'S NOT HURT, THEN WHERE'D HE GO? WHY WOULD HE RUN OFF AND LEAVE US? IS HE REALLY THAT SELFISH?
HELL WITH HIM. I CAN'T SIT AROUND WAITING FOR HIM. GOT TO FIND LILY.
PRETTY SURE I HEARD MJ AND HARRY SAY WHERE THEY WERE TAKING HER.
SOMEPLACE GOOD AND SAFE.
AT LEAST WE'RE ALL OUT OF DANGER NOW.
COFFEE

UNLEASHING THE RAMPAGING HORDES OF *SPIDER-HATERS* IS AN IMPRESSIVE *FEAT*, OCTAVIUS...

...BUT WHY NOT GO AFTER THE WALL-CRAWLER *YOURSELF*? YOU'RE STRONGER THAN *EVER*, AND YOU ALMOST *BEAT* HIM LAST TIME.

I NEARLY DID JUST *THAT* WHEN ONLY SECOND-STRINGERS LIKE THE SPOT AND FREAK RESPONDED TO MY OFFER...

Kravinoff Mansion.

...BUT WORD SPREAD QUICKLY, AND NOW SPIDER-MAN'S MOST FORMIDABLE FOES ARE GRINDING AWAY AT HIM.

SO LET *THEM* DIRTY THEIR HANDS AND WEAR HIM DOWN WHILE I PREPARE MY BIOCHEMICAL MASTERPIECE.

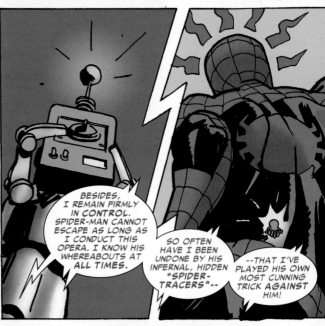

BESIDES, I REMAIN FIRMLY IN *CONTROL*. SPIDER-MAN CANNOT ESCAPE AS LONG AS I CONDUCT THIS OPERA. I KNOW HIS WHEREABOUTS AT ALL TIMES.

SO OFTEN HAVE I BEEN UNDONE BY HIS INFERNAL, HIDDEN *"SPIDER-TRACERS"*--

--THAT I'VE PLAYED HIS OWN MOST CUNNING TRICK AGAINST HIM!

AND NOW MY OCTO-TRACER HAS GIVEN YOU ALL YOU NEED TO KNOW...

...TO END THIS, SWIFTLY... AND IN OUR FAVOR.

HA.

GO.

587 Park Avenue.

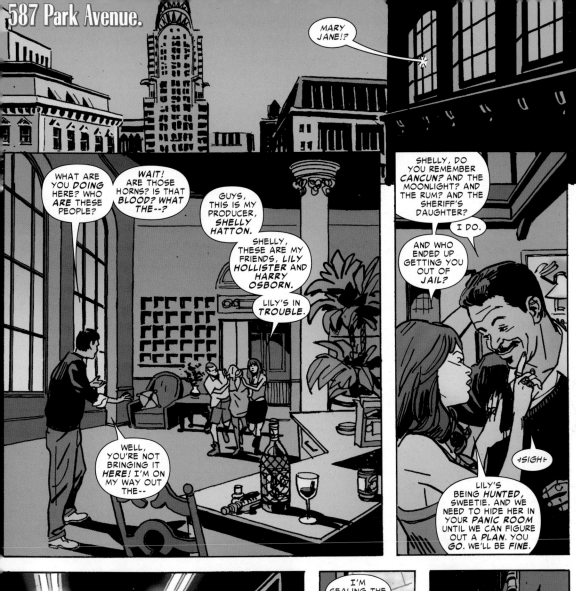

MARY JANE!?

WHAT ARE YOU *DOING* HERE? WHO *ARE* THESE PEOPLE?

WAIT! ARE THOSE HORNS? IS THAT *BLOOD?* WHAT THE--?

GUYS, THIS IS MY PRODUCER, *SHELLY HATTON.*

SHELLY, THESE ARE MY FRIENDS, *LILY HOLLISTER* AND *HARRY OSBORN.*

LILY'S IN *TROUBLE.*

SHELLY, DO YOU REMEMBER *CANCUN?* AND THE *MOONLIGHT?* AND THE *RUM?* AND THE *SHERIFF'S DAUGHTER?*

I DO.

AND WHO ENDED UP GETTING YOU OUT OF *JAIL?*

WELL, YOU'RE NOT BRINGING IT *HERE!* I'M ON MY WAY OUT THE--

‡SIGH‡

LILY'S BEING *HUNTED,* SWEETIE. AND WE NEED TO HIDE HER IN YOUR *PANIC ROOM* UNTIL WE CAN FIGURE OUT A *PLAN.* YOU *GO.* WE'LL BE *FINE.*

MJ WATSON, YOU COULD SELL WATER TO A DROWNING MAN.

IT'S TRUE. AND AGAIN, YOU *NEVER SAW US.*

I'M SEALING THE DOOR. *NOT* WITH ME *INSIDE.*

YOU STAY HERE WITH LILY. I... ...I HAVE A *PLAN.*

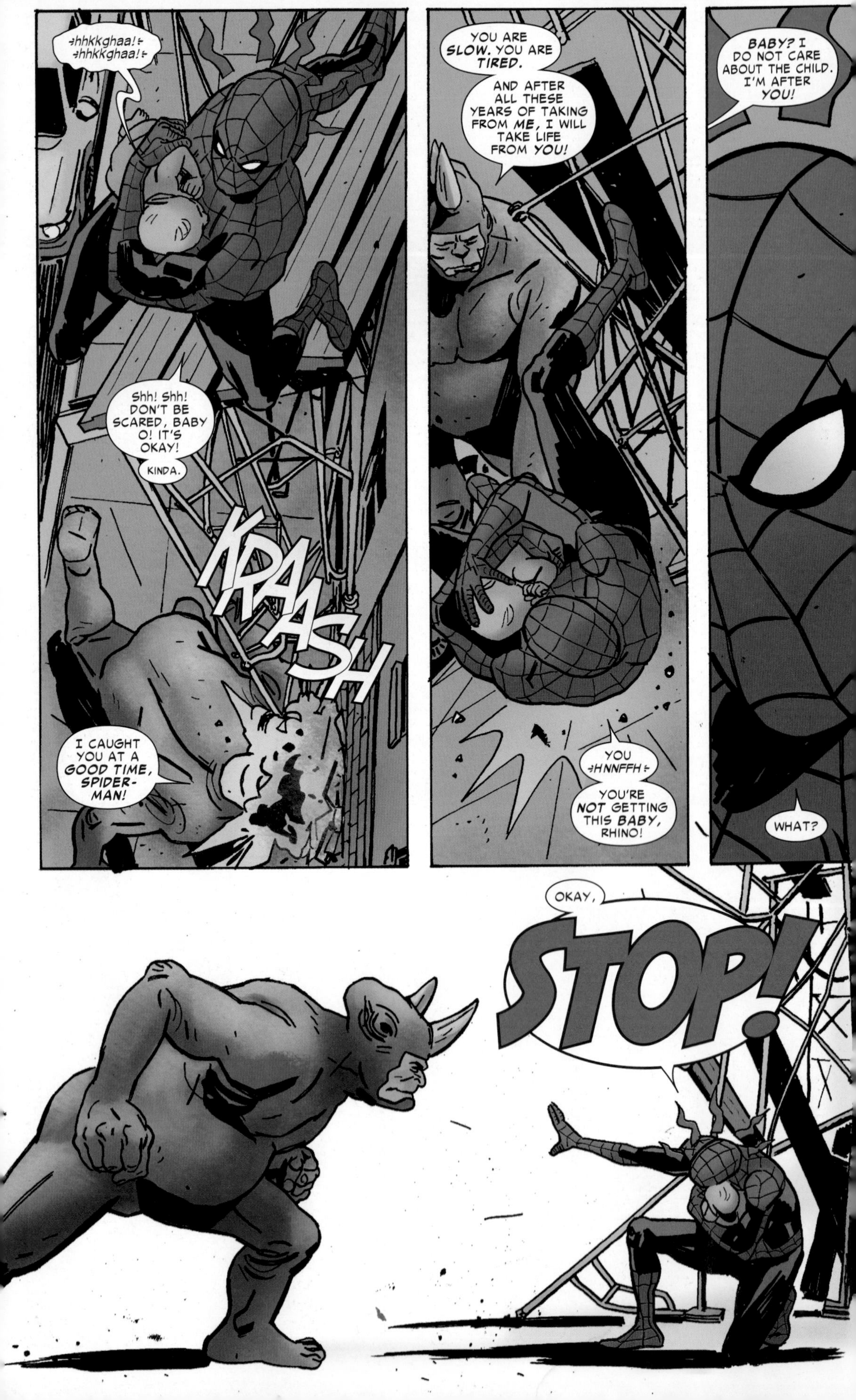

≠hhkkghaa!≠ ≠hhkkghaa!≠
Shh! Shh! DON'T BE SCARED, BABY O! IT'S OKAY!
KINDA.
KRAASH
I CAUGHT YOU AT A GOOD TIME, SPIDER-MAN!
YOU ARE SLOW. YOU ARE TIRED.
AND AFTER ALL THESE YEARS OF TAKING FROM ME, I WILL TAKE LIFE FROM YOU!
YOU ≠HNNFFH≠
YOU'RE NOT GETTING THIS BABY, RHINO!
BABY? I DO NOT CARE ABOUT THE CHILD. I'M AFTER YOU!
WHAT?
OKAY,
STOP!

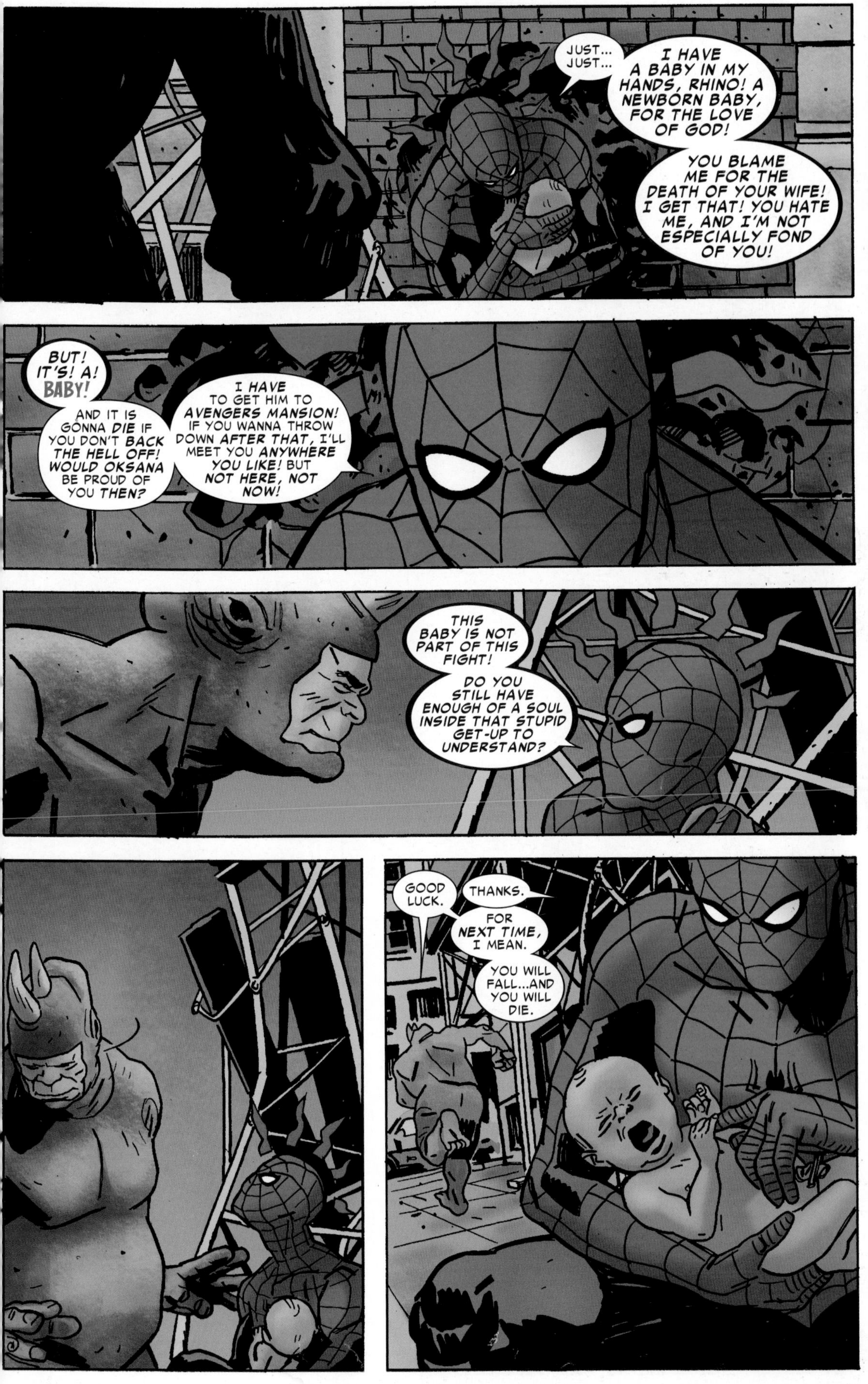
JUST... JUST...
I HAVE A BABY IN MY HANDS, RHINO! A NEWBORN BABY, FOR THE LOVE OF GOD!
YOU BLAME ME FOR THE DEATH OF YOUR WIFE! I GET THAT! YOU HATE ME, AND I'M NOT ESPECIALLY FOND OF YOU!
BUT! IT'S! A! BABY!
AND IT IS GONNA DIE IF YOU DON'T BACK THE HELL OFF! WOULD OKSANA BE PROUD OF YOU THEN?
I HAVE TO GET HIM TO AVENGERS MANSION! IF YOU WANNA THROW DOWN AFTER THAT, I'LL MEET YOU ANYWHERE YOU LIKE! BUT NOT HERE, NOT NOW!
THIS BABY IS NOT PART OF THIS FIGHT!
DO YOU STILL HAVE ENOUGH OF A SOUL INSIDE THAT STUPID GET-UP TO UNDERSTAND?
GOOD LUCK.
THANKS.
FOR NEXT TIME, I MEAN.
YOU WILL FALL...AND YOU WILL DIE.

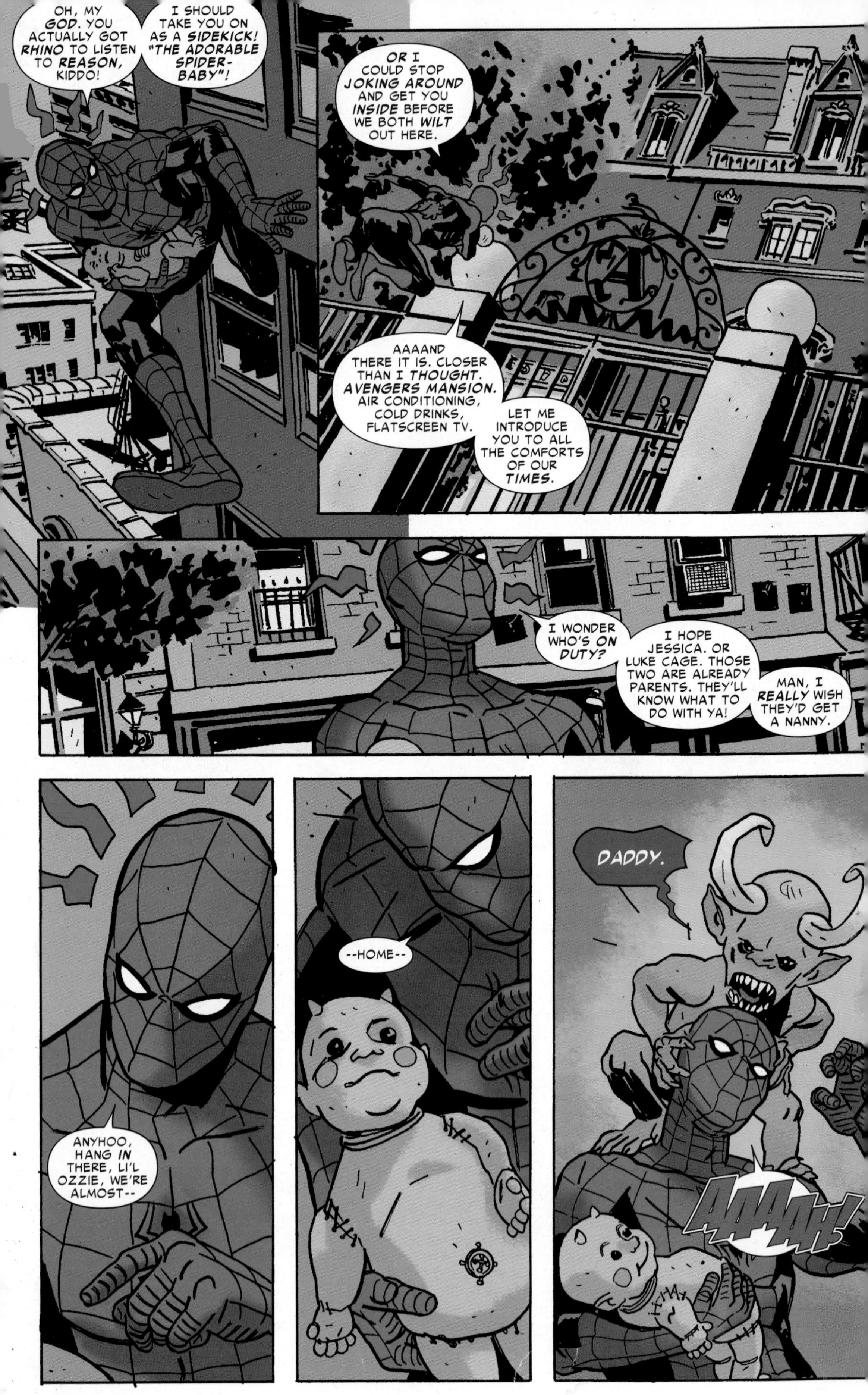

OH, MY GOD. YOU ACTUALLY GOT RHINO TO LISTEN TO REASON, KIDDO!
I SHOULD TAKE YOU ON AS A SIDEKICK! "THE ADORABLE SPIDER-BABY"!
OR I COULD STOP JOKING AROUND AND GET YOU INSIDE BEFORE WE BOTH WILT OUT HERE.
AAAAND THERE IT IS. CLOSER THAN I THOUGHT. AVENGERS MANSION. AIR CONDITIONING, COLD DRINKS, FLATSCREEN TV.
LET ME INTRODUCE YOU TO ALL THE COMFORTS OF OUR TIMES.
I WONDER WHO'S ON DUTY?
I HOPE JESSICA. OR LUKE CAGE. THOSE TWO ARE ALREADY PARENTS. THEY'LL KNOW WHAT TO DO WITH YA!
MAN, I REALLY WISH THEY'D GET A NANNY.
ANYHOO, HANG IN THERE, LI'L OZZIE, WE'RE ALMOST--
--HOME--
DADDY.
AAAAH!

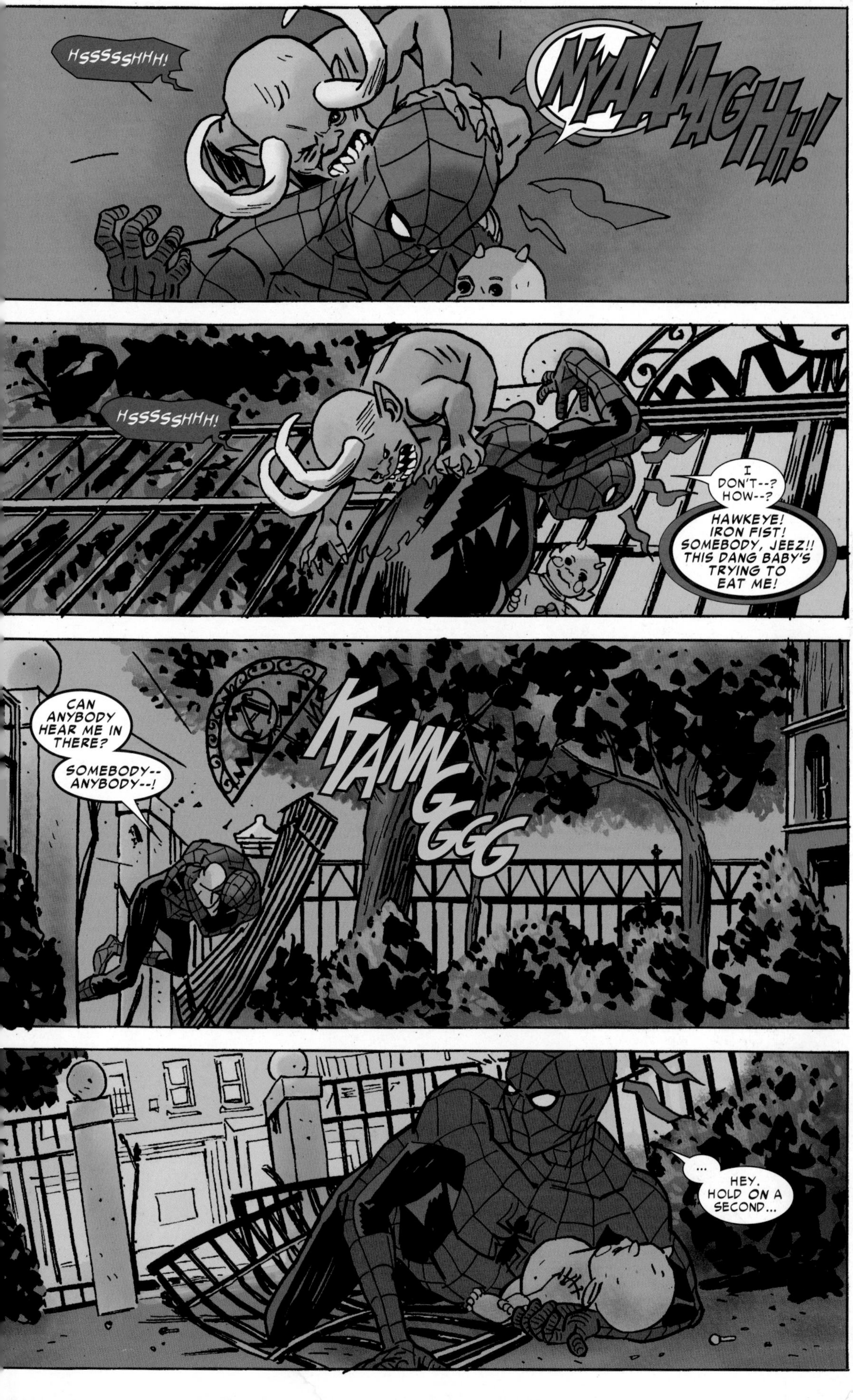
HSSSSSHHH!
NYAAAAGHH!
HSSSSSHHH!
I DON'T--? HOW--?
HAWKEYE! IRON FIST! SOMEBODY, JEEZ!! THIS DANG BABY'S TRYING TO EAT ME!
CAN ANYBODY HEAR ME IN THERE?
SOMEBODY-- ANYBODY--!
KTANNGGG
... HEY. HOLD ON A SECOND...

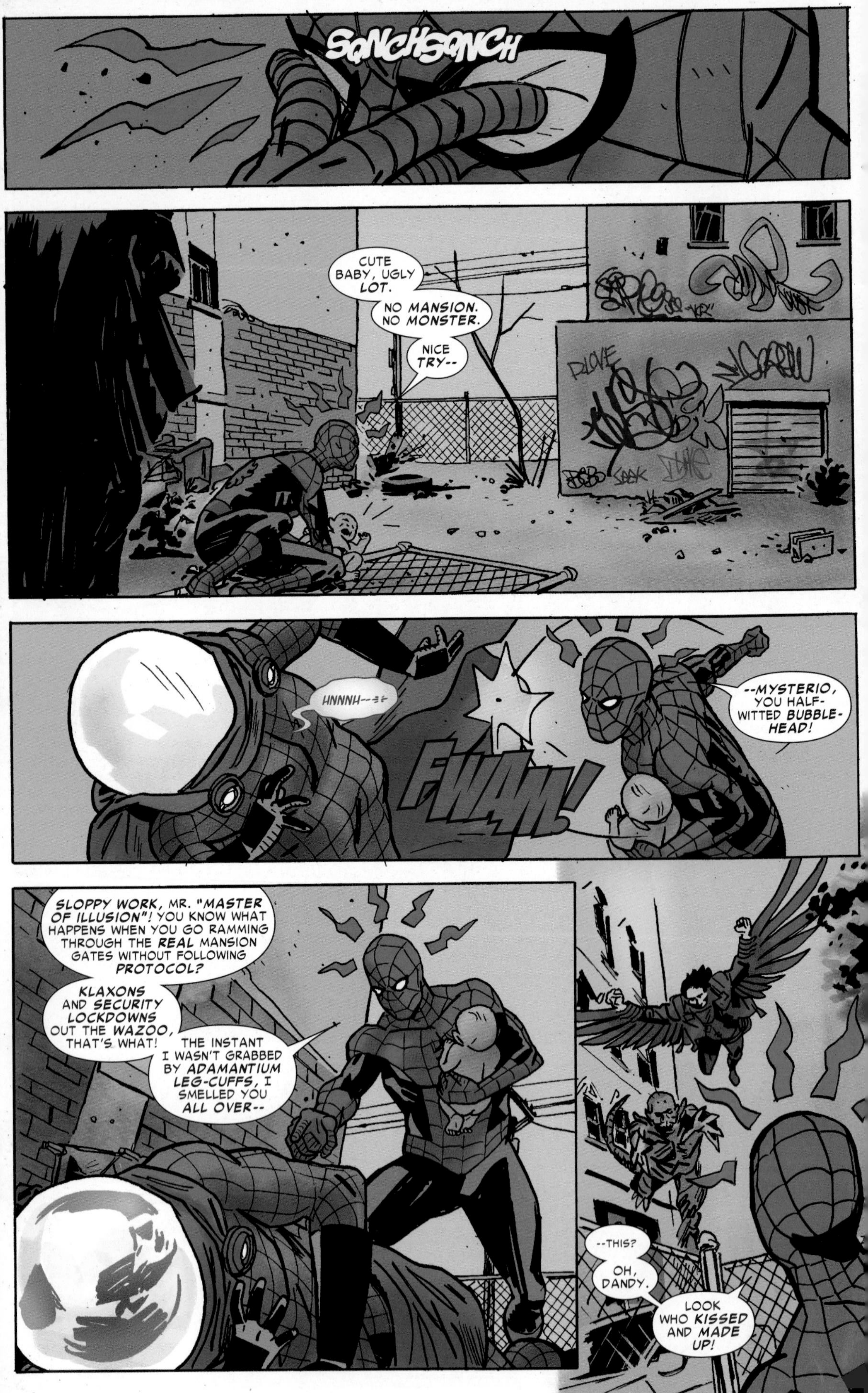
SQNCHSQNCH
CUTE BABY, UGLY LOT.
NO MANSION. NO MONSTER.
NICE TRY--
HNNNH--
--MYSTERIO, YOU HALF-WITTED BUBBLE-HEAD!
FWAM!
SLOPPY WORK, MR. "MASTER OF ILLUSION"! YOU KNOW WHAT HAPPENS WHEN YOU GO RAMMING THROUGH THE REAL MANSION GATES WITHOUT FOLLOWING PROTOCOL?
KLAXONS AND SECURITY LOCKDOWNS OUT THE WAZOO, THAT'S WHAT!
THE INSTANT I WASN'T GRABBED BY ADAMANTIUM LEG-CUFFS, I SMELLED YOU ALL OVER--
--THIS?
OH, DANDY.
LOOK WHO KISSED AND MADE UP!

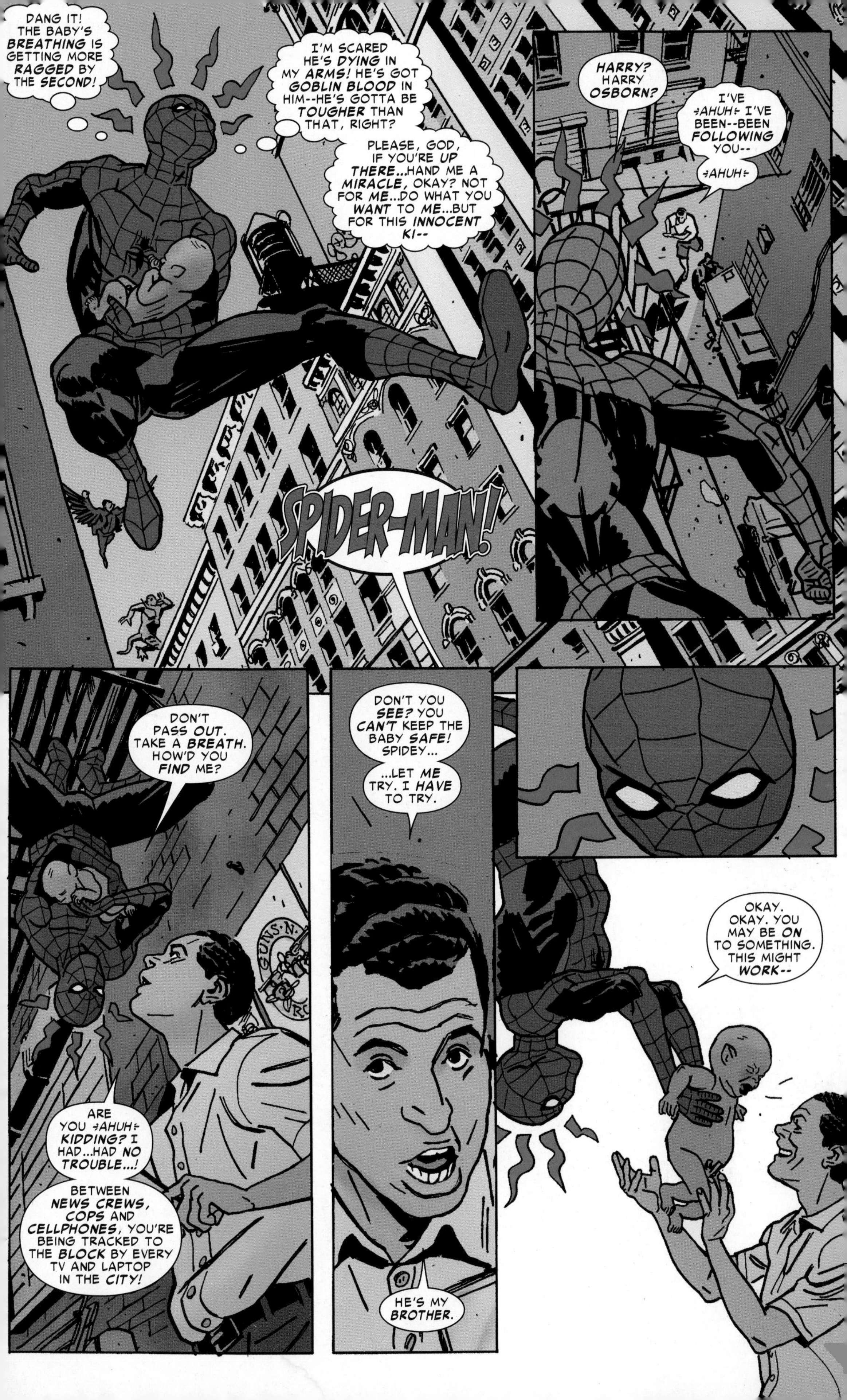
DANG IT! THE BABY'S BREATHING IS GETTING MORE RAGGED BY THE SECOND!
I'M SCARED HE'S DYING IN MY ARMS! HE'S GOT GOBLIN BLOOD IN HIM--HE'S GOTTA BE TOUGHER THAN THAT, RIGHT?
PLEASE, GOD, IF YOU'RE UP THERE...HAND ME A MIRACLE, OKAY? NOT FOR ME...DO WHAT YOU WANT TO ME...BUT FOR THIS INNOCENT KI--
SPIDER-MAN!
HARRY? HARRY OSBORN?
I'VE ≠AHUH≠ I'VE BEEN--BEEN FOLLOWING YOU--
≠AHUH≠
DON'T PASS OUT. TAKE A BREATH. HOW'D YOU FIND ME?
ARE YOU ≠AHUH≠ KIDDING? I HAD...HAD NO TROUBLE...!
BETWEEN NEWS CREWS, COPS AND CELLPHONES, YOU'RE BEING TRACKED TO THE BLOCK BY EVERY TV AND LAPTOP IN THE CITY!
DON'T YOU SEE? YOU CAN'T KEEP THE BABY SAFE! SPIDEY...
...LET ME TRY. I HAVE TO TRY.
HE'S MY BROTHER.
OKAY. OKAY. YOU MAY BE ON TO SOMETHING. THIS MIGHT WORK--

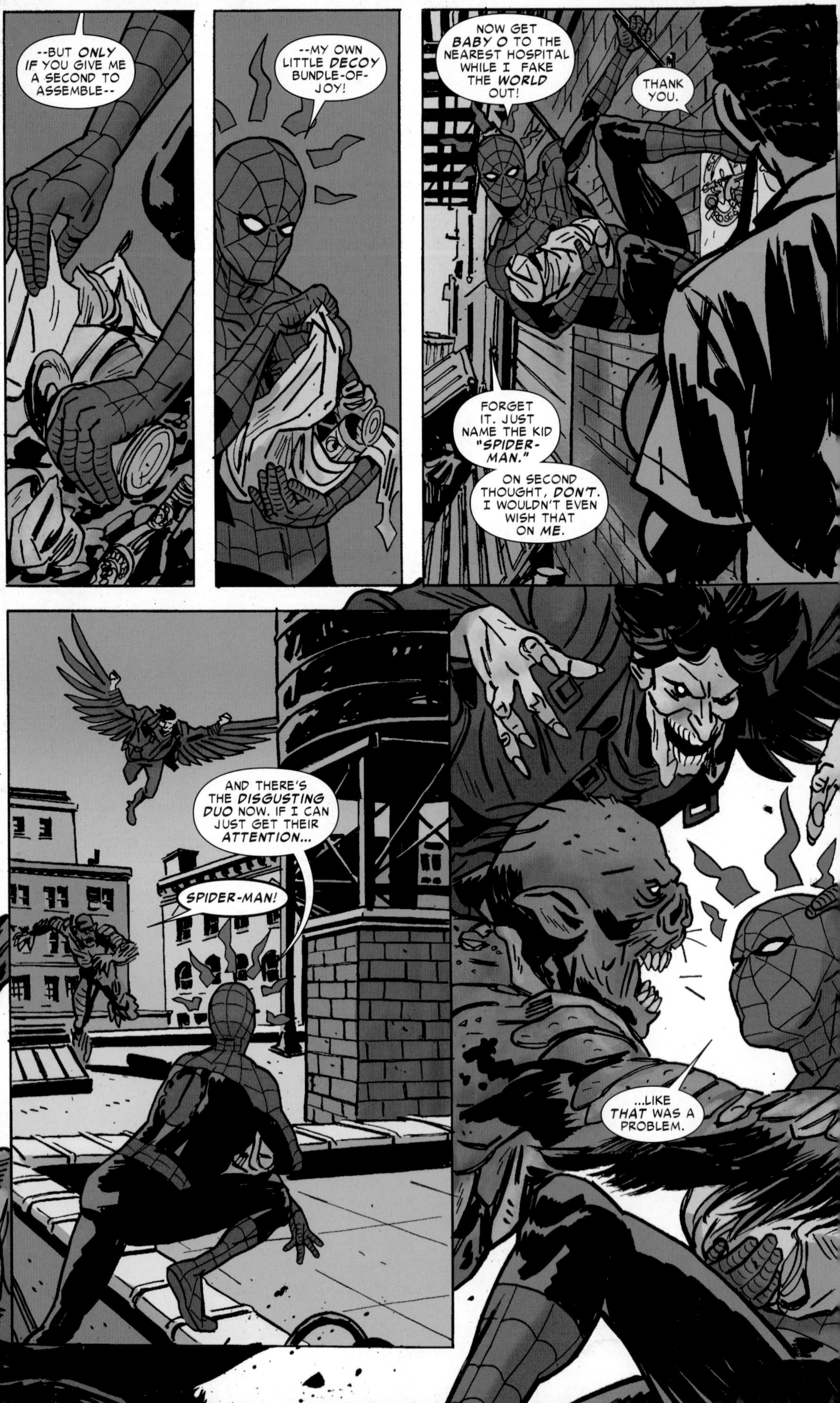
--BUT ONLY IF YOU GIVE ME A SECOND TO ASSEMBLE--
--MY OWN LITTLE DECOY BUNDLE-OF-JOY!
NOW GET BABY O TO THE NEAREST HOSPITAL WHILE I FAKE THE WORLD OUT!
THANK YOU.
FORGET IT. JUST NAME THE KID "SPIDER-MAN."
ON SECOND THOUGHT, DON'T. I WOULDN'T EVEN WISH THAT ON ME.
AND THERE'S THE DISGUSTING DUO NOW. IF I CAN JUST GET THEIR ATTENTION...
SPIDER-MAN!
...LIKE THAT WAS A PROBLEM.

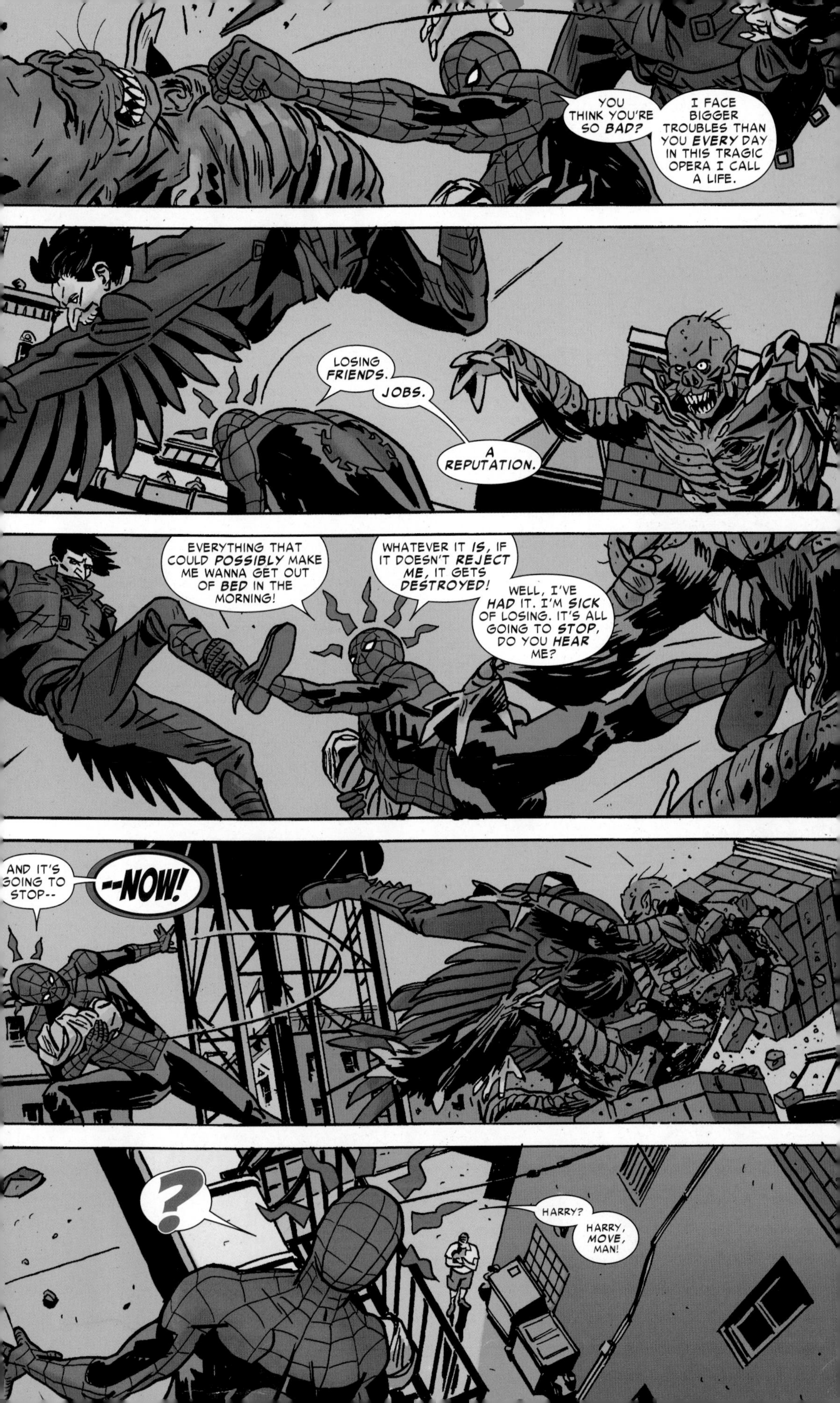
YOU THINK YOU'RE SO BAD?
I FACE BIGGER TROUBLES THAN YOU EVERY DAY IN THIS TRAGIC OPERA I CALL A LIFE.
LOSING FRIENDS.
JOBS.
A REPUTATION.
EVERYTHING THAT COULD POSSIBLY MAKE ME WANNA GET OUT OF BED IN THE MORNING!
WHATEVER IT IS, IF IT DOESN'T REJECT ME, IT GETS DESTROYED!
WELL, I'VE HAD IT. I'M SICK OF LOSING. IT'S ALL GOING TO STOP, DO YOU HEAR ME?
AND IT'S GOING TO STOP--
--NOW!
?
HARRY?
HARRY, MOVE, MAN!

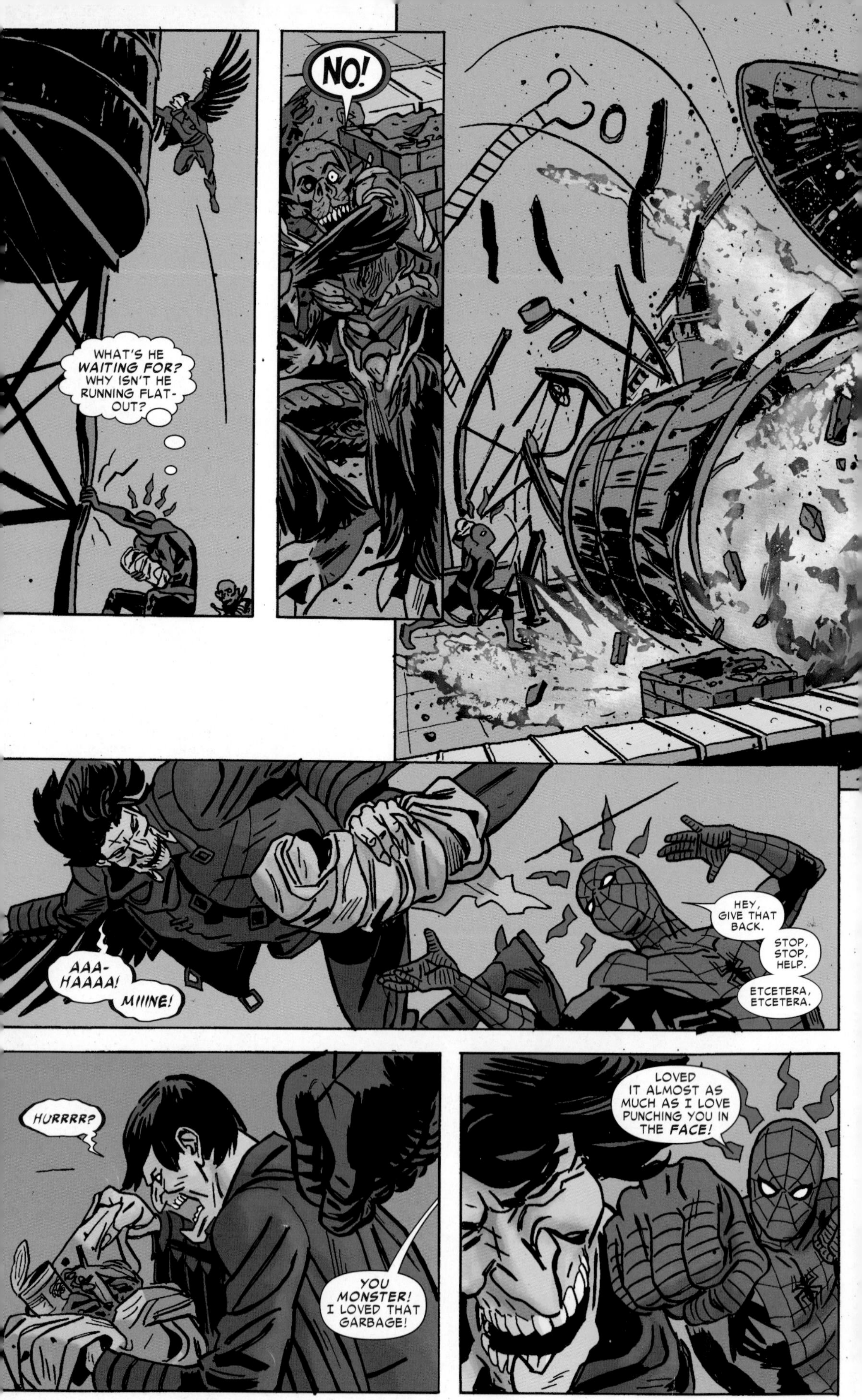
WHAT'S HE *WAITING FOR?* WHY ISN'T HE RUNNING FLAT-OUT?
NO!
AAA-HAAAA!
MIIINE!
HEY, GIVE THAT BACK.
STOP, STOP, HELP.
ETCETERA, ETCETERA.
HURRRR?
YOU *MONSTER!* I LOVED THAT GARBAGE!
LOVED IT ALMOST AS MUCH AS I LOVE PUNCHING YOU IN THE *FACE!*

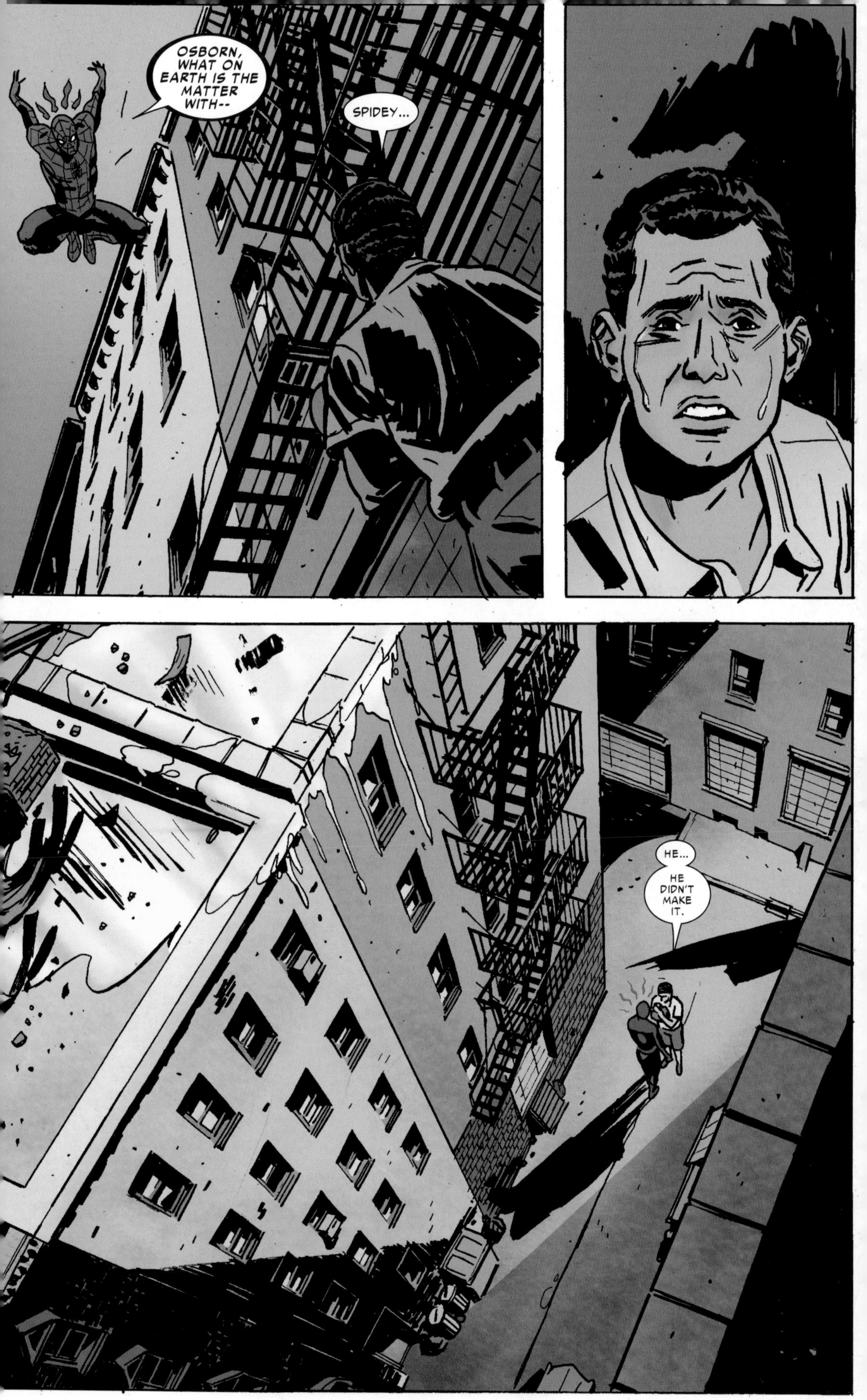
OSBORN, WHAT ON EARTH IS THE MATTER WITH--
SPIDEY...
HE...
HE DIDN'T MAKE IT.

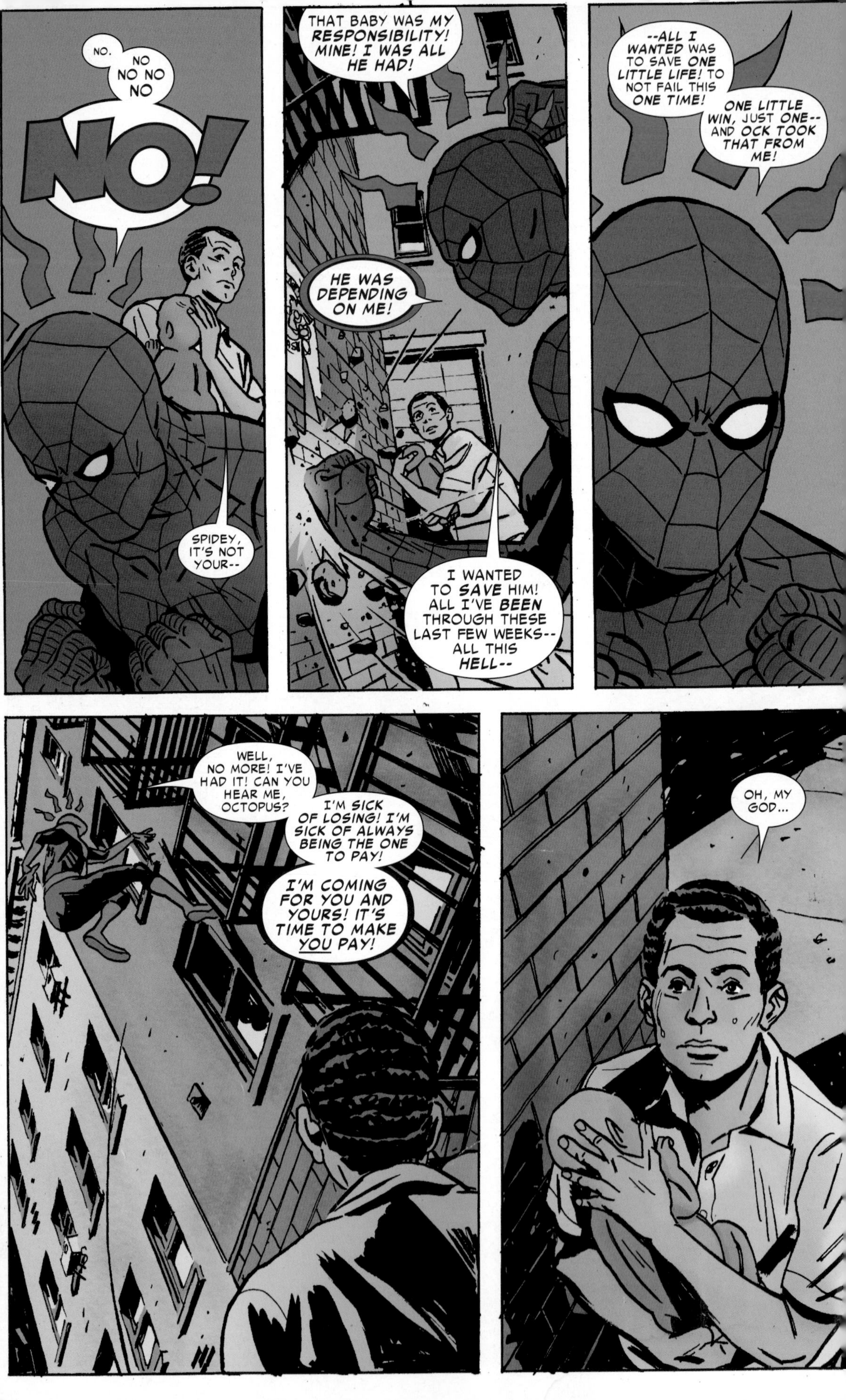

NO.
NO NO NO NO
NO!
SPIDEY, IT'S NOT YOUR--
THAT BABY WAS MY RESPONSIBILITY! MINE! I WAS ALL HE HAD!
HE WAS DEPENDING ON ME!
I WANTED TO SAVE HIM! ALL I'VE BEEN THROUGH THESE LAST FEW WEEKS-- ALL THIS HELL--
--ALL I WANTED WAS TO SAVE ONE LITTLE LIFE! TO NOT FAIL THIS ONE TIME!
ONE LITTLE WIN, JUST ONE-- AND OCK TOOK THAT FROM ME!
WELL, NO MORE! I'VE HAD IT! CAN YOU HEAR ME, OCTOPUS?
I'M SICK OF LOSING! I'M SICK OF ALWAYS BEING THE ONE TO PAY!
I'M COMING FOR YOU AND YOURS! IT'S TIME TO MAKE YOU PAY!
OH, MY GOD...

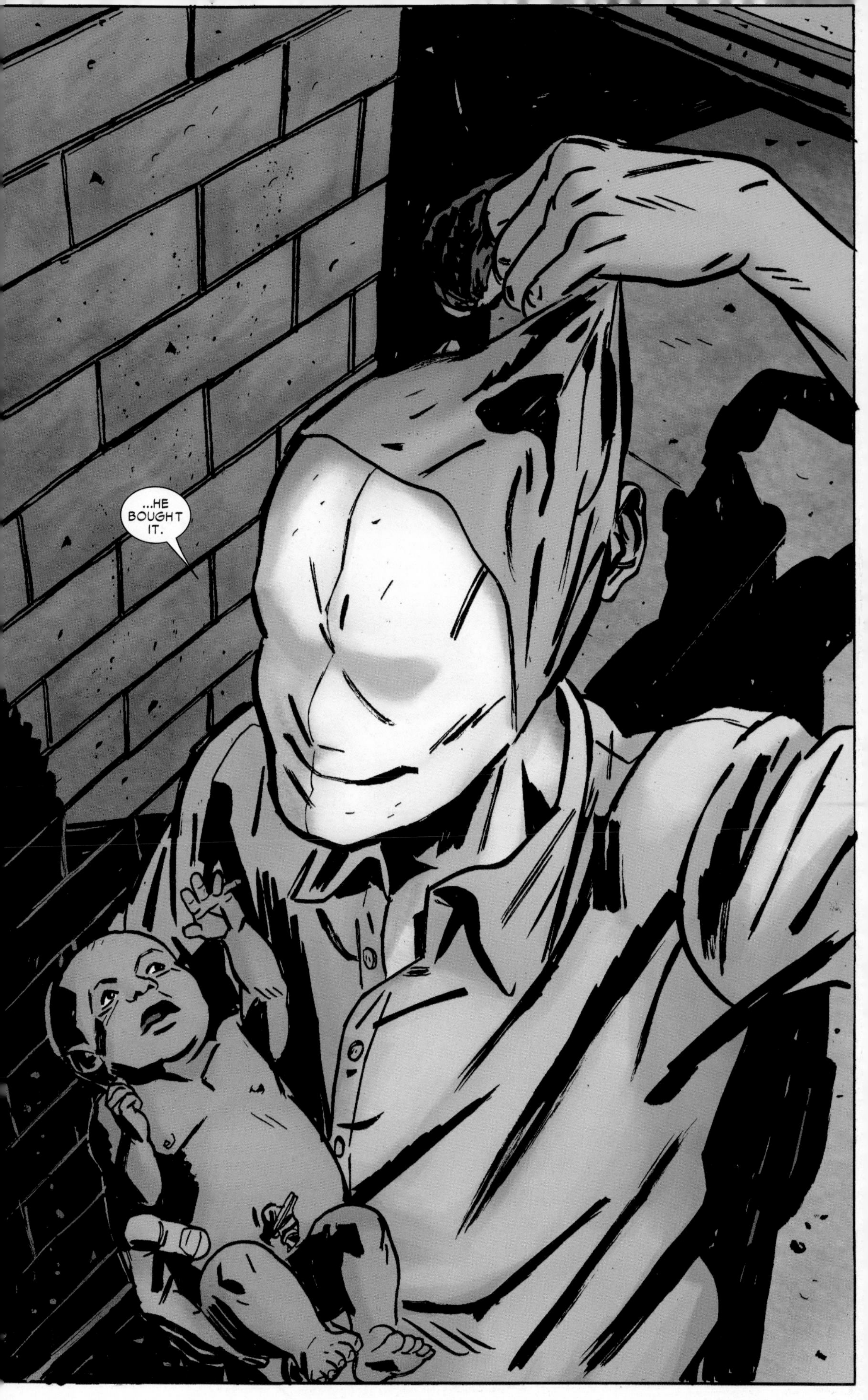
...HE BOUGHT IT.

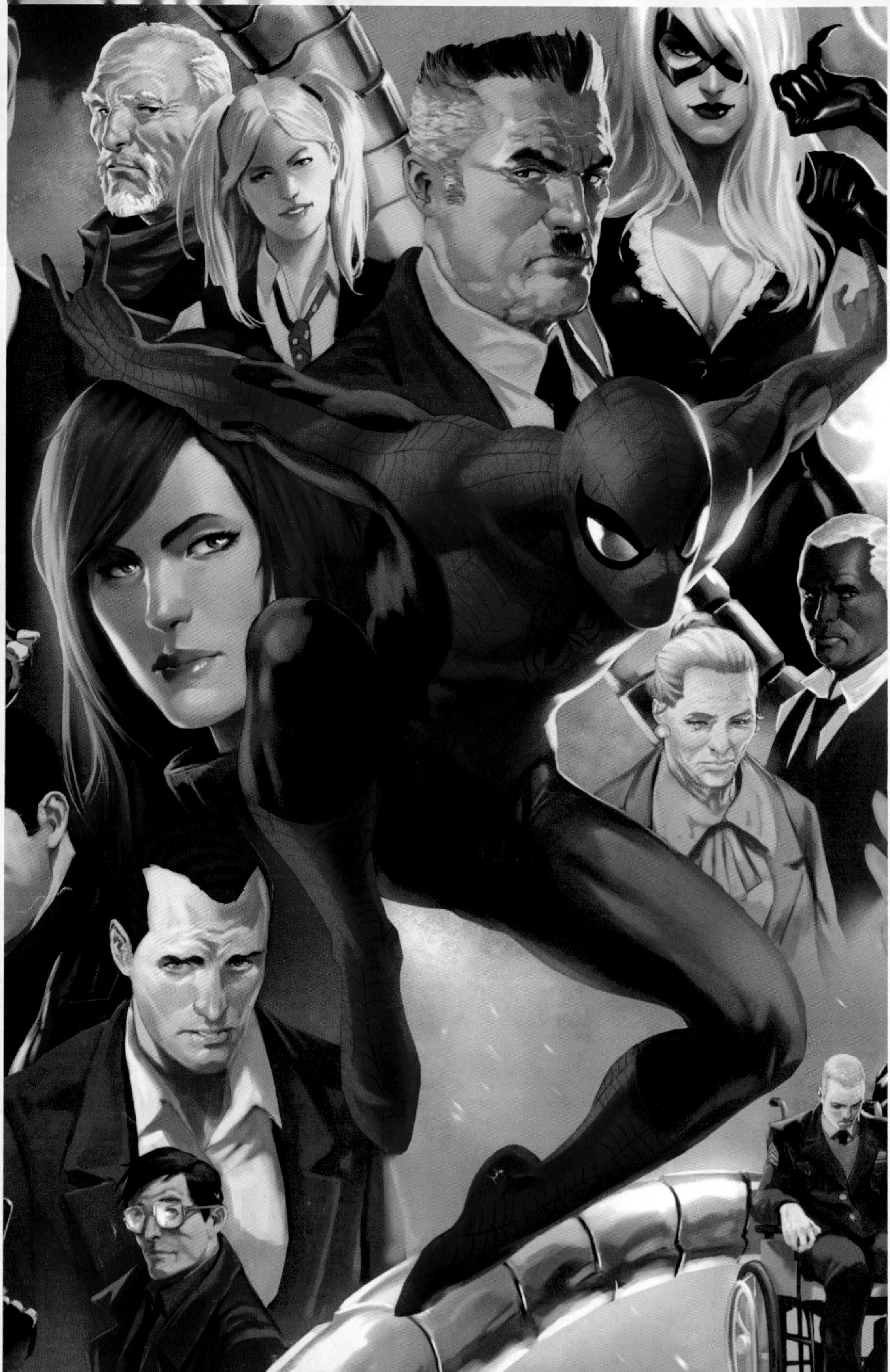

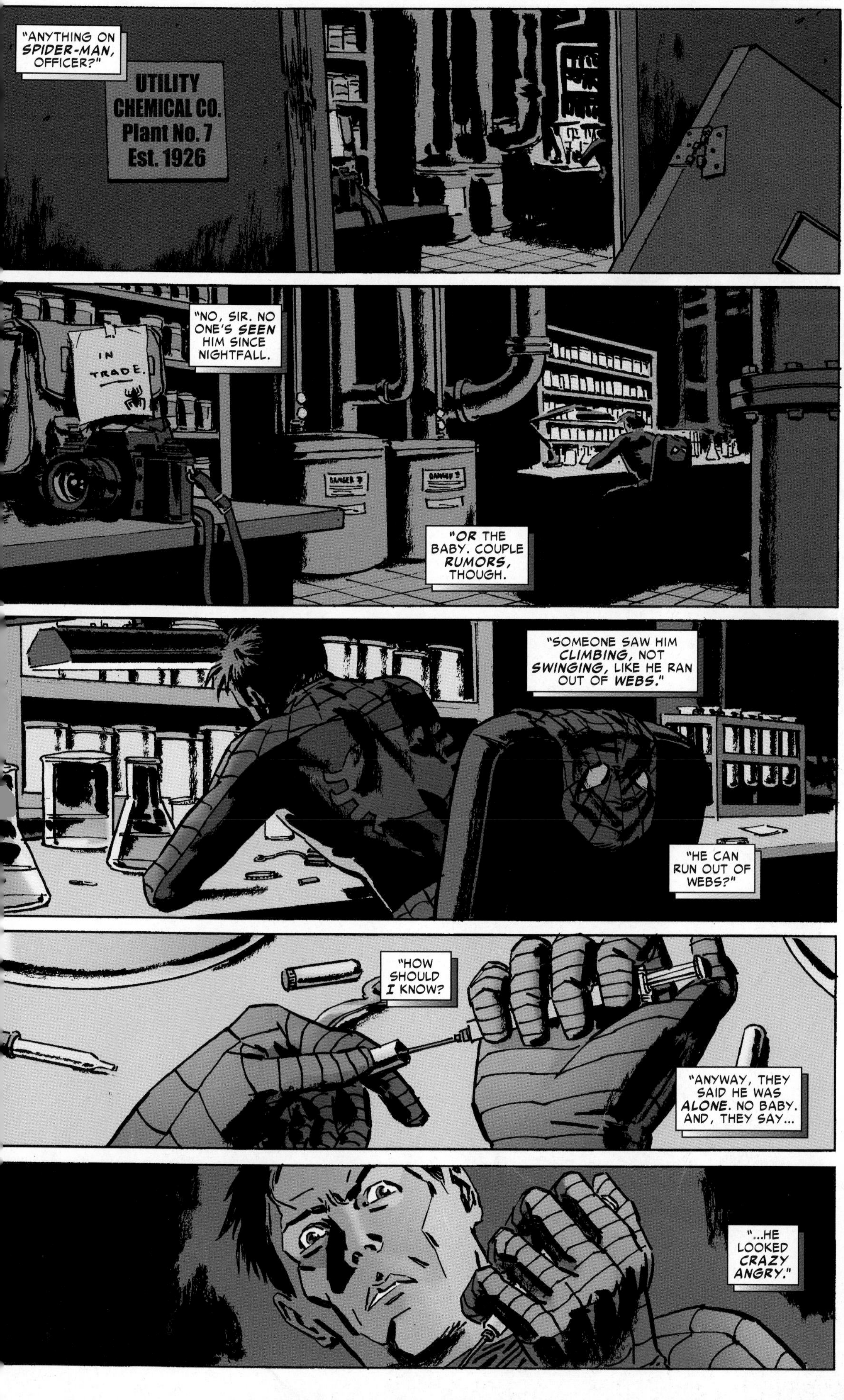
"ANYTHING ON SPIDER-MAN, OFFICER?"
UTILITY CHEMICAL CO. Plant No. 7 Est. 1926
IN TRADE.
"NO, SIR. NO ONE'S SEEN HIM SINCE NIGHTFALL.
"OR THE BABY. COUPLE RUMORS, THOUGH.
"SOMEONE SAW HIM CLIMBING, NOT SWINGING, LIKE HE RAN OUT OF WEBS."
"HE CAN RUN OUT OF WEBS?"
"HOW SHOULD I KNOW?
"ANYWAY, THEY SAID HE WAS ALONE. NO BABY. AND, THEY SAY...
"...HE LOOKED CRAZY ANGRY."

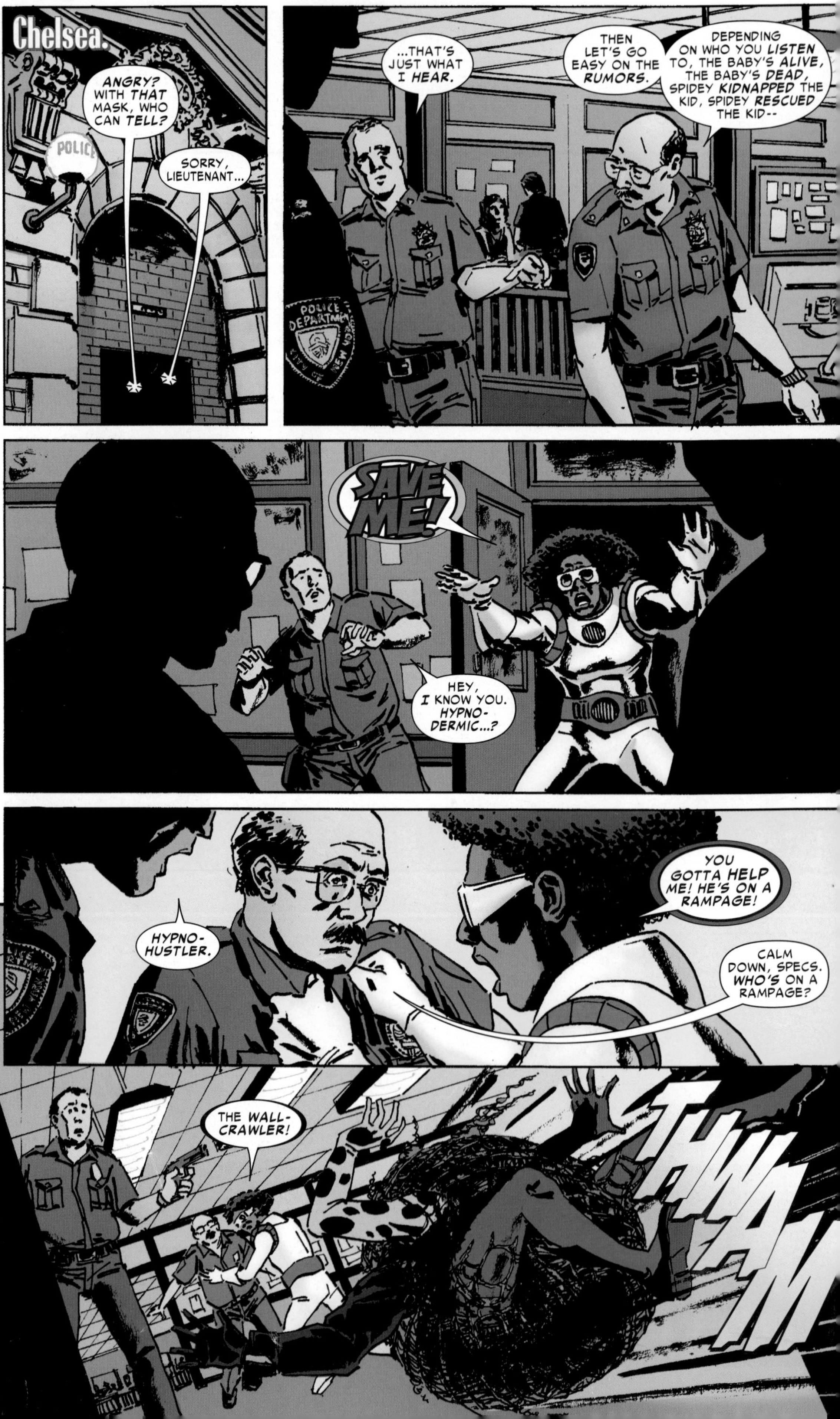
Chelsea.
ANGRY? WITH THAT MASK, WHO CAN TELL?
SORRY, LIEUTENANT...
POLICE
...THAT'S JUST WHAT I HEAR.
THEN LET'S GO EASY ON THE RUMORS.
DEPENDING ON WHO YOU LISTEN TO, THE BABY'S ALIVE, THE BABY'S DEAD, SPIDEY KIDNAPPED THE KID, SPIDEY RESCUED THE KID--
POLICE DEPARTMENT
SAVE ME!
HEY, I KNOW YOU. HYPNO-DERMIC...?
HYPNO-HUSTLER.
YOU GOTTA HELP ME! HE'S ON A RAMPAGE!
CALM DOWN, SPECS. WHO'S ON A RAMPAGE?
THE WALL-CRAWLER!
THWAM

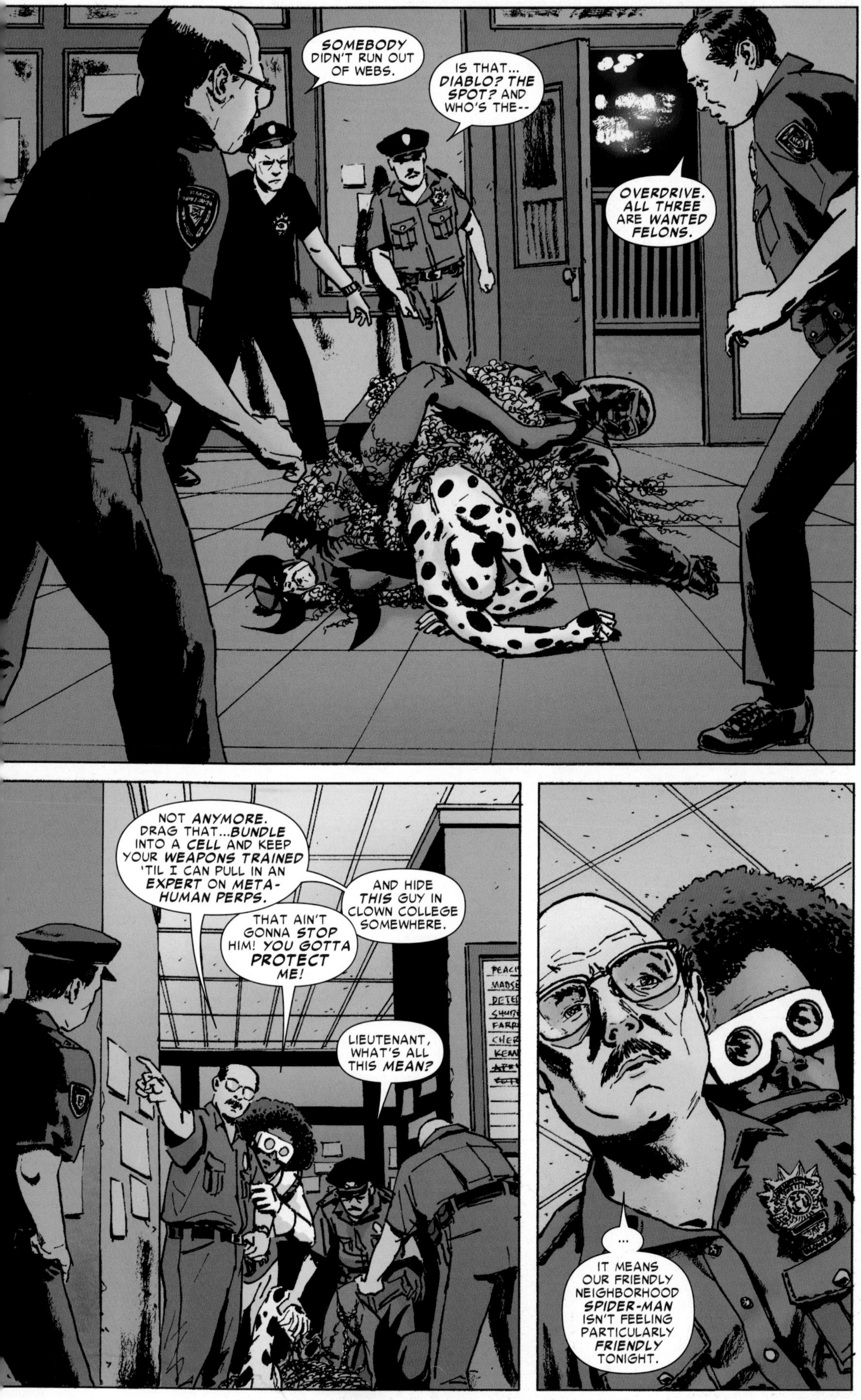
SOMEBODY DIDN'T RUN OUT OF WEBS.
IS THAT... DIABLO? THE SPOT? AND WHO'S THE--
OVERDRIVE. ALL THREE ARE WANTED FELONS.
NOT ANYMORE. DRAG THAT...BUNDLE INTO A CELL AND KEEP YOUR WEAPONS TRAINED 'TIL I CAN PULL IN AN EXPERT ON META-HUMAN PERPS.
AND HIDE THIS GUY IN CLOWN COLLEGE SOMEWHERE.
THAT AIN'T GONNA STOP HIM! YOU GOTTA PROTECT ME!
LIEUTENANT, WHAT'S ALL THIS MEAN?
...
IT MEANS OUR FRIENDLY NEIGHBORHOOD SPIDER-MAN ISN'T FEELING PARTICULARLY FRIENDLY TONIGHT.

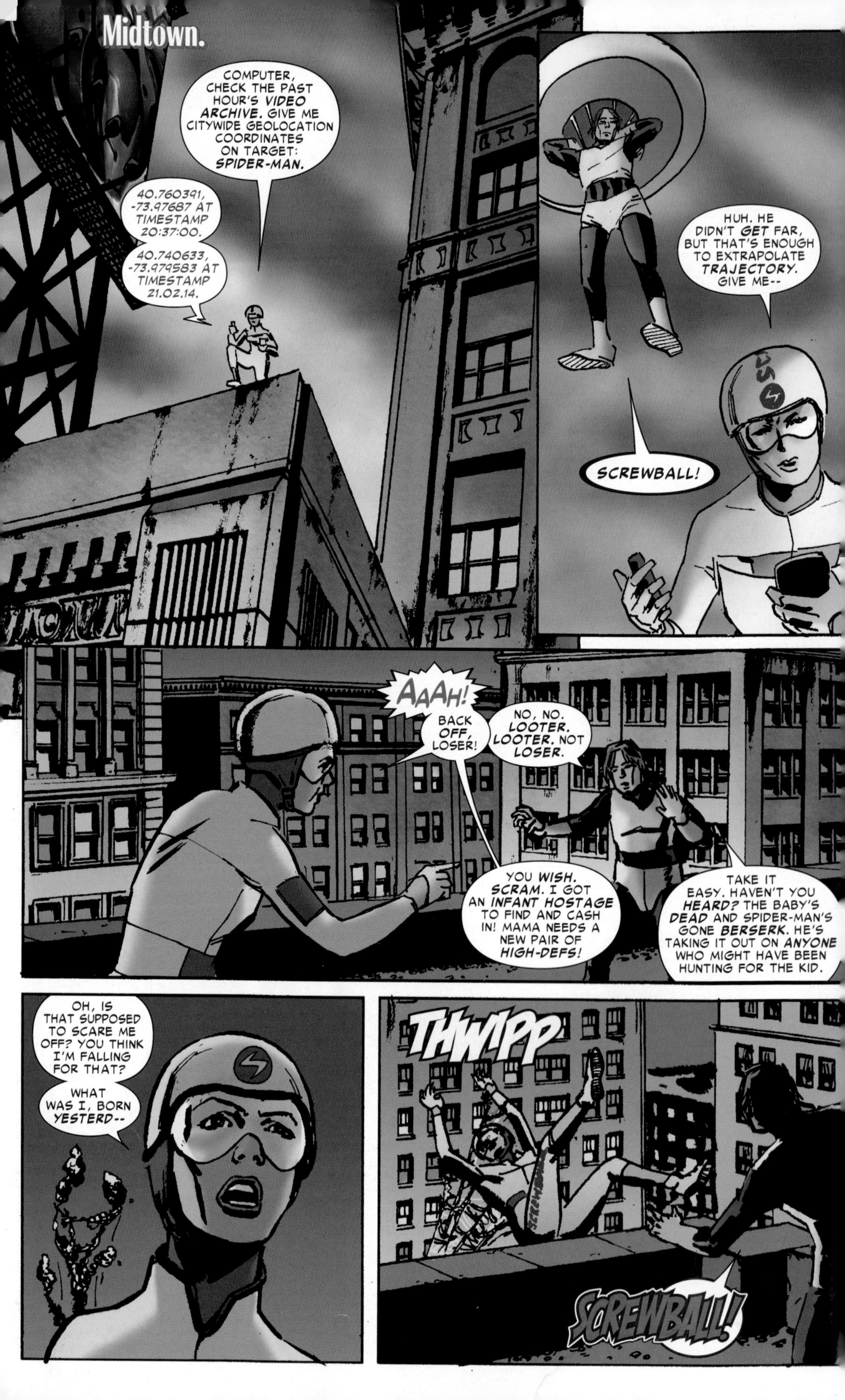

Midtown.
COMPUTER, CHECK THE PAST HOUR'S VIDEO ARCHIVE. GIVE ME CITYWIDE GEOLOCATION COORDINATES ON TARGET: SPIDER-MAN.
40.760391, -73.97687 AT TIMESTAMP 20:37:00.
40.740633, -73.979583 AT TIMESTAMP 21.02.14.
HUH. HE DIDN'T GET FAR, BUT THAT'S ENOUGH TO EXTRAPOLATE TRAJECTORY. GIVE ME--
SCREWBALL!
AAAH!
BACK OFF, LOSER!
NO, NO. LOOTER. LOOTER. NOT LOSER.
YOU WISH. SCRAM. I GOT AN INFANT HOSTAGE TO FIND AND CASH IN! MAMA NEEDS A NEW PAIR OF HIGH-DEFS!
TAKE IT EASY. HAVEN'T YOU HEARD? THE BABY'S DEAD AND SPIDER-MAN'S GONE BERSERK. HE'S TAKING IT OUT ON ANYONE WHO MIGHT HAVE BEEN HUNTING FOR THE KID.
OH, IS THAT SUPPOSED TO SCARE ME OFF? YOU THINK I'M FALLING FOR THAT?
WHAT WAS I, BORN YESTERD--
THWIPP
SCREWBALL!

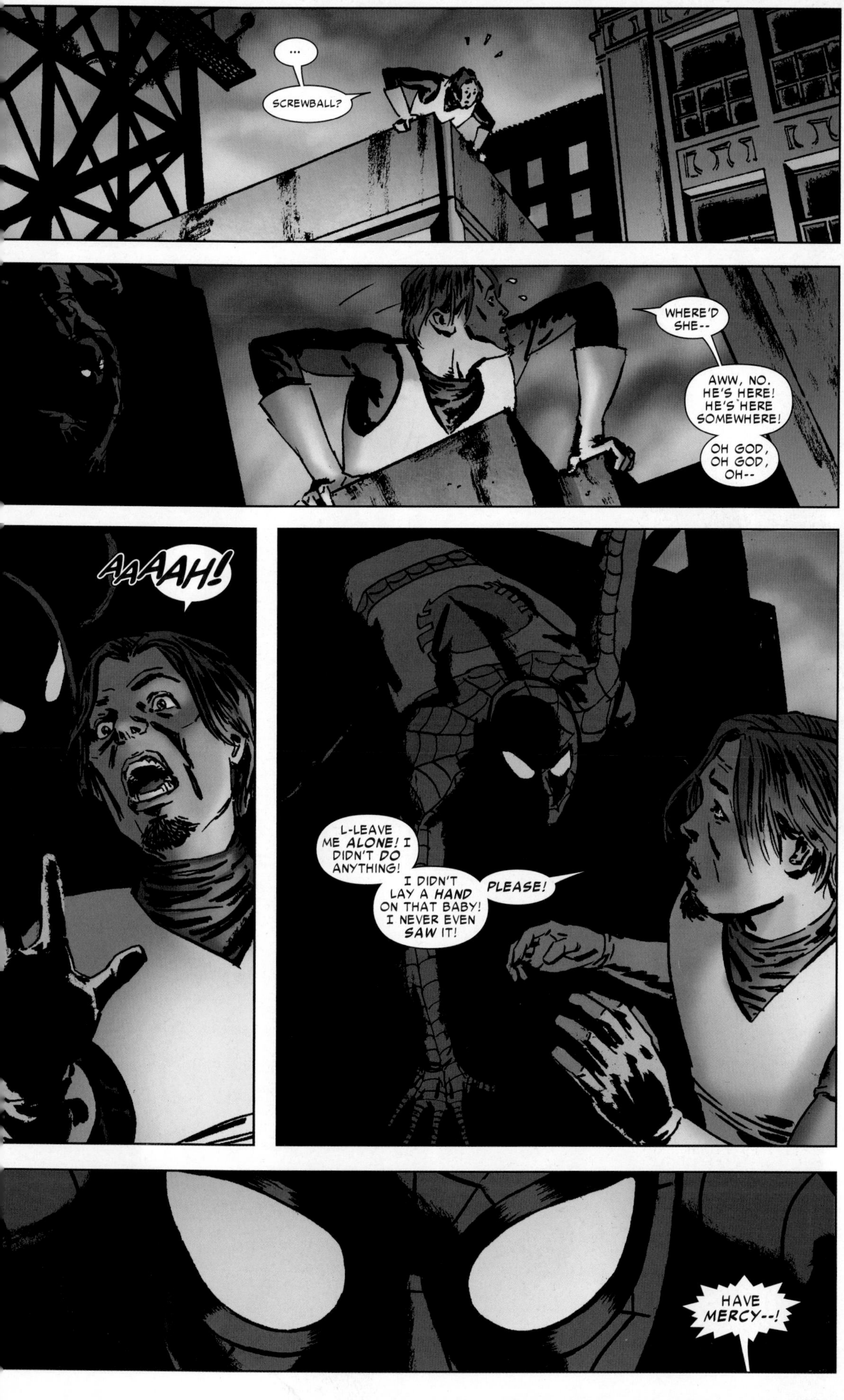
...
SCREWBALL?
WHERE'D SHE--
AWW, NO. HE'S HERE! HE'S HERE SOMEWHERE!
OH GOD, OH GOD, OH--
AAAAH!
L-LEAVE ME ALONE! I DIDN'T DO ANYTHING!
I DIDN'T LAY A HAND ON THAT BABY! I NEVER EVEN SAW IT!
PLEASE!
HAVE MERCY--!

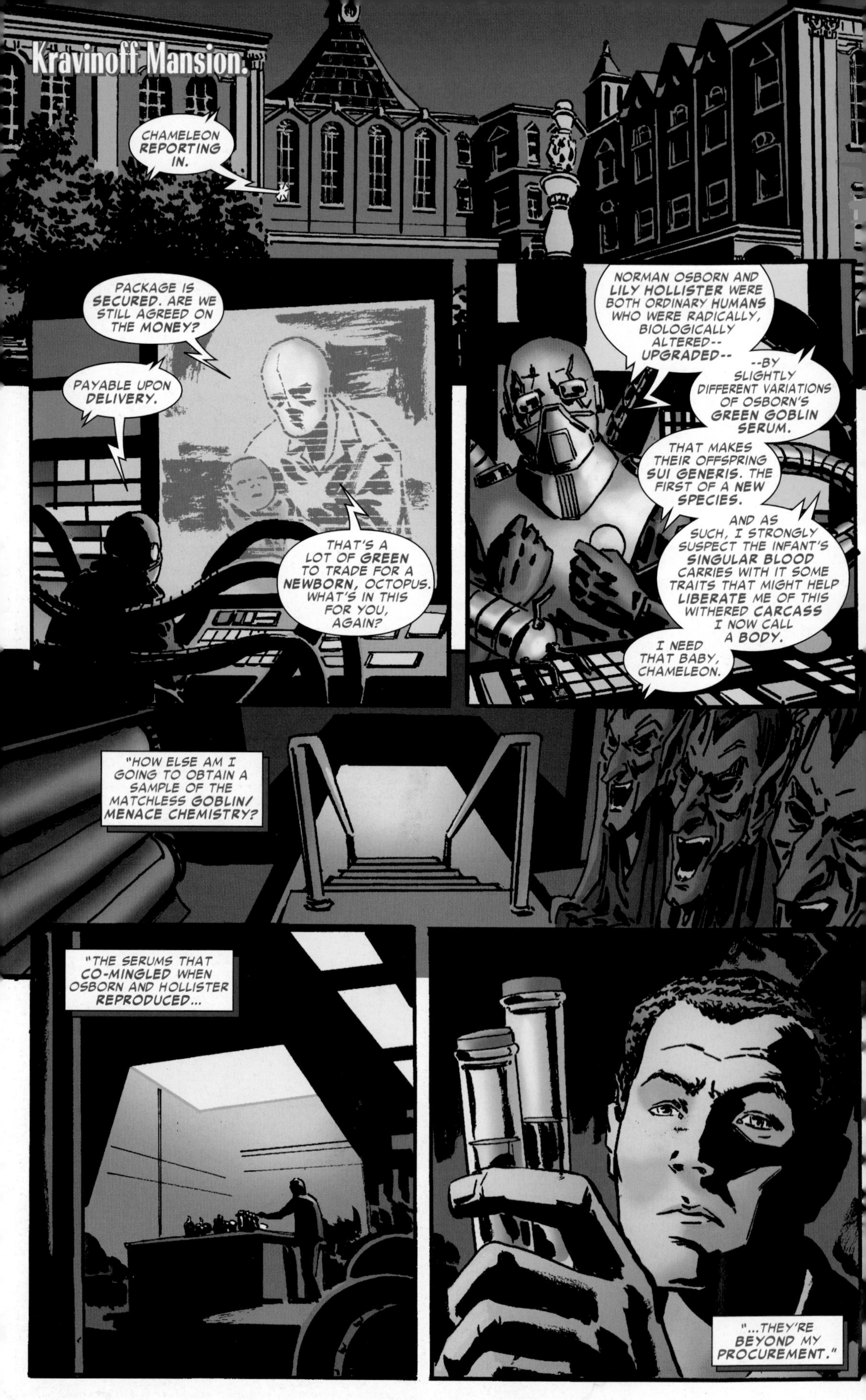
Kravinoff Mansion.
CHAMELEON REPORTING IN.
PACKAGE IS SECURED. ARE WE STILL AGREED ON THE MONEY?
PAYABLE UPON DELIVERY.
THAT'S A LOT OF GREEN TO TRADE FOR A NEWBORN, OCTOPUS. WHAT'S IN THIS FOR YOU, AGAIN?
NORMAN OSBORN AND LILY HOLLISTER WERE BOTH ORDINARY HUMANS WHO WERE RADICALLY, BIOLOGICALLY ALTERED-- UPGRADED--
--BY SLIGHTLY DIFFERENT VARIATIONS OF OSBORN'S GREEN GOBLIN SERUM.
THAT MAKES THEIR OFFSPRING SUI GENERIS. THE FIRST OF A NEW SPECIES.
AND AS SUCH, I STRONGLY SUSPECT THE INFANT'S SINGULAR BLOOD CARRIES WITH IT SOME TRAITS THAT MIGHT HELP LIBERATE ME OF THIS WITHERED CARCASS I NOW CALL A BODY.
I NEED THAT BABY, CHAMELEON.
"HOW ELSE AM I GOING TO OBTAIN A SAMPLE OF THE MATCHLESS GOBLIN/ MENACE CHEMISTRY?
"THE SERUMS THAT CO-MINGLED WHEN OSBORN AND HOLLISTER REPRODUCED...
"...THEY'RE BEYOND MY PROCUREMENT."

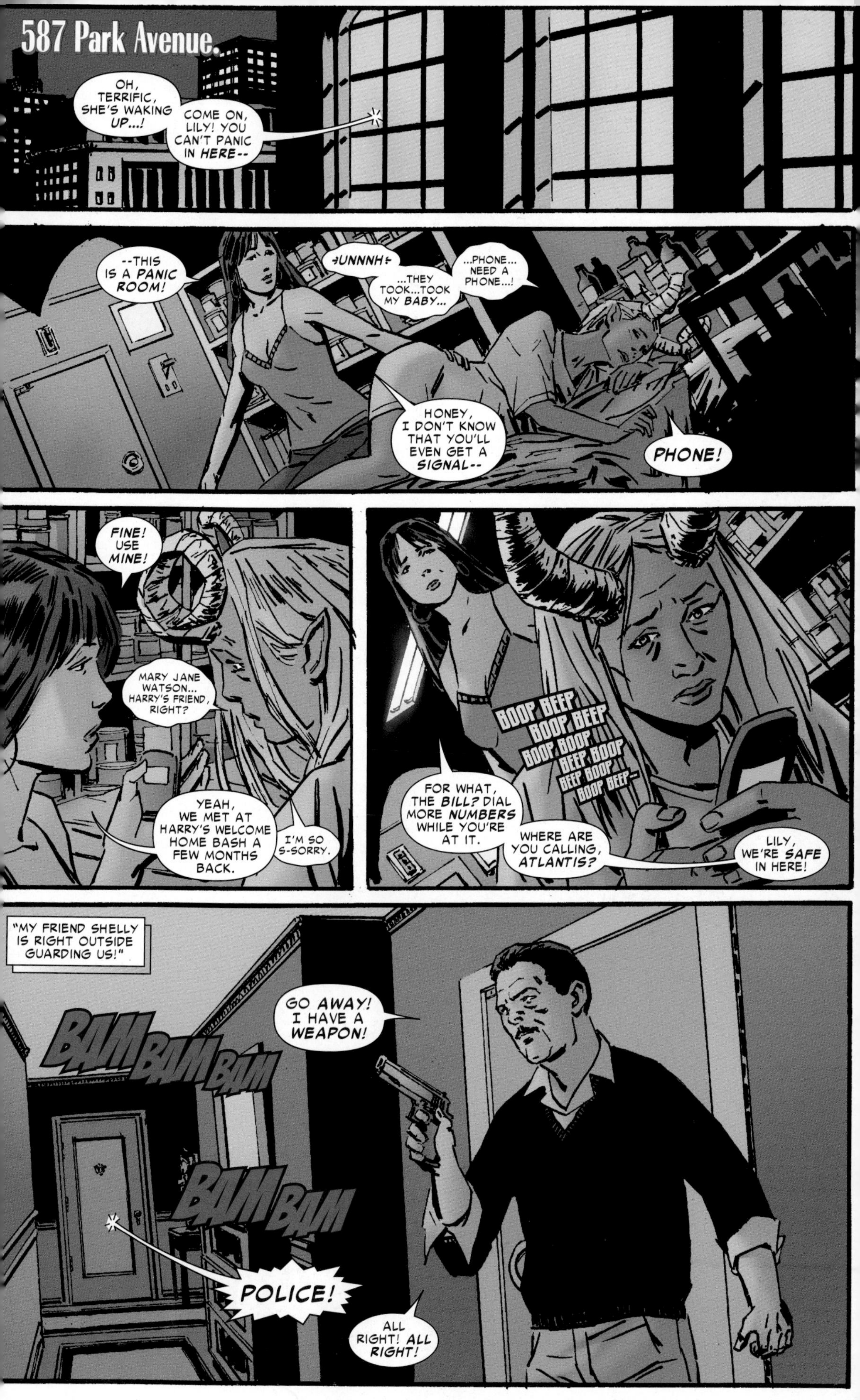
587 Park Avenue.
OH, TERRIFIC, SHE'S WAKING UP...!
COME ON, LILY! YOU CAN'T PANIC IN HERE--
--THIS IS A PANIC ROOM!
UNNNH
...THEY TOOK...TOOK MY BABY...
...PHONE... NEED A PHONE...!
HONEY, I DON'T KNOW THAT YOU'LL EVEN GET A SIGNAL--
PHONE!
FINE! USE MINE!
MARY JANE WATSON... HARRY'S FRIEND, RIGHT?
YEAH, WE MET AT HARRY'S WELCOME HOME BASH A FEW MONTHS BACK.
I'M SO S-SORRY.
BOOP BEEP BOOP BEEP BOOP BOOP BEEP BOOP BEEP BOOP BOOP BEEP--
FOR WHAT, THE BILL? DIAL MORE NUMBERS WHILE YOU'RE AT IT.
WHERE ARE YOU CALLING, ATLANTIS?
LILY, WE'RE SAFE IN HERE!
"MY FRIEND SHELLY IS RIGHT OUTSIDE GUARDING US!"
BAM BAM BAM
GO AWAY! I HAVE A WEAPON!
BAM BAM
POLICE!
ALL RIGHT! ALL RIGHT!

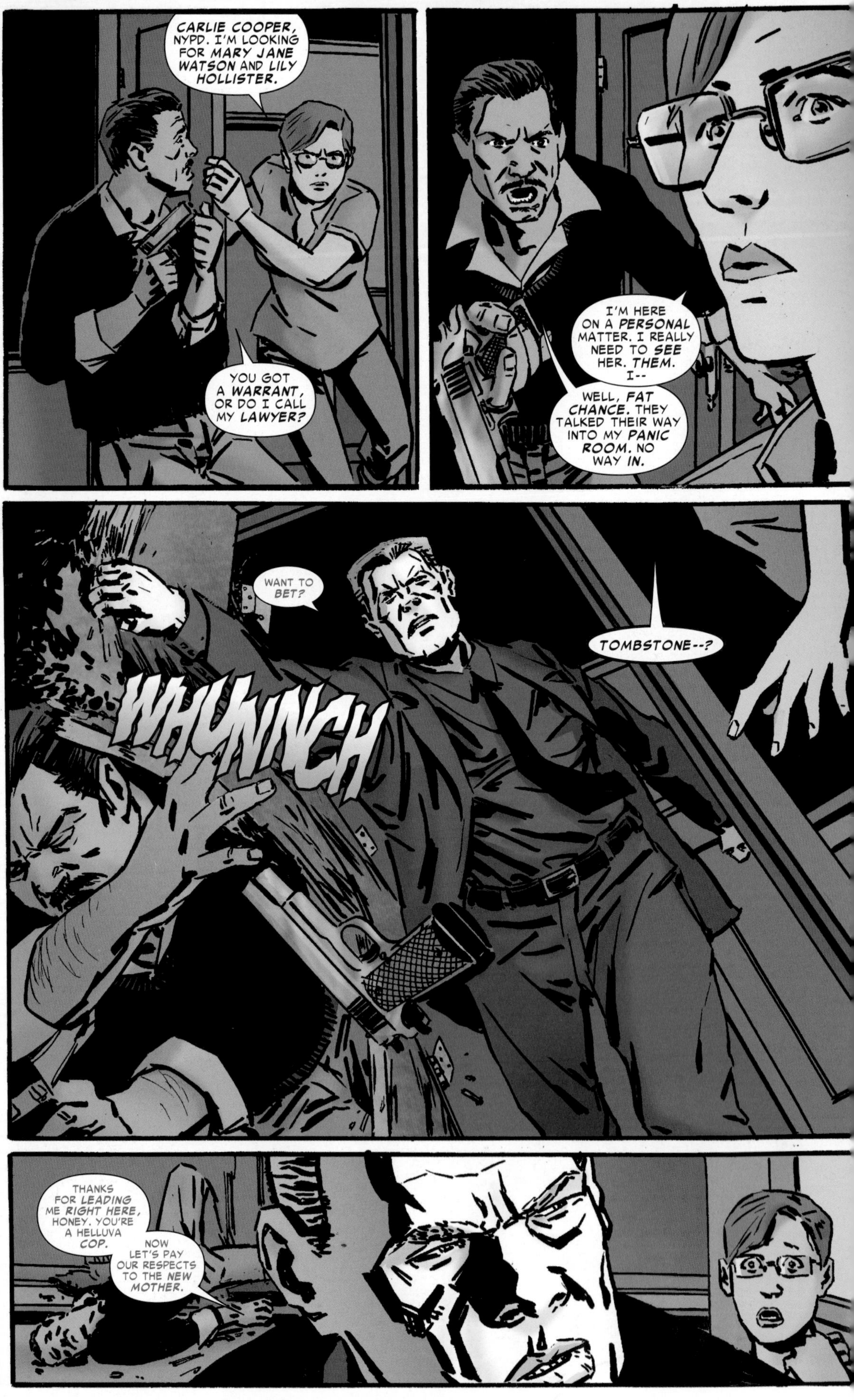
CARLIE COOPER, NYPD. I'M LOOKING FOR MARY JANE WATSON AND LILY HOLLISTER.
YOU GOT A WARRANT, OR DO I CALL MY LAWYER?
I'M HERE ON A PERSONAL MATTER. I REALLY NEED TO SEE HER. THEM. I--
WELL, FAT CHANCE. THEY TALKED THEIR WAY INTO MY PANIC ROOM. NO WAY IN.
WANT TO BET?
TOMBSTONE--?
WHUNNCH
THANKS FOR LEADING ME RIGHT HERE, HONEY. YOU'RE A HELLUVA COP.
NOW LET'S PAY OUR RESPECTS TO THE NEW MOTHER.

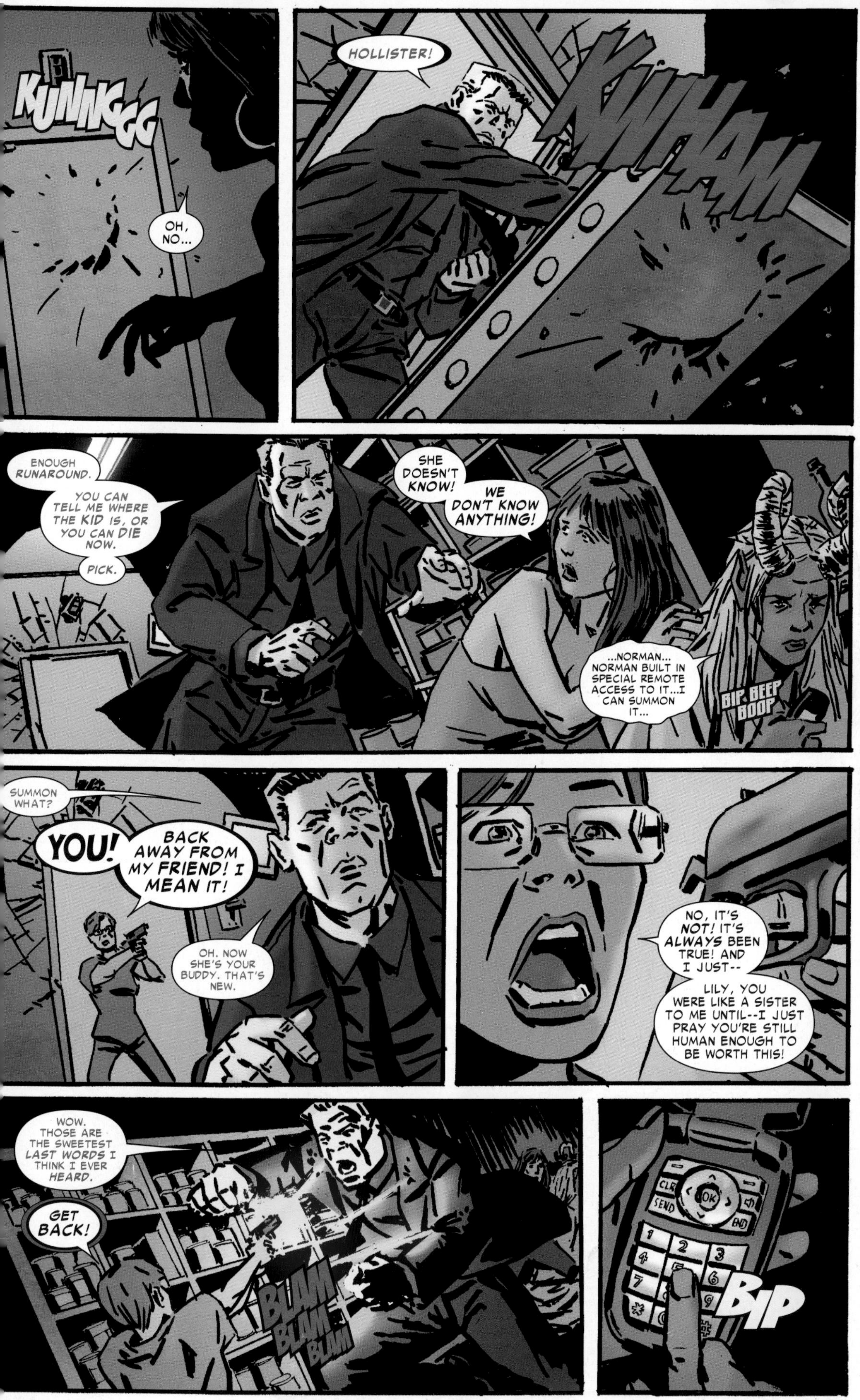
KUNNNGGG
OH, NO...
HOLLISTER!
KWHAM
ENOUGH RUNAROUND.
YOU CAN TELL ME WHERE THE KID IS, OR YOU CAN DIE NOW.
PICK.
SHE DOESN'T KNOW!
WE DON'T KNOW ANYTHING!
...NORMAN... NORMAN BUILT IN SPECIAL REMOTE ACCESS TO IT...I CAN SUMMON IT...
BIP BEEP BOOP
SUMMON WHAT?
YOU!
BACK AWAY FROM MY FRIEND! I MEAN IT!
OH. NOW SHE'S YOUR BUDDY. THAT'S NEW.
NO, IT'S NOT! IT'S ALWAYS BEEN TRUE! AND I JUST--
LILY, YOU WERE LIKE A SISTER TO ME UNTIL--I JUST PRAY YOU'RE STILL HUMAN ENOUGH TO BE WORTH THIS!
WOW. THOSE ARE THE SWEETEST LAST WORDS I THINK I EVER HEARD.
GET BACK!
BLAM BLAM BLAM
BIP

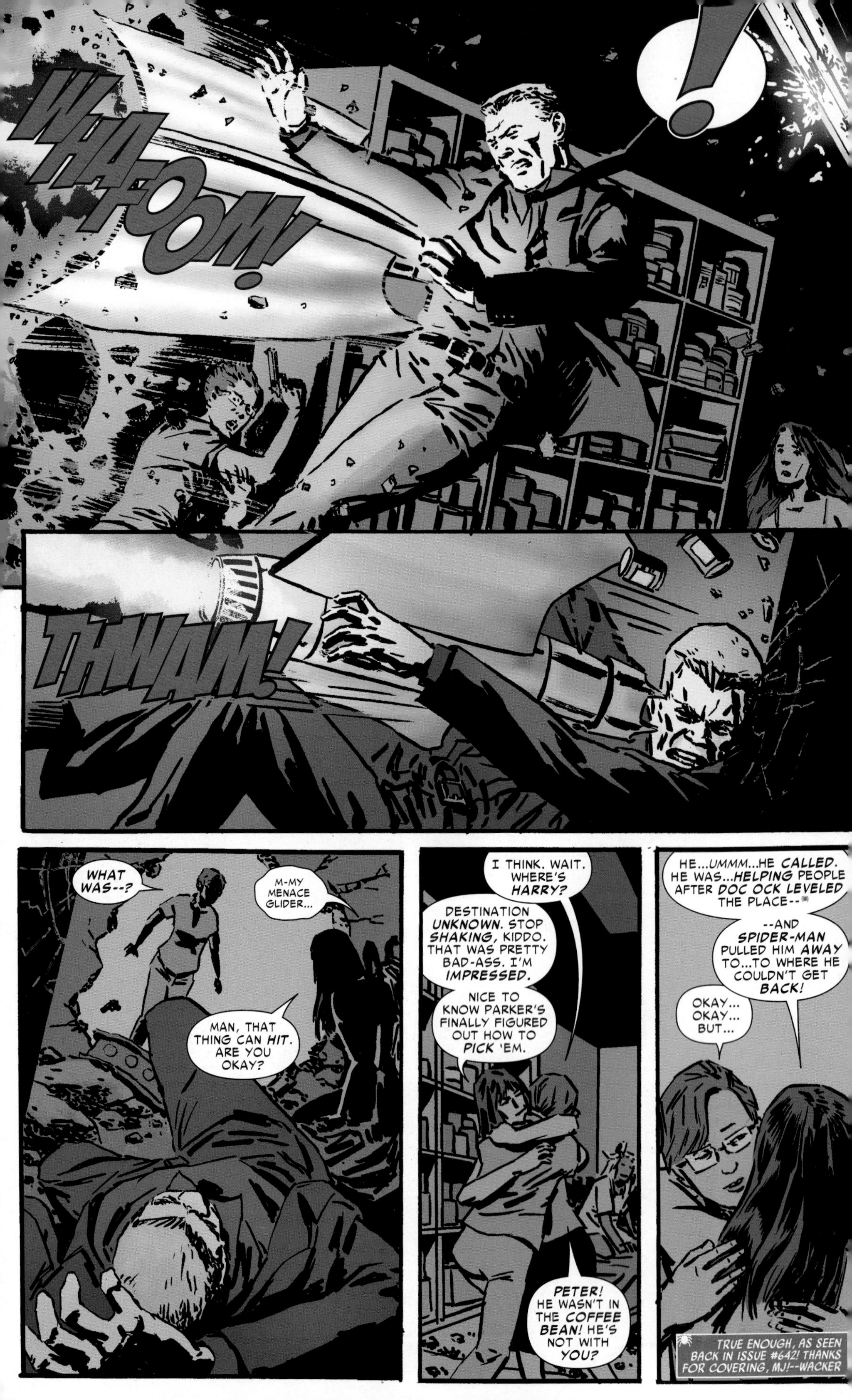

WHAFOOM!
!
THWAM!
WHAT WAS--?
M-MY MENACE GLIDER...
MAN, THAT THING CAN HIT. ARE YOU OKAY?
I THINK. WAIT. WHERE'S HARRY?
DESTINATION UNKNOWN. STOP SHAKING, KIDDO. THAT WAS PRETTY BAD-ASS. I'M IMPRESSED.
NICE TO KNOW PARKER'S FINALLY FIGURED OUT HOW TO PICK 'EM.
PETER! HE WASN'T IN THE COFFEE BEAN! HE'S NOT WITH YOU?
HE...UMMM...HE CALLED. HE WAS...HELPING PEOPLE AFTER DOC OCK LEVELED THE PLACE--
--AND SPIDER-MAN PULLED HIM AWAY TO...TO WHERE HE COULDN'T GET BACK!
OKAY... OKAY... BUT...
TRUE ENOUGH, AS SEEN BACK IN ISSUE #642! THANKS FOR COVERING, MJ!--WACKER

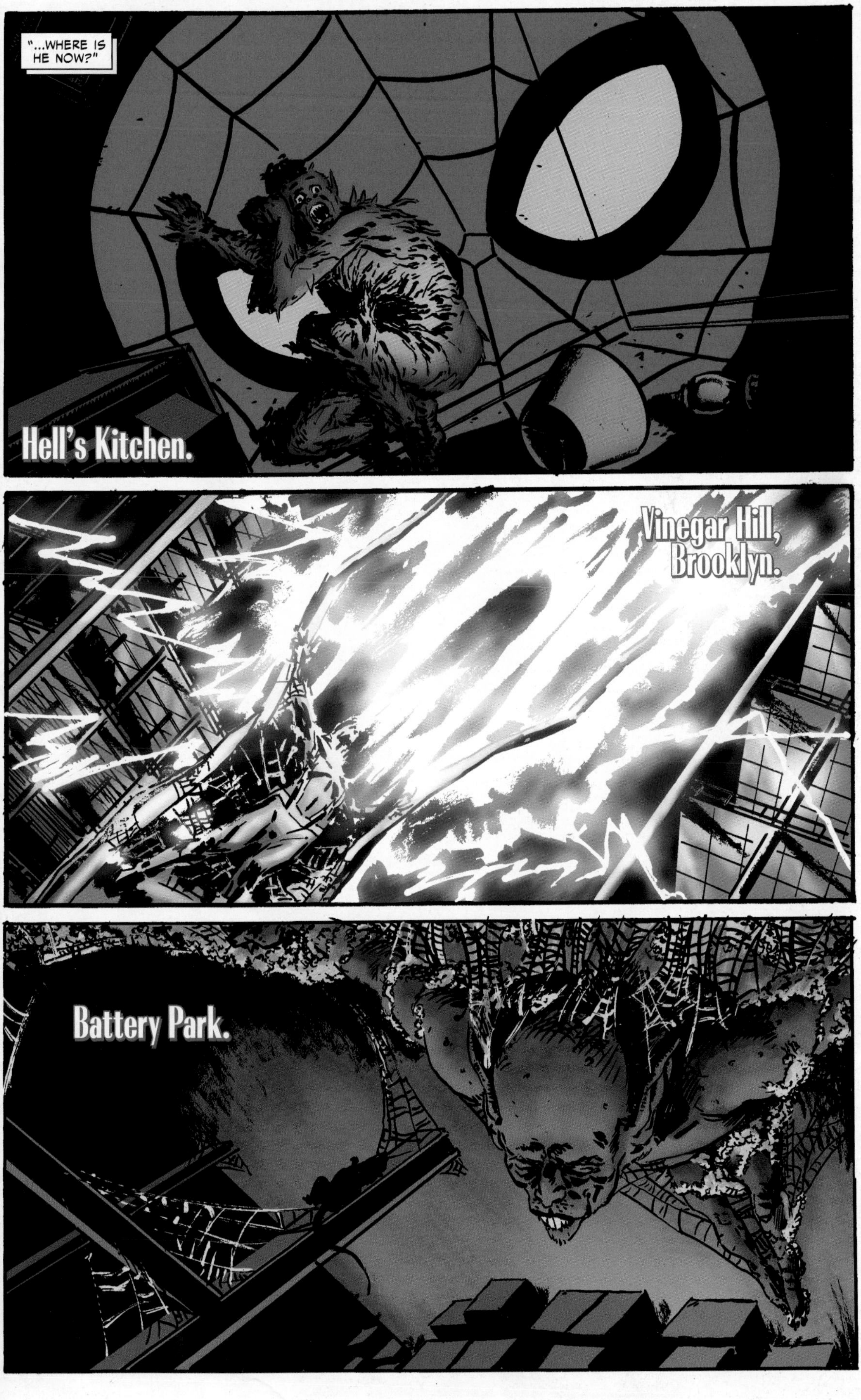
"...WHERE IS HE NOW?"
Hell's Kitchen.
Vinegar Hill, Brooklyn.
Battery Park.

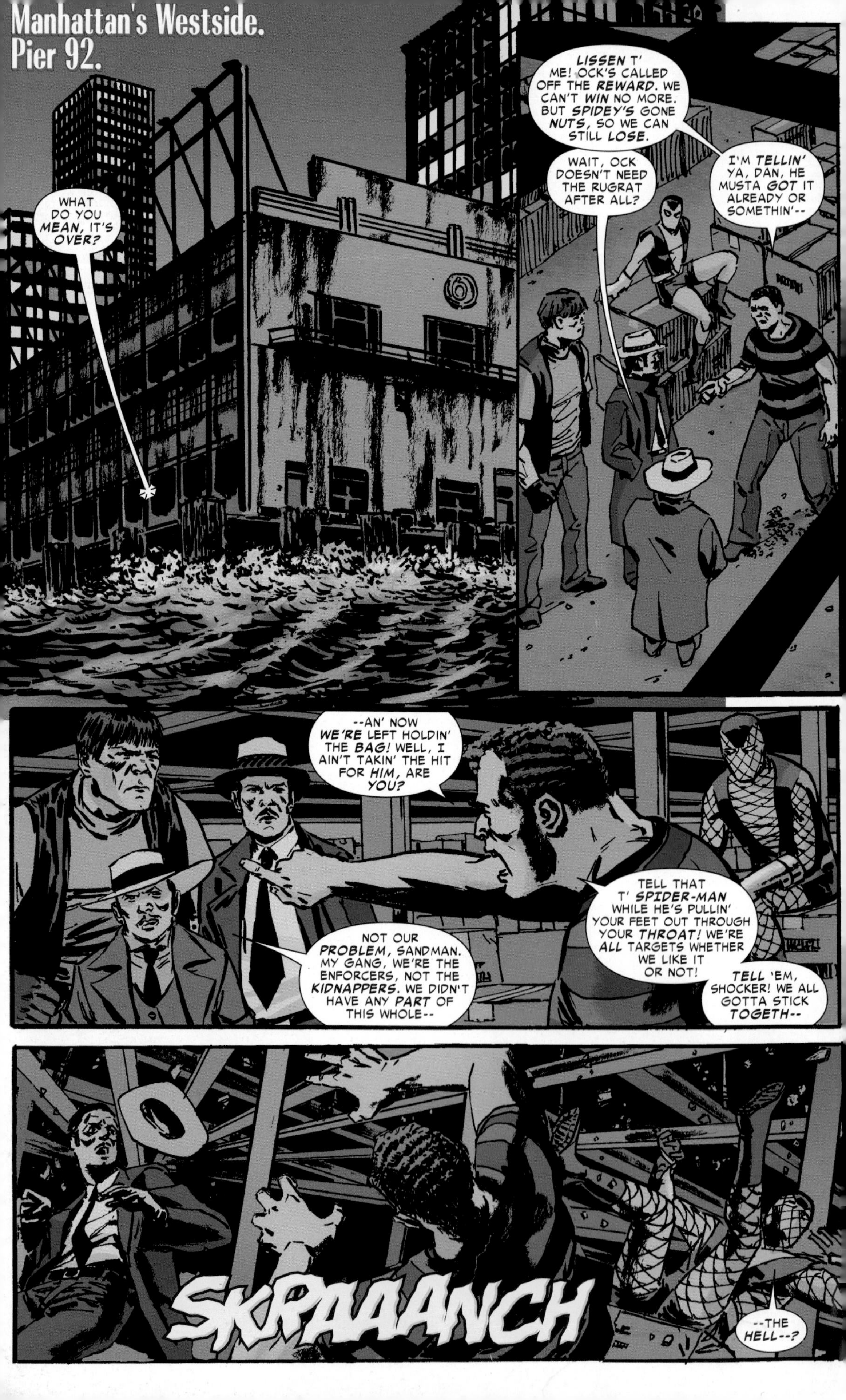

Manhattan's Westside. Pier 92.
WHAT DO YOU MEAN, IT'S OVER?
LISSEN T' ME! OCK'S CALLED OFF THE REWARD. WE CAN'T WIN NO MORE. BUT SPIDEY'S GONE NUTS, SO WE CAN STILL LOSE.
WAIT, OCK DOESN'T NEED THE RUGRAT AFTER ALL?
I'M TELLIN' YA, DAN, HE MUSTA GOT IT ALREADY OR SOMETHIN'--
--AN' NOW WE'RE LEFT HOLDIN' THE BAG! WELL, I AIN'T TAKIN' THE HIT FOR HIM, ARE YOU?
NOT OUR PROBLEM, SANDMAN. MY GANG, WE'RE THE ENFORCERS, NOT THE KIDNAPPERS. WE DIDN'T HAVE ANY PART OF THIS WHOLE--
TELL THAT T' SPIDER-MAN WHILE HE'S PULLIN' YOUR FEET OUT THROUGH YOUR THROAT! WE'RE ALL TARGETS WHETHER WE LIKE IT OR NOT!
TELL 'EM, SHOCKER! WE ALL GOTTA STICK TOGETH--
SKRAAANCH
--THE HELL--?

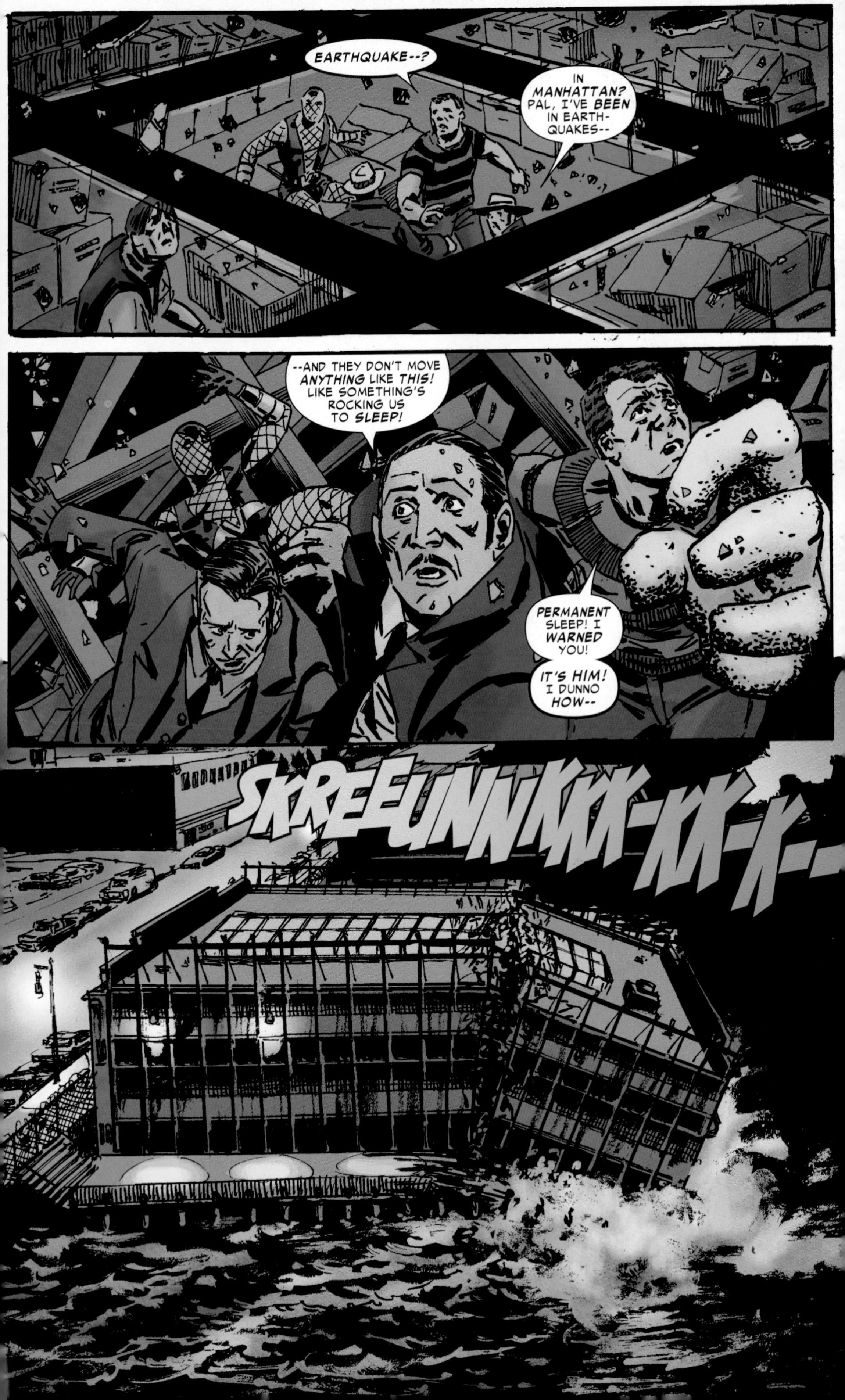
EARTHQUAKE--?
IN MANHATTAN? PAL, I'VE BEEN IN EARTH-QUAKES--
--AND THEY DON'T MOVE ANYTHING LIKE THIS! LIKE SOMETHING'S ROCKING US TO SLEEP!
PERMANENT SLEEP! I WARNED YOU!
IT'S HIM! I DUNNO HOW--
SKREEUNNNKKK-KK-K--

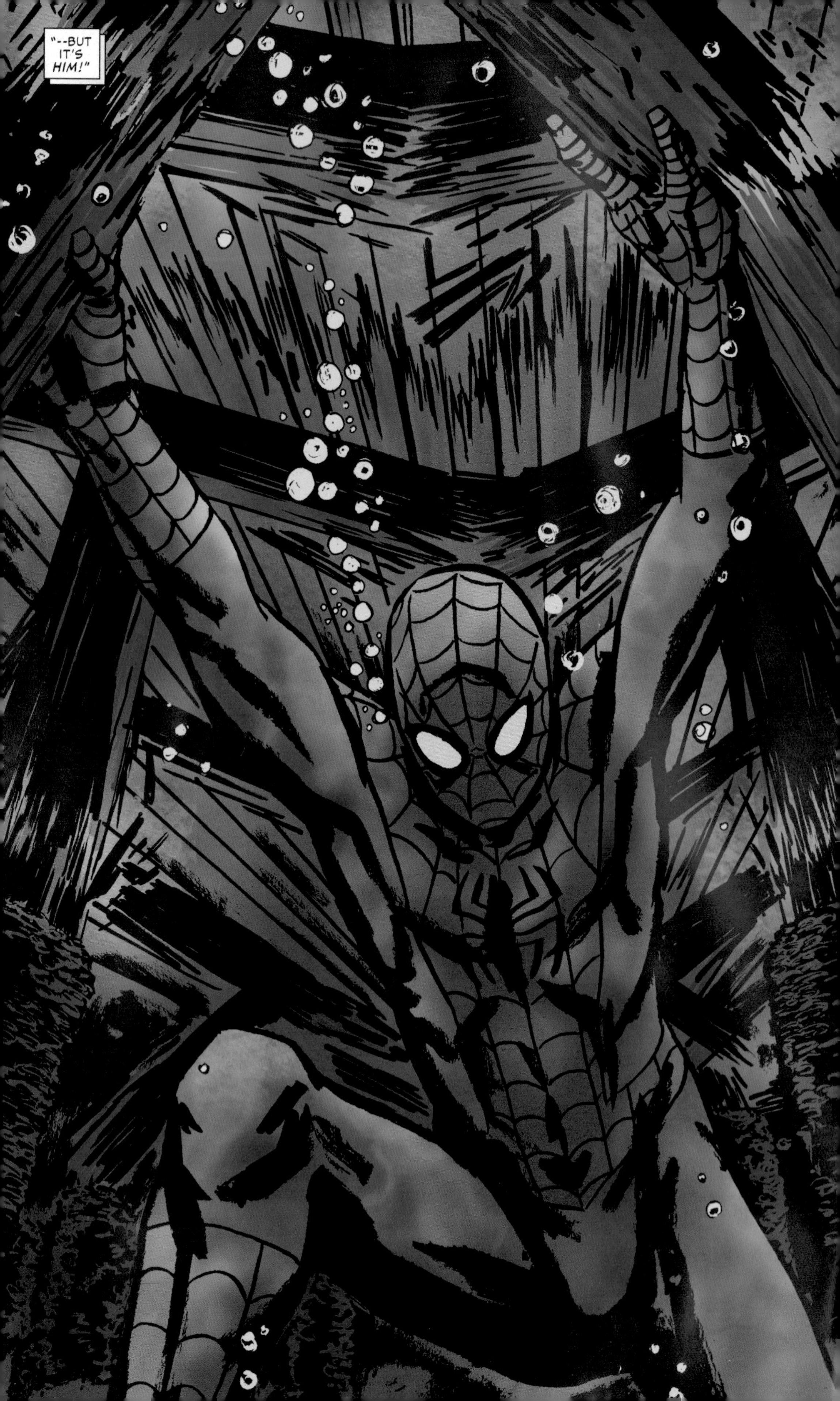
"--BUT IT'S *HIM!*"

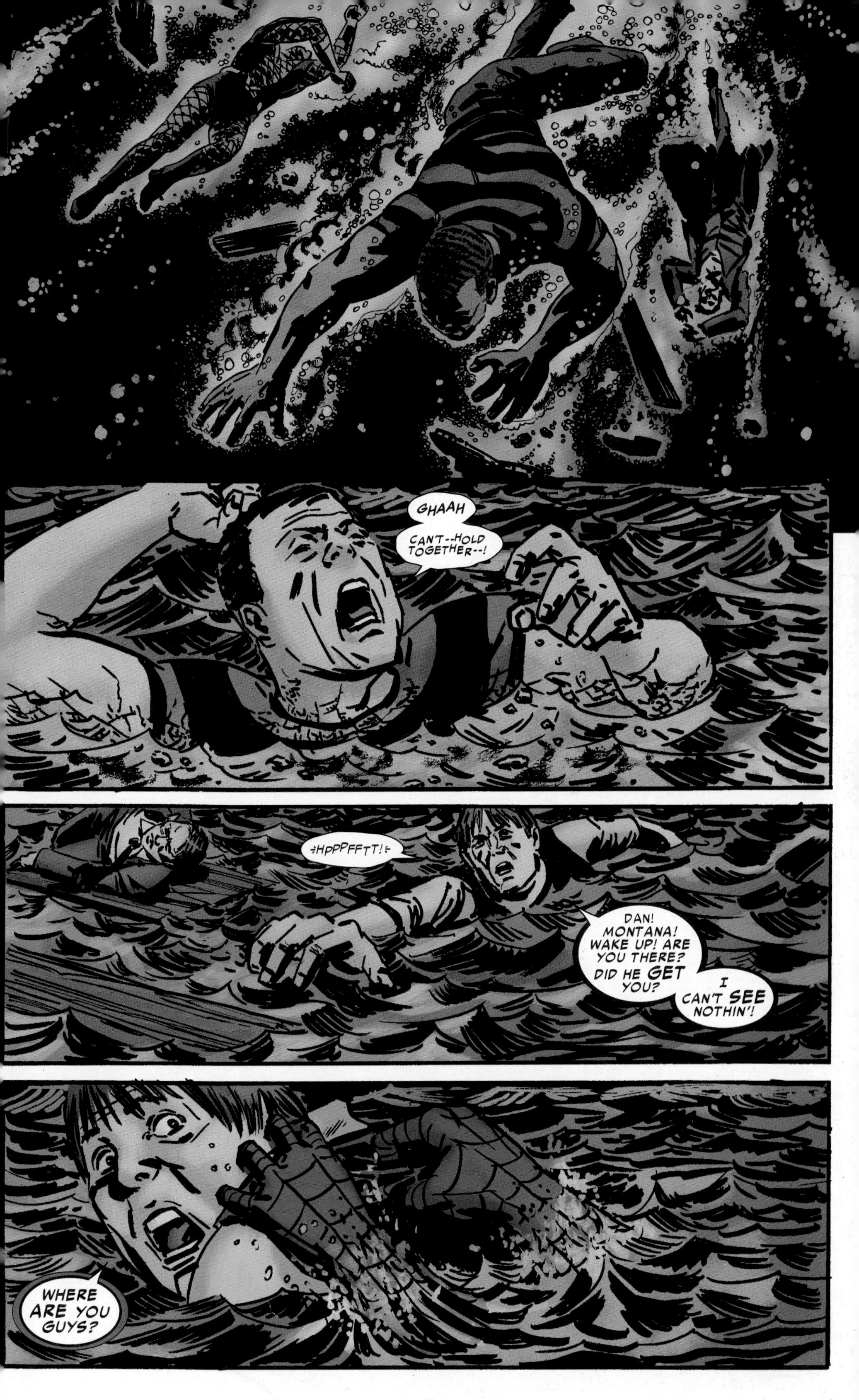
GHAAH
CAN'T--HOLD TOGETHER--!
≠HPPPFFTT!≠
DAN! MONTANA! WAKE UP! ARE YOU THERE? DID HE GET YOU?
I CAN'T SEE NOTHIN'!
WHERE ARE YOU GUYS?

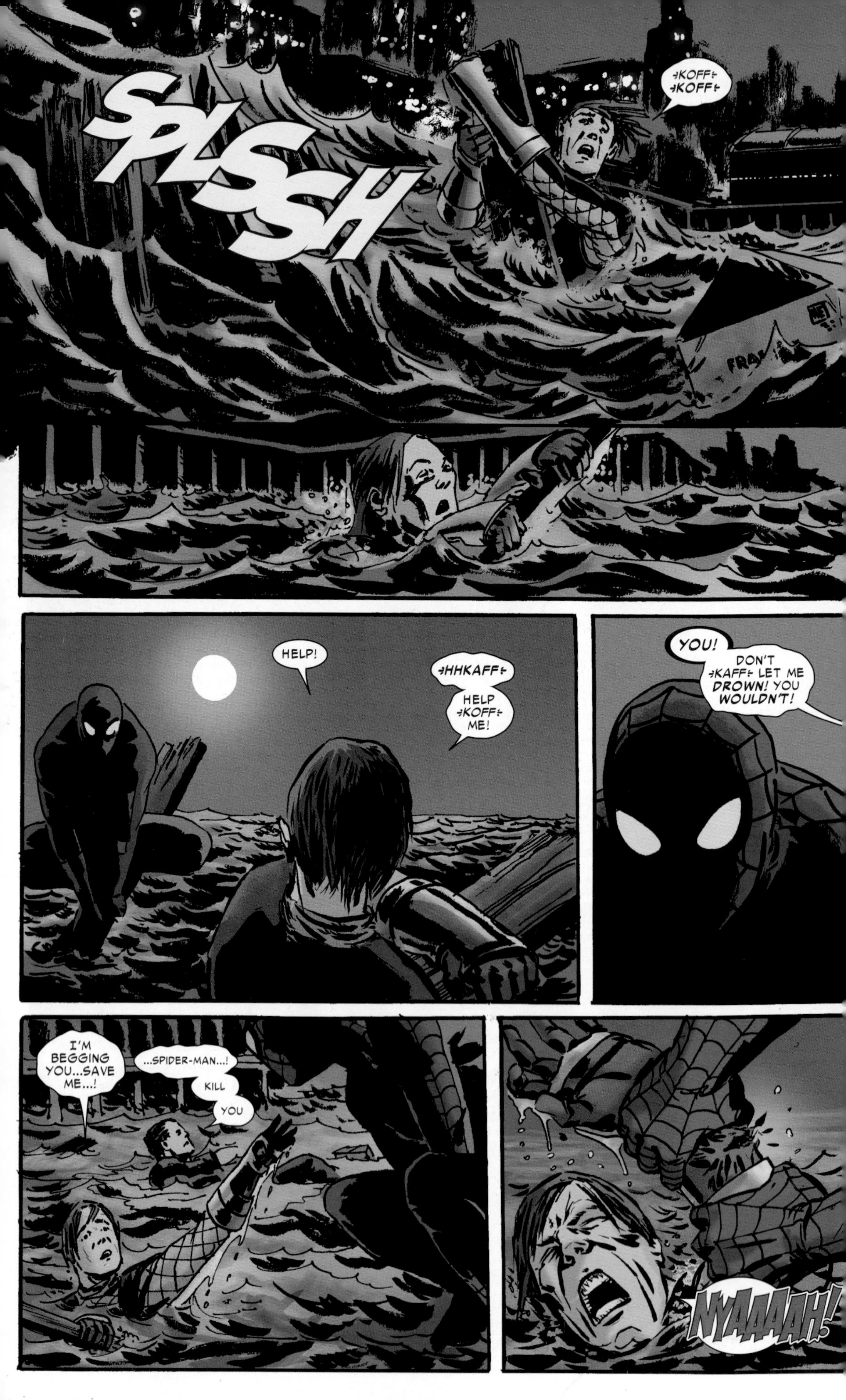
SPLSSH
KOFF KOFF
HELP!
HHKAFF HELP KOFF ME!
YOU!
DON'T KAFF LET ME DROWN! YOU WOULDN'T!
I'M BEGGING YOU...SAVE ME...!
...SPIDER-MAN...!
KILL
YOU
NYAAAAH!

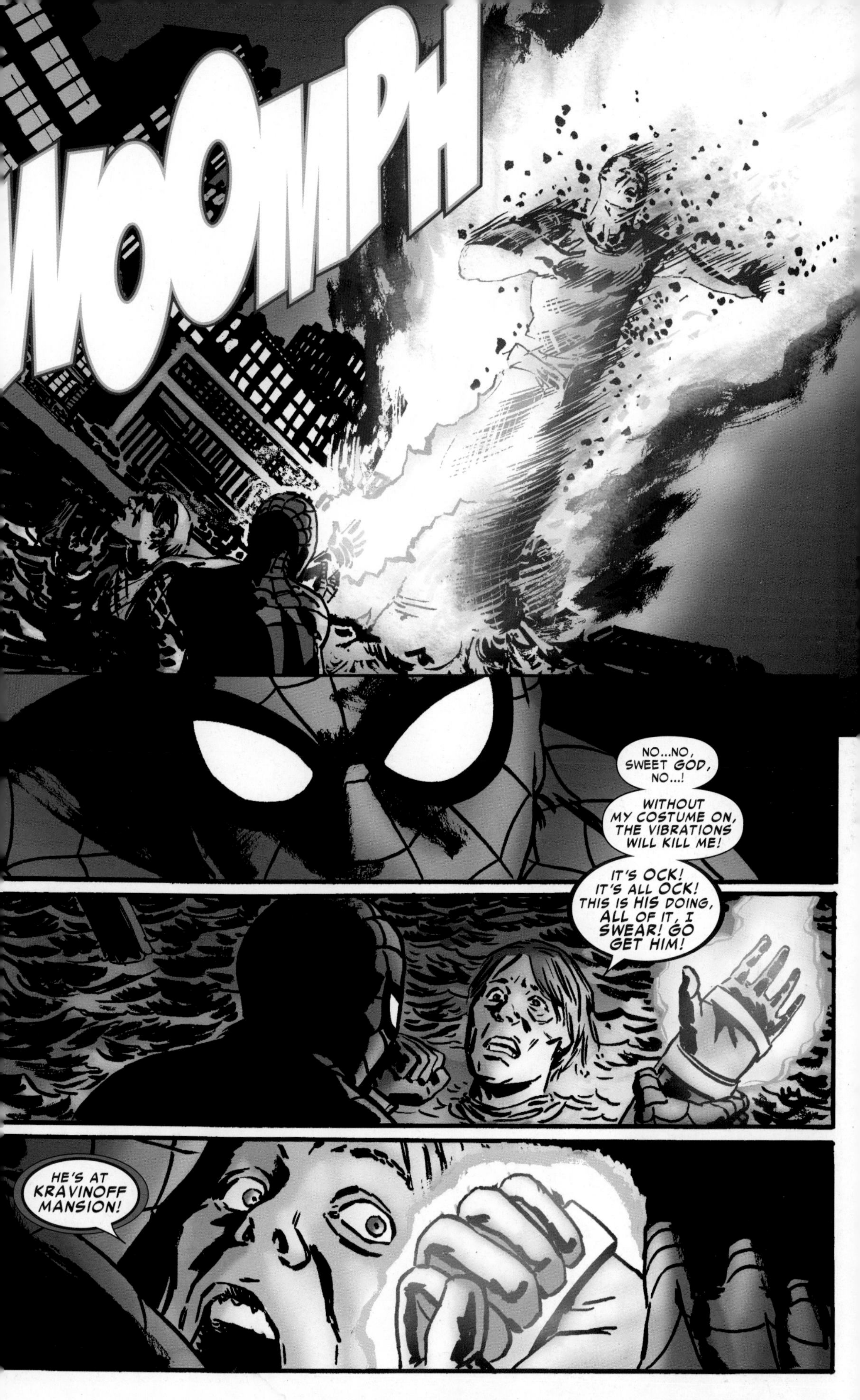
WOOMPH
NO...NO, SWEET GOD, NO...!
WITHOUT MY COSTUME ON, THE VIBRATIONS WILL KILL ME!
IT'S OCK! IT'S ALL OCK! THIS IS HIS DOING, ALL OF IT, I SWEAR! GO GET HIM!
HE'S AT KRAVINOFF MANSION!

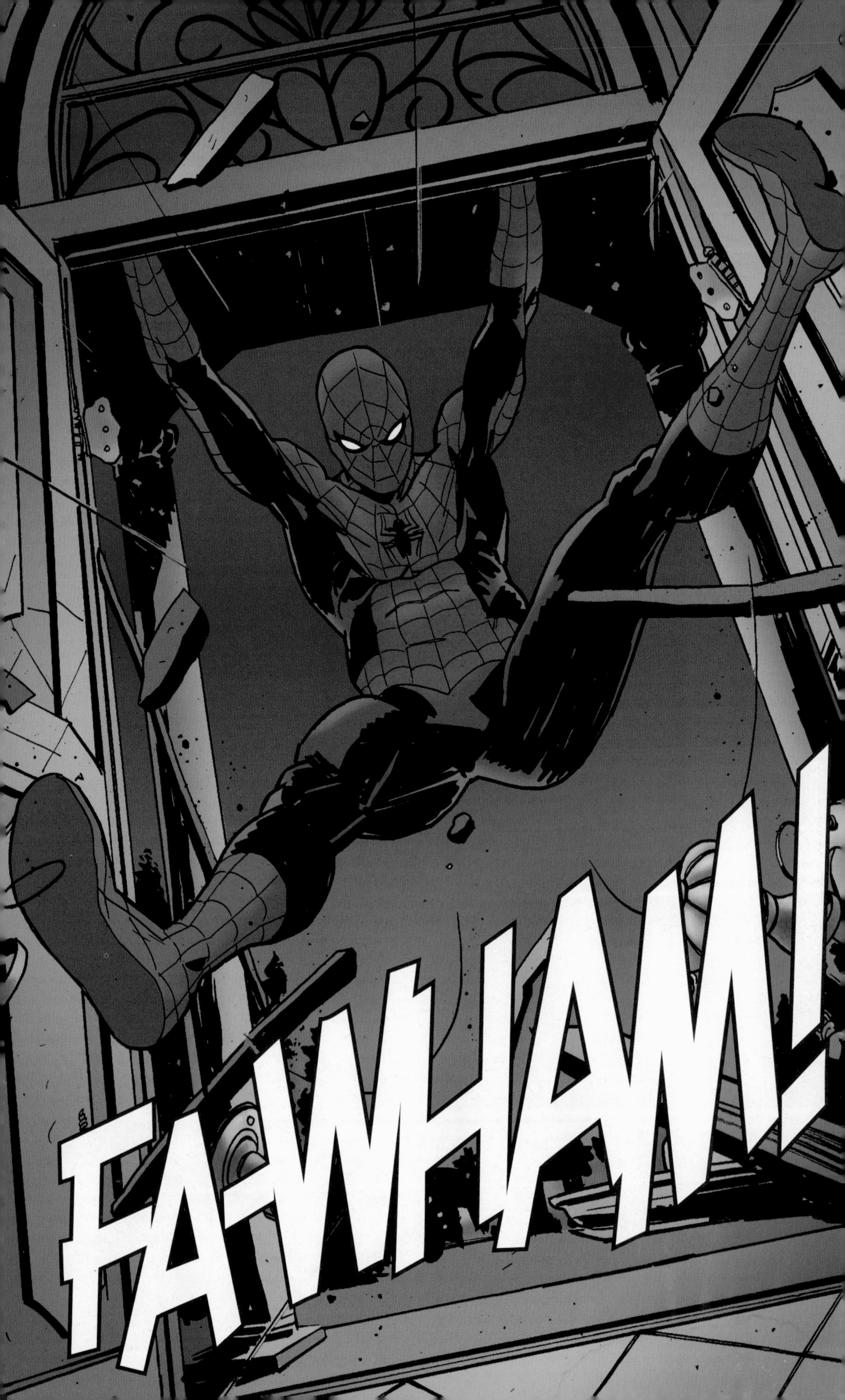
FA-WHAM!

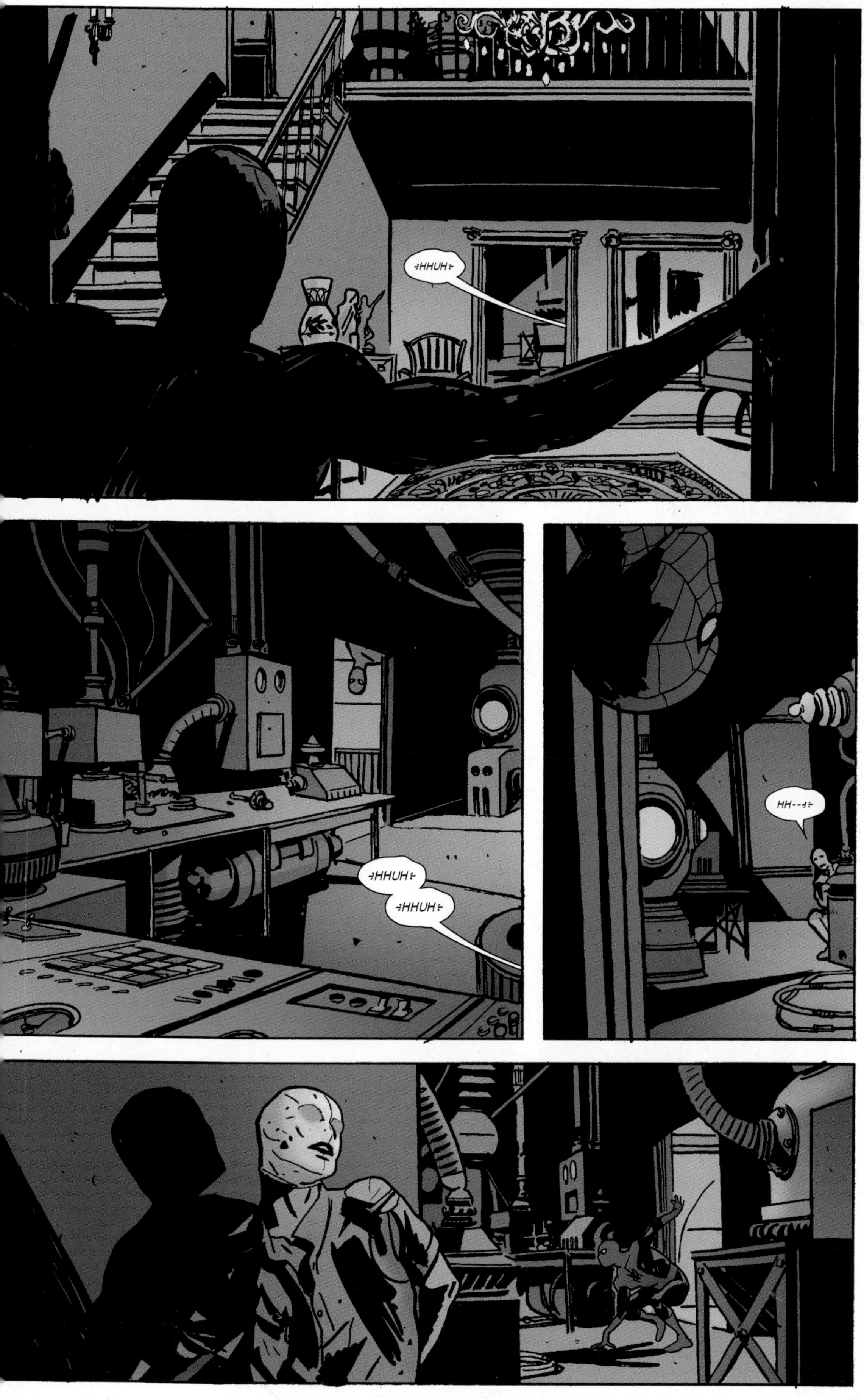
HHUH
HHUH
HHUH
HH--

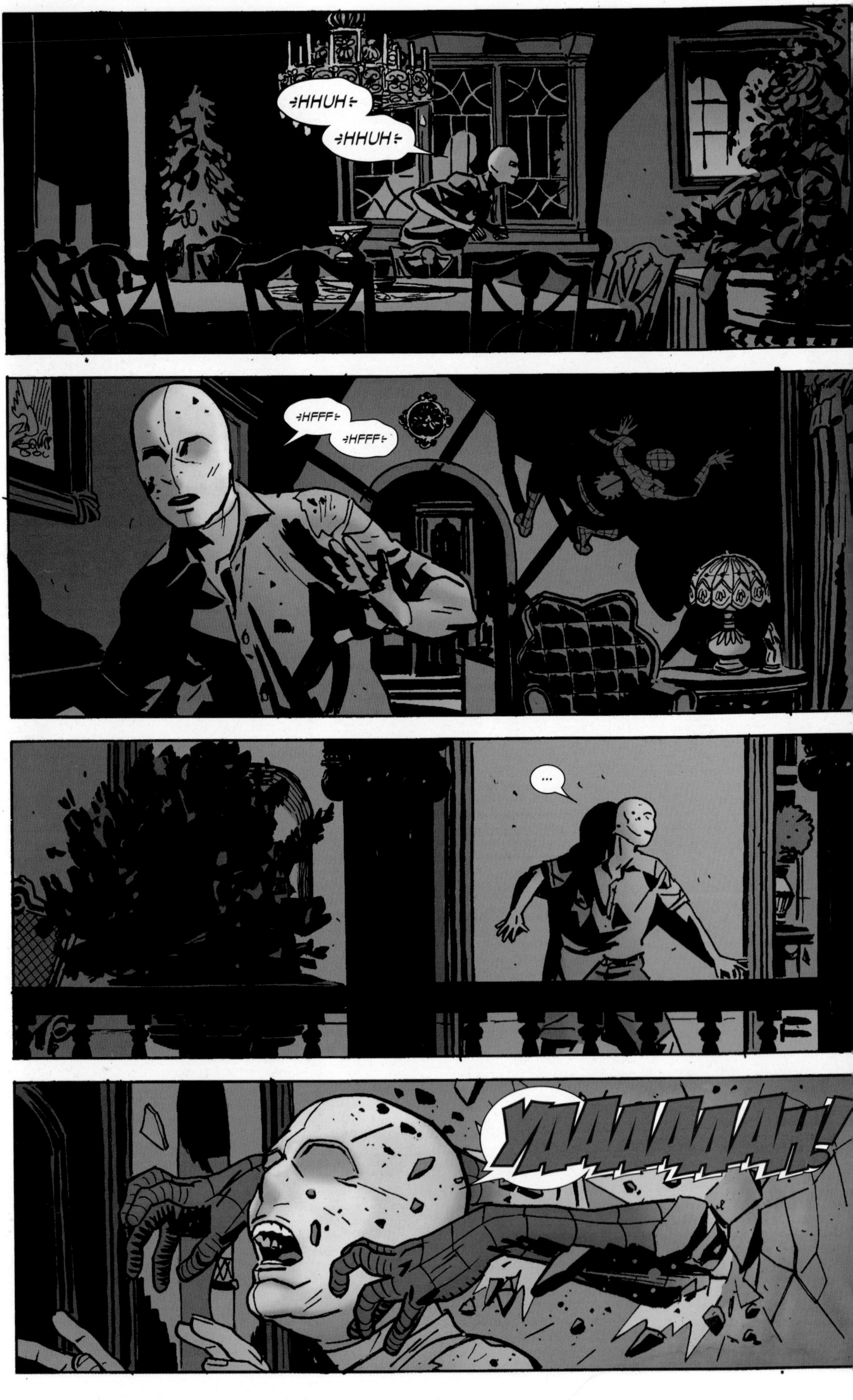

HHUH
HHUH
HFFF
HFFF
...
YAAAAAAH!

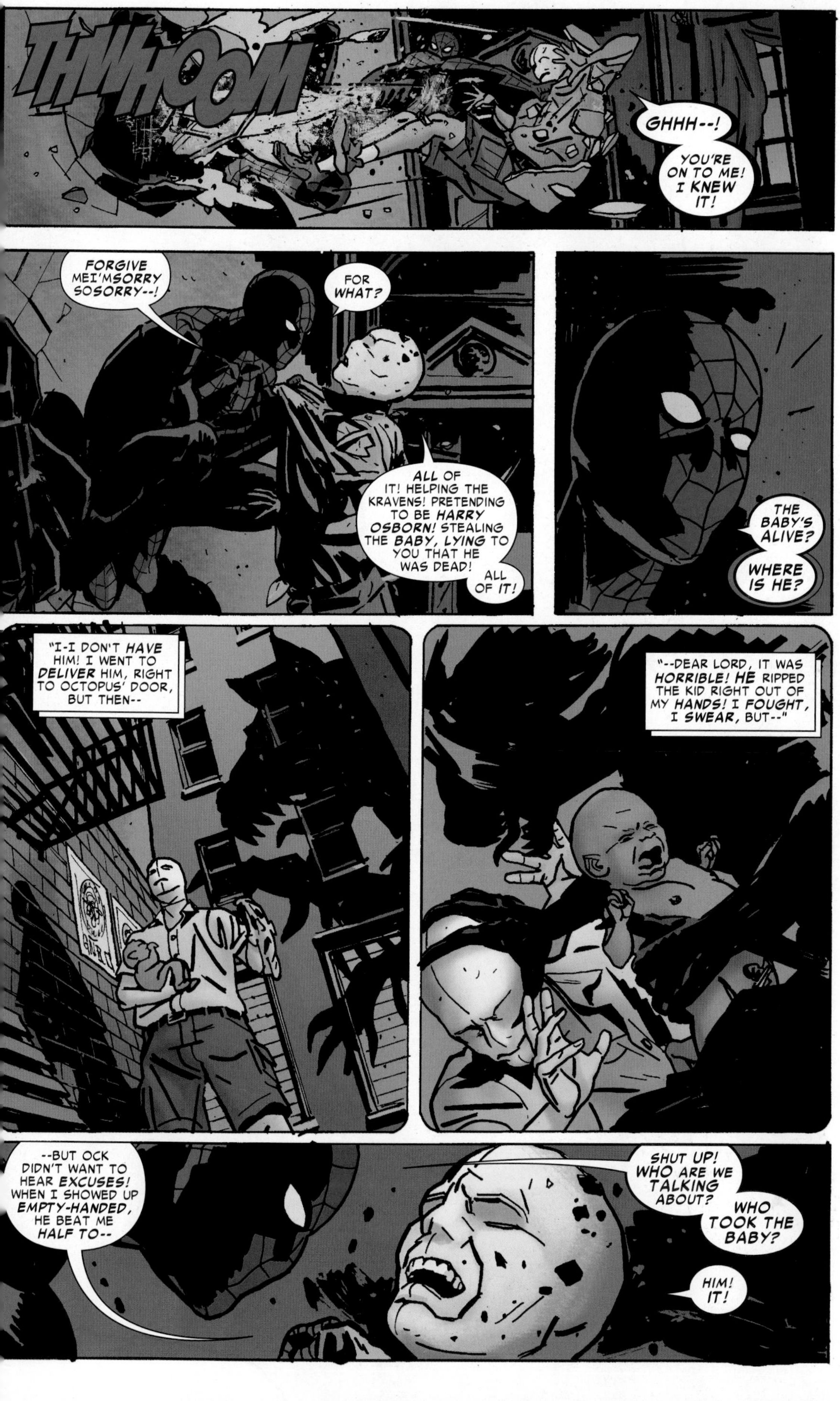
THWHOOM
GHHH--!
YOU'RE ON TO ME! I KNEW IT!
FORGIVE MEI'MSORRY SOSORRY--!
FOR WHAT?
ALL OF IT! HELPING THE KRAVENS! PRETENDING TO BE HARRY OSBORN! STEALING THE BABY, LYING TO YOU THAT HE WAS DEAD!
ALL OF IT!
THE BABY'S ALIVE?
WHERE IS HE?
"I-I DON'T HAVE HIM! I WENT TO DELIVER HIM, RIGHT TO OCTOPUS' DOOR, BUT THEN--
"--DEAR LORD, IT WAS HORRIBLE! HE RIPPED THE KID RIGHT OUT OF MY HANDS! I FOUGHT, I SWEAR, BUT--"
--BUT OCK DIDN'T WANT TO HEAR EXCUSES! WHEN I SHOWED UP EMPTY-HANDED, HE BEAT ME HALF TO--
SHUT UP! WHO ARE WE TALKING ABOUT?
WHO TOOK THE BABY?
HIM! IT!

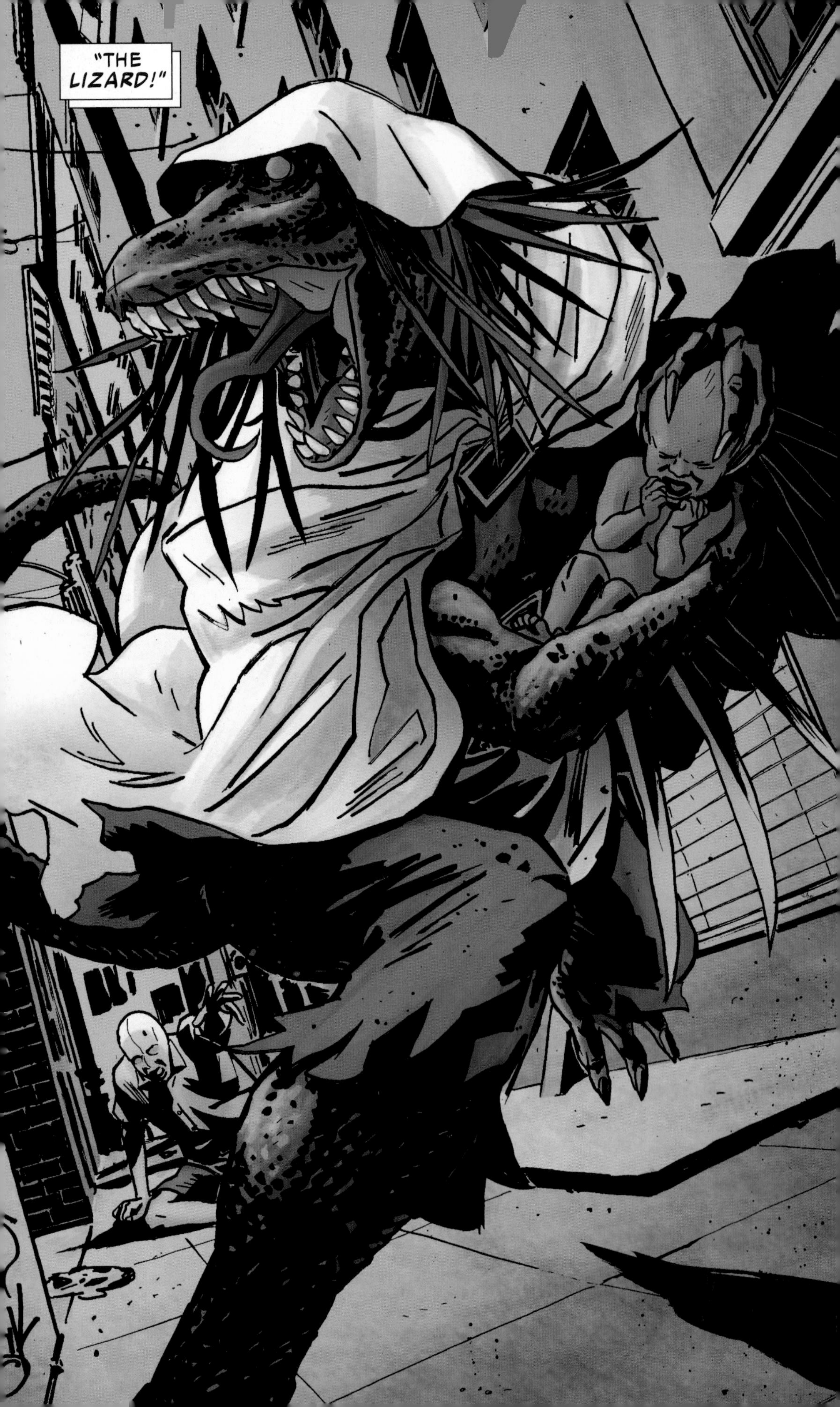
"THE LIZARD!"

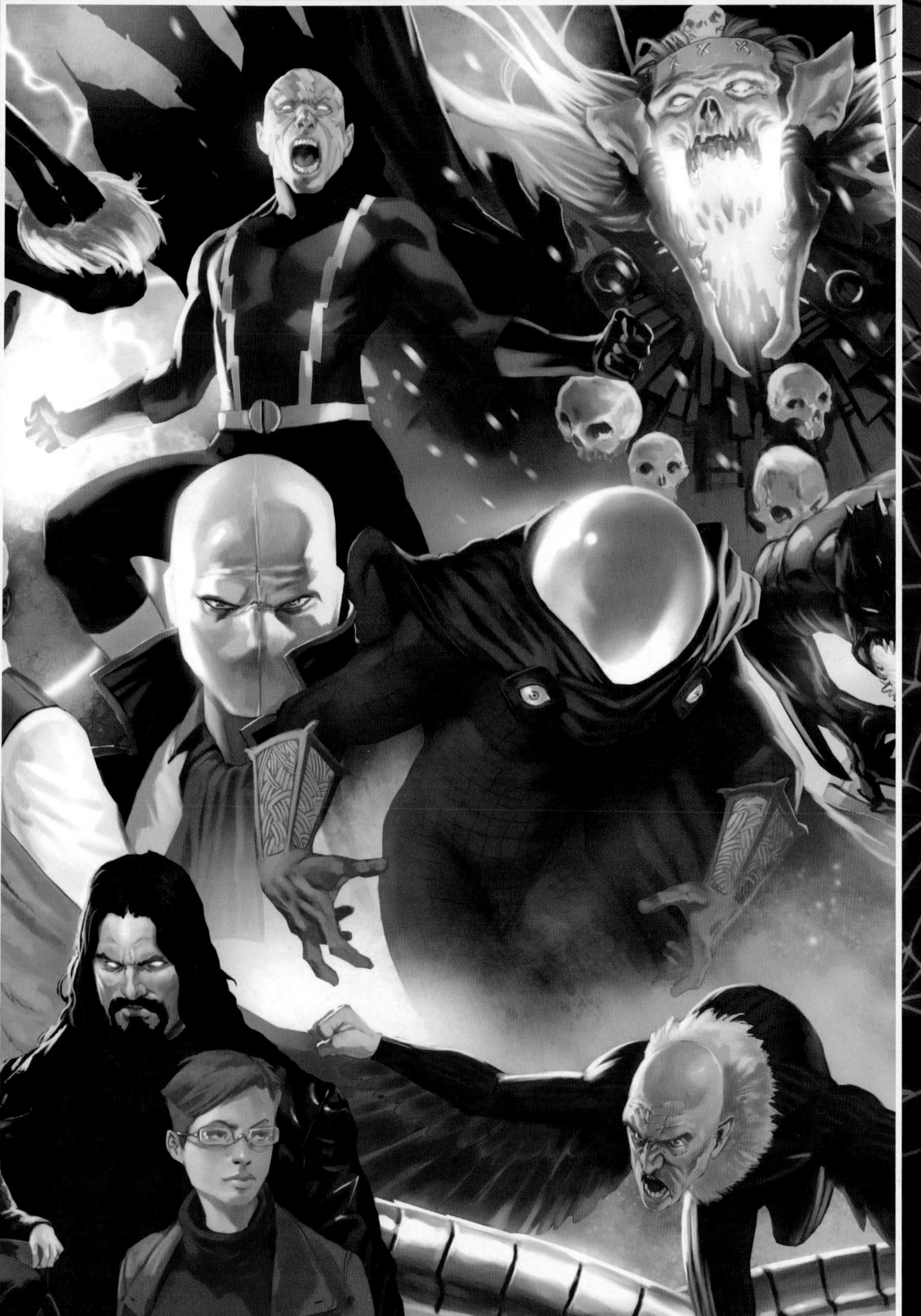

AMAZING SPIDER-MAN #646
COVER BY MARKO DJURDJEVIC

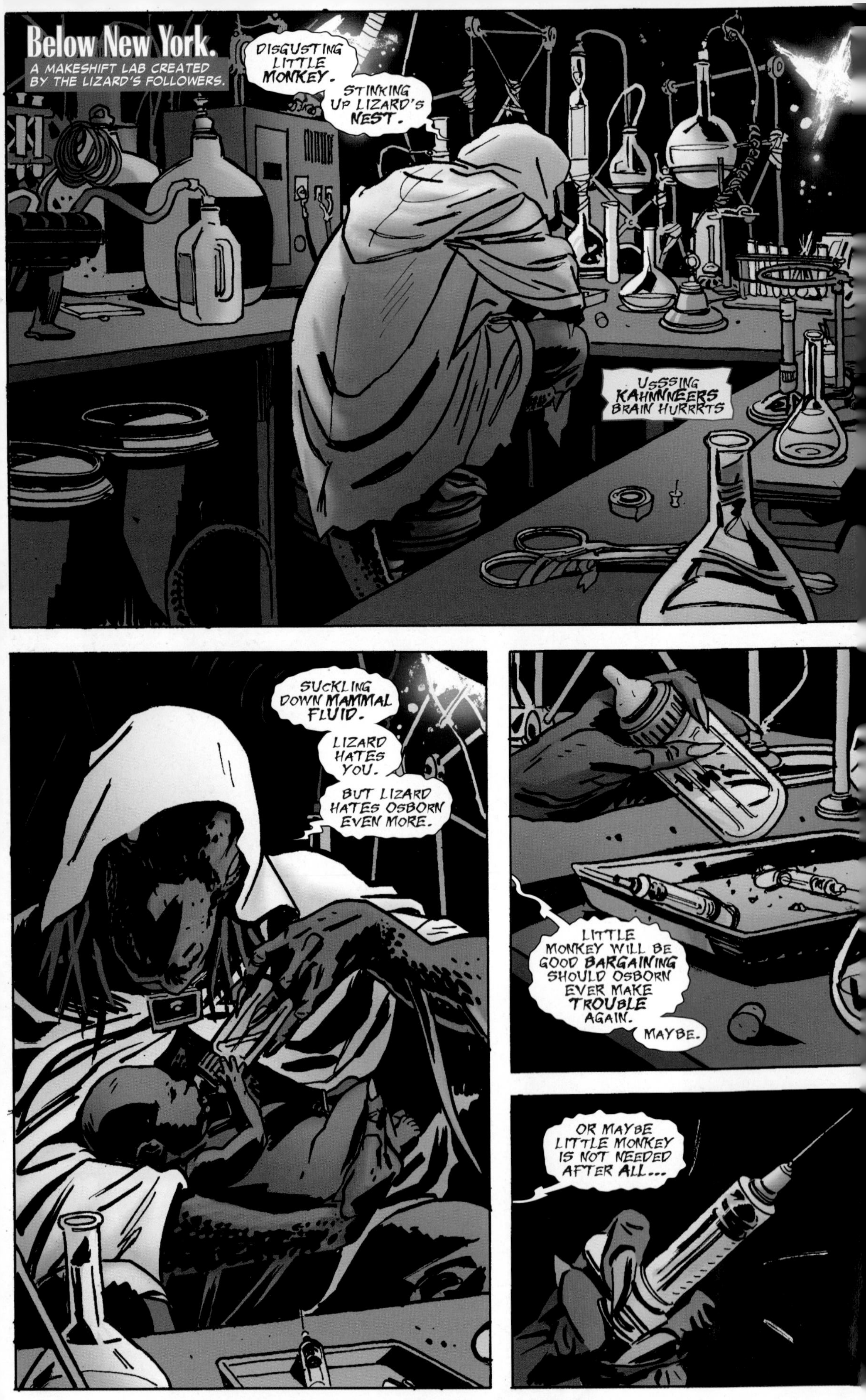
Below New York.
A MAKESHIFT LAB CREATED BY THE LIZARD'S FOLLOWERS.
DISGUSTING LITTLE MONKEY.
STINKING UP LIZARD'S NEST.
USSSING KAHNNNEERS BRAIN HURRRTS
SUCKLING DOWN MAMMAL FLUID.
LIZARD HATES YOU.
BUT LIZARD HATES OSBORN EVEN MORE.
LITTLE MONKEY WILL BE GOOD BARGAINING SHOULD OSBORN EVER MAKE TROUBLE AGAIN.
MAYBE.
OR MAYBE LITTLE MONKEY IS NOT NEEDED AFTER ALL...

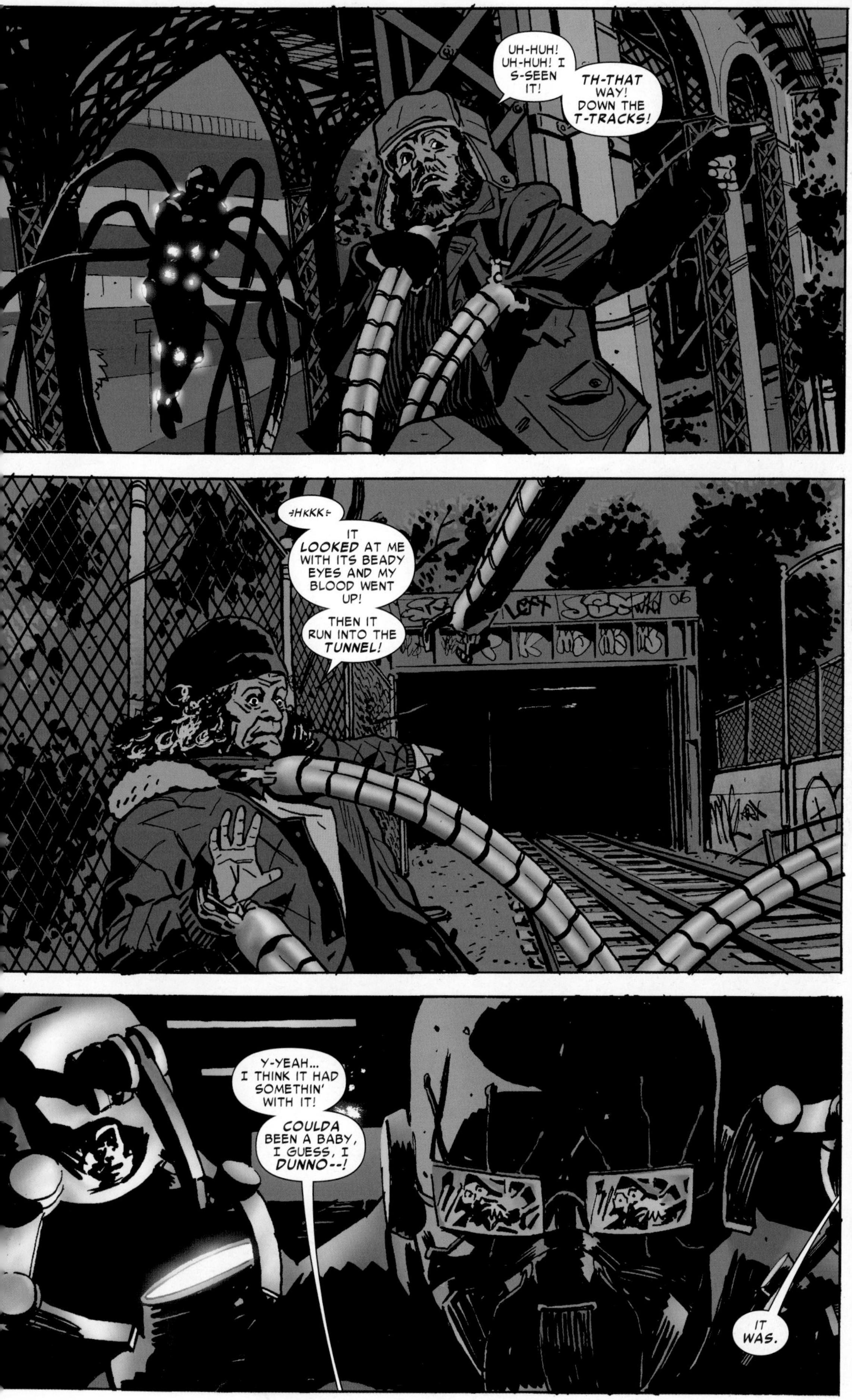

UH-HUH! UH-HUH! I S-SEEN IT!
TH-THAT WAY! DOWN THE T-TRACKS!
HKKK
IT LOOKED AT ME WITH ITS BEADY EYES AND MY BLOOD WENT UP!
THEN IT RUN INTO THE TUNNEL!
Y-YEAH... I THINK IT HAD SOMETHIN' WITH IT!
COULDA BEEN A BABY, I GUESS, I DUNNO--!
IT WAS.

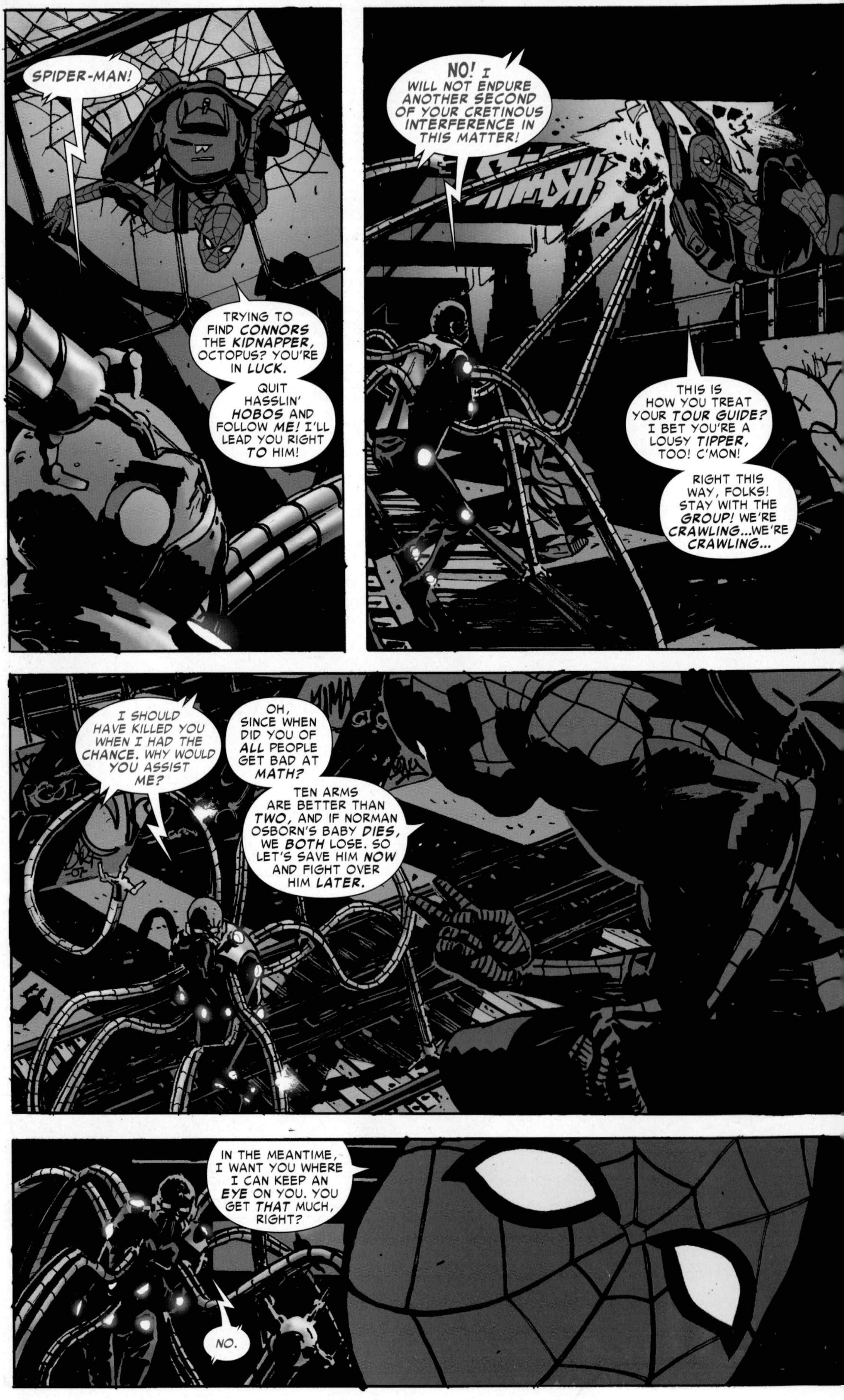
SPIDER-MAN!
TRYING TO FIND CONNORS THE KIDNAPPER, OCTOPUS? YOU'RE IN LUCK.
QUIT HASSLIN' HOBOS AND FOLLOW ME! I'LL LEAD YOU RIGHT TO HIM!
NO! I WILL NOT ENDURE ANOTHER SECOND OF YOUR CRETINOUS INTERFERENCE IN THIS MATTER!
THIS IS HOW YOU TREAT YOUR TOUR GUIDE? I BET YOU'RE A LOUSY TIPPER, TOO! C'MON!
RIGHT THIS WAY, FOLKS! STAY WITH THE GROUP! WE'RE CRAWLING...WE'RE CRAWLING...
I SHOULD HAVE KILLED YOU WHEN I HAD THE CHANCE. WHY WOULD YOU ASSIST ME?
OH, SINCE WHEN DID YOU OF ALL PEOPLE GET BAD AT MATH?
TEN ARMS ARE BETTER THAN TWO, AND IF NORMAN OSBORN'S BABY DIES, WE BOTH LOSE. SO LET'S SAVE HIM NOW AND FIGHT OVER HIM LATER.
IN THE MEANTIME, I WANT YOU WHERE I CAN KEEP AN EYE ON YOU. YOU GET THAT MUCH, RIGHT?
NO.

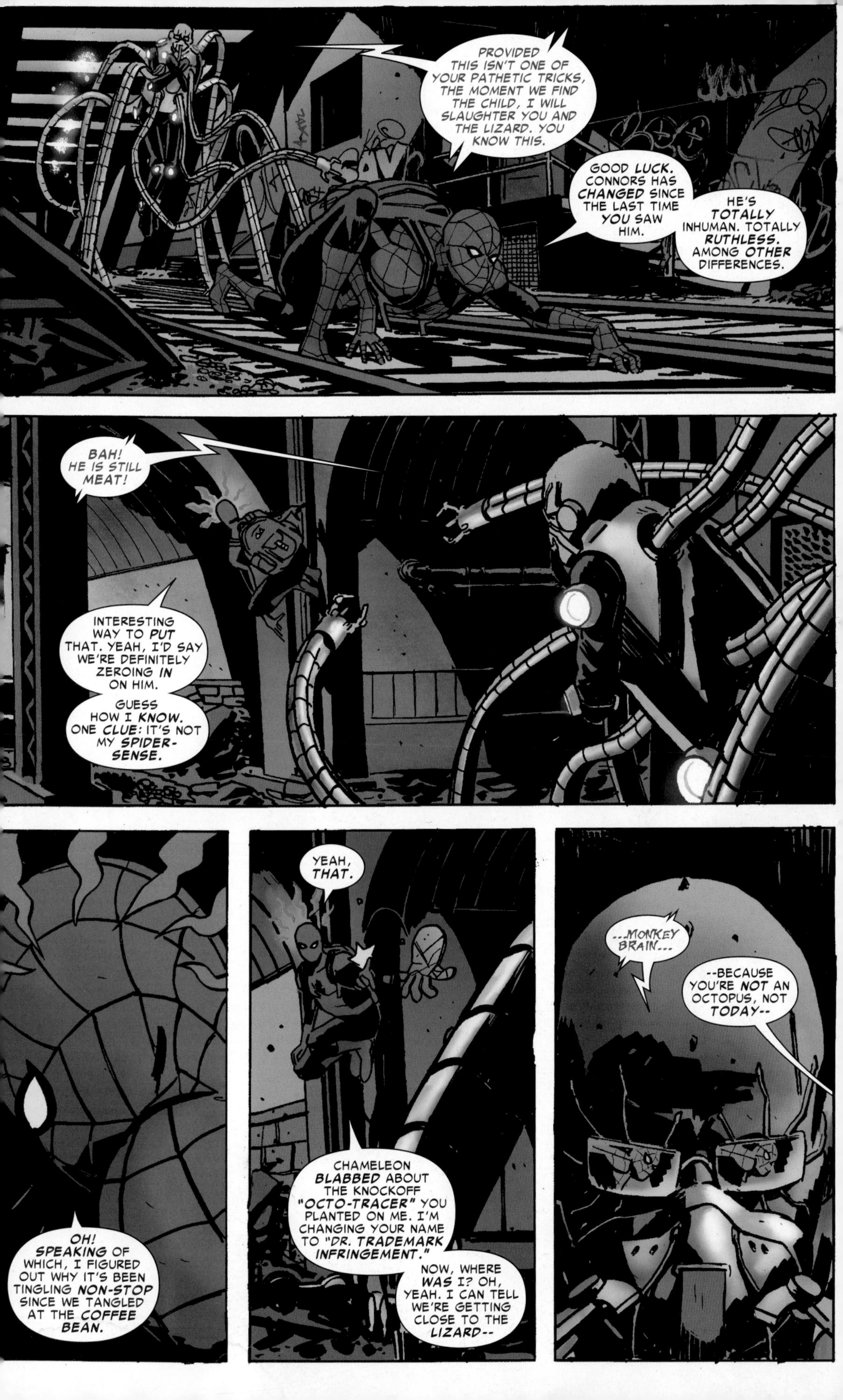
PROVIDED THIS ISN'T ONE OF YOUR PATHETIC TRICKS, THE MOMENT WE FIND THE CHILD, I WILL SLAUGHTER YOU AND THE LIZARD. YOU KNOW THIS.
GOOD LUCK. CONNORS HAS CHANGED SINCE THE LAST TIME YOU SAW HIM.
HE'S TOTALLY INHUMAN. TOTALLY RUTHLESS. AMONG OTHER DIFFERENCES.
BAH! HE IS STILL MEAT!
INTERESTING WAY TO PUT THAT. YEAH, I'D SAY WE'RE DEFINITELY ZEROING IN ON HIM.
GUESS HOW I KNOW. ONE CLUE: IT'S NOT MY SPIDER-SENSE.
OH! SPEAKING OF WHICH, I FIGURED OUT WHY IT'S BEEN TINGLING NON-STOP SINCE WE TANGLED AT THE COFFEE BEAN.
YEAH, THAT.
CHAMELEON BLABBED ABOUT THE KNOCKOFF "OCTO-TRACER" YOU PLANTED ON ME. I'M CHANGING YOUR NAME TO "DR. TRADEMARK INFRINGEMENT."
NOW, WHERE WAS I? OH, YEAH. I CAN TELL WE'RE GETTING CLOSE TO THE LIZARD--
--BECAUSE YOU'RE NOT AN OCTOPUS, NOT TODAY--
...MONKEY BRAIN...

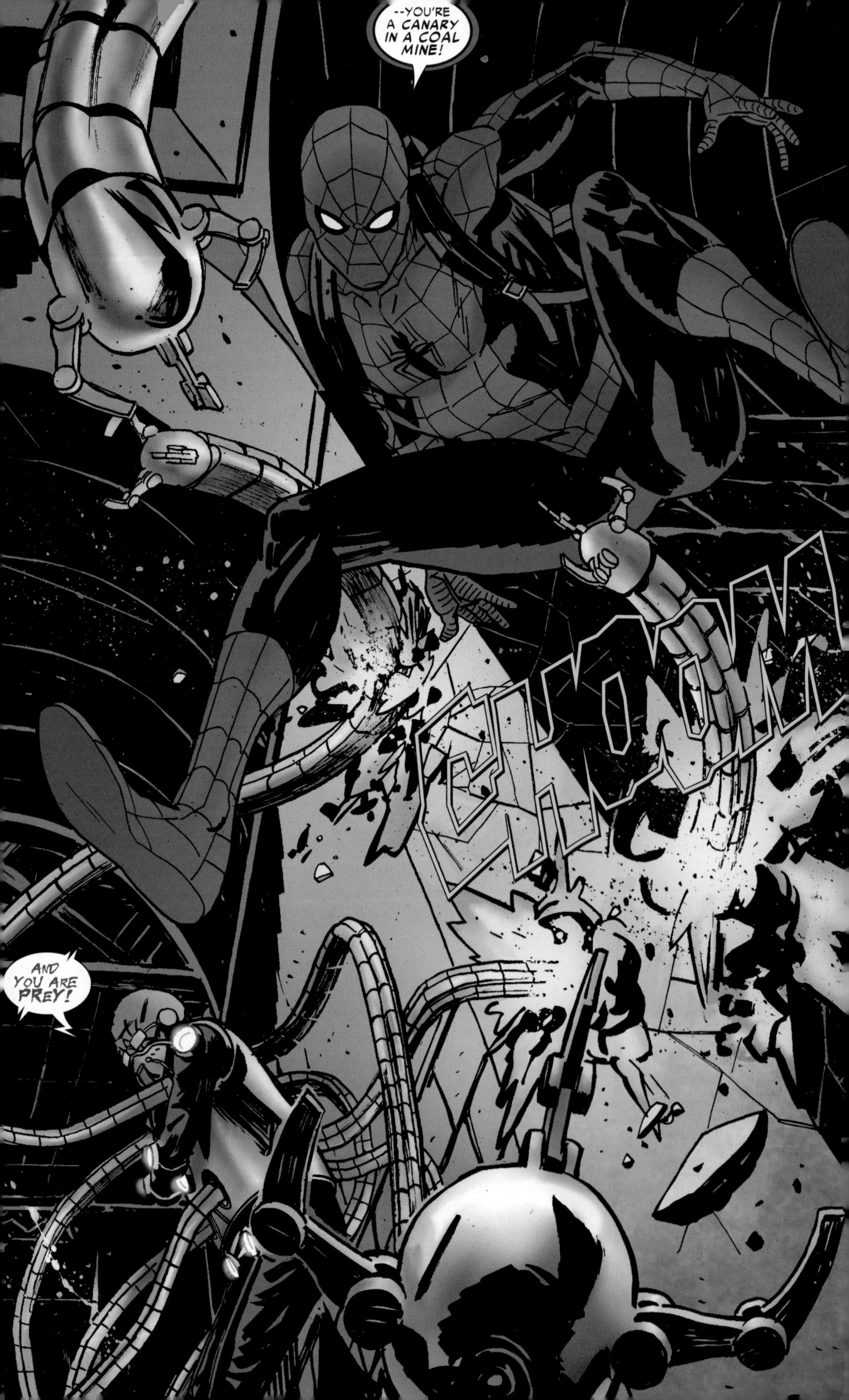
--YOU'RE A CANARY IN A COAL MINE!
AND YOU ARE PREY!

YOU TALK TOO MUCH!
YOU SHOULD SEE MY TWITTER FEED.
IF YOU'D BOTHERED TO DO AN ADEQUATE AMOUNT OF OPPOSITION RESEARCH, DOC, YOU'D HAVE KNOWN--
--THAT NOWADAYS, LIZARD'S PROXIMITY BRINGS OUT THE BRAIN'S PRIMITIVE REPTILIAN INSTINCTS! IN OTHER WORDS--
KILL YOU!
--WHEN HE'S NEAR, YOU GET IMPULSIVE, YOU FOLLOW BASE URGES, YOUR ID KICKS YOUR SUPEREGO IN THE FACE--
--AND WHAT'S MOST DELIGHTFUL FOR A SMART GUY LIKE ME WATCHING IT HAPPEN TO YOU--
DIE!
--YOU GET STUPID!

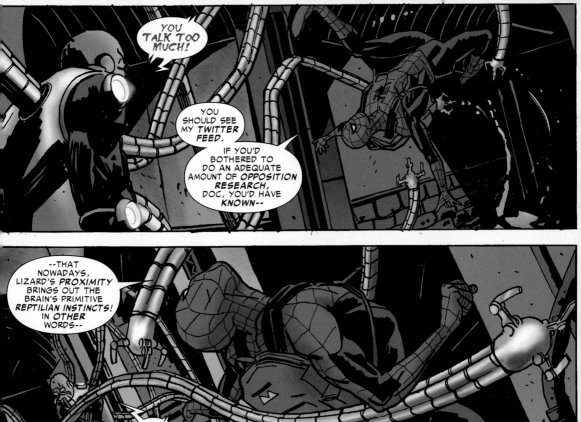

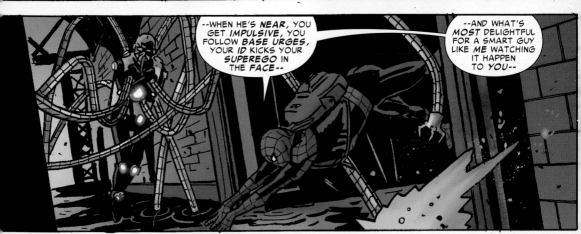

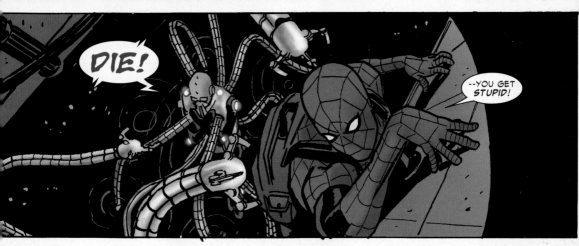

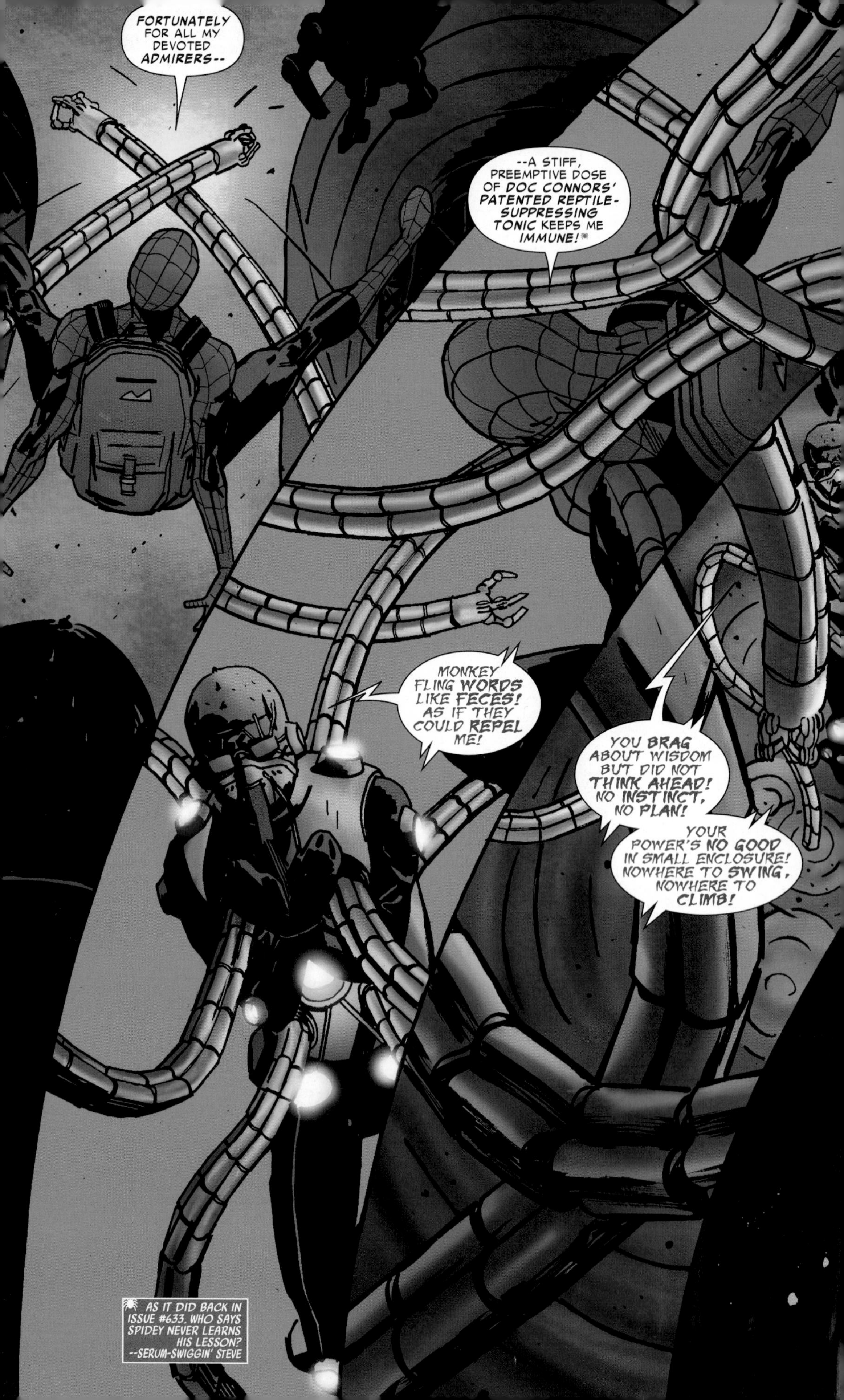
FORTUNATELY FOR ALL MY DEVOTED ADMIRERS--
--A STIFF, PREEMPTIVE DOSE OF DOC CONNORS' PATENTED REPTILE-SUPPRESSING TONIC KEEPS ME IMMUNE!
MONKEY FLING WORDS LIKE FECES! AS IF THEY COULD REPEL ME!
YOU BRAG ABOUT WISDOM BUT DID NOT THINK AHEAD! NO INSTINCT, NO PLAN!
YOUR POWER'S NO GOOD IN SMALL ENCLOSURE! NOWHERE TO SWING, NOWHERE TO CLIMB!
AS IT DID BACK IN ISSUE #633. WHO SAYS SPIDEY NEVER LEARNS HIS LESSON? --SERUM-SWIGGIN' STEVE

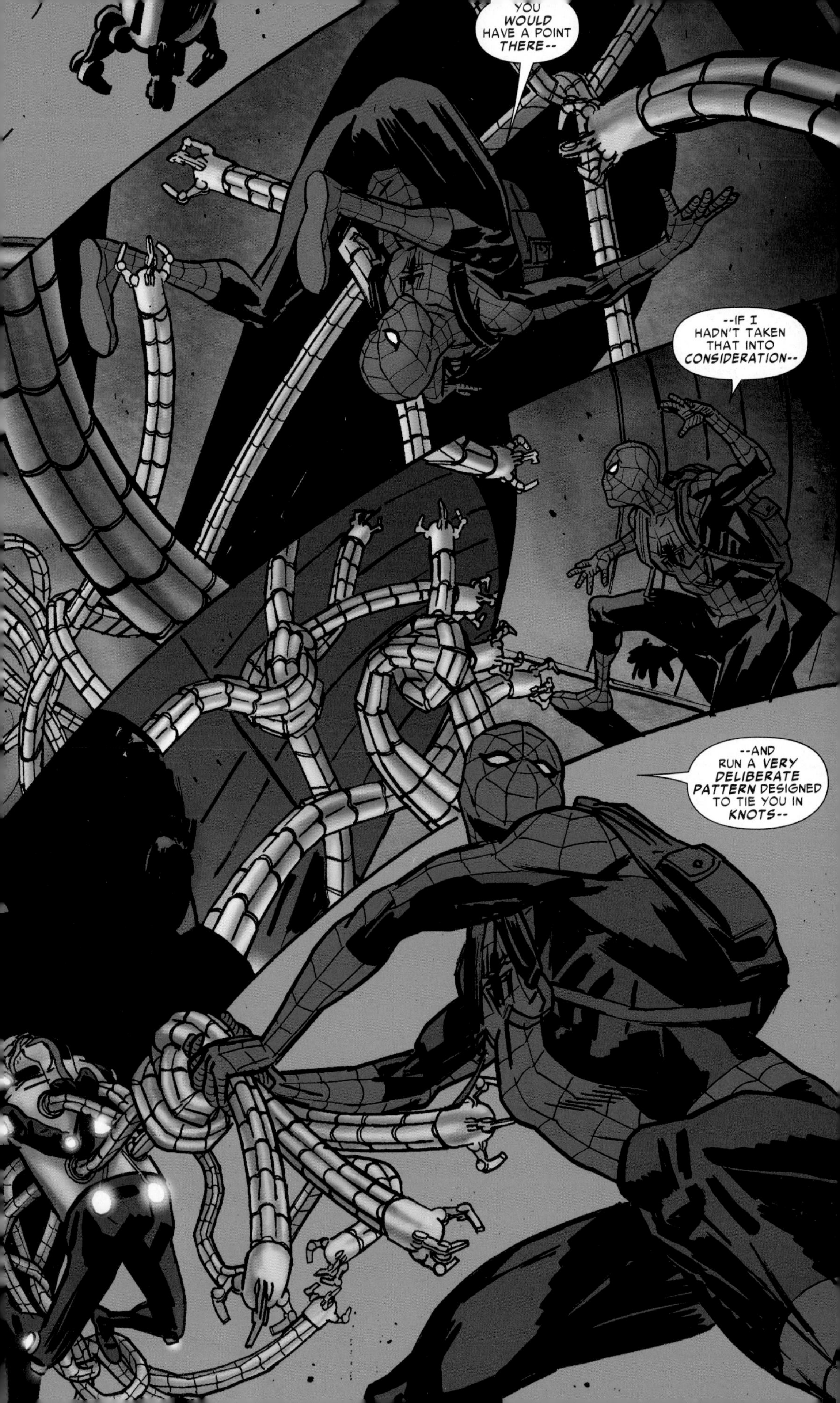
YOU *WOULD* HAVE A POINT *THERE*--
--IF I HADN'T TAKEN THAT INTO *CONSIDERATION*--
--AND RUN A *VERY DELIBERATE PATTERN* DESIGNED TO TIE YOU IN *KNOTS*--

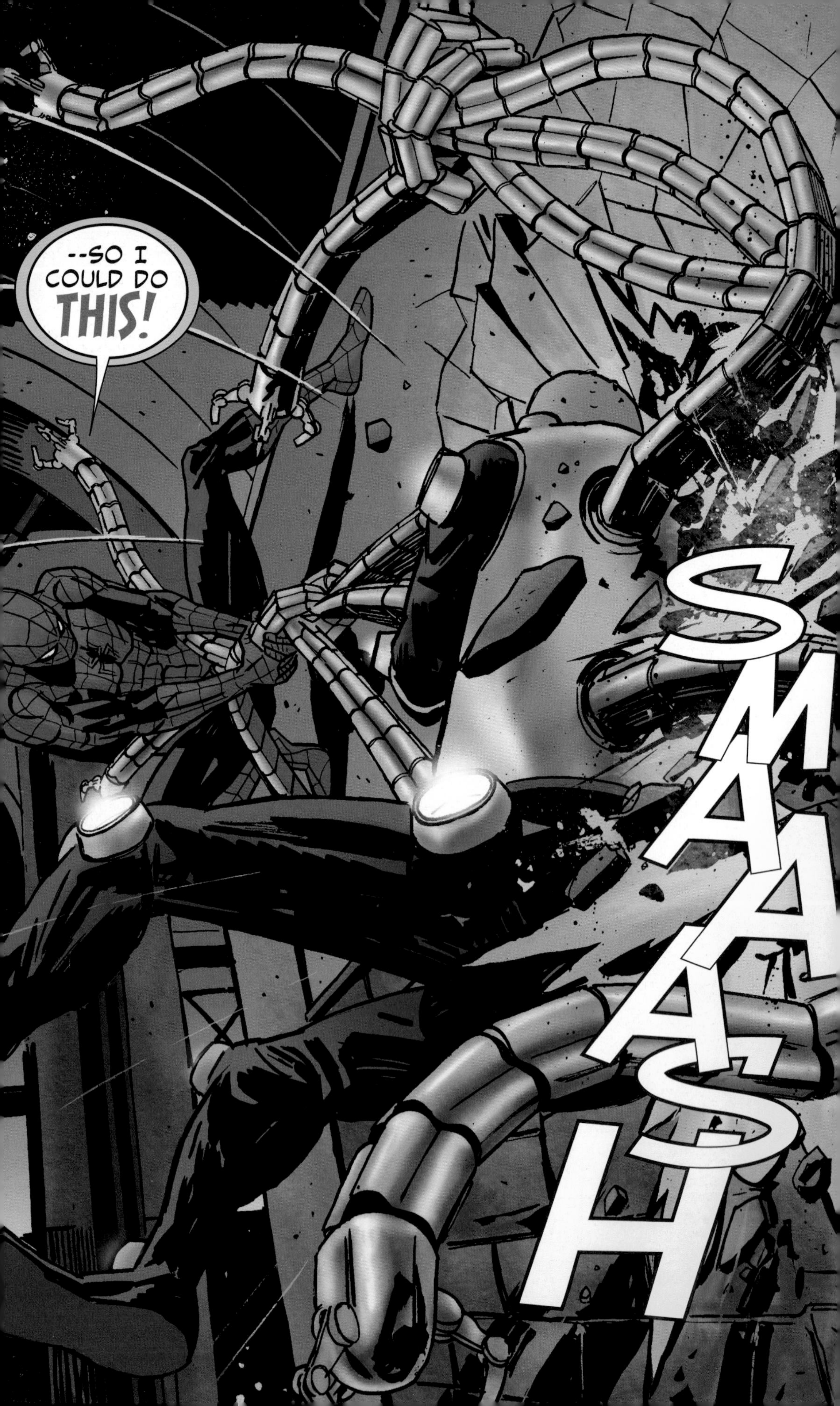
--SO I COULD DO THIS!
SMAAAASH

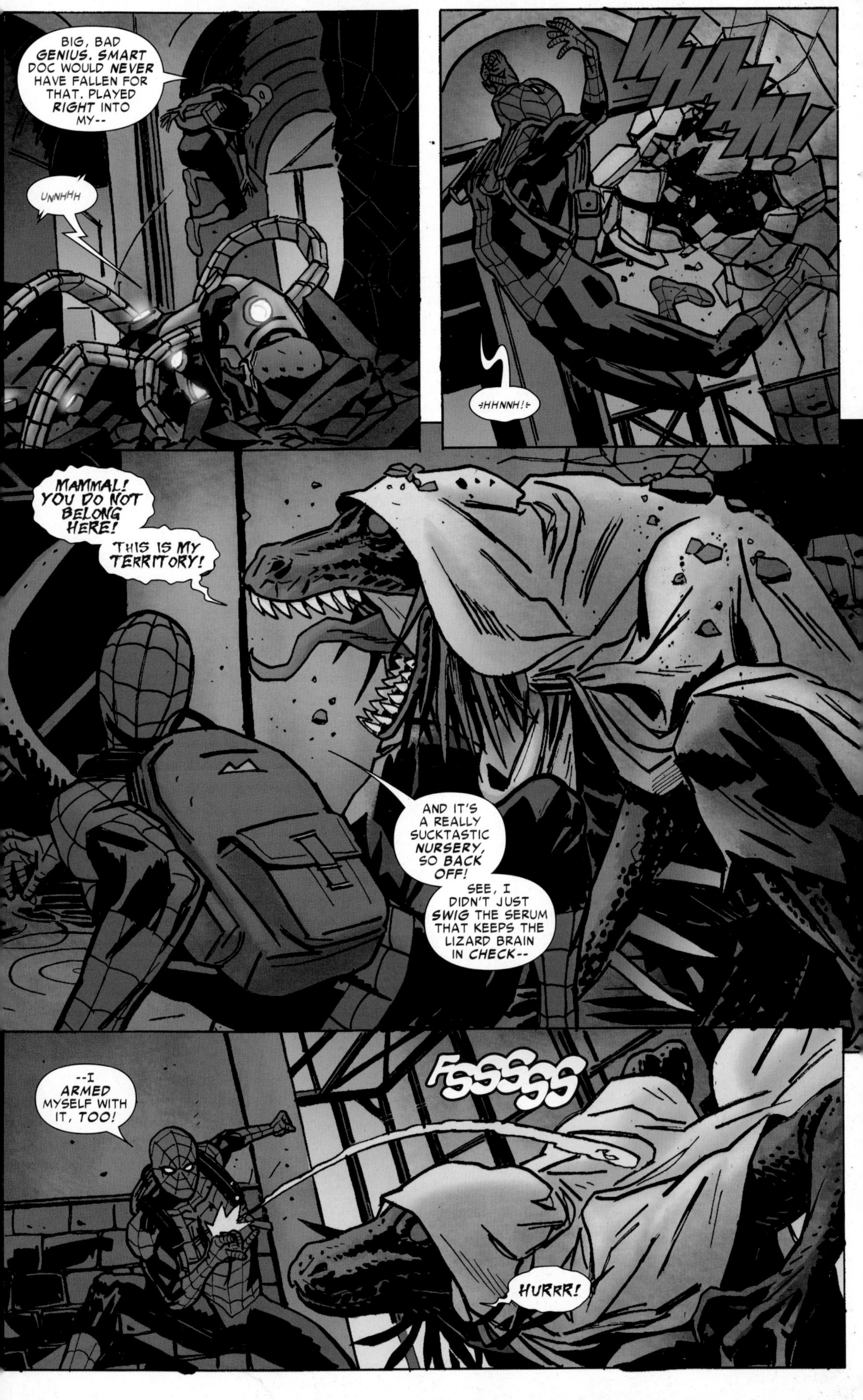
BIG, BAD GENIUS. SMART DOC WOULD NEVER HAVE FALLEN FOR THAT. PLAYED RIGHT INTO MY--
UNNHHH
WHAM!
HHNNH!
MAMMAL! YOU DO NOT BELONG HERE!
THIS IS MY TERRITORY!
AND IT'S A REALLY SUCKTASTIC NURSERY, SO BACK OFF!
SEE, I DIDN'T JUST SWIG THE SERUM THAT KEEPS THE LIZARD BRAIN IN CHECK--
--I ARMED MYSELF WITH IT, TOO!
FSSSSS
HURRR!

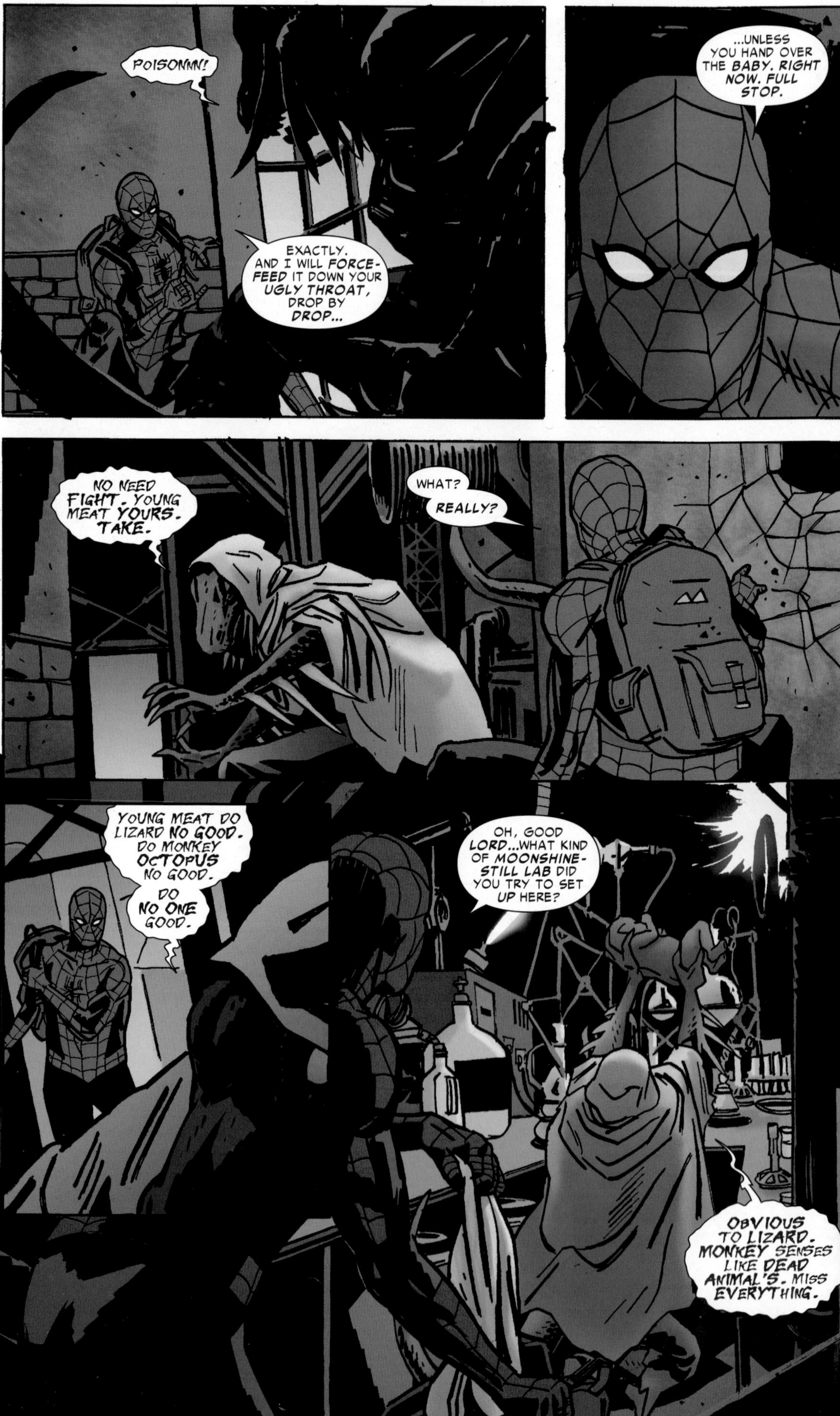
POISONNN!
EXACTLY. AND I WILL FORCE-FEED IT DOWN YOUR UGLY THROAT, DROP BY DROP...
...UNLESS YOU HAND OVER THE BABY. RIGHT NOW. FULL STOP.
NO NEED FIGHT. YOUNG MEAT YOURS. TAKE.
WHAT?
REALLY?
YOUNG MEAT DO LIZARD NO GOOD. DO MONKEY OCTOPUS NO GOOD.
DO NO ONE GOOD.
OH, GOOD LORD...WHAT KIND OF MOONSHINE-STILL LAB DID YOU TRY TO SET UP HERE?
OBVIOUS TO LIZARD. MONKEY SENSES LIKE DEAD ANIMAL'S. MISS EVERYTHING.

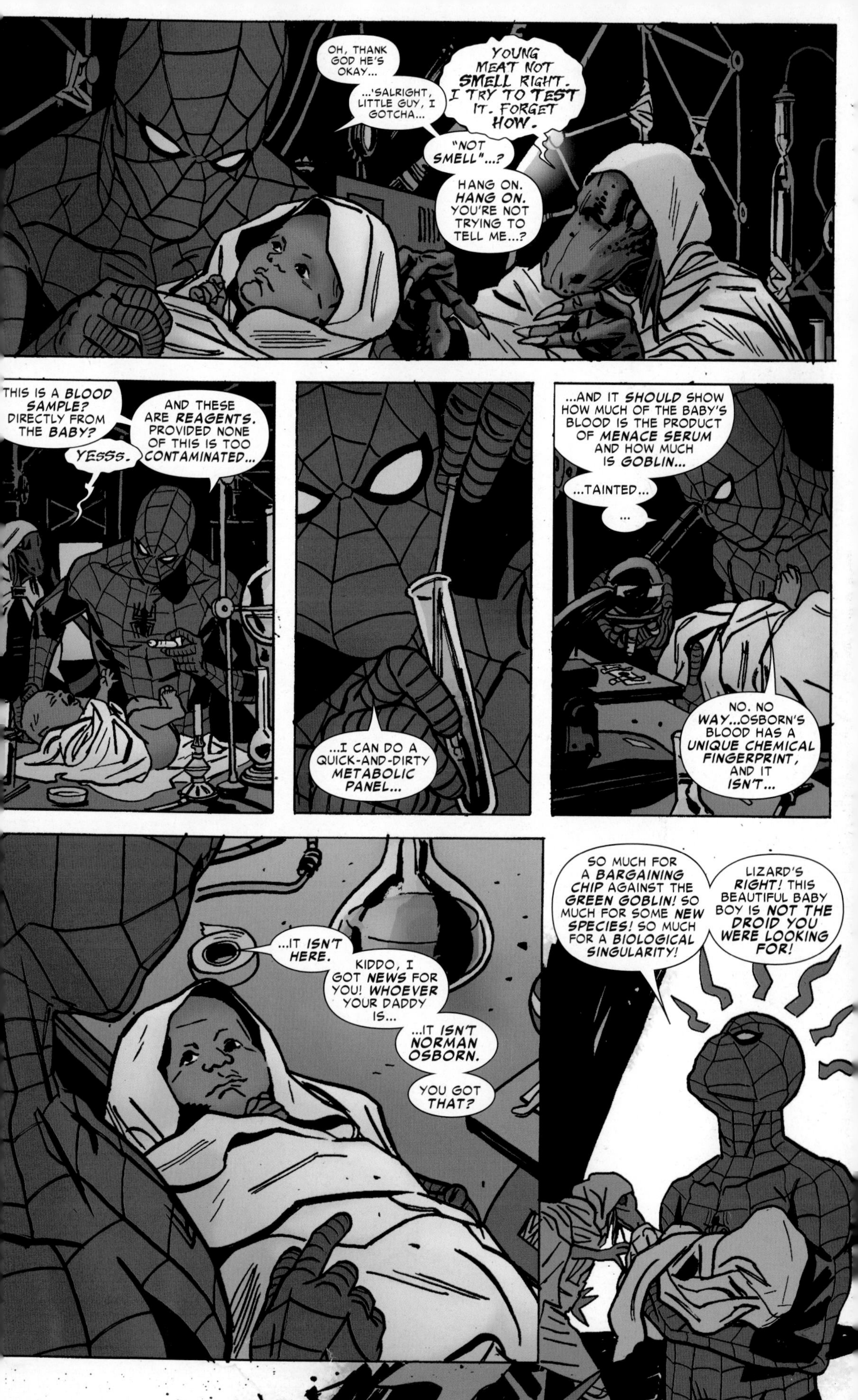
OH, THANK GOD HE'S OKAY...
...'SALRIGHT, LITTLE GUY, I GOTCHA...
YOUNG MEAT NOT SMELL RIGHT. I TRY TO TEST IT. FORGET HOW.
"NOT SMELL"...?
HANG ON. HANG ON. YOU'RE NOT TRYING TO TELL ME...?
THIS IS A BLOOD SAMPLE? DIRECTLY FROM THE BABY?
YESSs.
AND THESE ARE REAGENTS. PROVIDED NONE OF THIS IS TOO CONTAMINATED...
...I CAN DO A QUICK-AND-DIRTY METABOLIC PANEL...
...AND IT SHOULD SHOW HOW MUCH OF THE BABY'S BLOOD IS THE PRODUCT OF MENACE SERUM AND HOW MUCH IS GOBLIN...
...TAINTED...
...
NO. NO WAY...OSBORN'S BLOOD HAS A UNIQUE CHEMICAL FINGERPRINT, AND IT ISN'T...
...IT ISN'T HERE.
KIDDO, I GOT NEWS FOR YOU! WHOEVER YOUR DADDY IS...
...IT ISN'T NORMAN OSBORN.
YOU GOT THAT?
SO MUCH FOR A BARGAINING CHIP AGAINST THE GREEN GOBLIN! SO MUCH FOR SOME NEW SPECIES! SO MUCH FOR A BIOLOGICAL SINGULARITY!
LIZARD'S RIGHT! THIS BEAUTIFUL BABY BOY IS NOT THE DROID YOU WERE LOOKING FOR!

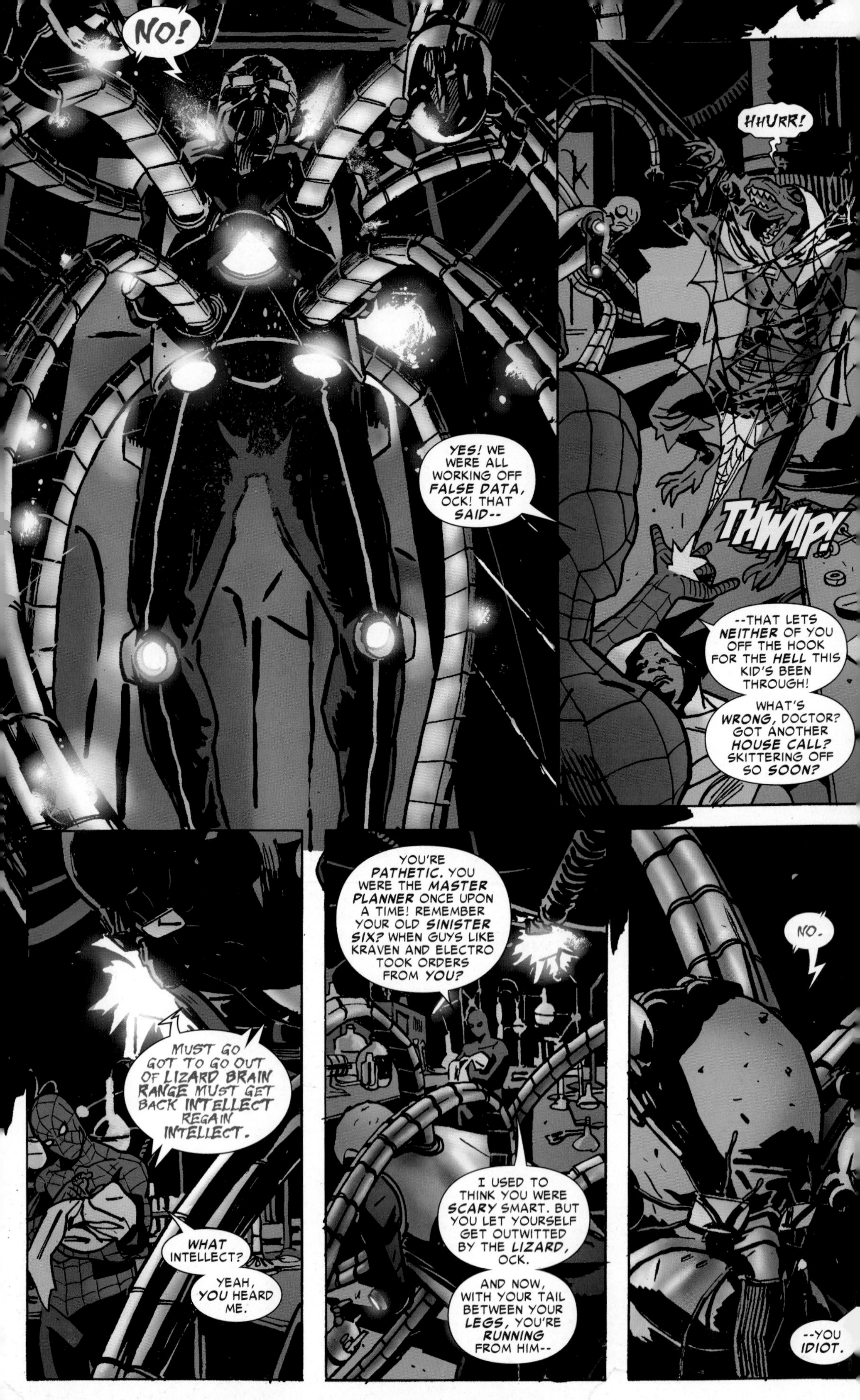
NO!
HHURR!
YES! WE WERE ALL WORKING OFF FALSE DATA, OCK! THAT SAID--
THWIIP!
--THAT LETS NEITHER OF YOU OFF THE HOOK FOR THE HELL THIS KID'S BEEN THROUGH!
WHAT'S WRONG, DOCTOR? GOT ANOTHER HOUSE CALL? SKITTERING OFF SO SOON?
MUST GO GOT TO GO OUT OF LIZARD BRAIN RANGE MUST GET BACK INTELLECT REGAIN INTELLECT.
WHAT INTELLECT?
YEAH, YOU HEARD ME.
YOU'RE PATHETIC. YOU WERE THE MASTER PLANNER ONCE UPON A TIME! REMEMBER YOUR OLD SINISTER SIX? WHEN GUYS LIKE KRAVEN AND ELECTRO TOOK ORDERS FROM YOU?
I USED TO THINK YOU WERE SCARY SMART. BUT YOU LET YOURSELF GET OUTWITTED BY THE LIZARD, OCK.
AND NOW, WITH YOUR TAIL BETWEEN YOUR LEGS, YOU'RE RUNNING FROM HIM--
NO.
--YOU IDIOT.

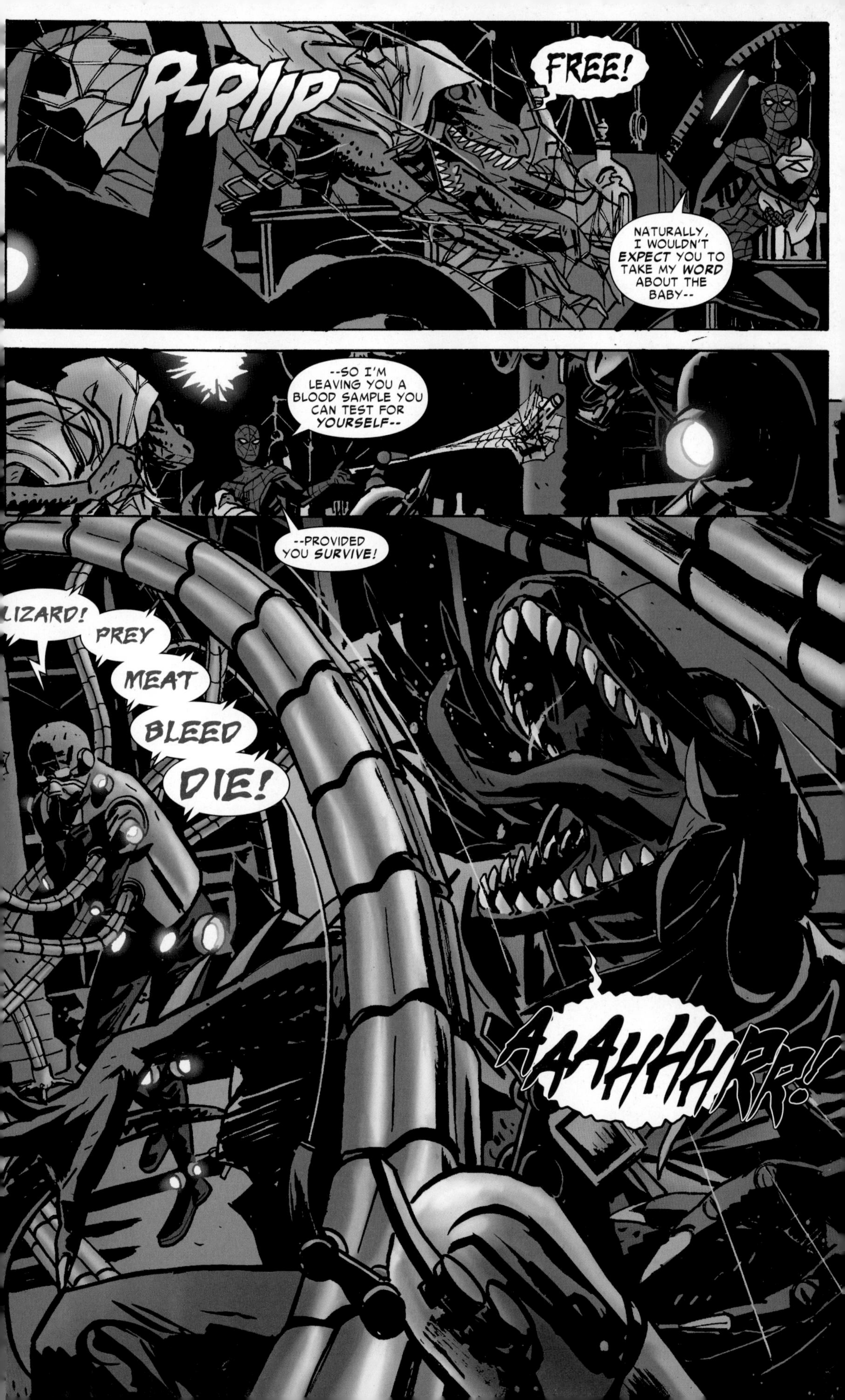
R-RIIP
FREE!
NATURALLY, I WOULDN'T EXPECT YOU TO TAKE MY WORD ABOUT THE BABY--
--SO I'M LEAVING YOU A BLOOD SAMPLE YOU CAN TEST FOR YOURSELF--
--PROVIDED YOU SURVIVE!
LIZARD!
PREY
MEAT
BLEED
DIE!
AAAHHHRR!

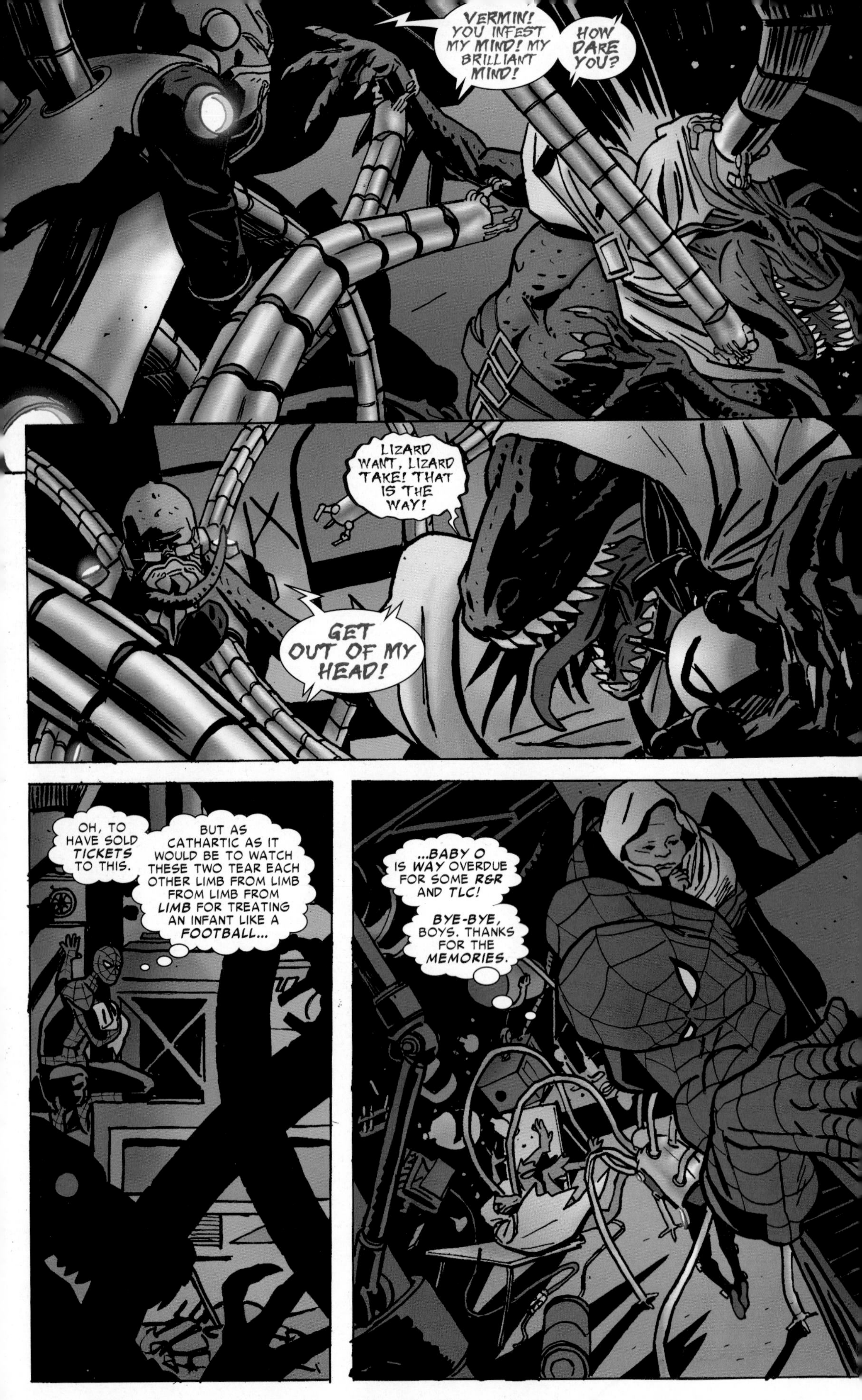
VERMIN! YOU INFEST MY MIND! MY BRILLIANT MIND!
HOW DARE YOU?
LIZARD WANT, LIZARD TAKE! THAT IS THE WAY!
GET OUT OF MY HEAD!
OH, TO HAVE SOLD TICKETS TO THIS.
BUT AS CATHARTIC AS IT WOULD BE TO WATCH THESE TWO TEAR EACH OTHER LIMB FROM LIMB FROM LIMB FROM LIMB FOR TREATING AN INFANT LIKE A FOOTBALL...
...BABY O IS WAY OVERDUE FOR SOME R&R AND TLC!
BYE-BYE, BOYS. THANKS FOR THE MEMORIES.

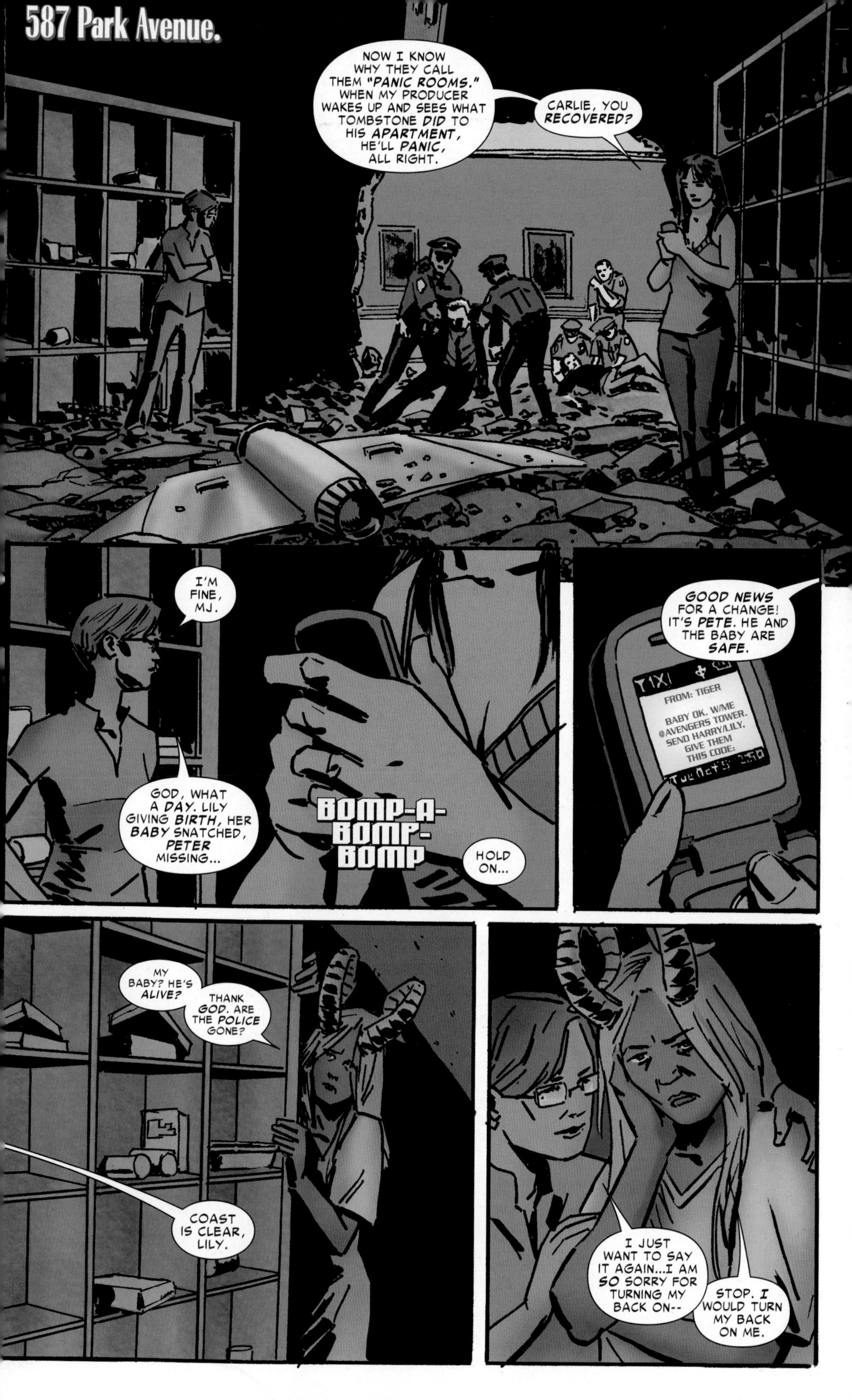
587 Park Avenue.
NOW I KNOW WHY THEY CALL THEM "PANIC ROOMS." WHEN MY PRODUCER WAKES UP AND SEES WHAT TOMBSTONE DID TO HIS APARTMENT, HE'LL PANIC, ALL RIGHT.
CARLIE, YOU RECOVERED?
I'M FINE, MJ.
GOD, WHAT A DAY. LILY GIVING BIRTH, HER BABY SNATCHED, PETER MISSING...
BOMP-A-BOMP-BOMP
HOLD ON...
GOOD NEWS FOR A CHANGE! IT'S PETE. HE AND THE BABY ARE SAFE.
FROM: TIGER
BABY OK. W/ME @AVENGERS TOWER. SEND HARRY/LILY. GIVE THEM THIS CODE:
MY BABY? HE'S ALIVE?
THANK GOD. ARE THE POLICE GONE?
COAST IS CLEAR, LILY.
I JUST WANT TO SAY IT AGAIN...I AM SO SORRY FOR TURNING MY BACK ON--
STOP. I WOULD TURN MY BACK ON ME.

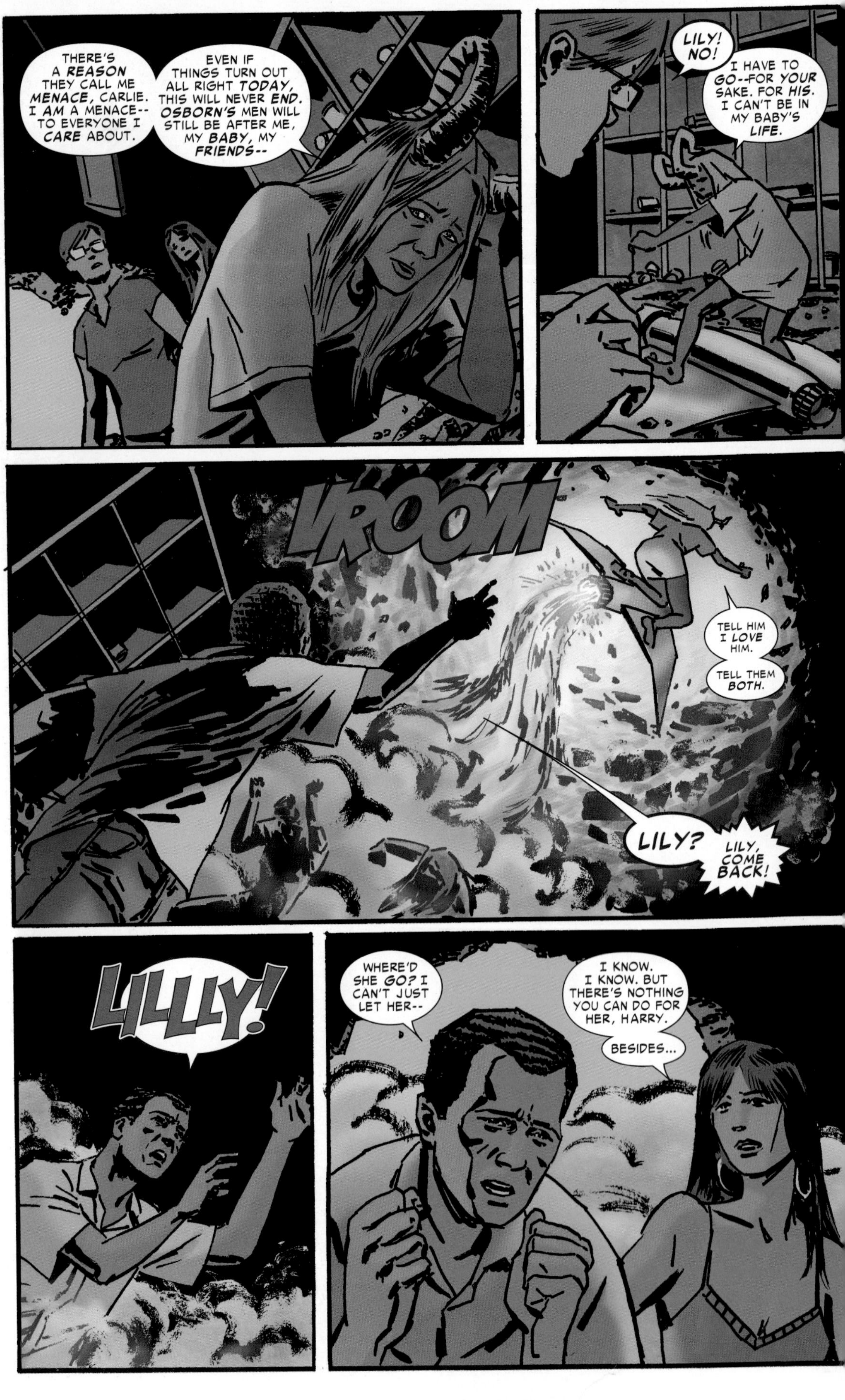
THERE'S A REASON THEY CALL ME MENACE, CARLIE. I AM A MENACE-- TO EVERYONE I CARE ABOUT.
EVEN IF THINGS TURN OUT ALL RIGHT TODAY, THIS WILL NEVER END. OSBORN'S MEN WILL STILL BE AFTER ME, MY BABY, MY FRIENDS--
LILY! NO!
I HAVE TO GO--FOR YOUR SAKE. FOR HIS. I CAN'T BE IN MY BABY'S LIFE.
VROOM
TELL HIM I LOVE HIM.
TELL THEM BOTH.
LILY?
LILY, COME BACK!
LILLY!
WHERE'D SHE GO? I CAN'T JUST LET HER--
I KNOW. I KNOW. BUT THERE'S NOTHING YOU CAN DO FOR HER, HARRY.
BESIDES...

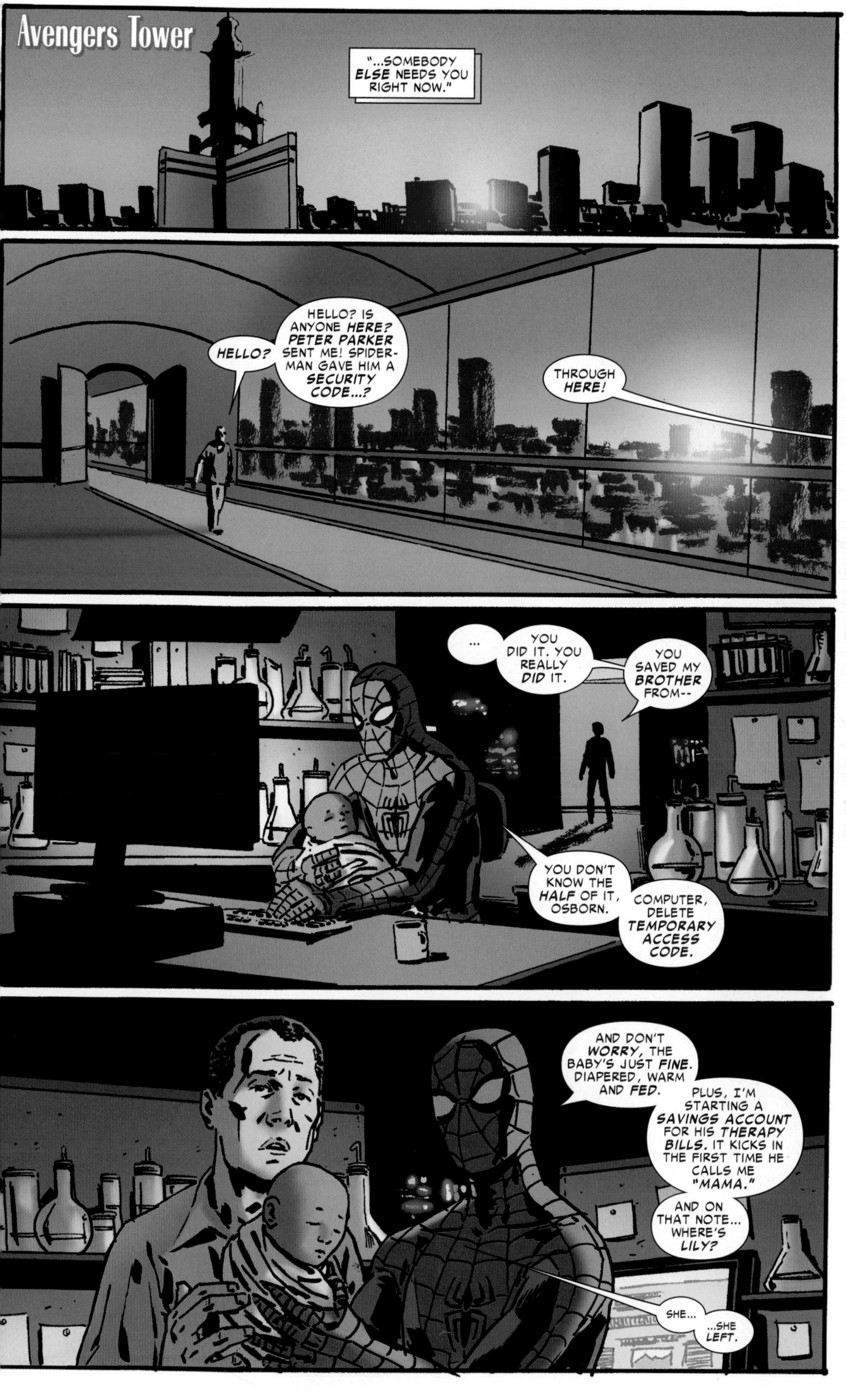
Avengers Tower
"...SOMEBODY ELSE NEEDS YOU RIGHT NOW."
HELLO?
HELLO? IS ANYONE HERE? PETER PARKER SENT ME! SPIDER-MAN GAVE HIM A SECURITY CODE...?
THROUGH HERE!
...
YOU DID IT. YOU REALLY DID IT.
YOU SAVED MY BROTHER FROM--
YOU DON'T KNOW THE HALF OF IT, OSBORN.
COMPUTER, DELETE TEMPORARY ACCESS CODE.
AND DON'T WORRY, THE BABY'S JUST FINE. DIAPERED, WARM AND FED.
PLUS, I'M STARTING A SAVINGS ACCOUNT FOR HIS THERAPY BILLS. IT KICKS IN THE FIRST TIME HE CALLS ME "MAMA."
AND ON THAT NOTE... WHERE'S LILY?
SHE...
...SHE LEFT.

IS THE BABY STILL BEING *HUNTED?* BECAUSE I HAD AN *IDEA* ABOUT HOW TO DEAL WITH *OCTOPUS...*

HE'S OFF THE TABLE. COAST IS *CLEAR.* FINGER.

WHAT?

FINGER. OW!

THAT'S THE BIG BOY. NOW *RELAX.*

RELAX? WHO *ELSE* IS AFTER THIS BABY WITH HIS FATHER BEING--

--NOT WHO WE *BELIEVED.*

THAT'S WHY WE CAME *HERE.* I NEEDED A STATE-OF-THE-ART *DNA LAB* TO PLAY OUT A *THEORY.*

YOUR POP DID *NOT* BESTOW UPON THIS WORLD A LI'L *MINI-GOBLIN,* TURNS OUT. APPARENTLY, NOT EVEN *LILY* KNOWS WHO THE FATHER IS, TSK, TSK...

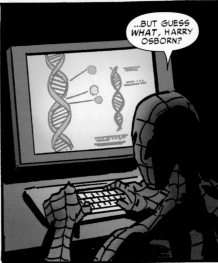

...BUT GUESS *WHAT,* HARRY OSBORN?

IT'S *YOU.*

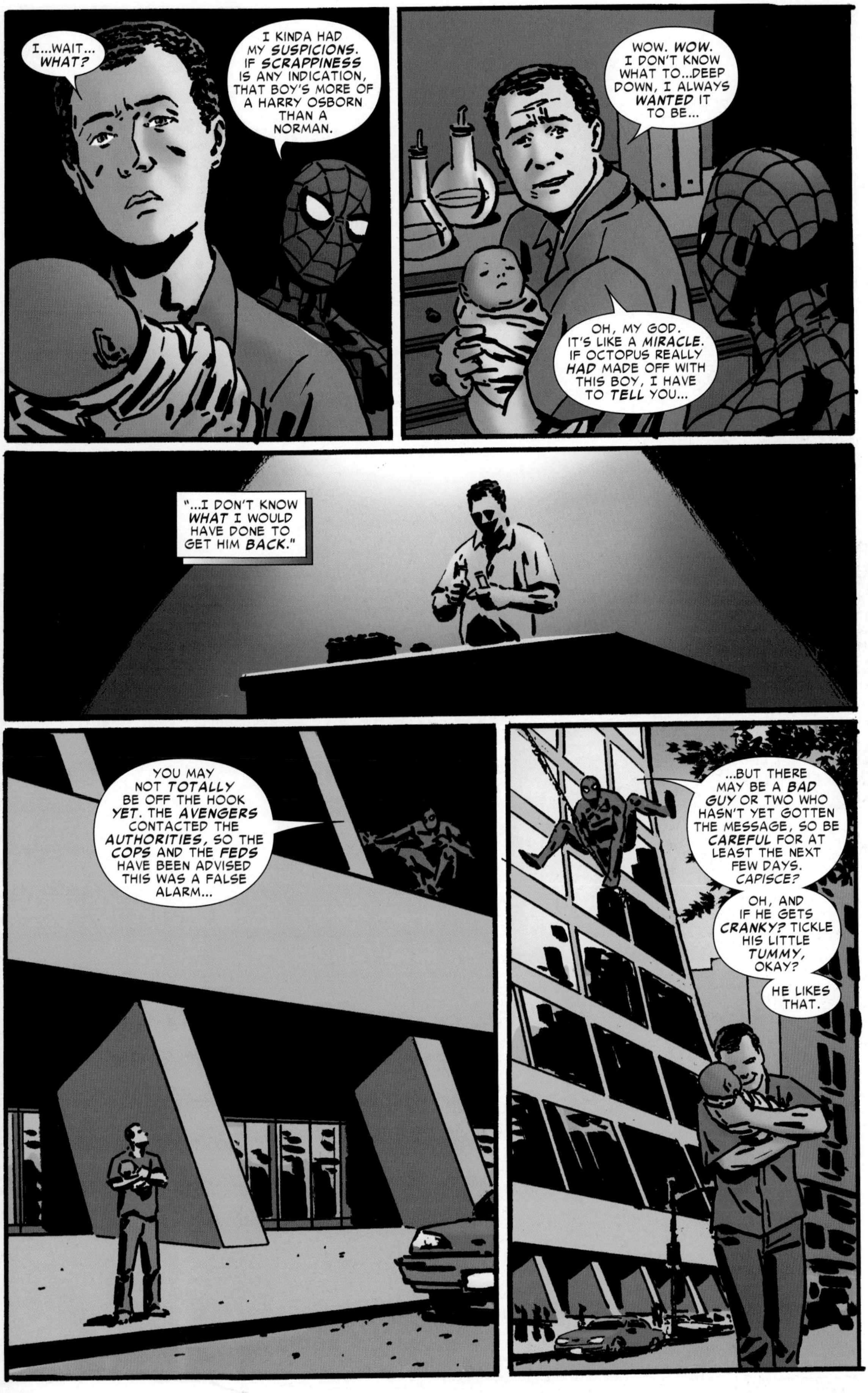
I...WAIT... WHAT?
I KINDA HAD MY SUSPICIONS. IF SCRAPPINESS IS ANY INDICATION, THAT BOY'S MORE OF A HARRY OSBORN THAN A NORMAN.
WOW. WOW. I DON'T KNOW WHAT TO...DEEP DOWN, I ALWAYS WANTED IT TO BE...
OH, MY GOD. IT'S LIKE A MIRACLE. IF OCTOPUS REALLY HAD MADE OFF WITH THIS BOY, I HAVE TO TELL YOU...
"...I DON'T KNOW WHAT I WOULD HAVE DONE TO GET HIM BACK."
YOU MAY NOT TOTALLY BE OFF THE HOOK YET. THE AVENGERS CONTACTED THE AUTHORITIES, SO THE COPS AND THE FEDS HAVE BEEN ADVISED THIS WAS A FALSE ALARM...
...BUT THERE MAY BE A BAD GUY OR TWO WHO HASN'T YET GOTTEN THE MESSAGE, SO BE CAREFUL FOR AT LEAST THE NEXT FEW DAYS. CAPISCE?
OH, AND IF HE GETS CRANKY? TICKLE HIS LITTLE TUMMY, OKAY?
HE LIKES THAT.

THIS MIGHT JUST BE THE KICK INTO ADULTHOOD THAT OL' HARRY'S BEEN *NEEDING.*

A WHOLE *NEW* HARRY.

ORIGIN OF A SPECIES, INDEED.

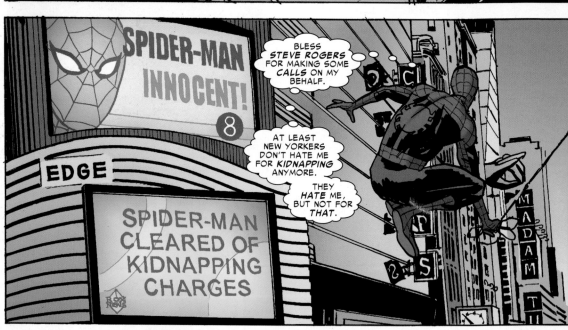

SPIDER-MAN INNOCENT!

8

EDGE

SPIDER-MAN CLEARED OF KIDNAPPING CHARGES

BLESS STEVE ROGERS FOR MAKING SOME *CALLS* ON MY BEHALF.

AT LEAST NEW YORKERS DON'T HATE ME FOR *KIDNAPPING* ANYMORE.

THEY *HATE* ME, BUT NOT FOR *THAT.*

SILVER LININGS *EVERYWHERE.* I STILL HAVE A *SEMI-EVIL* ROOMMATE, NO JOB, NO CLOTHES, NO CAMERA AND NO DOUGH--

--BUT MAYBE *CAPTAIN AMERICA* HAS SOME CHAIN MAIL I COULD WEAR. MAYBE *IRON MAN* WOULD LOAN ME A FEW BUCKS. MAYBE *AUNT MAY'LL* COOK ME SOME *WHEATCAKES.*

AND MAYBE *MJ* WILL PUT IN A GOOD WORD WITH *CARLIE.* 'CAUSE UGLY AS MY LIFE *GETS*-- AND IT'S RARELY PRETTY--IT'S ALWAYS SOMETHING *ELSE,* TOO:

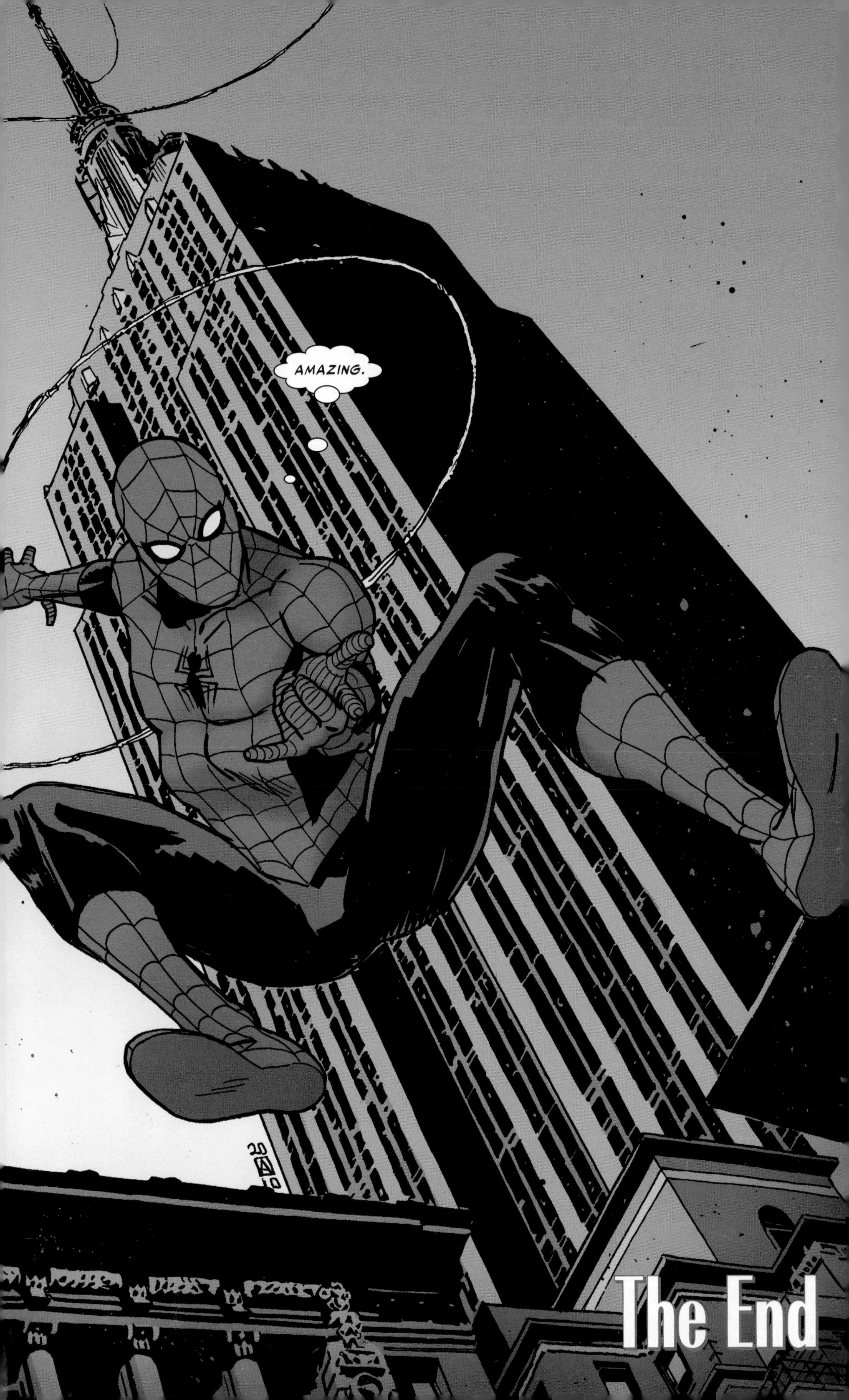
AMAZING.
The End

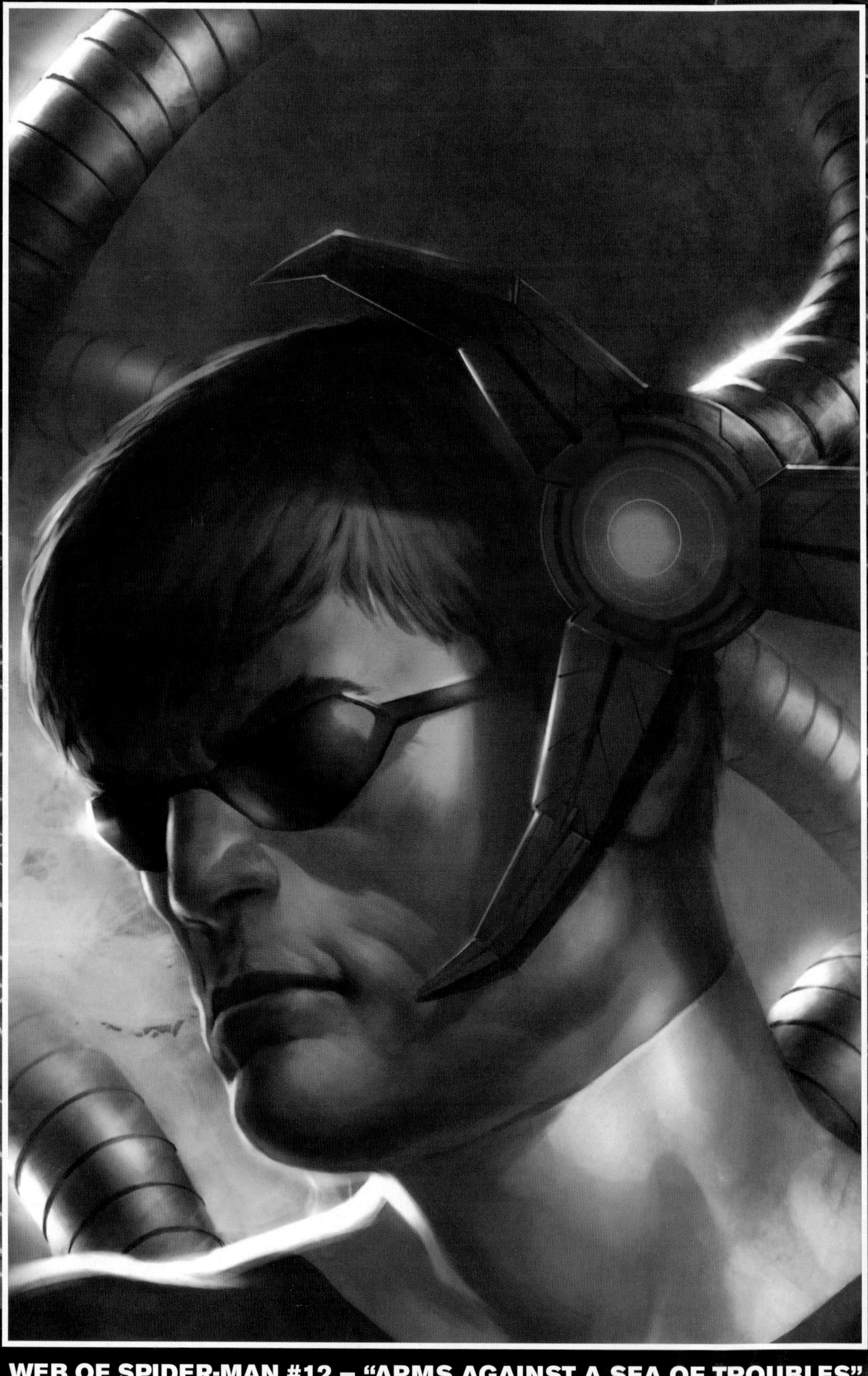

WEB OF SPIDER-MAN #12 – "ARMS AGAINST A SEA OF TROUBLES"
COVER BY JELENA KEVIC DJURDJEVIC

"I WAS ALWAYS A GOOD STUDENT. EVERYTHING FASCINATED ME.

"I REMEMBER ONE CLASS TRIP TO AN AQUARIUM... I WAS MESMERIZED BY THE OCTOPUS."

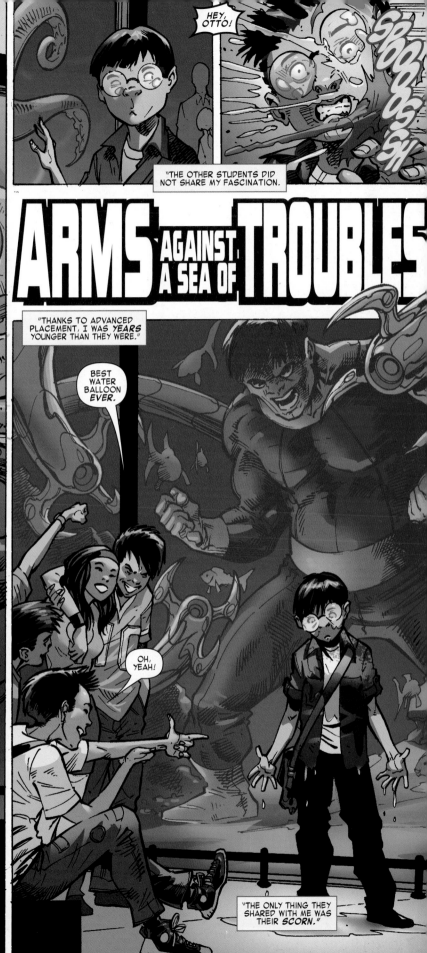

HEY, OTTO!

SPOOOSH

"THE OTHER STUDENTS DID NOT SHARE MY FASCINATION.

ARMS AGAINST A SEA OF TROUBLES

"THANKS TO ADVANCED PLACEMENT, I WAS *YEARS* YOUNGER THAN THEY WERE."

BEST WATER BALLOON *EVER.*

OH, YEAH!

ROGER STERN--WRITER
HILIPPE BRIONES--ARTIST
RIS SOTOMAYOR--COLORIST
?AVE SHARPE--LETTERER
TOM BRENNAN--EDITOR

"THE ONLY THING THEY SHARED WITH ME WAS THEIR *SCORN.*"

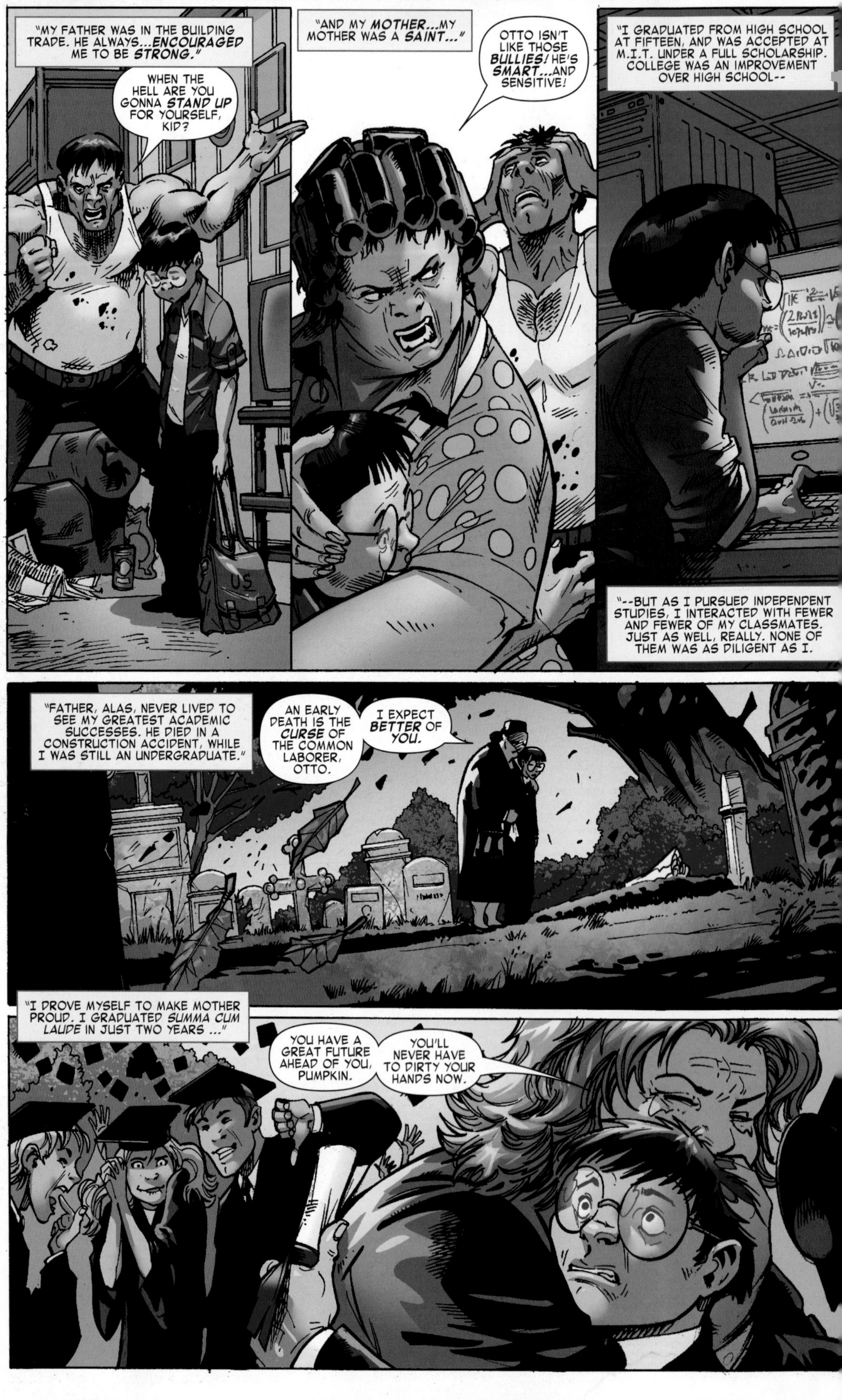
"MY FATHER WAS IN THE BUILDING TRADE. HE ALWAYS...ENCOURAGED ME TO BE STRONG."
WHEN THE HELL ARE YOU GONNA STAND UP FOR YOURSELF, KID?
"AND MY MOTHER...MY MOTHER WAS A SAINT..."
OTTO ISN'T LIKE THOSE BULLIES! HE'S SMART...AND SENSITIVE!
"I GRADUATED FROM HIGH SCHOOL AT FIFTEEN, AND WAS ACCEPTED AT M.I.T. UNDER A FULL SCHOLARSHIP. COLLEGE WAS AN IMPROVEMENT OVER HIGH SCHOOL--
"--BUT AS I PURSUED INDEPENDENT STUDIES, I INTERACTED WITH FEWER AND FEWER OF MY CLASSMATES. JUST AS WELL, REALLY. NONE OF THEM WAS AS DILIGENT AS I.
"FATHER, ALAS, NEVER LIVED TO SEE MY GREATEST ACADEMIC SUCCESSES. HE DIED IN A CONSTRUCTION ACCIDENT, WHILE I WAS STILL AN UNDERGRADUATE."
AN EARLY DEATH IS THE CURSE OF THE COMMON LABORER, OTTO.
I EXPECT BETTER OF YOU.
"I DROVE MYSELF TO MAKE MOTHER PROUD. I GRADUATED SUMMA CUM LAUDE IN JUST TWO YEARS ..."
YOU HAVE A GREAT FUTURE AHEAD OF YOU, PUMPKIN.
YOU'LL NEVER HAVE TO DIRTY YOUR HANDS NOW.

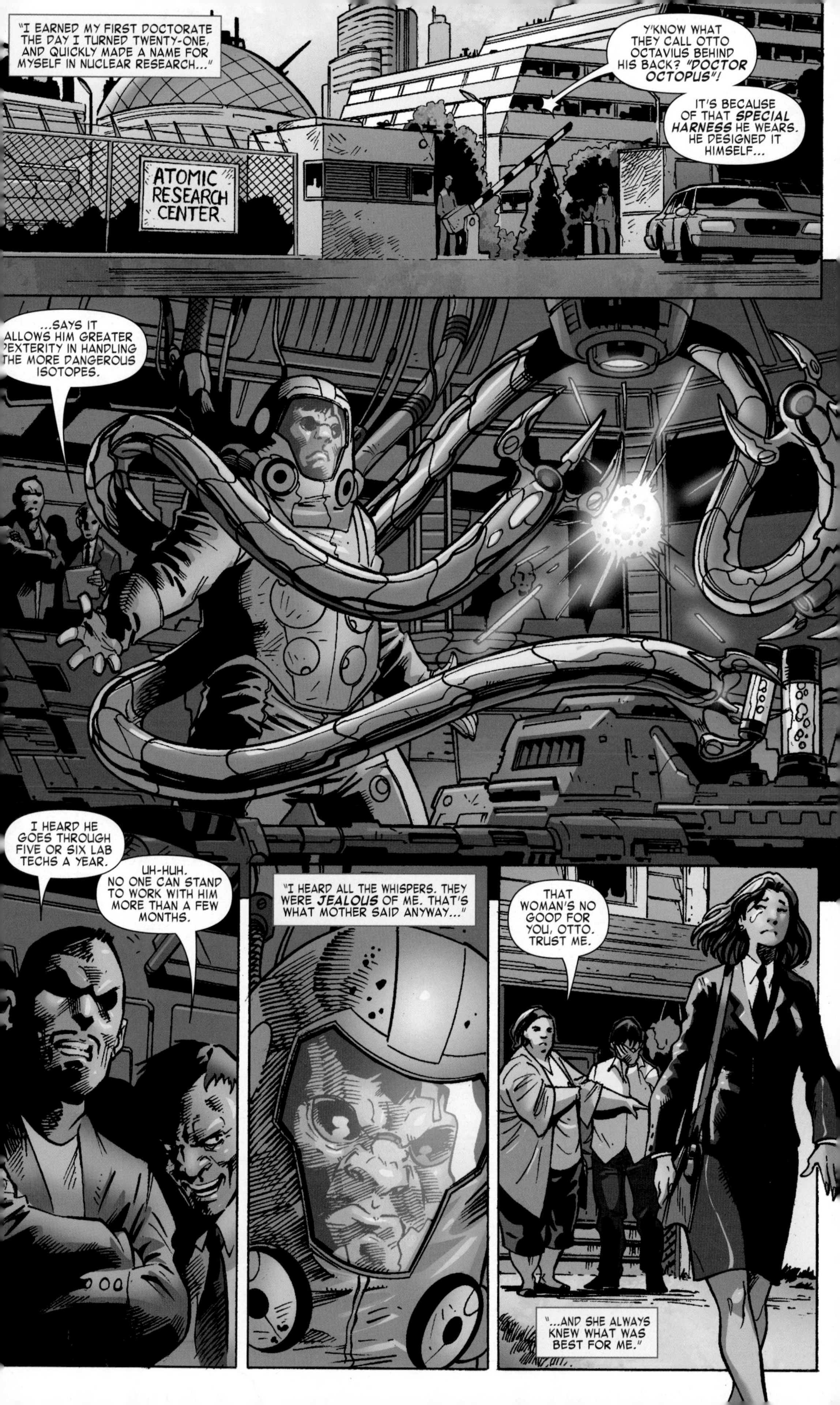
"I EARNED MY FIRST DOCTORATE THE DAY I TURNED TWENTY-ONE, AND QUICKLY MADE A NAME FOR MYSELF IN NUCLEAR RESEARCH..."
ATOMIC RESEARCH CENTER
Y'KNOW WHAT THEY CALL OTTO OCTAVIUS BEHIND HIS BACK? "DOCTOR OCTOPUS"!
IT'S BECAUSE OF THAT SPECIAL HARNESS HE WEARS. HE DESIGNED IT HIMSELF...
...SAYS IT ALLOWS HIM GREATER DEXTERITY IN HANDLING THE MORE DANGEROUS ISOTOPES.
I HEARD HE GOES THROUGH FIVE OR SIX LAB TECHS A YEAR.
UH-HUH. NO ONE CAN STAND TO WORK WITH HIM MORE THAN A FEW MONTHS.
"I HEARD ALL THE WHISPERS. THEY WERE JEALOUS OF ME. THAT'S WHAT MOTHER SAID ANYWAY..."
THAT WOMAN'S NO GOOD FOR YOU, OTTO. TRUST ME.
"...AND SHE ALWAYS KNEW WHAT WAS BEST FOR ME."

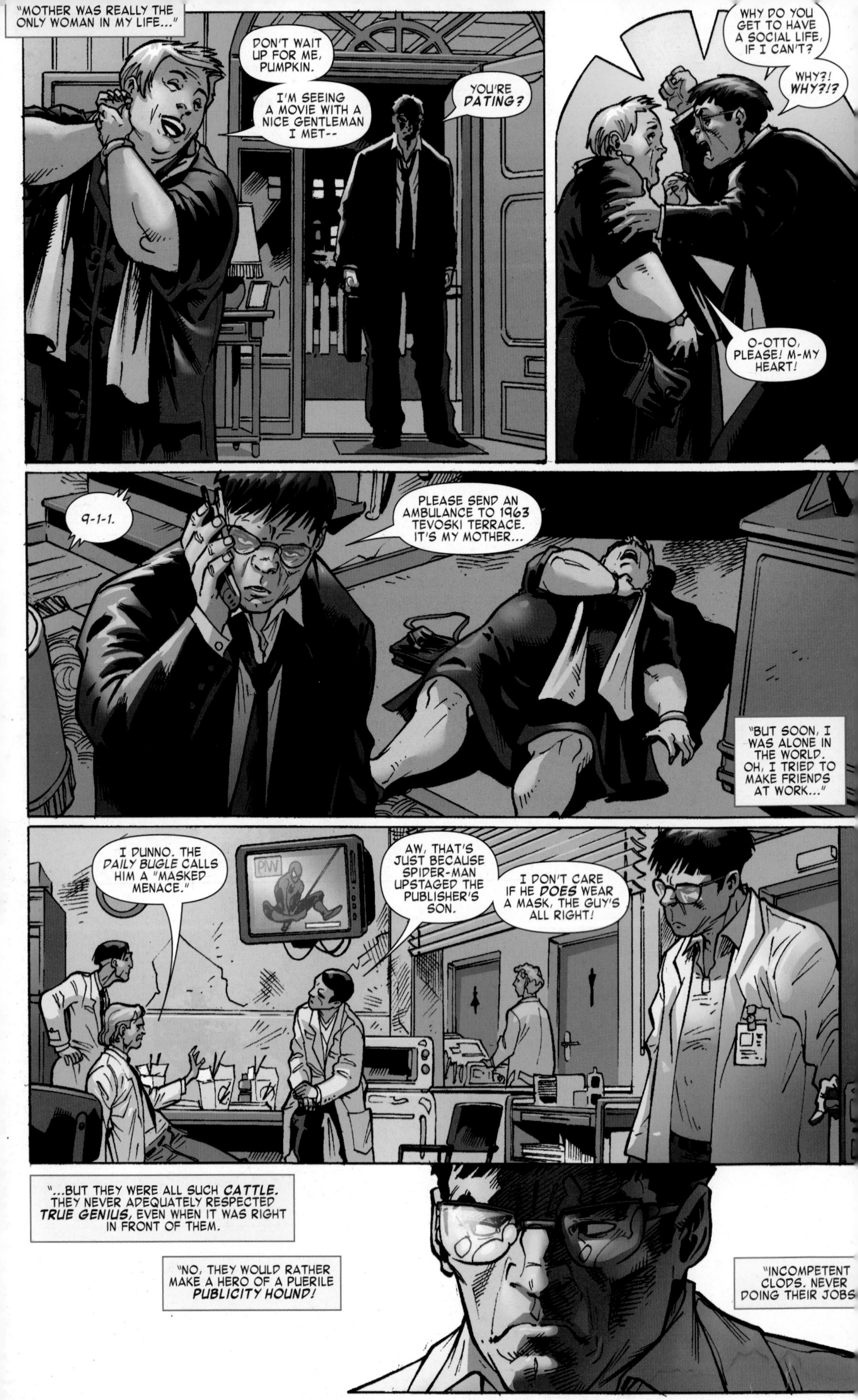

"MOTHER WAS REALLY THE ONLY WOMAN IN MY LIFE..."
DON'T WAIT UP FOR ME, PUMPKIN.
I'M SEEING A MOVIE WITH A NICE GENTLEMAN I MET--
YOU'RE DATING?
WHY DO YOU GET TO HAVE A SOCIAL LIFE, IF I CAN'T?
WHY?! WHY?!?
O-OTTO, PLEASE! M-MY HEART!
9-1-1.
PLEASE SEND AN AMBULANCE TO 1963 TEVOSKI TERRACE. IT'S MY MOTHER...
"BUT SOON, I WAS ALONE IN THE WORLD. OH, I TRIED TO MAKE FRIENDS AT WORK..."
I DUNNO. THE DAILY BUGLE CALLS HIM A "MASKED MENACE."
AW, THAT'S JUST BECAUSE SPIDER-MAN UPSTAGED THE PUBLISHER'S SON.
I DON'T CARE IF HE DOES WEAR A MASK, THE GUY'S ALL RIGHT!
"...BUT THEY WERE ALL SUCH CATTLE. THEY NEVER ADEQUATELY RESPECTED TRUE GENIUS, EVEN WHEN IT WAS RIGHT IN FRONT OF THEM.
"NO, THEY WOULD RATHER MAKE A HERO OF A PUERILE PUBLICITY HOUND!
"INCOMPETENT CLODS. NEVER DOING THEIR JOBS

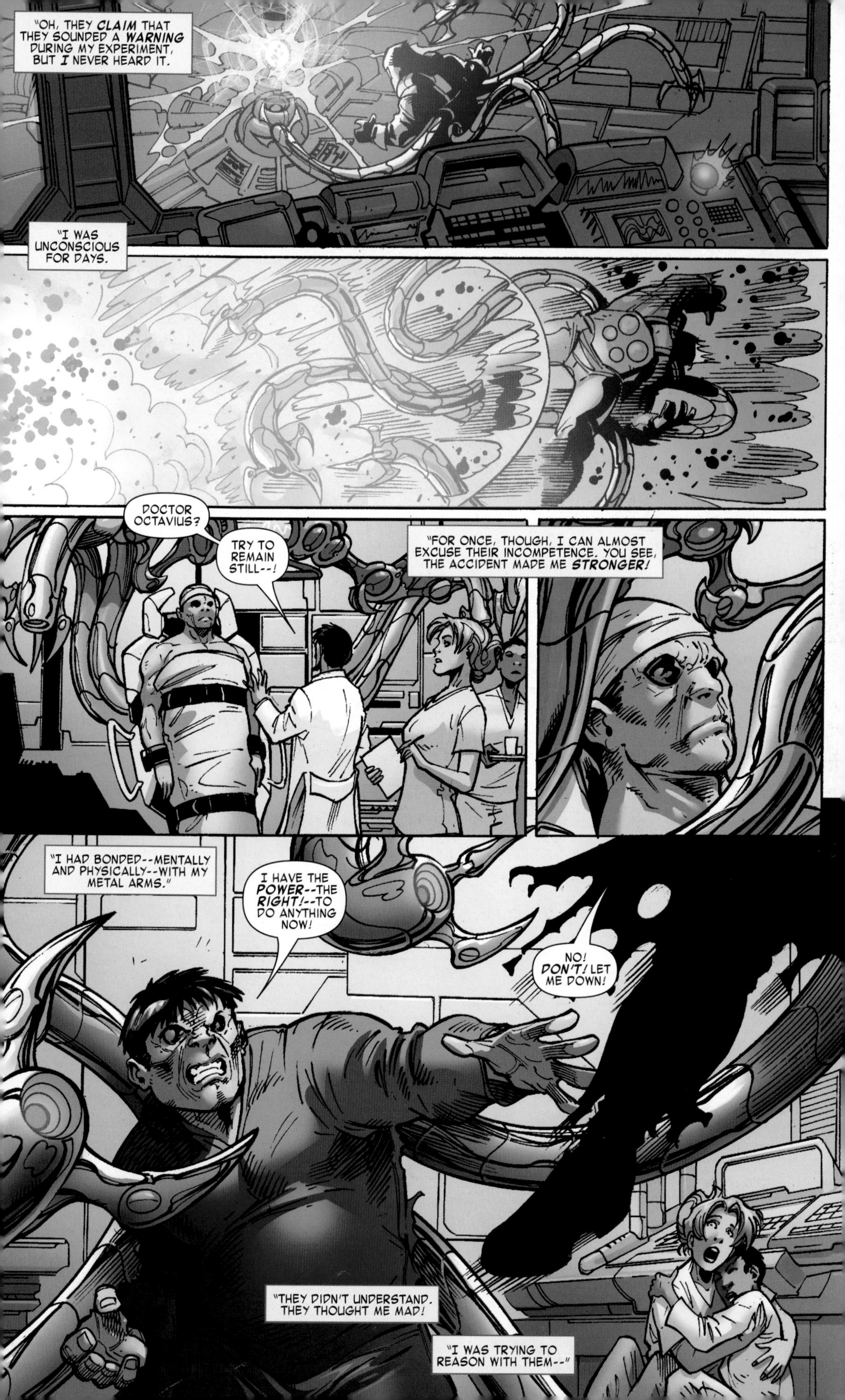
"OH, THEY CLAIM THAT THEY SOUNDED A WARNING DURING MY EXPERIMENT, BUT I NEVER HEARD IT.
"I WAS UNCONSCIOUS FOR DAYS.
DOCTOR OCTAVIUS?
TRY TO REMAIN STILL--!
"FOR ONCE, THOUGH, I CAN ALMOST EXCUSE THEIR INCOMPETENCE. YOU SEE, THE ACCIDENT MADE ME STRONGER!
"I HAD BONDED--MENTALLY AND PHYSICALLY--WITH MY METAL ARMS."
I HAVE THE POWER--THE RIGHT!--TO DO ANYTHING NOW!
NO! DON'T! LET ME DOWN!
"THEY DIDN'T UNDERSTAND. THEY THOUGHT ME MAD!
"I WAS TRYING TO REASON WITH THEM--"

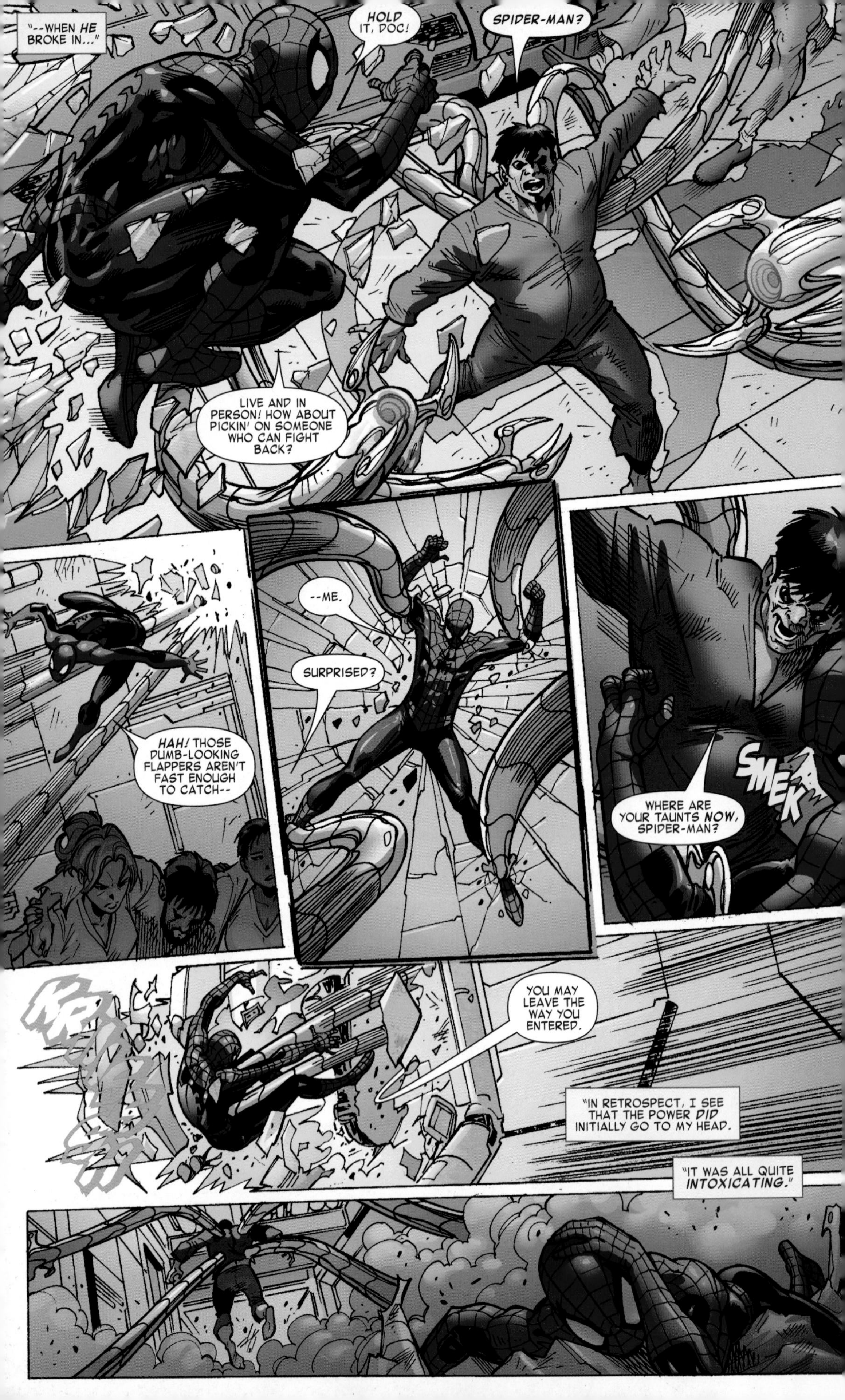
"--WHEN HE BROKE IN..."
HOLD IT, DOC!
SPIDER-MAN?
LIVE AND IN PERSON! HOW ABOUT PICKIN' ON SOMEONE WHO CAN FIGHT BACK?
HAH! THOSE DUMB-LOOKING FLAPPERS AREN'T FAST ENOUGH TO CATCH--
--ME.
SURPRISED?
SMEK
WHERE ARE YOUR TAUNTS NOW, SPIDER-MAN?
YOU MAY LEAVE THE WAY YOU ENTERED.
"IN RETROSPECT, I SEE THAT THE POWER DID INITIALLY GO TO MY HEAD.
"IT WAS ALL QUITE INTOXICATING."

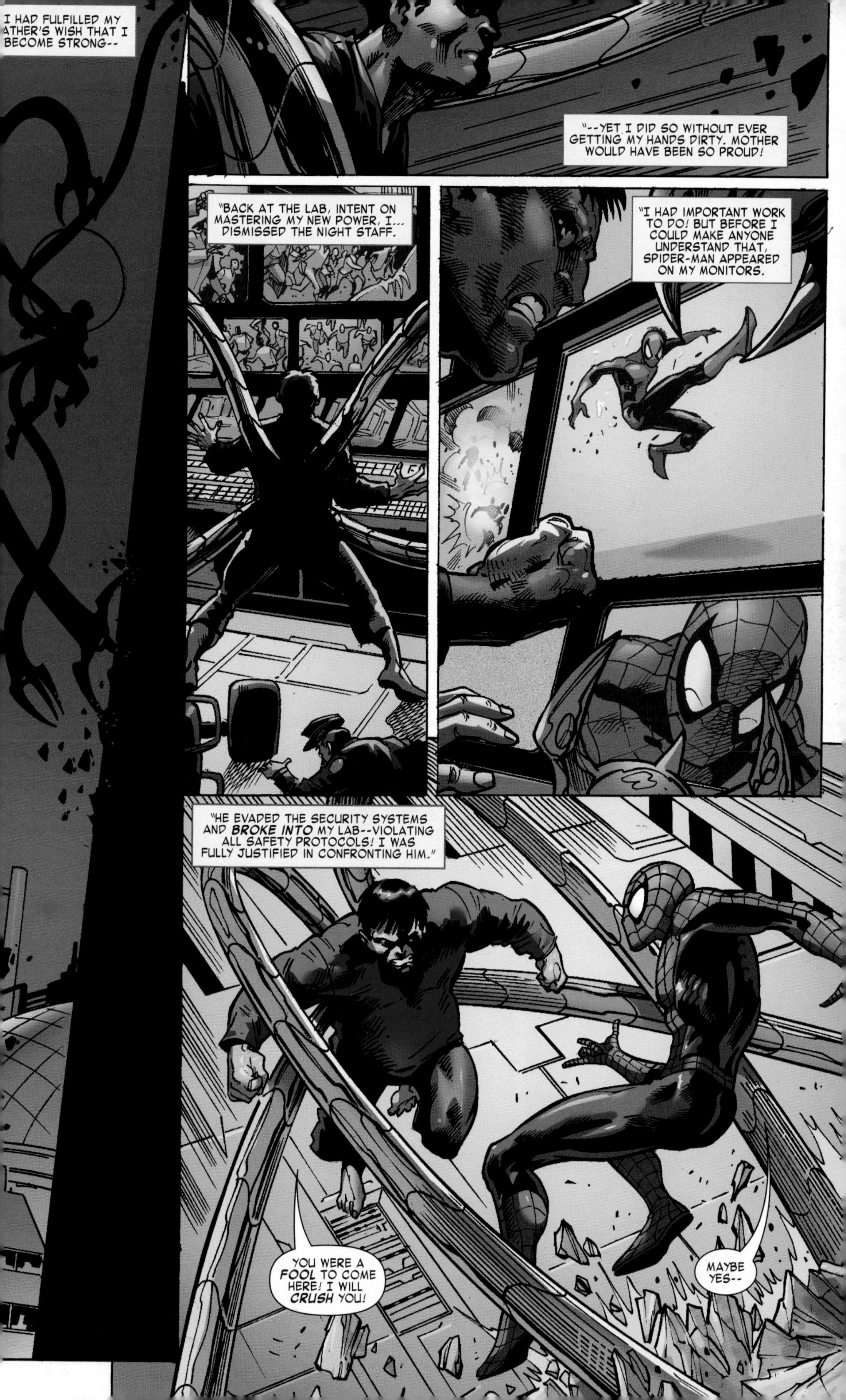
I HAD FULFILLED MY FATHER'S WISH THAT I BECOME STRONG--
"--YET I DID SO WITHOUT EVER GETTING MY HANDS DIRTY. MOTHER WOULD HAVE BEEN SO PROUD!
"BACK AT THE LAB, INTENT ON MASTERING MY NEW POWER, I... DISMISSED THE NIGHT STAFF.
"I HAD IMPORTANT WORK TO DO! BUT BEFORE I COULD MAKE ANYONE UNDERSTAND THAT, SPIDER-MAN APPEARED ON MY MONITORS.
"HE EVADED THE SECURITY SYSTEMS AND BROKE INTO MY LAB--VIOLATING ALL SAFETY PROTOCOLS! I WAS FULLY JUSTIFIED IN CONFRONTING HIM."
YOU WERE A FOOL TO COME HERE! I WILL CRUSH YOU!
MAYBE YES--

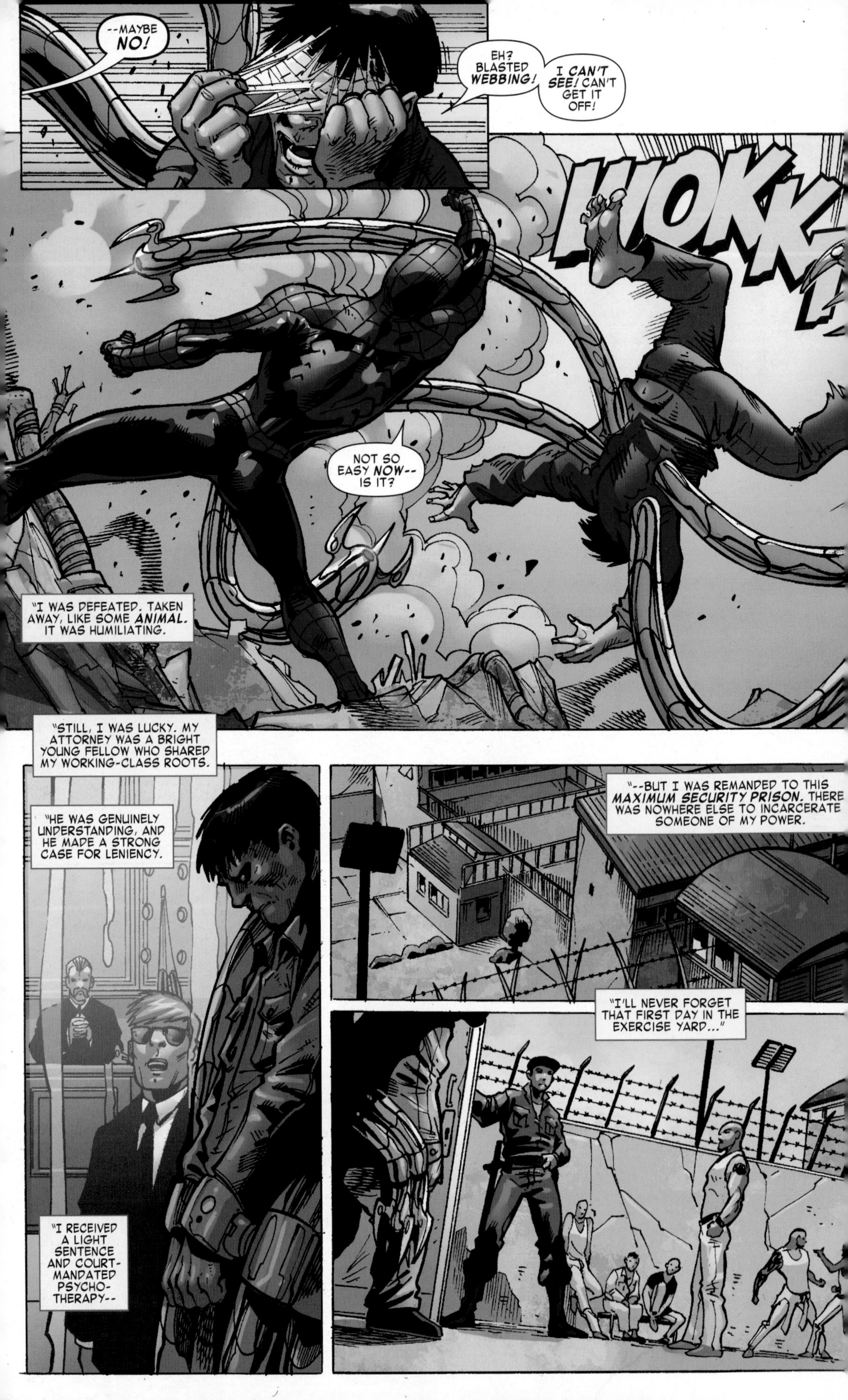
--MAYBE NO!
EH? BLASTED WEBBING!
I CAN'T SEE! CAN'T GET IT OFF!
WOKK
NOT SO EASY NOW-- IS IT?
"I WAS DEFEATED. TAKEN AWAY, LIKE SOME ANIMAL. IT WAS HUMILIATING.
"STILL, I WAS LUCKY. MY ATTORNEY WAS A BRIGHT YOUNG FELLOW WHO SHARED MY WORKING-CLASS ROOTS.
"HE WAS GENUINELY UNDERSTANDING, AND HE MADE A STRONG CASE FOR LENIENCY.
"I RECEIVED A LIGHT SENTENCE AND COURT-MANDATED PSYCHO-THERAPY--
"--BUT I WAS REMANDED TO THIS MAXIMUM SECURITY PRISON. THERE WAS NOWHERE ELSE TO INCARCERATE SOMEONE OF MY POWER.
"I'LL NEVER FORGET THAT FIRST DAY IN THE EXERCISE YARD..."

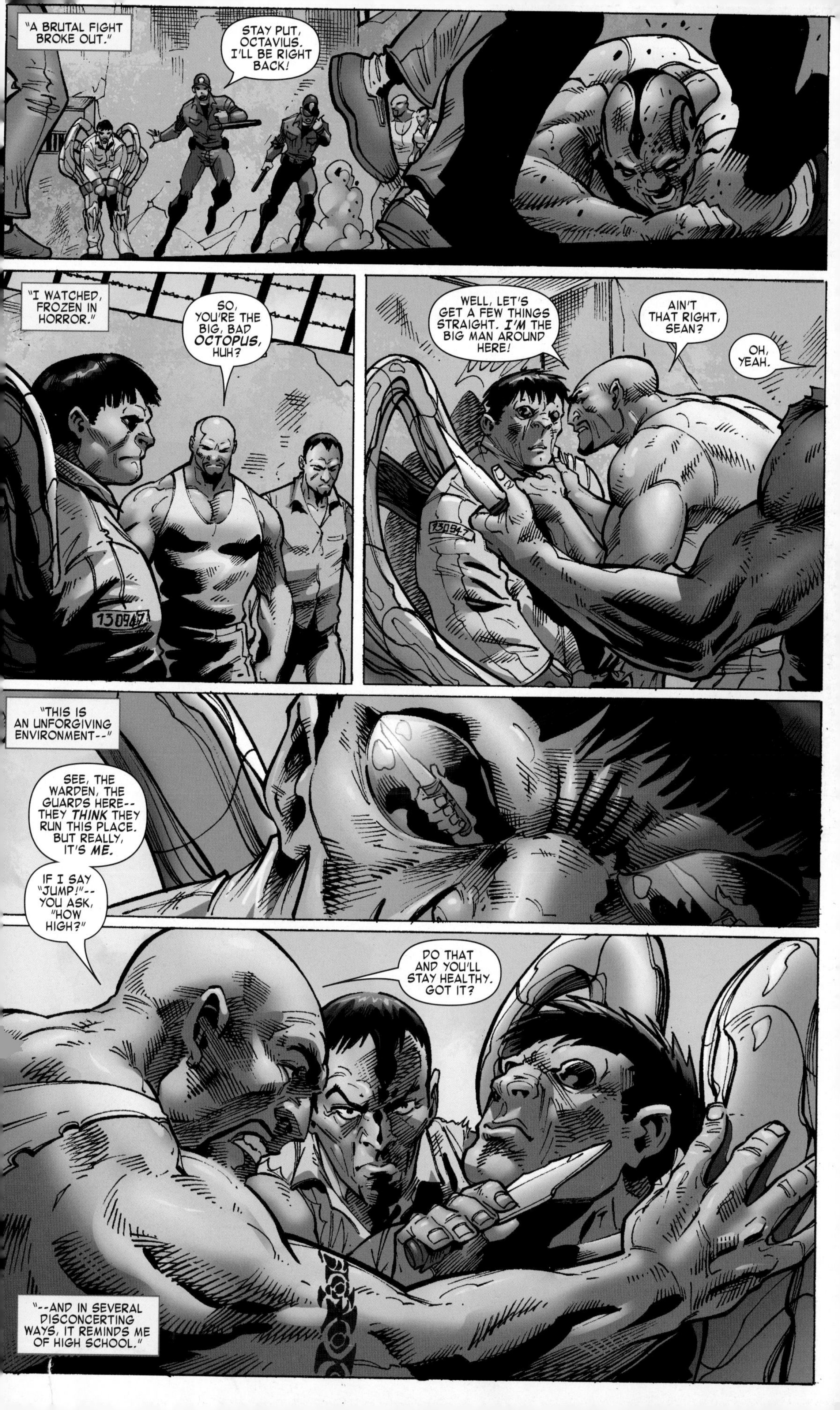
"A BRUTAL FIGHT BROKE OUT."
STAY PUT, OCTAVIUS. I'LL BE RIGHT BACK!
"I WATCHED, FROZEN IN HORROR."
SO, YOU'RE THE BIG, BAD OCTOPUS, HUH?
130947
WELL, LET'S GET A FEW THINGS STRAIGHT. I'M THE BIG MAN AROUND HERE!
AIN'T THAT RIGHT, SEAN?
OH, YEAH.
"THIS IS AN UNFORGIVING ENVIRONMENT--"
SEE, THE WARDEN, THE GUARDS HERE-- THEY THINK THEY RUN THIS PLACE. BUT REALLY, IT'S ME.
IF I SAY "JUMP!"-- YOU ASK, "HOW HIGH?"
DO THAT AND YOU'LL STAY HEALTHY. GOT IT?
"--AND IN SEVERAL DISCONCERTING WAYS, IT REMINDS ME OF HIGH SCHOOL."

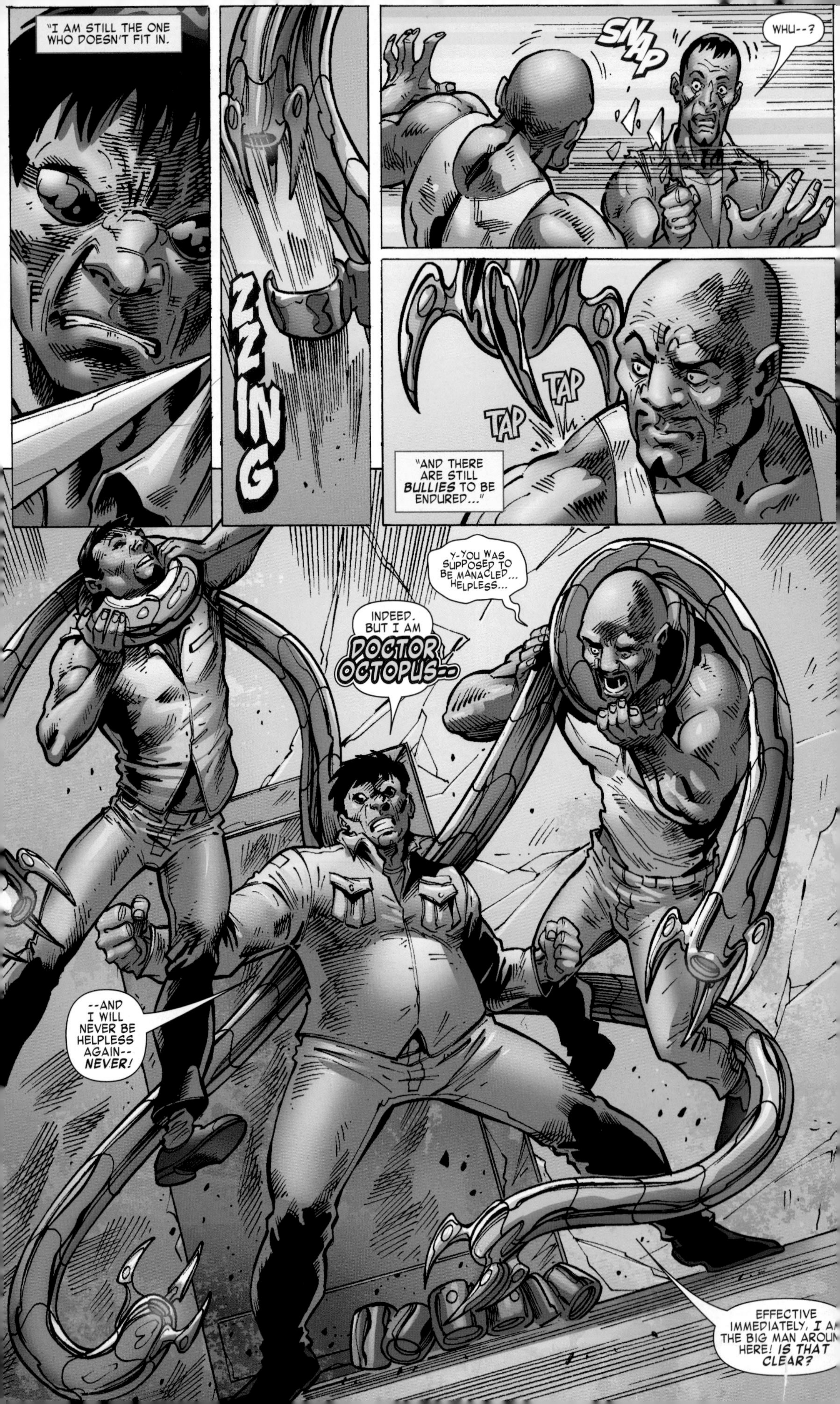
"I AM STILL THE ONE WHO DOESN'T FIT IN.
ZZING
SNAP
WHU--?
TAP
TAP
"AND THERE ARE STILL BULLIES TO BE ENDURED..."
Y-YOU WAS SUPPOSED TO BE MANACLED... HELPLESS...
INDEED. BUT I AM DOCTOR OCTOPUS--
--AND I WILL NEVER BE HELPLESS AGAIN-- NEVER!
EFFECTIVE IMMEDIATELY, I A THE BIG MAN AROUN HERE! IS THAT CLEAR?

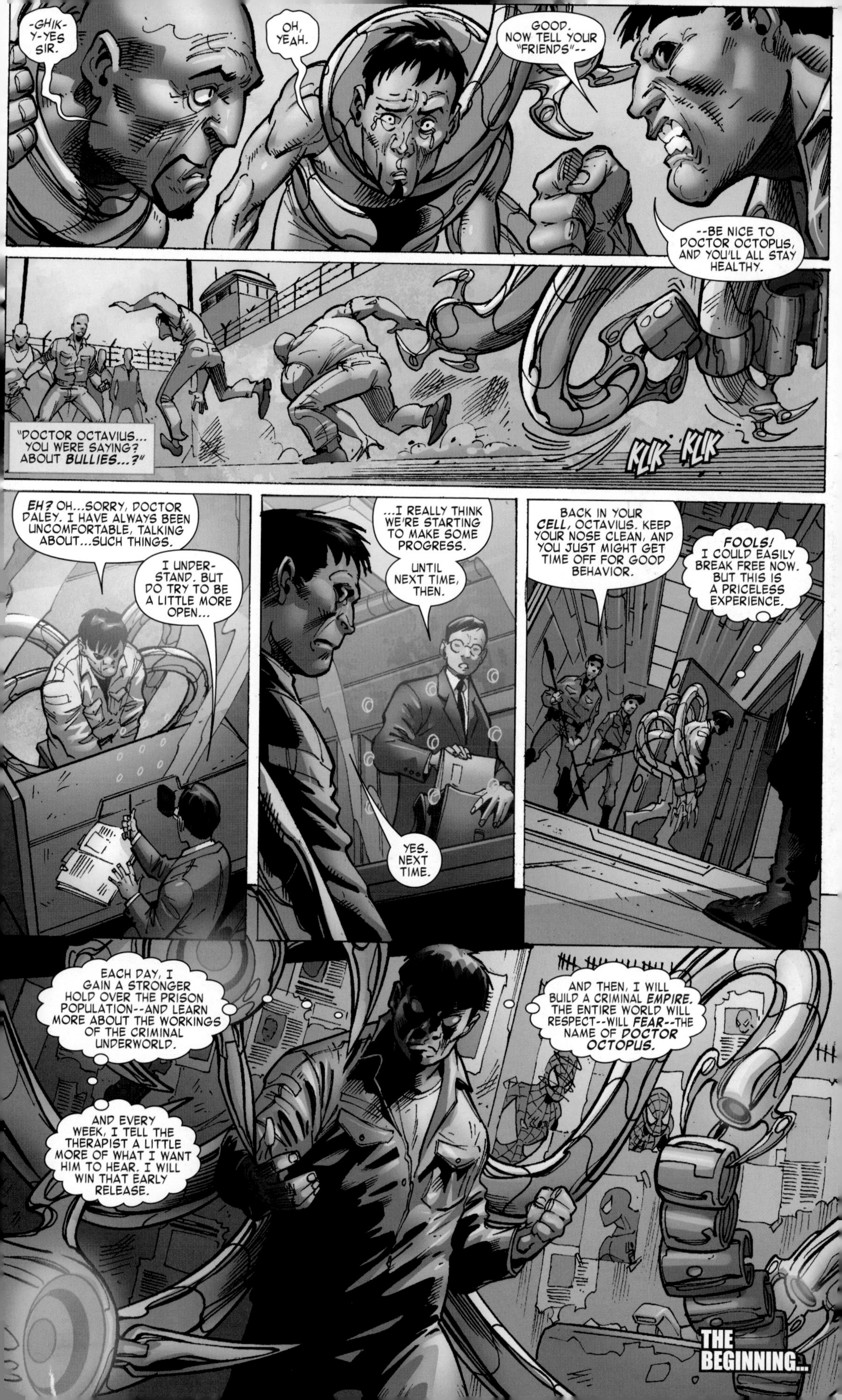
-GHIK-Y-YES SIR.
OH, YEAH.
GOOD. NOW TELL YOUR "FRIENDS"--
--BE NICE TO DOCTOR OCTOPUS, AND YOU'LL ALL STAY HEALTHY.
"DOCTOR OCTAVIUS... YOU WERE SAYING? ABOUT BULLIES...?"
KLIK KLIK
EH? OH...SORRY, DOCTOR DALEY. I HAVE ALWAYS BEEN UNCOMFORTABLE, TALKING ABOUT...SUCH THINGS.
I UNDER-STAND. BUT DO TRY TO BE A LITTLE MORE OPEN...
...I REALLY THINK WE'RE STARTING TO MAKE SOME PROGRESS.
UNTIL NEXT TIME, THEN.
YES. NEXT TIME.
BACK IN YOUR CELL, OCTAVIUS. KEEP YOUR NOSE CLEAN, AND YOU JUST MIGHT GET TIME OFF FOR GOOD BEHAVIOR.
FOOLS! I COULD EASILY BREAK FREE NOW. BUT THIS IS A PRICELESS EXPERIENCE.
EACH DAY, I GAIN A STRONGER HOLD OVER THE PRISON POPULATION--AND LEARN MORE ABOUT THE WORKINGS OF THE CRIMINAL UNDERWORLD.
AND EVERY WEEK, I TELL THE THERAPIST A LITTLE MORE OF WHAT I WANT HIM TO HEAR. I WILL WIN THAT EARLY RELEASE.
AND THEN, I WILL BUILD A CRIMINAL EMPIRE. THE ENTIRE WORLD WILL RESPECT--WILL FEAR--THE NAME OF DOCTOR OCTOPUS.
THE BEGINNING...

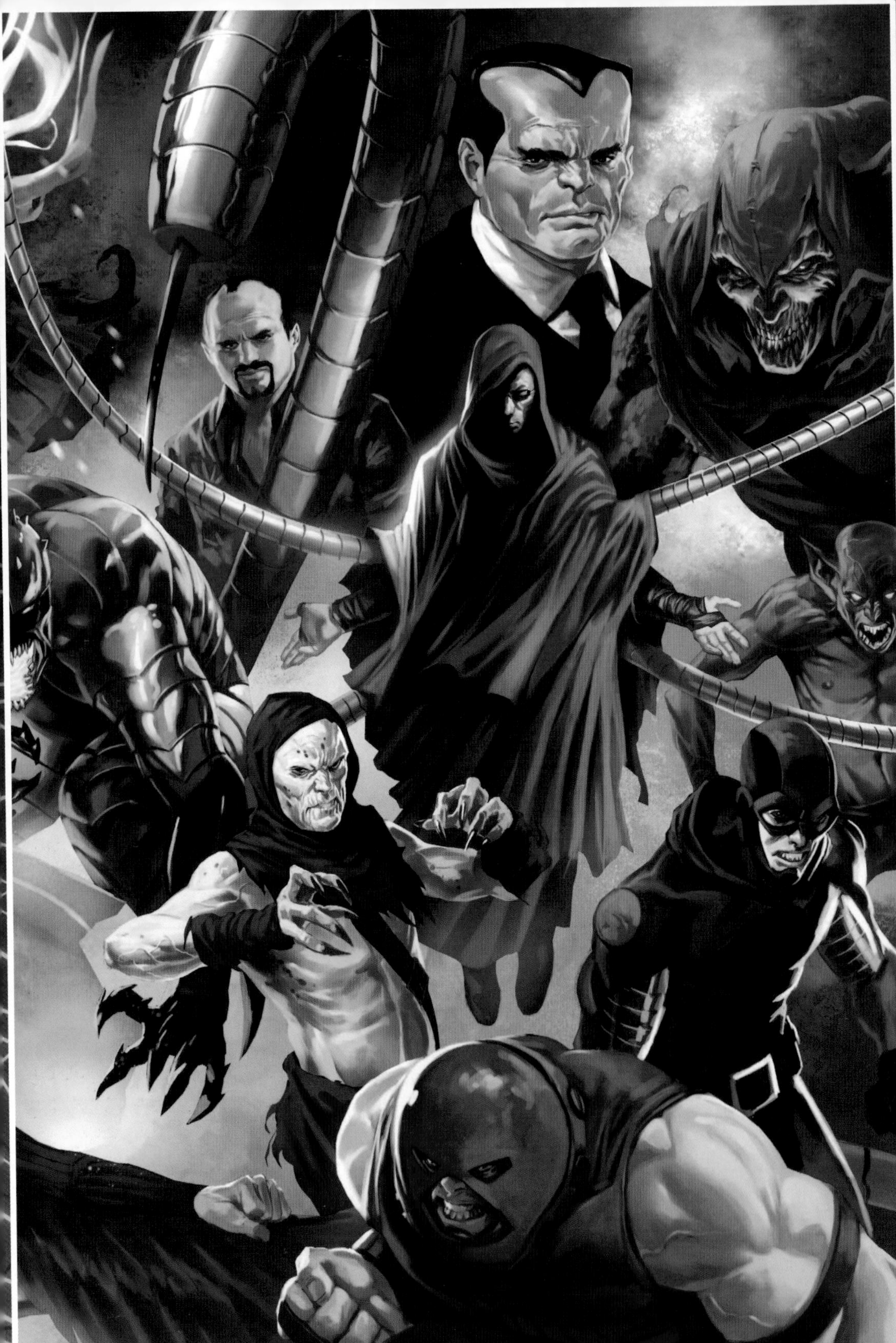

THE AMAZING SPIDER-MAN

After the Superhuman Civil War, Spider-Man took a brief hiatus from crime-fighting. His ex-girlfriend, Mary Jane Watson, had left New York City to make her name in Hollywood, and his best friend, Harry Osborn, had returned from a prolonged stint in rehab. It seemed like a good time to take some time off.

But the responsibility his great powers gave him couldn't be ignored, and as new threats and menaces reared their vile heads, he slapped on his web-shooters and got back to doing whatever a Spider can to protect the streets of the Big Apple.

Along the way, old friends have returned, new friends have been made and his greatest villains have come back stronger than ever. His beloved Aunt May is now married to J. Jonah Jameson, Sr., father of Pete's former boss, Mayor J. Jonah Jameson. Harry Osborn is again a father – having a child with Lily Hollister, the super-villain known as Menace. And last (but not least) Pete has resolved his relationship with Mary Jane Watson, regaining his best friend. Now if only he can get it together to ask NYPD CSI sleuth Carlie Cooper on a date...

It's truly a brand new day.

AMAZING SPIDER-MAN #647

Gale, Kelly, Slott, Van Lente, Waid & Wells — Web-Heads

Featuring:

ANOTHER DOOR
Fred Van Lente — Writer
Max Fiumara — Artist
Morry Hollowell — Colorist

HONOR THY FATHER...
Zeb Wells — Writer
Michael Del Mundo — Artist

STAND OFF
Bob Gale — Writer
Karl Kesel — Artist
Antonio Fabela — Colorist

NORAH'S LAST NIGHT IN NYC
Joe Kelly — Writer
J.M Ken Niimura — Art & Letters

J. JONAH JAMESON — THE MUSICAL
Mark Waid — Writer
Paul Azaceta — Artist
Morry Hollowell — Color Artist

AMERICAN HERO
Marc Guggenheim — Writer
Graham Nolan — Pencils
Mark Pennington — Inks
Antonio Fabela — Colorist

YOU AGAIN
Fred Van Lente & Dan Slott — Writers
Adam Archer — Artist
Antonio Fabela — Colorist

Lettering by VC's Joe Caramagna (unless otherwise indicated)
Cover by Marko Djurdjevic
Variant Cover by Steve McNiven, Dexter Vines and Justin Ponsor

Tom Brennan — Associate Editor
Stephen Wacker — Editor
Tom Brevoort — Executive Editor
Joe Quesada — Editor in Chief
Dan Buckley — Publisher
Alan Fine — Executive Producer

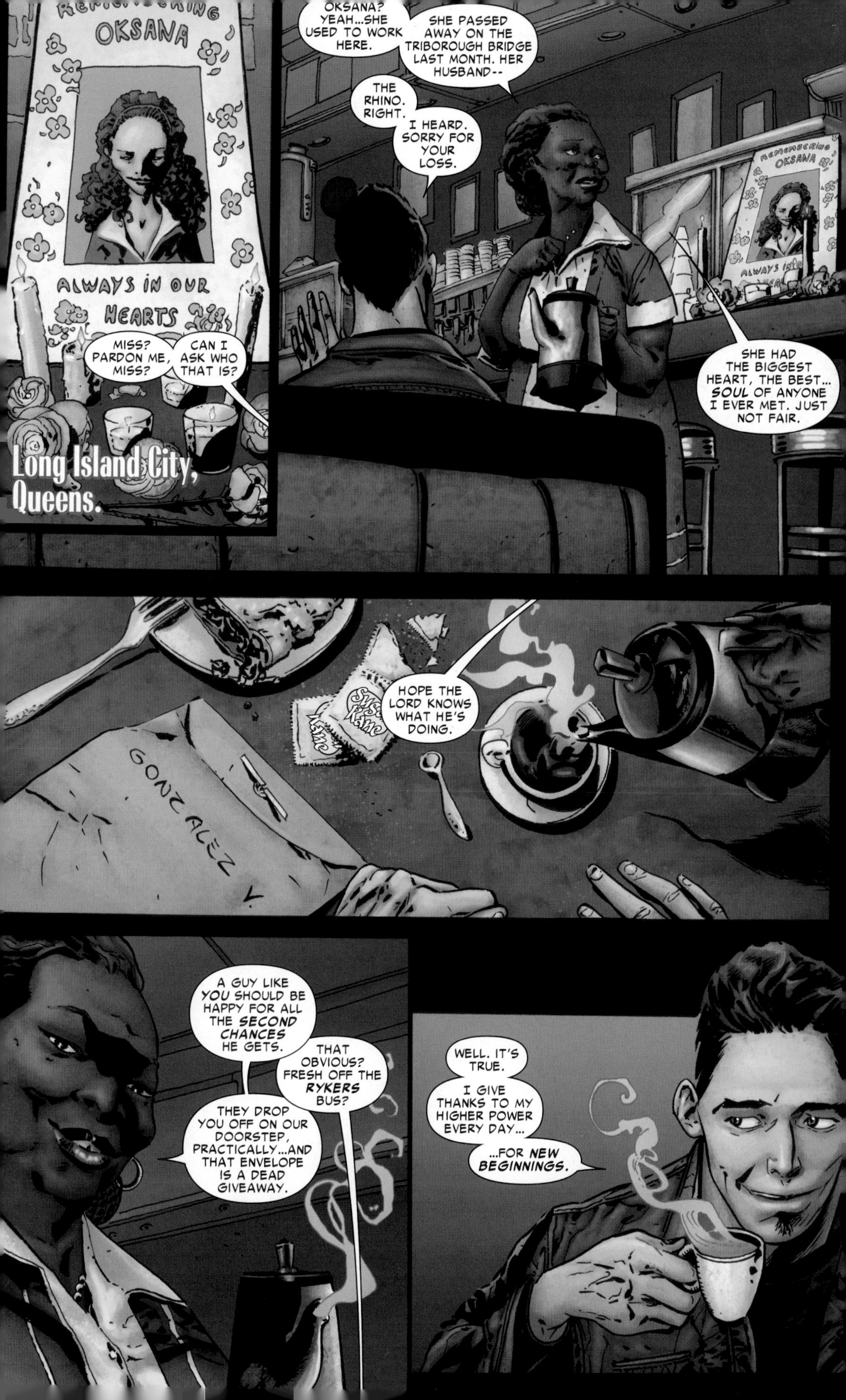
REMEMBERING
OKSANA
ALWAYS IN OUR HEARTS
Long Island City, Queens.
MISS? PARDON ME, MISS?
CAN I ASK WHO THAT IS?
OKSANA? YEAH...SHE USED TO WORK HERE.
SHE PASSED AWAY ON THE TRIBOROUGH BRIDGE LAST MONTH. HER HUSBAND--
THE RHINO. RIGHT.
I HEARD. SORRY FOR YOUR LOSS.
REMEMBERING OKSANA
SHE HAD THE BIGGEST HEART, THE BEST... SOUL OF ANYONE I EVER MET. JUST NOT FAIR.
HOPE THE LORD KNOWS WHAT HE'S DOING.
GONZALEZ
A GUY LIKE YOU SHOULD BE HAPPY FOR ALL THE SECOND CHANCES HE GETS.
THAT OBVIOUS? FRESH OFF THE RYKERS BUS?
THEY DROP YOU OFF ON OUR DOORSTEP, PRACTICALLY...AND THAT ENVELOPE IS A DEAD GIVEAWAY.
WELL. IT'S TRUE.
I GIVE THANKS TO MY HIGHER POWER EVERY DAY...
...FOR NEW BEGINNINGS.

WHILE ATTENDING A DEMONSTRATION IN RADIOLOGY, HIGH SCHOOL STUDENT **PETER PARKER** WAS BITTEN BY A SPIDER WHICH HAD ACCIDENTALLY BEEN EXPOSED TO **RADIOACTIVE RAYS.** THROUGH A MIRACLE OF SCIENCE, PETER SOON FOUND THAT HE HAD **GAINED** THE SPIDER'S POWERS...AND HAD, IN EFFECT, BECOME A HUMAN SPIDER! FROM THAT DAY ON HE WAS...

THE AMAZING SPIDER-MAN™

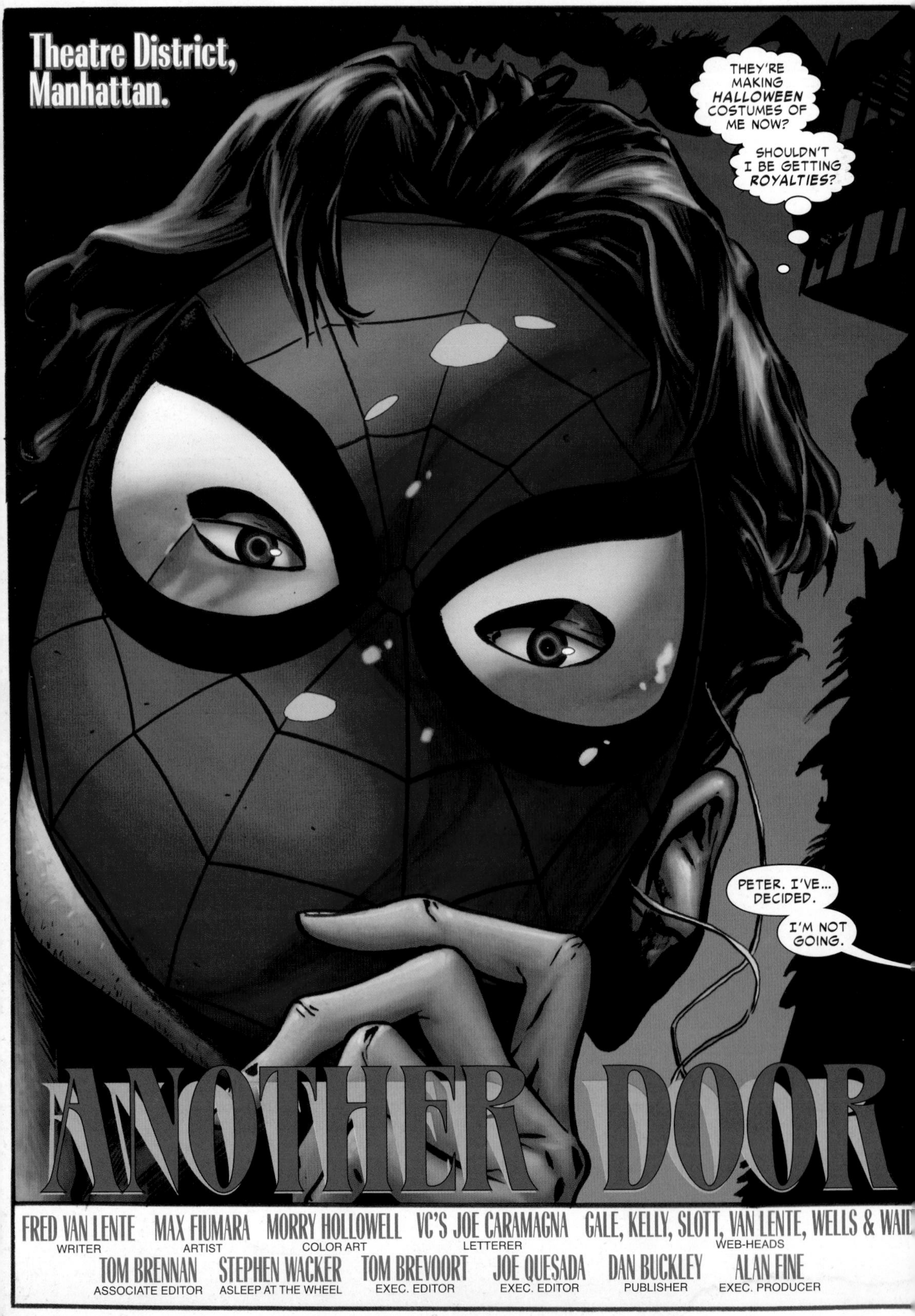
Theatre District, Manhattan.
THEY'RE MAKING *HALLOWEEN* COSTUMES OF ME NOW?
SHOULDN'T I BE GETTING *ROYALTIES?*
PETER. I'VE... DECIDED.
I'M NOT GOING.
ANOTHER DOOR

FRED VAN LENTE WRITER · MAX FIUMARA ARTIST · MORRY HOLLOWELL COLOR ART · VC'S JOE CARAMAGNA LETTERER · GALE, KELLY, SLOTT, VAN LENTE, WELLS & WAID WEB-HEADS

TOM BRENNAN ASSOCIATE EDITOR · STEPHEN WACKER ASLEEP AT THE WHEEL · TOM BREVOORT EXEC. EDITOR · JOE QUESADA EXEC. EDITOR · DAN BUCKLEY PUBLISHER · ALAN FINE EXEC. PRODUCER

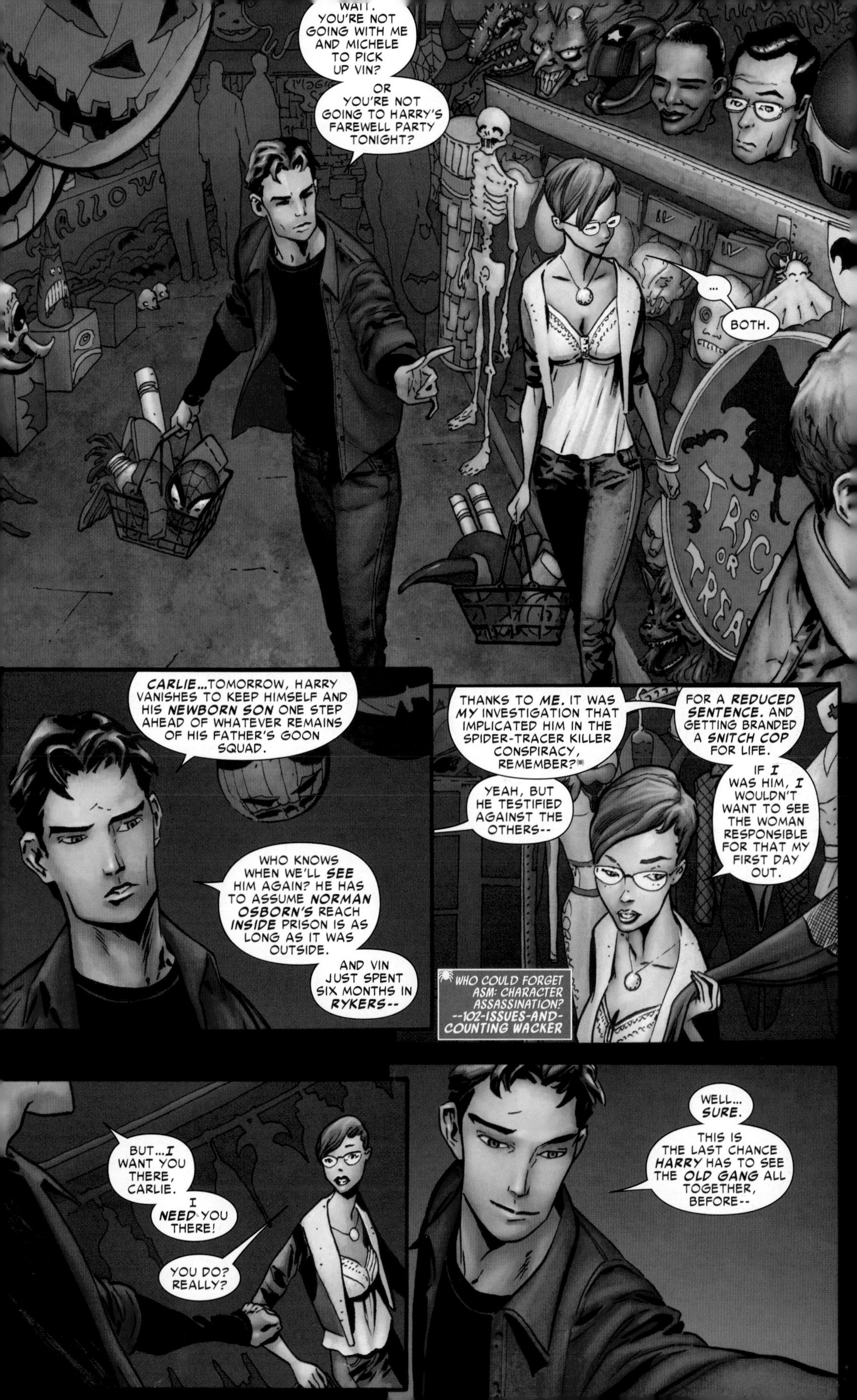
WAIT. YOU'RE NOT GOING WITH ME AND MICHELE TO PICK UP VIN?
OR YOU'RE NOT GOING TO HARRY'S FAREWELL PARTY TONIGHT?
...
BOTH.
CARLIE...TOMORROW, HARRY VANISHES TO KEEP HIMSELF AND HIS NEWBORN SON ONE STEP AHEAD OF WHATEVER REMAINS OF HIS FATHER'S GOON SQUAD.
WHO KNOWS WHEN WE'LL SEE HIM AGAIN? HE HAS TO ASSUME NORMAN OSBORN'S REACH INSIDE PRISON IS AS LONG AS IT WAS OUTSIDE.
AND VIN JUST SPENT SIX MONTHS IN RYKERS--
THANKS TO ME. IT WAS MY INVESTIGATION THAT IMPLICATED HIM IN THE SPIDER-TRACER KILLER CONSPIRACY, REMEMBER?
YEAH, BUT HE TESTIFIED AGAINST THE OTHERS--
FOR A REDUCED SENTENCE. AND GETTING BRANDED A SNITCH COP FOR LIFE.
IF I WAS HIM, I WOULDN'T WANT TO SEE THE WOMAN RESPONSIBLE FOR THAT MY FIRST DAY OUT.
WHO COULD FORGET ASM: CHARACTER ASSASSINATION? --102-ISSUES-AND-COUNTING WACKER
BUT...I WANT YOU THERE, CARLIE.
I NEED YOU THERE!
YOU DO? REALLY?
WELL... SURE.
THIS IS THE LAST CHANCE HARRY HAS TO SEE THE OLD GANG ALL TOGETHER, BEFORE--

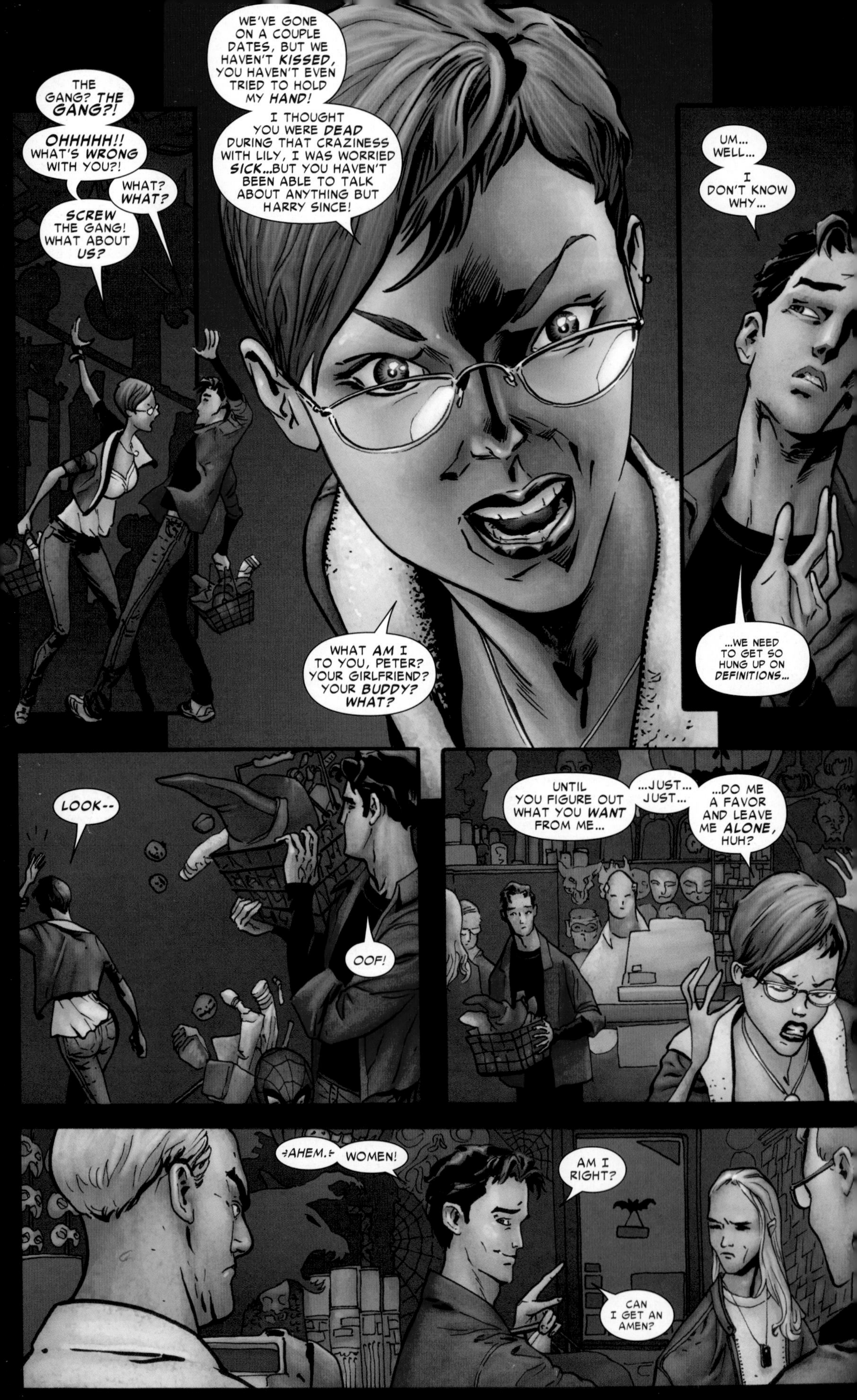
THE GANG? THE GANG?!
OHHHHH!! WHAT'S WRONG WITH YOU?!
WHAT? WHAT?
SCREW THE GANG! WHAT ABOUT US?
WE'VE GONE ON A COUPLE DATES, BUT WE HAVEN'T KISSED, YOU HAVEN'T EVEN TRIED TO HOLD MY HAND!
I THOUGHT YOU WERE DEAD DURING THAT CRAZINESS WITH LILY, I WAS WORRIED SICK...BUT YOU HAVEN'T BEEN ABLE TO TALK ABOUT ANYTHING BUT HARRY SINCE!
WHAT AM I TO YOU, PETER? YOUR GIRLFRIEND? YOUR BUDDY? WHAT?
UM... WELL...
I DON'T KNOW WHY...
...WE NEED TO GET SO HUNG UP ON DEFINITIONS...
LOOK--
OOF!
UNTIL YOU FIGURE OUT WHAT YOU WANT FROM ME...
...JUST... JUST...
...DO ME A FAVOR AND LEAVE ME ALONE, HUH?
AHEM.
WOMEN!
AM I RIGHT?
CAN I GET AN AMEN?

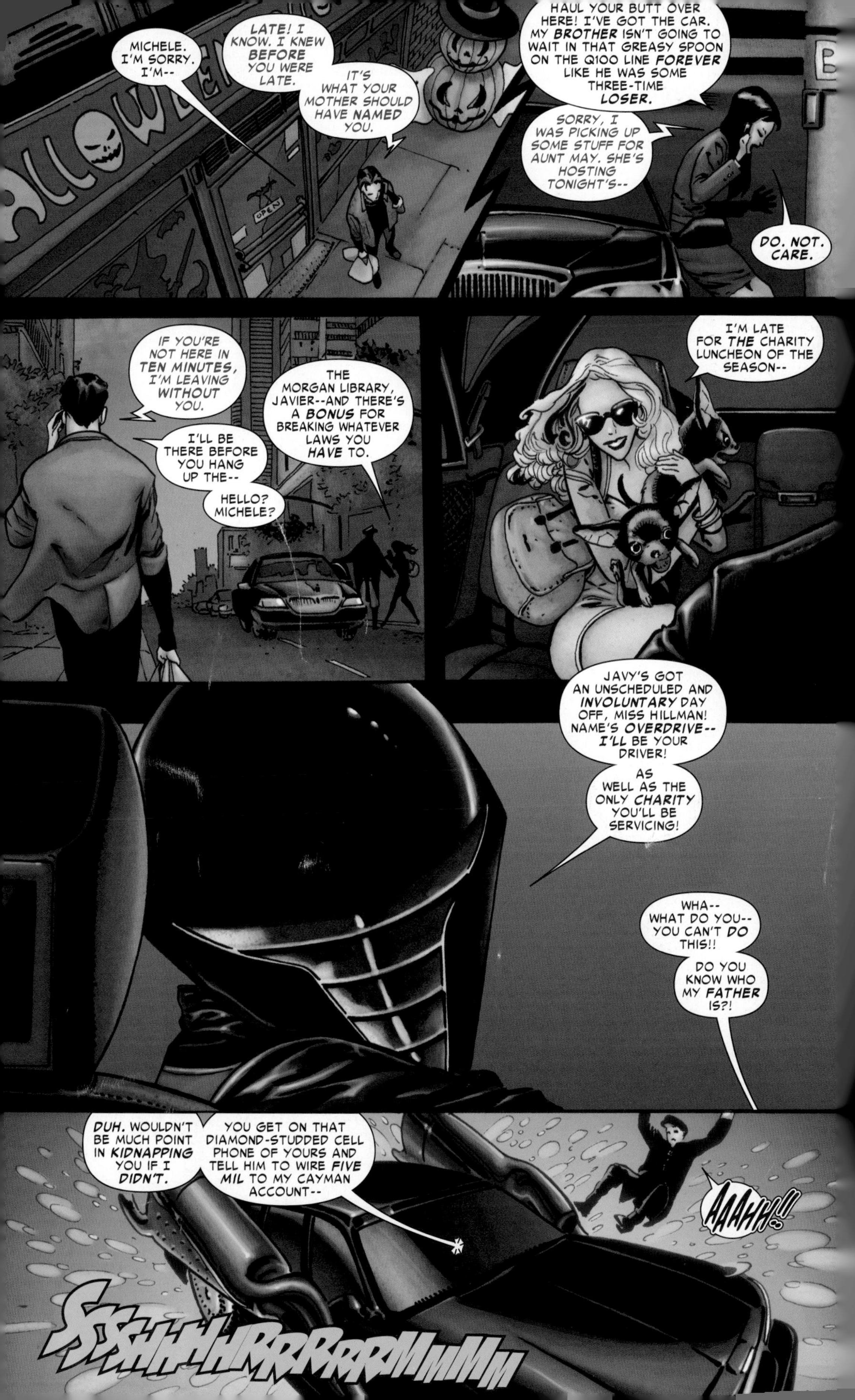
MICHELE. I'M SORRY. I'M--
LATE! I KNOW. I KNEW BEFORE YOU WERE LATE.
IT'S WHAT YOUR MOTHER SHOULD HAVE NAMED YOU.
HAUL YOUR BUTT OVER HERE! I'VE GOT THE CAR. MY BROTHER ISN'T GOING TO WAIT IN THAT GREASY SPOON ON THE Q100 LINE FOREVER LIKE HE WAS SOME THREE-TIME LOSER.
SORRY, I WAS PICKING UP SOME STUFF FOR AUNT MAY. SHE'S HOSTING TONIGHT'S--
DO. NOT. CARE.
OPEN
IF YOU'RE NOT HERE IN TEN MINUTES, I'M LEAVING WITHOUT YOU.
I'LL BE THERE BEFORE YOU HANG UP THE--
HELLO? MICHELE?
THE MORGAN LIBRARY, JAVIER--AND THERE'S A BONUS FOR BREAKING WHATEVER LAWS YOU HAVE TO.
I'M LATE FOR THE CHARITY LUNCHEON OF THE SEASON--
JAVY'S GOT AN UNSCHEDULED AND INVOLUNTARY DAY OFF, MISS HILLMAN! NAME'S OVERDRIVE-- I'LL BE YOUR DRIVER!
AS WELL AS THE ONLY CHARITY YOU'LL BE SERVICING!
WHA-- WHAT DO YOU-- YOU CAN'T DO THIS!!
DO YOU KNOW WHO MY FATHER IS?!
DUH. WOULDN'T BE MUCH POINT IN KIDNAPPING YOU IF I DIDN'T.
YOU GET ON THAT DIAMOND-STUDDED CELL PHONE OF YOURS AND TELL HIM TO WIRE FIVE MIL TO MY CAYMAN ACCOUNT--
AAAHH!!
SSSHHHHRRRRRRRMMMMM

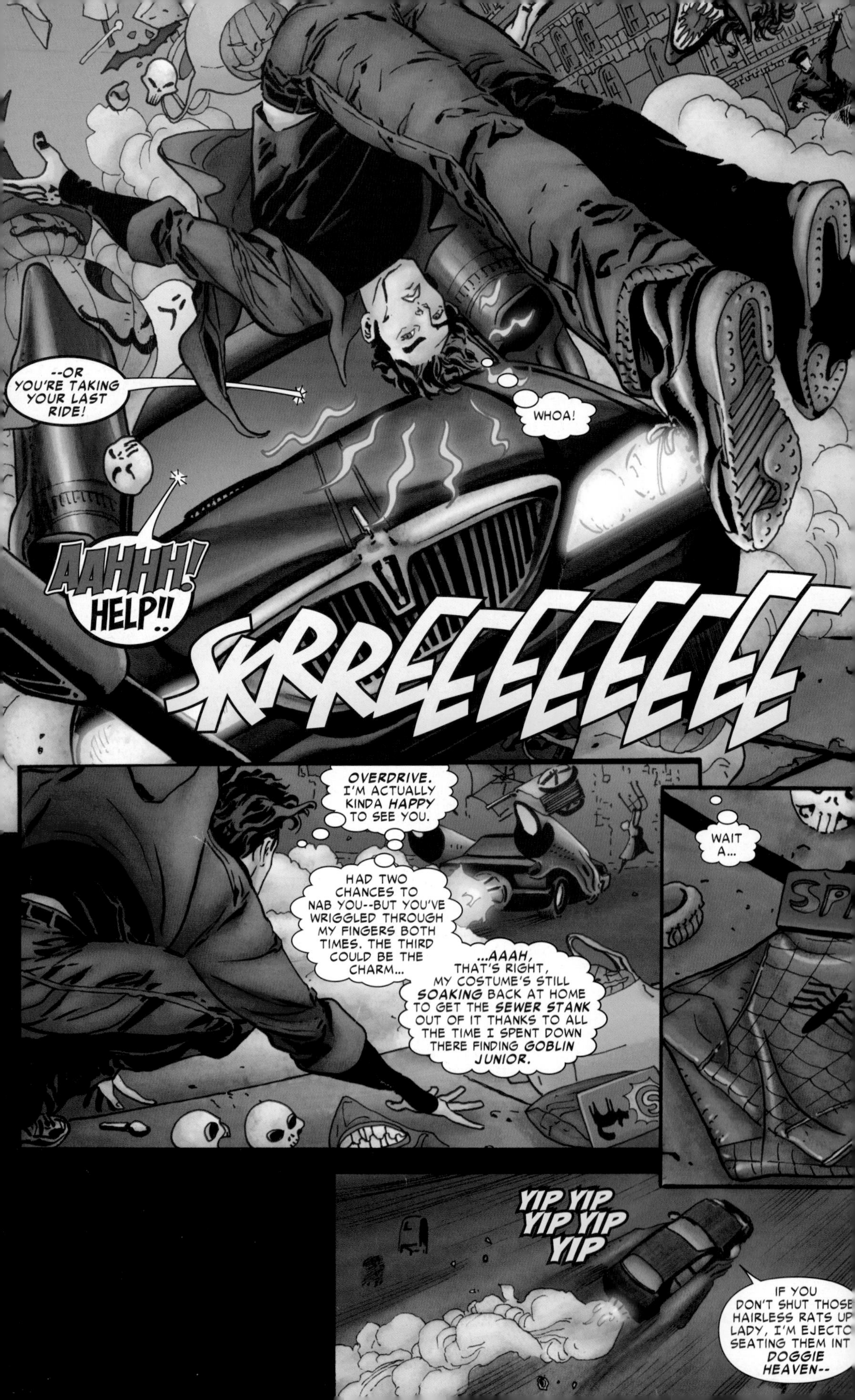
--OR YOU'RE TAKING YOUR LAST RIDE!
WHOA!
AAHHH! HELP!!
SKRREEEEEEEEE
OVERDRIVE. I'M ACTUALLY KINDA HAPPY TO SEE YOU.
HAD TWO CHANCES TO NAB YOU--BUT YOU'VE WRIGGLED THROUGH MY FINGERS BOTH TIMES. THE THIRD COULD BE THE CHARM...
...AAAH, THAT'S RIGHT, MY COSTUME'S STILL SOAKING BACK AT HOME TO GET THE SEWER STANK OUT OF IT THANKS TO ALL THE TIME I SPENT DOWN THERE FINDING GOBLIN JUNIOR.
WAIT A...
YIP YIP YIP YIP YIP
IF YOU DON'T SHUT THOSE HAIRLESS RATS UP LADY, I'M EJECTO SEATING THEM INT DOGGIE HEAVEN--

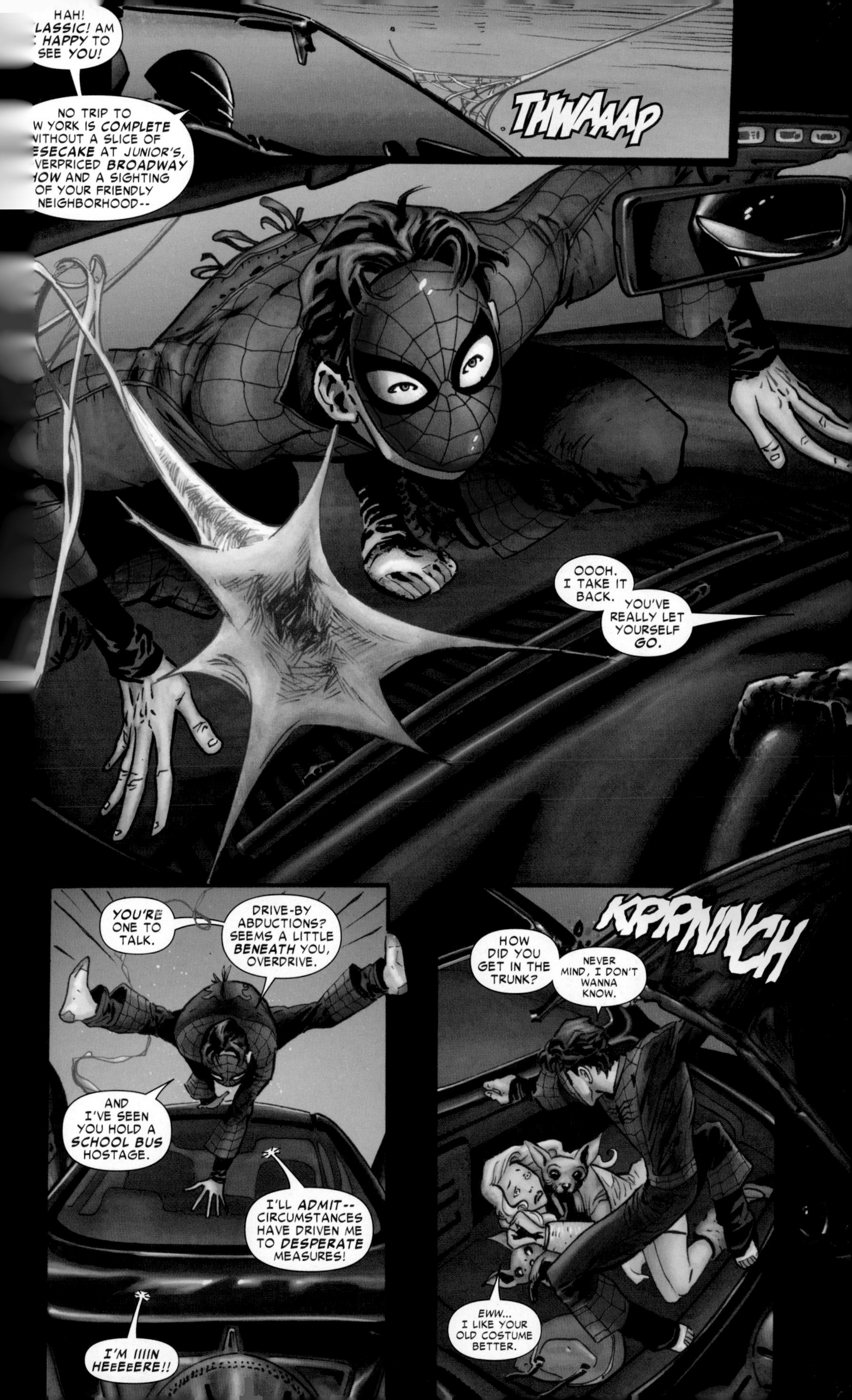
HAH!
LASSIC! AM
: HAPPY TO
SEE YOU!
NO TRIP TO
W YORK IS COMPLETE
WITHOUT A SLICE OF
ESECAKE AT JUNIOR'S,
VERPRICED BROADWAY
HOW AND A SIGHTING
OF YOUR FRIENDLY
NEIGHBORHOOD--
THWAAAP
OOOH. I TAKE IT BACK.
YOU'VE REALLY LET YOURSELF GO.
DRIVE-BY ABDUCTIONS? SEEMS A LITTLE BENEATH YOU, OVERDRIVE.
YOU'RE ONE TO TALK.
AND I'VE SEEN YOU HOLD A SCHOOL BUS HOSTAGE.
I'LL ADMIT-- CIRCUMSTANCES HAVE DRIVEN ME TO DESPERATE MEASURES!
I'M IIIIN HEEEEERE!!
KRRNNCH
HOW DID YOU GET IN THE TRUNK?
NEVER MIND, I DON'T WANNA KNOW.
EWW... I LIKE YOUR OLD COSTUME BETTER.

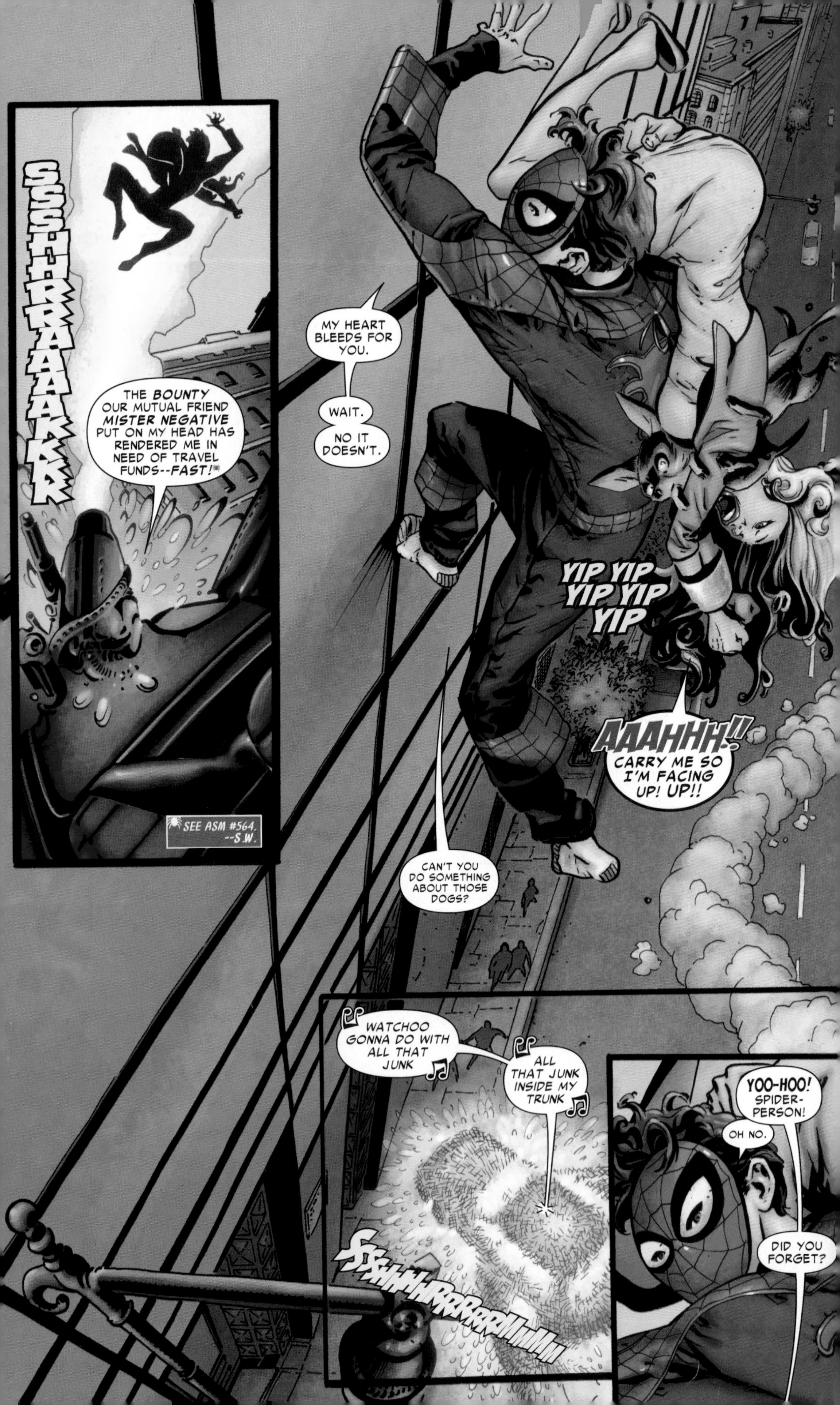

SSSHHRRAAAAKKK
THE BOUNTY OUR MUTUAL FRIEND MISTER NEGATIVE PUT ON MY HEAD HAS RENDERED ME IN NEED OF TRAVEL FUNDS--FAST!
SEE ASM #564. --S.W.
MY HEART BLEEDS FOR YOU.
WAIT.
NO IT DOESN'T.
YIP YIP YIP YIP YIP
AAAHHH!! CARRY ME SO I'M FACING UP! UP!!
CAN'T YOU DO SOMETHING ABOUT THOSE DOGS?
WATCHOO GONNA DO WITH ALL THAT JUNK
ALL THAT JUNK INSIDE MY TRUNK
SSSHHHRRRRMMMM
YOO-HOO! SPIDER-PERSON!
OH NO.
DID YOU FORGET?

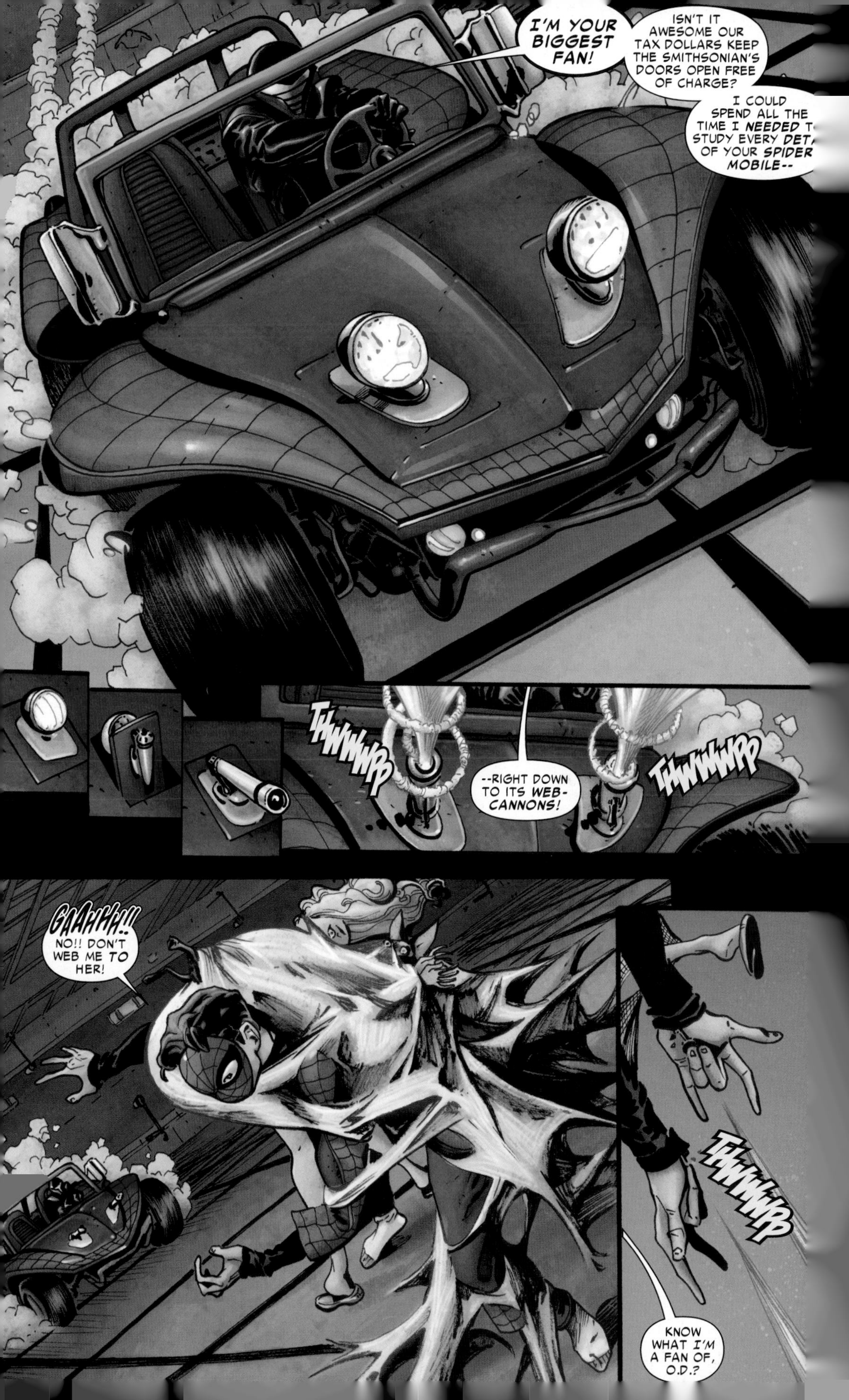

I'M YOUR BIGGEST FAN!
ISN'T IT AWESOME OUR TAX DOLLARS KEEP THE SMITHSONIAN'S DOORS OPEN FREE OF CHARGE?
I COULD SPEND ALL THE TIME I NEEDED TO STUDY EVERY DETAIL OF YOUR SPIDER MOBILE--
THWWWPP
--RIGHT DOWN TO ITS WEB-CANNONS!
THWWWPP
GAAHHH!! NO!! DON'T WEB ME TO HER!
THWWWPP
KNOW WHAT I'M A FAN OF, O.D.?

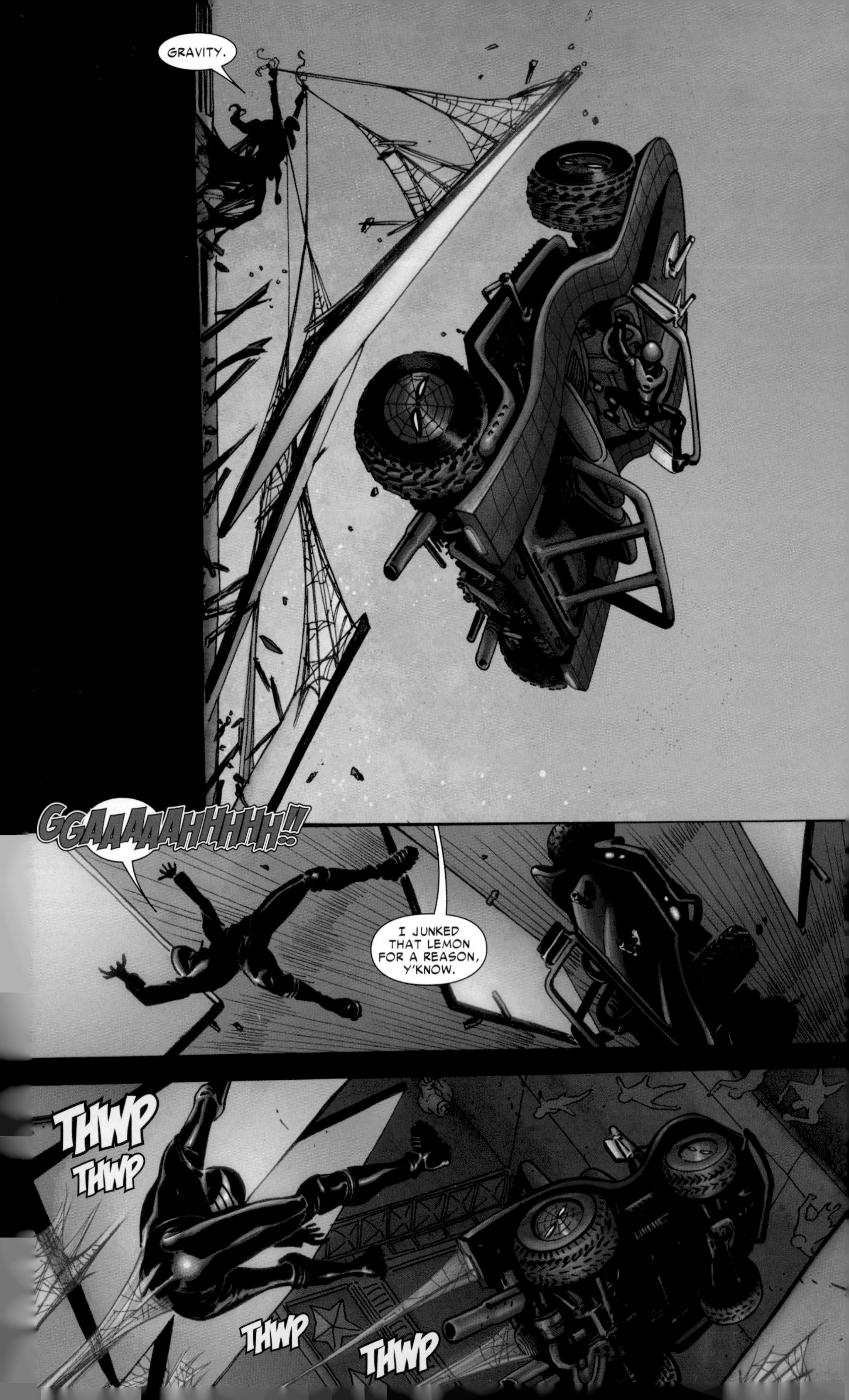
GRAVITY.
GGAAAAAHHHHH!!
I JUNKED THAT LEMON FOR A REASON, Y'KNOW.
THWP
THWP
THWP
THWP

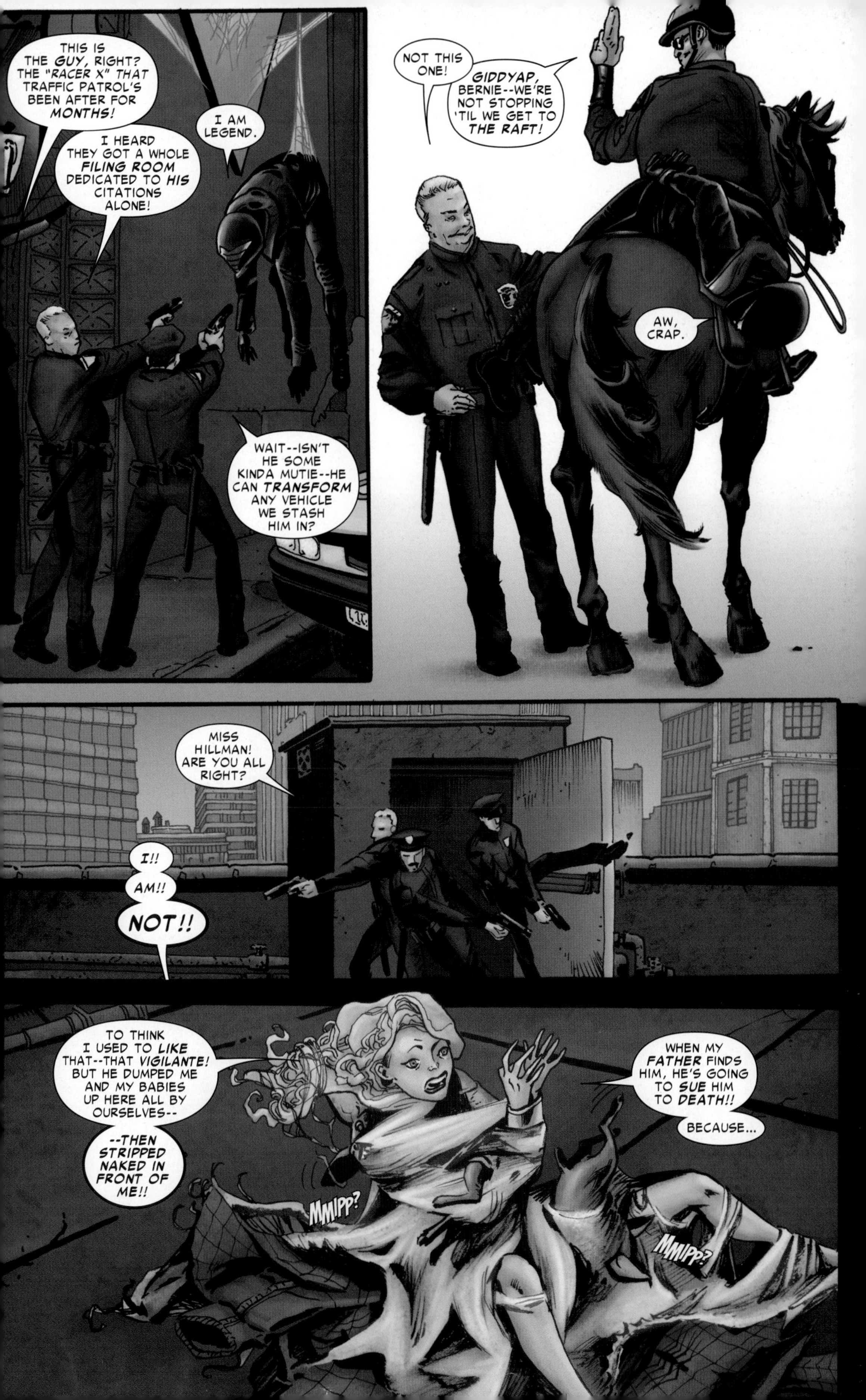

THIS IS THE *GUY*, RIGHT? THE "*RACER X*" *THAT* TRAFFIC PATROL'S BEEN AFTER FOR *MONTHS!*
I HEARD THEY GOT A WHOLE *FILING ROOM* DEDICATED TO *HIS* CITATIONS ALONE!
I AM LEGEND.
WAIT--ISN'T HE SOME KINDA MUTIE--HE CAN *TRANSFORM* ANY VEHICLE WE STASH HIM IN?
NOT THIS ONE!
GIDDYAP, BERNIE--WE'RE NOT STOPPING 'TIL WE GET TO *THE RAFT!*
AW, CRAP.
MISS HILLMAN! ARE YOU ALL RIGHT?
I!!
AM!!
NOT!!
TO THINK I USED TO *LIKE* THAT--THAT *VIGILANTE!* BUT HE DUMPED ME AND MY BABIES UP HERE ALL BY OURSELVES--
--THEN STRIPPED NAKED IN FRONT OF ME!!
MMIPP?
MMIPP?
WHEN MY *FATHER* FINDS HIM, HE'S GOING TO *SUE* HIM TO *DEATH!!*
BECAUSE...

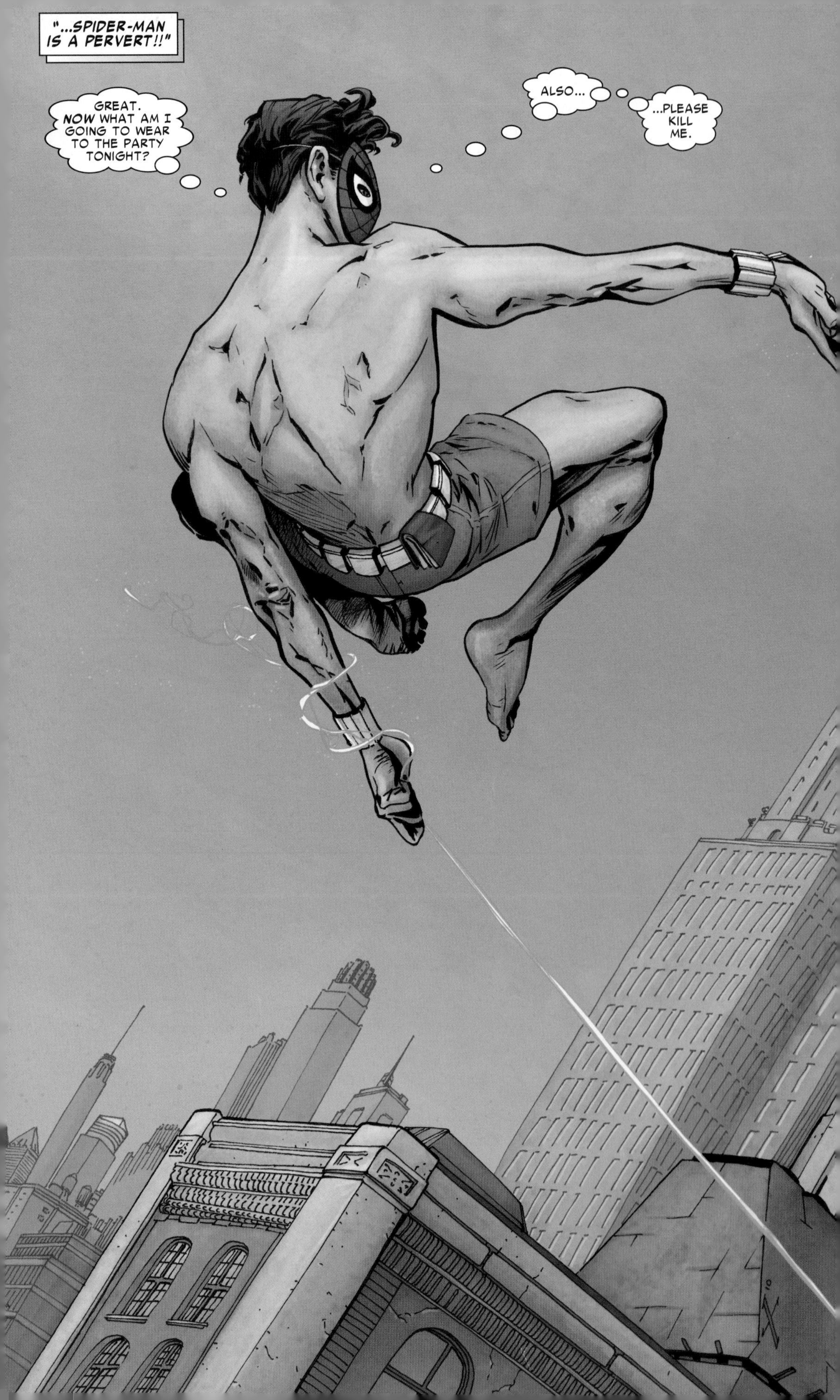
"...SPIDER-MAN IS A PERVERT!!"
GREAT. NOW WHAT AM I GOING TO WEAR TO THE PARTY TONIGHT?
ALSO...
...PLEASE KILL ME.

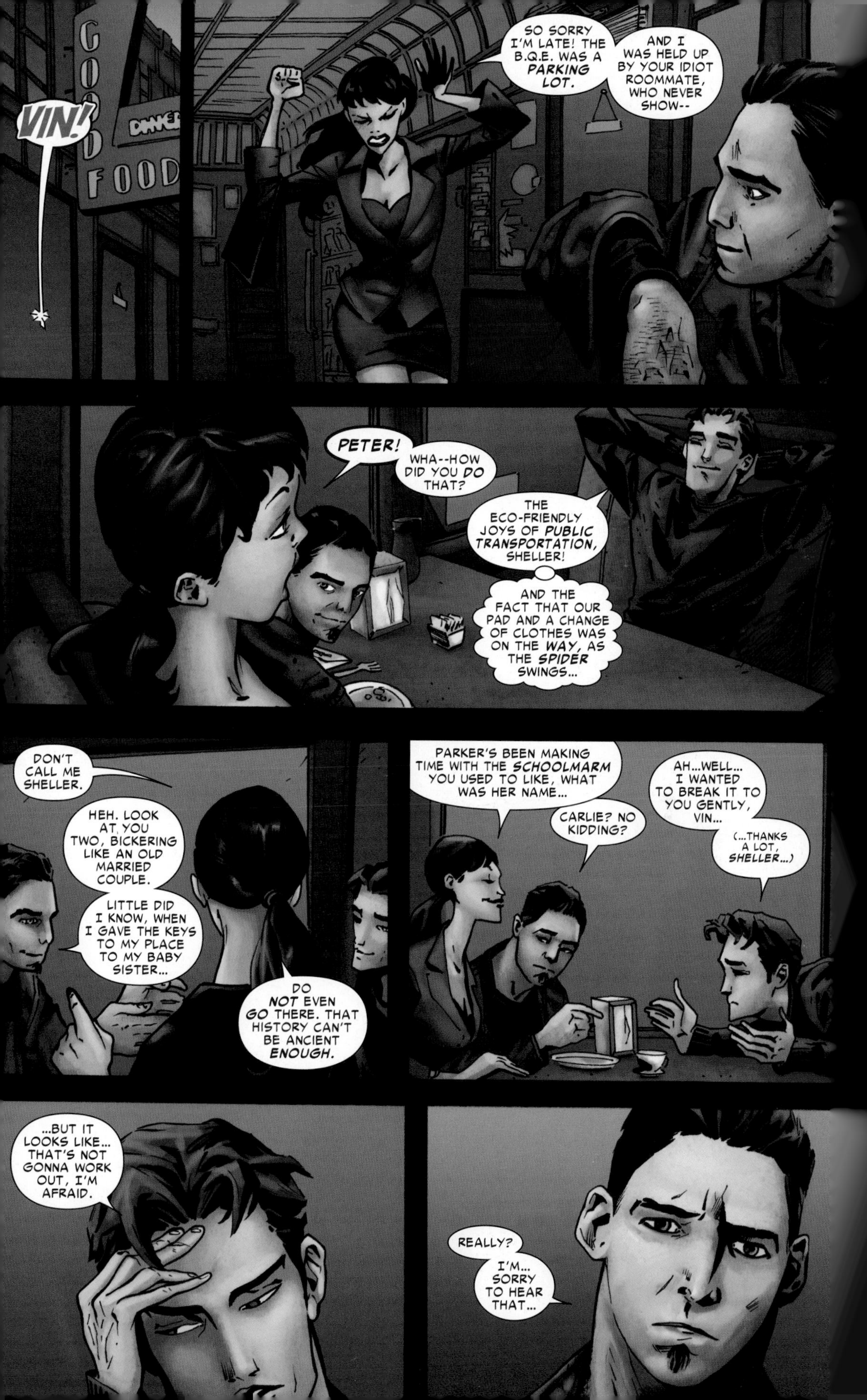

VIN!
GOOD FOOD
DINER
SO SORRY I'M LATE! THE B.Q.E. WAS A PARKING LOT.
AND I WAS HELD UP BY YOUR IDIOT ROOMMATE, WHO NEVER SHOW--
PETER!
WHA--HOW DID YOU DO THAT?
THE ECO-FRIENDLY JOYS OF PUBLIC TRANSPORTATION, SHELLER!
AND THE FACT THAT OUR PAD AND A CHANGE OF CLOTHES WAS ON THE WAY, AS THE SPIDER SWINGS...
DON'T CALL ME SHELLER.
HEH. LOOK AT YOU TWO, BICKERING LIKE AN OLD MARRIED COUPLE.
LITTLE DID I KNOW, WHEN I GAVE THE KEYS TO MY PLACE TO MY BABY SISTER...
DO NOT EVEN GO THERE. THAT HISTORY CAN'T BE ANCIENT ENOUGH.
PARKER'S BEEN MAKING TIME WITH THE SCHOOLMARM YOU USED TO LIKE, WHAT WAS HER NAME...
CARLIE? NO KIDDING?
AH...WELL... I WANTED TO BREAK IT TO YOU GENTLY, VIN...
(...THANKS A LOT, SHELLER...)
...BUT IT LOOKS LIKE... THAT'S NOT GONNA WORK OUT, I'M AFRAID.
REALLY?
I'M... SORRY TO HEAR THAT...

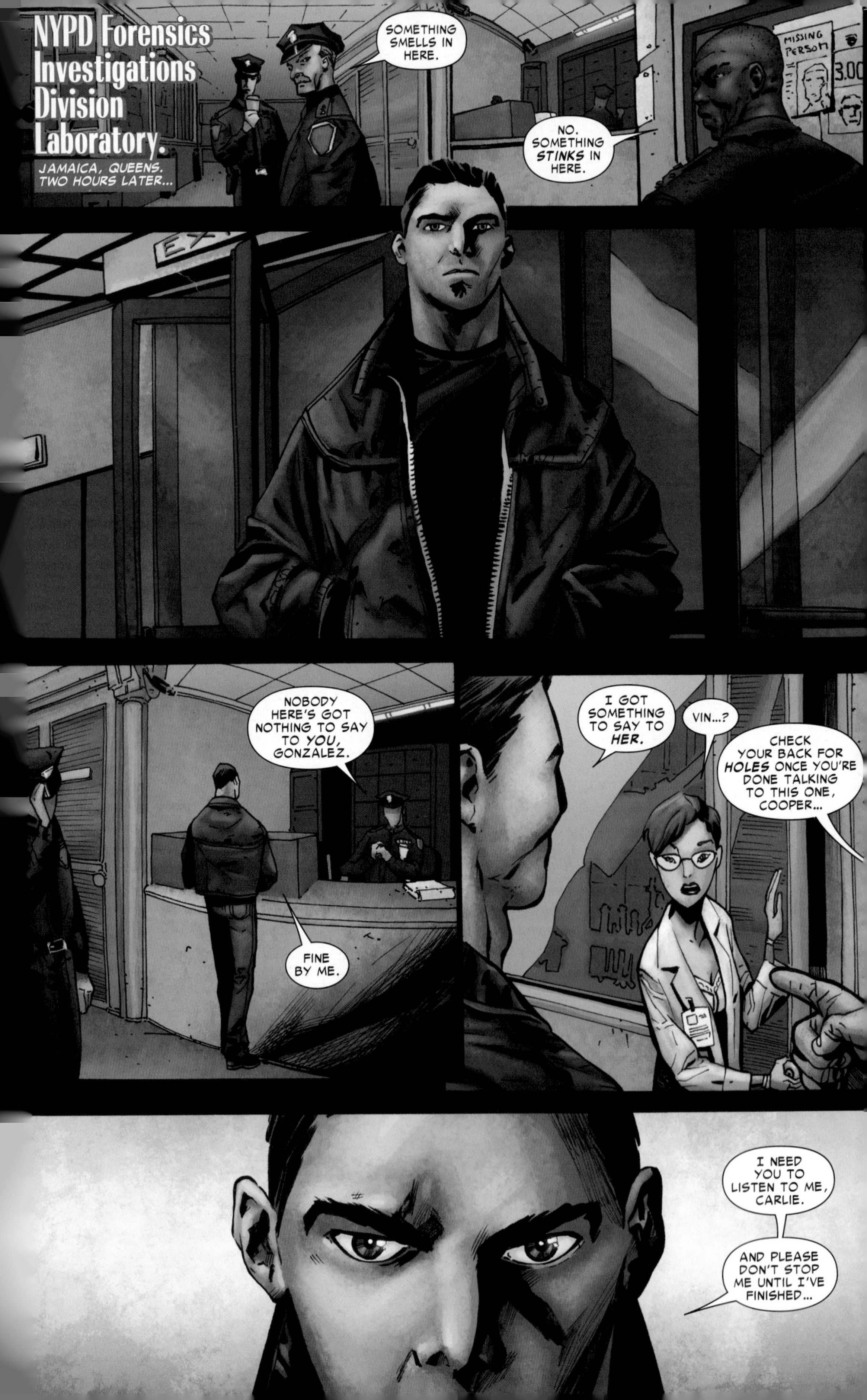
NYPD Forensics Investigations Division Laboratory.
JAMAICA, QUEENS. TWO HOURS LATER...
SOMETHING SMELLS IN HERE.
NO. SOMETHING STINKS IN HERE.
MISSING PERSON
NOBODY HERE'S GOT NOTHING TO SAY TO YOU, GONZALEZ.
FINE BY ME.
I GOT SOMETHING TO SAY TO HER.
VIN...?
CHECK YOUR BACK FOR HOLES ONCE YOU'RE DONE TALKING TO THIS ONE, COOPER...
I NEED YOU TO LISTEN TO ME, CARLIE.
AND PLEASE DON'T STOP ME UNTIL I'VE FINISHED...

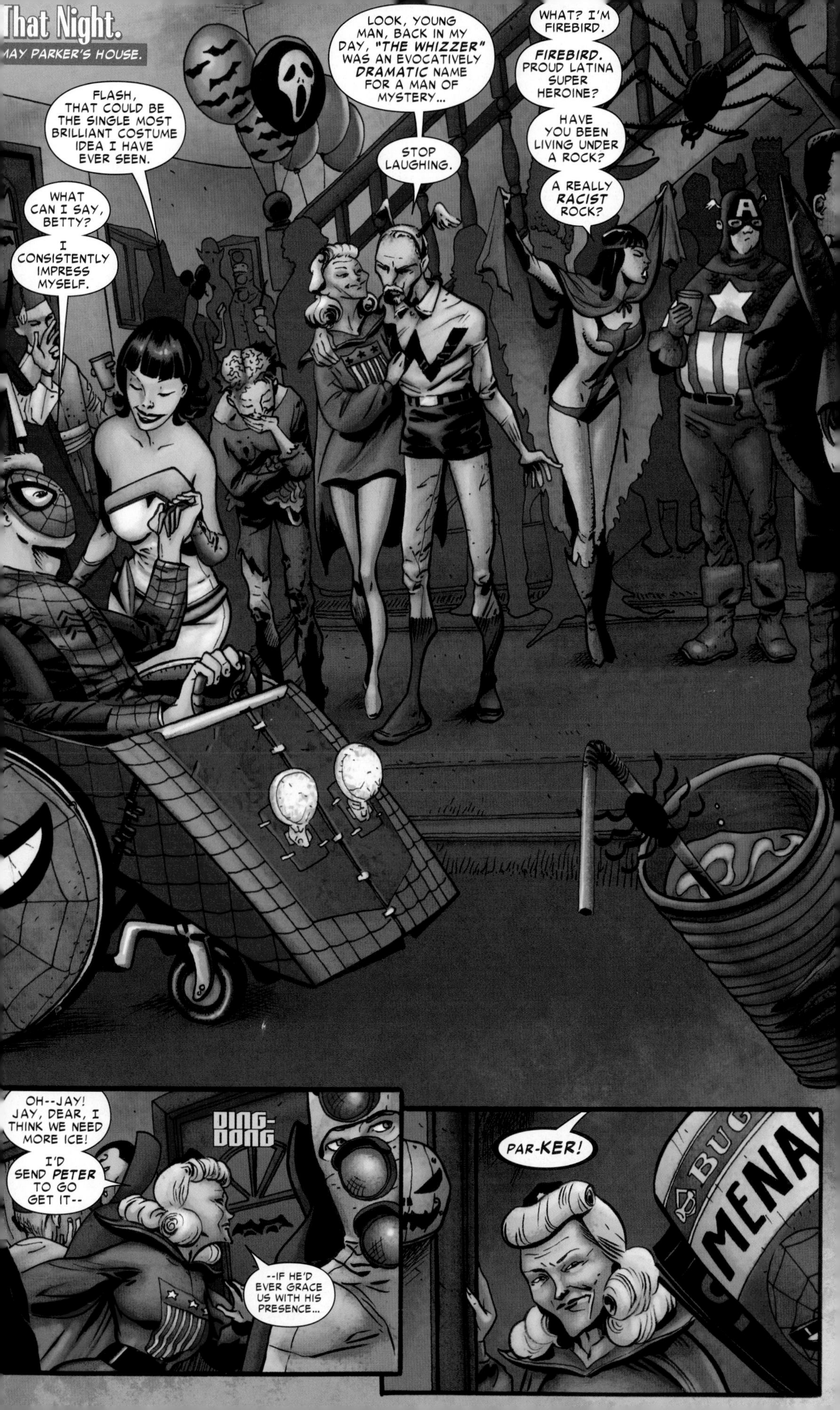

That Night.
MAY PARKER'S HOUSE.
FLASH, THAT COULD BE THE SINGLE MOST BRILLIANT COSTUME IDEA I HAVE EVER SEEN.
WHAT CAN I SAY, BETTY?
I CONSISTENTLY IMPRESS MYSELF.
LOOK, YOUNG MAN, BACK IN MY DAY, "THE WHIZZER" WAS AN EVOCATIVELY DRAMATIC NAME FOR A MAN OF MYSTERY...
STOP LAUGHING.
WHAT? I'M FIREBIRD.
FIREBIRD. PROUD LATINA SUPER HEROINE?
HAVE YOU BEEN LIVING UNDER A ROCK?
A REALLY RACIST ROCK?
OH--JAY! JAY, DEAR, I THINK WE NEED MORE ICE!
I'D SEND PETER TO GO GET IT--
DING-DONG
--IF HE'D EVER GRACE US WITH HIS PRESENCE...
PAR-KER!

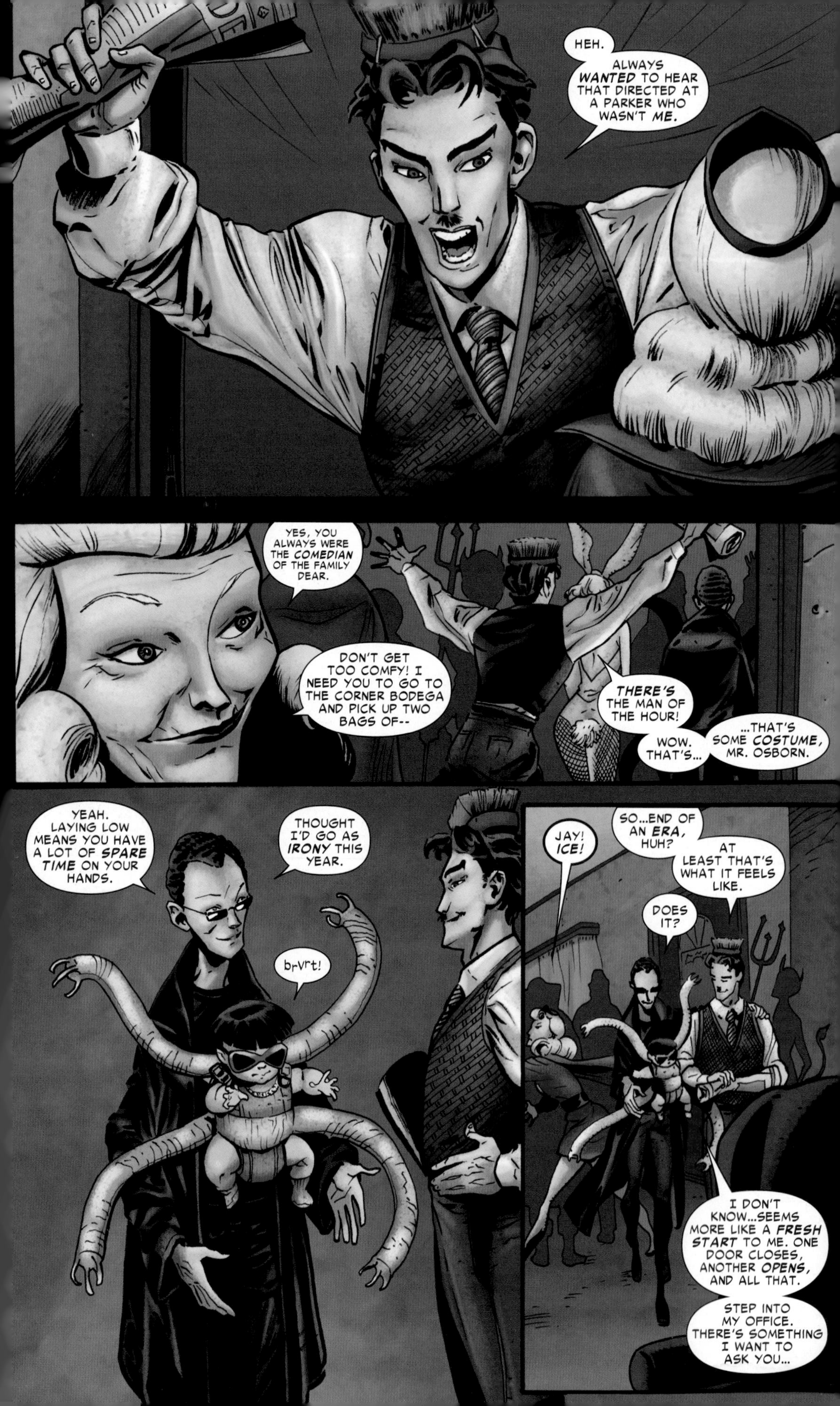
HEH.
ALWAYS WANTED TO HEAR THAT DIRECTED AT A PARKER WHO WASN'T ME.
YES, YOU ALWAYS WERE THE COMEDIAN OF THE FAMILY DEAR.
DON'T GET TOO COMFY! I NEED YOU TO GO TO THE CORNER BODEGA AND PICK UP TWO BAGS OF--
THERE'S THE MAN OF THE HOUR!
WOW. THAT'S...
...THAT'S SOME COSTUME, MR. OSBORN.
THOUGHT I'D GO AS IRONY THIS YEAR.
YEAH. LAYING LOW MEANS YOU HAVE A LOT OF SPARE TIME ON YOUR HANDS.
brvrt!
JAY! ICE!
SO...END OF AN ERA, HUH?
AT LEAST THAT'S WHAT IT FEELS LIKE.
DOES IT?
I DON'T KNOW...SEEMS MORE LIKE A FRESH START TO ME. ONE DOOR CLOSES, ANOTHER OPENS, AND ALL THAT.
STEP INTO MY OFFICE. THERE'S SOMETHING I WANT TO ASK YOU...

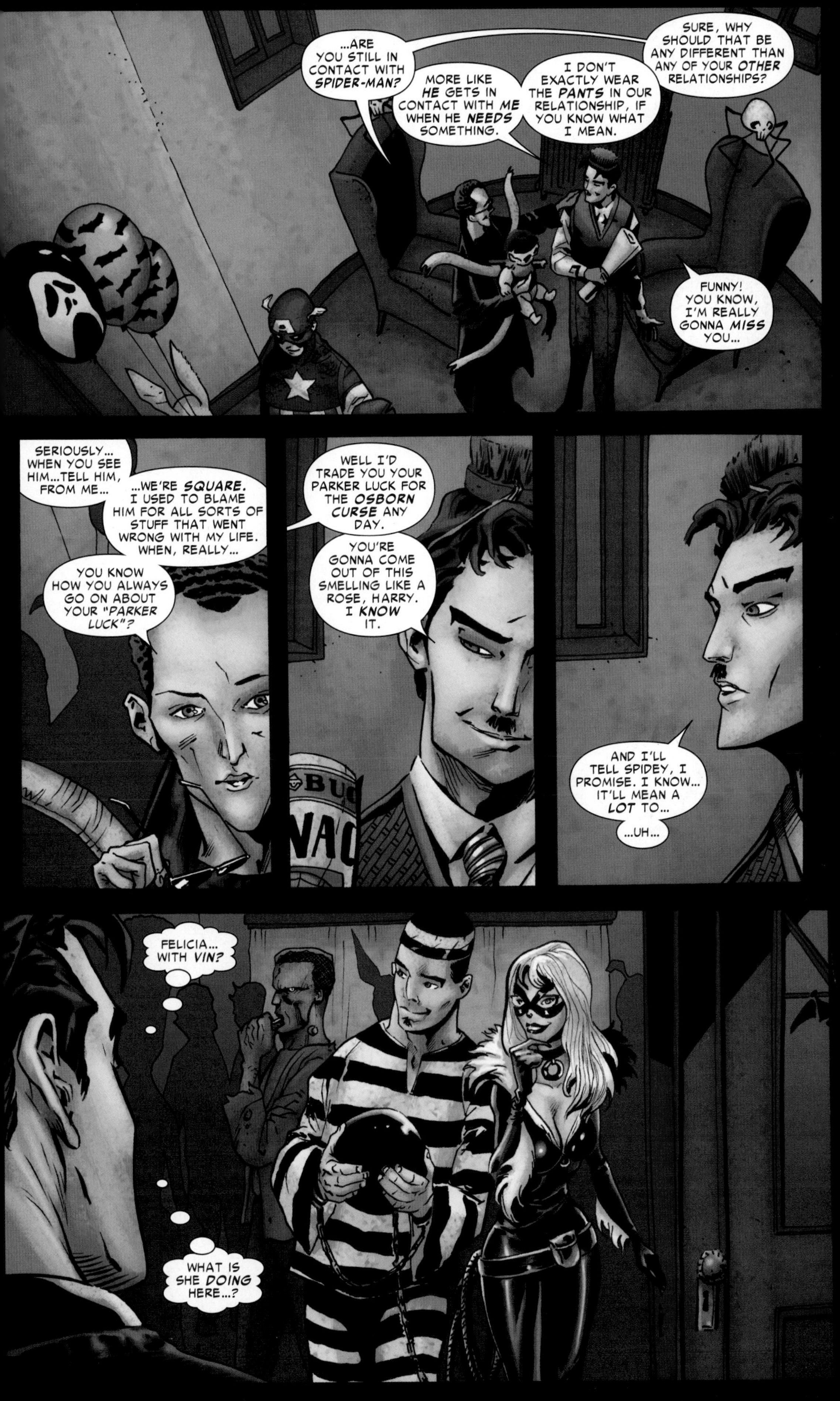
...ARE YOU STILL IN CONTACT WITH SPIDER-MAN?
MORE LIKE HE GETS IN CONTACT WITH ME WHEN HE NEEDS SOMETHING.
I DON'T EXACTLY WEAR THE PANTS IN OUR RELATIONSHIP, IF YOU KNOW WHAT I MEAN.
SURE, WHY SHOULD THAT BE ANY DIFFERENT THAN ANY OF YOUR OTHER RELATIONSHIPS?
FUNNY! YOU KNOW, I'M REALLY GONNA MISS YOU...
SERIOUSLY... WHEN YOU SEE HIM...TELL HIM, FROM ME...
...WE'RE SQUARE. I USED TO BLAME HIM FOR ALL SORTS OF STUFF THAT WENT WRONG WITH MY LIFE. WHEN, REALLY...
YOU KNOW HOW YOU ALWAYS GO ON ABOUT YOUR "PARKER LUCK"?
WELL I'D TRADE YOU YOUR PARKER LUCK FOR THE OSBORN CURSE ANY DAY.
YOU'RE GONNA COME OUT OF THIS SMELLING LIKE A ROSE, HARRY. I KNOW IT.
AND I'LL TELL SPIDEY, I PROMISE. I KNOW... IT'LL MEAN A LOT TO...
...UH...
FELICIA... WITH VIN?
WHAT IS SHE DOING HERE...?

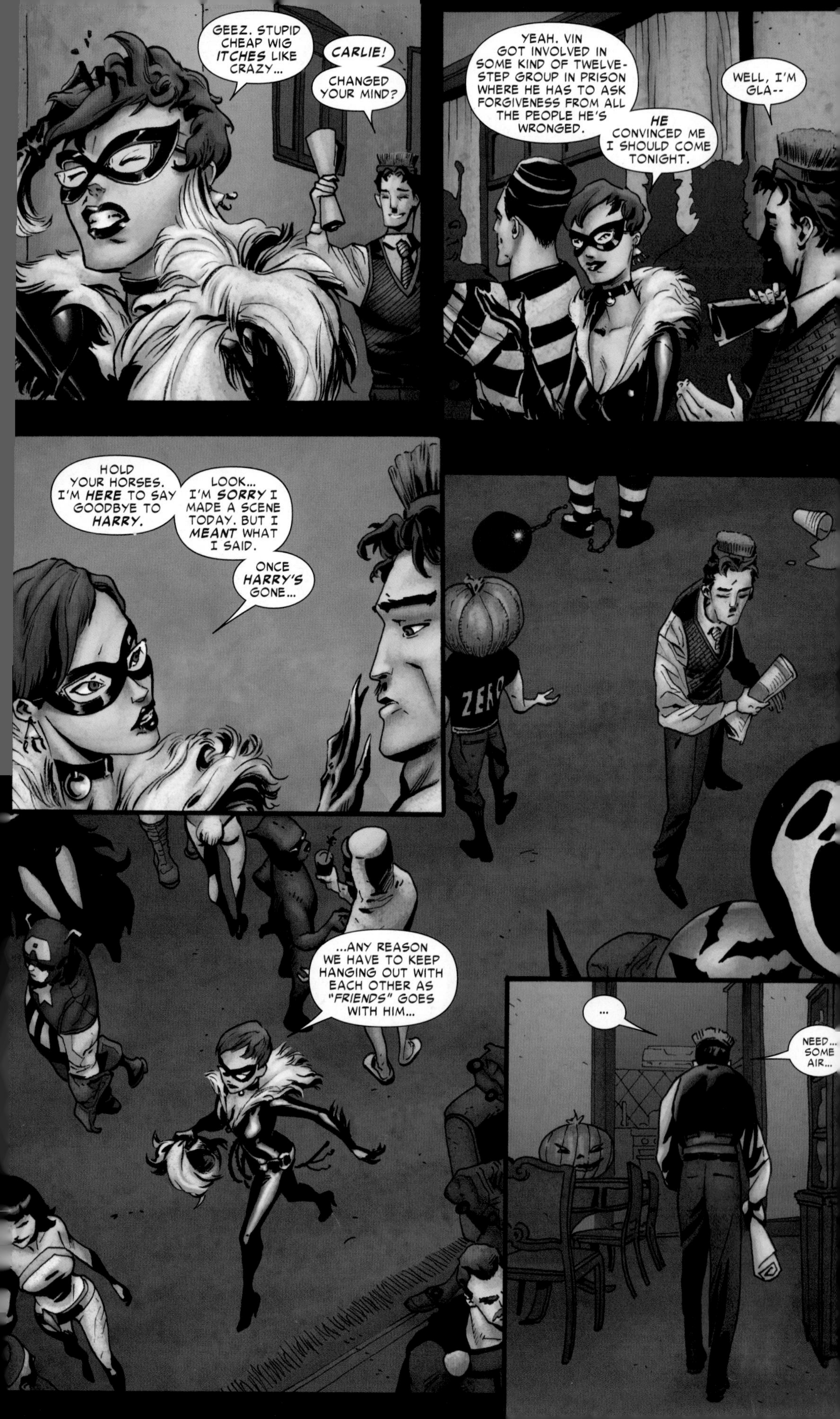
GEEZ. STUPID CHEAP WIG ITCHES LIKE CRAZY...
CARLIE!
CHANGED YOUR MIND?
YEAH. VIN GOT INVOLVED IN SOME KIND OF TWELVE-STEP GROUP IN PRISON WHERE HE HAS TO ASK FORGIVENESS FROM ALL THE PEOPLE HE'S WRONGED.
HE CONVINCED ME I SHOULD COME TONIGHT.
WELL, I'M GLA--
HOLD YOUR HORSES. I'M HERE TO SAY GOODBYE TO HARRY.
LOOK... I'M SORRY I MADE A SCENE TODAY. BUT I MEANT WHAT I SAID.
ONCE HARRY'S GONE...
...ANY REASON WE HAVE TO KEEP HANGING OUT WITH EACH OTHER AS "FRIENDS" GOES WITH HIM...
...
NEED... SOME AIR...
ZERO

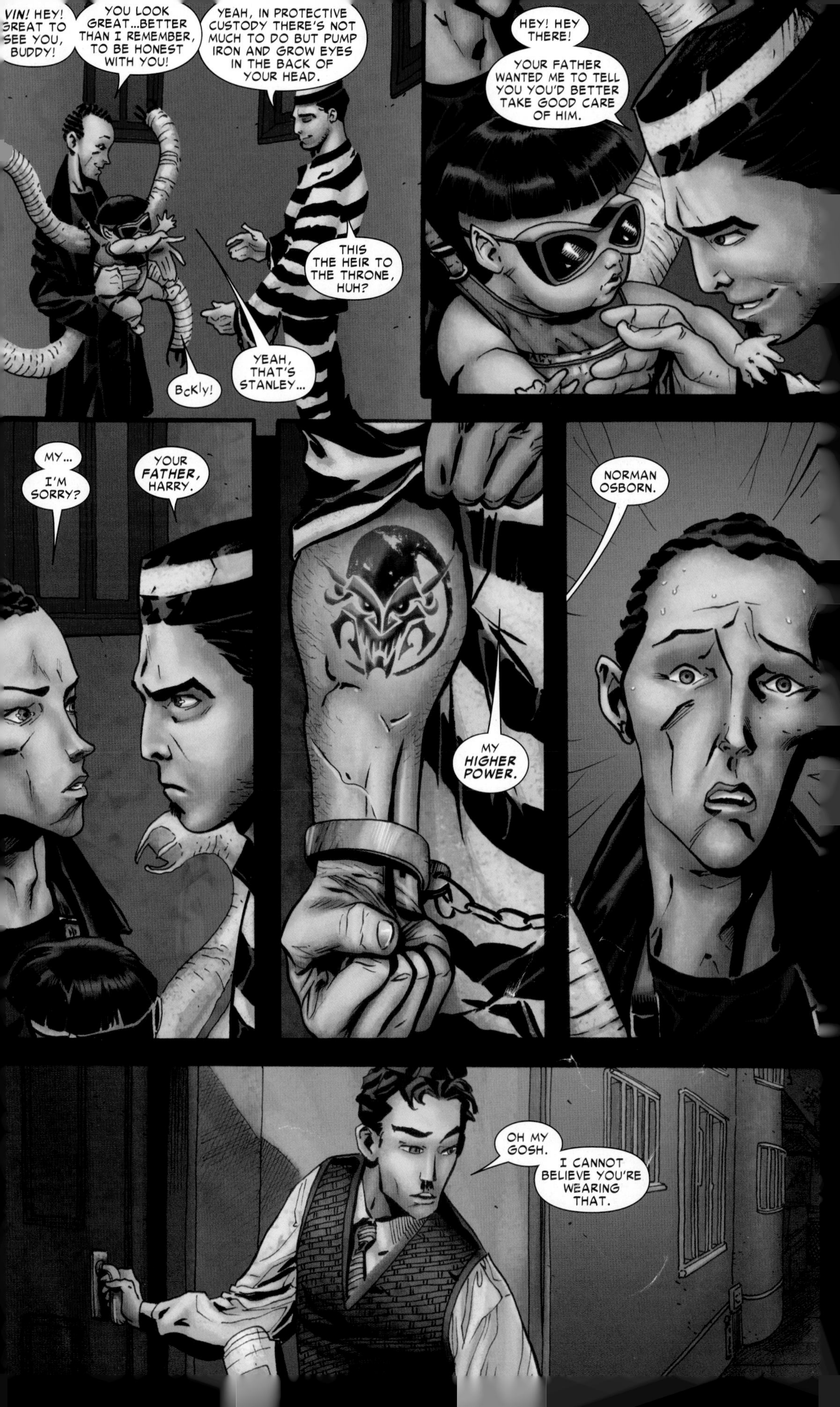

VIN! HEY! GREAT TO SEE YOU, BUDDY!
YOU LOOK GREAT...BETTER THAN I REMEMBER, TO BE HONEST WITH YOU!
YEAH, IN PROTECTIVE CUSTODY THERE'S NOT MUCH TO DO BUT PUMP IRON AND GROW EYES IN THE BACK OF YOUR HEAD.
THIS THE HEIR TO THE THRONE, HUH?
YEAH, THAT'S STANLEY...
BcKly!
HEY! HEY THERE!
YOUR FATHER WANTED ME TO TELL YOU YOU'D BETTER TAKE GOOD CARE OF HIM.
MY... I'M SORRY?
YOUR FATHER, HARRY.
MY HIGHER POWER.
NORMAN OSBORN.
OH MY GOSH.
I CANNOT BELIEVE YOU'RE WEARING THAT.

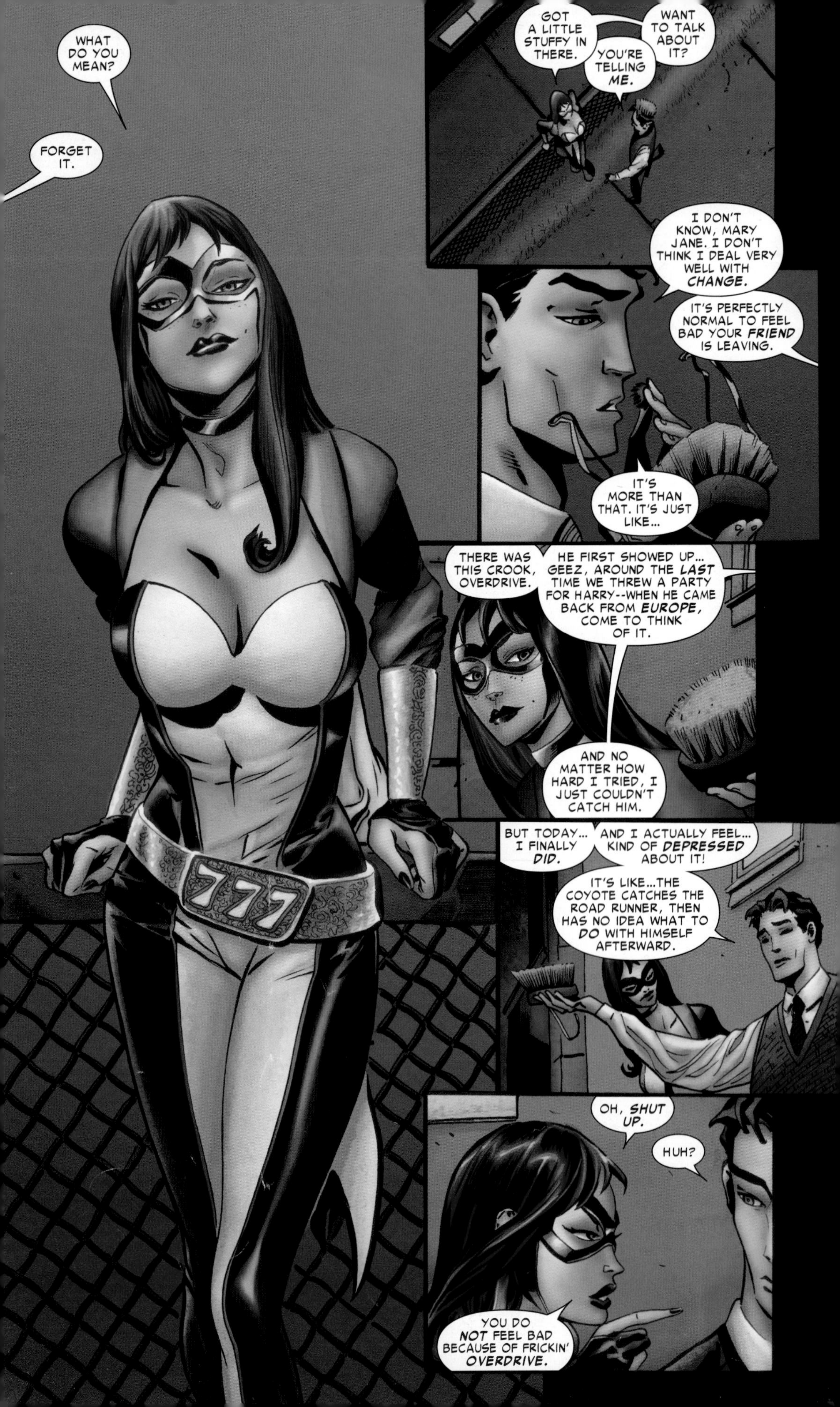
WHAT DO YOU MEAN?
FORGET IT.
GOT A LITTLE STUFFY IN THERE.
WANT TO TALK ABOUT IT?
YOU'RE TELLING ME.
I DON'T KNOW, MARY JANE. I DON'T THINK I DEAL VERY WELL WITH CHANGE.
IT'S PERFECTLY NORMAL TO FEEL BAD YOUR FRIEND IS LEAVING.
IT'S MORE THAN THAT. IT'S JUST LIKE...
THERE WAS THIS CROOK, OVERDRIVE.
HE FIRST SHOWED UP... GEEZ, AROUND THE LAST TIME WE THREW A PARTY FOR HARRY--WHEN HE CAME BACK FROM EUROPE, COME TO THINK OF IT.
AND NO MATTER HOW HARD I TRIED, I JUST COULDN'T CATCH HIM.
BUT TODAY... I FINALLY DID.
AND I ACTUALLY FEEL... KIND OF DEPRESSED ABOUT IT!
IT'S LIKE...THE COYOTE CATCHES THE ROAD RUNNER, THEN HAS NO IDEA WHAT TO DO WITH HIMSELF AFTERWARD.
OH, SHUT UP.
HUH?
YOU DO NOT FEEL BAD BECAUSE OF FRICKIN' OVERDRIVE.

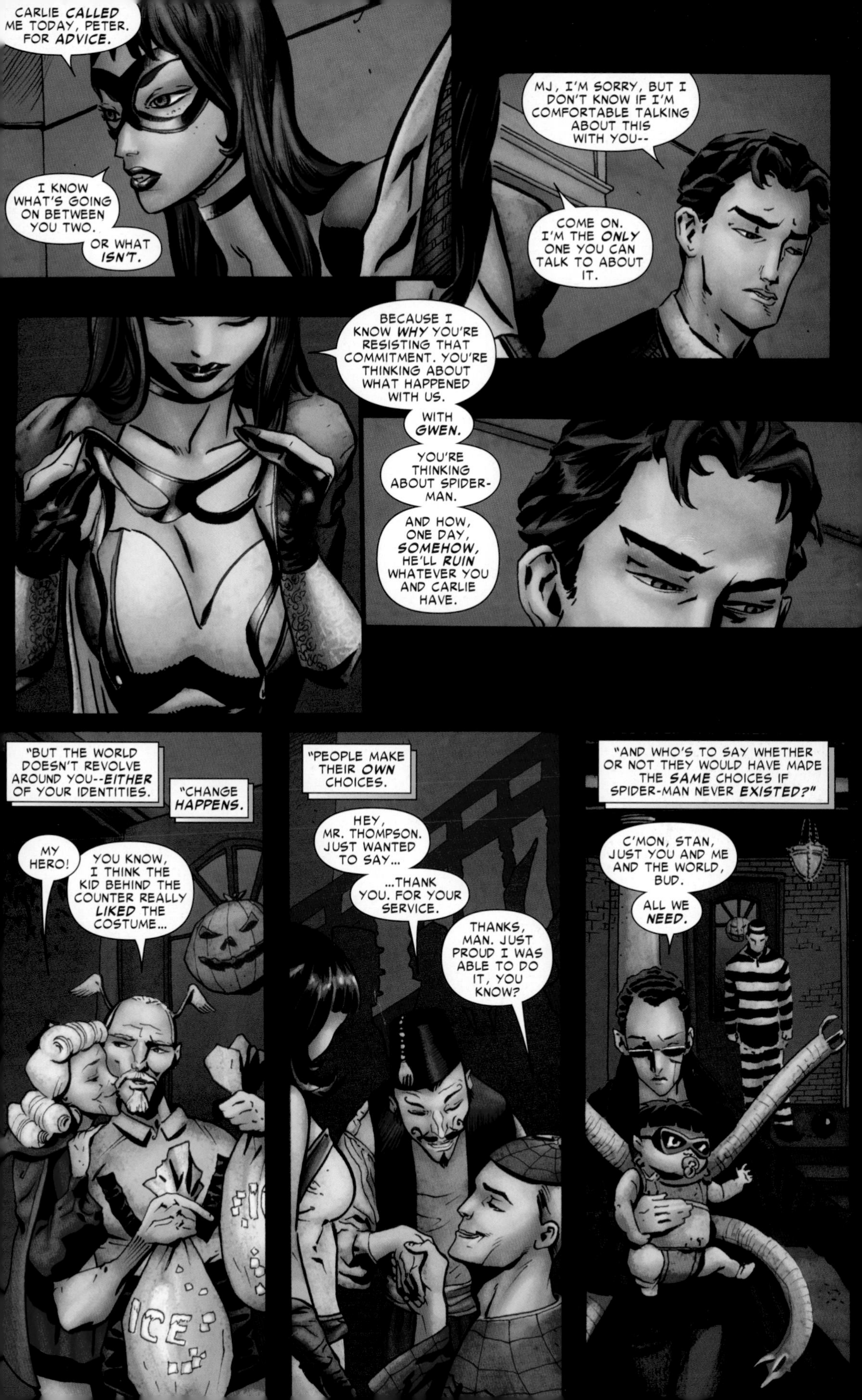
CARLIE CALLED ME TODAY, PETER. FOR ADVICE.
I KNOW WHAT'S GOING ON BETWEEN YOU TWO.
OR WHAT ISN'T.
MJ, I'M SORRY, BUT I DON'T KNOW IF I'M COMFORTABLE TALKING ABOUT THIS WITH YOU--
COME ON. I'M THE ONLY ONE YOU CAN TALK TO ABOUT IT.
BECAUSE I KNOW WHY YOU'RE RESISTING THAT COMMITMENT. YOU'RE THINKING ABOUT WHAT HAPPENED WITH US.
WITH GWEN.
YOU'RE THINKING ABOUT SPIDER-MAN.
AND HOW, ONE DAY, SOMEHOW, HE'LL RUIN WHATEVER YOU AND CARLIE HAVE.
"BUT THE WORLD DOESN'T REVOLVE AROUND YOU--EITHER OF YOUR IDENTITIES.
"CHANGE HAPPENS.
MY HERO!
YOU KNOW, I THINK THE KID BEHIND THE COUNTER REALLY LIKED THE COSTUME...
ICE
"PEOPLE MAKE THEIR OWN CHOICES.
HEY, MR. THOMPSON. JUST WANTED TO SAY...
...THANK YOU. FOR YOUR SERVICE.
THANKS, MAN. JUST PROUD I WAS ABLE TO DO IT, YOU KNOW?
"AND WHO'S TO SAY WHETHER OR NOT THEY WOULD HAVE MADE THE SAME CHOICES IF SPIDER-MAN NEVER EXISTED?"
C'MON, STAN, JUST YOU AND ME AND THE WORLD, BUD.
ALL WE NEED.

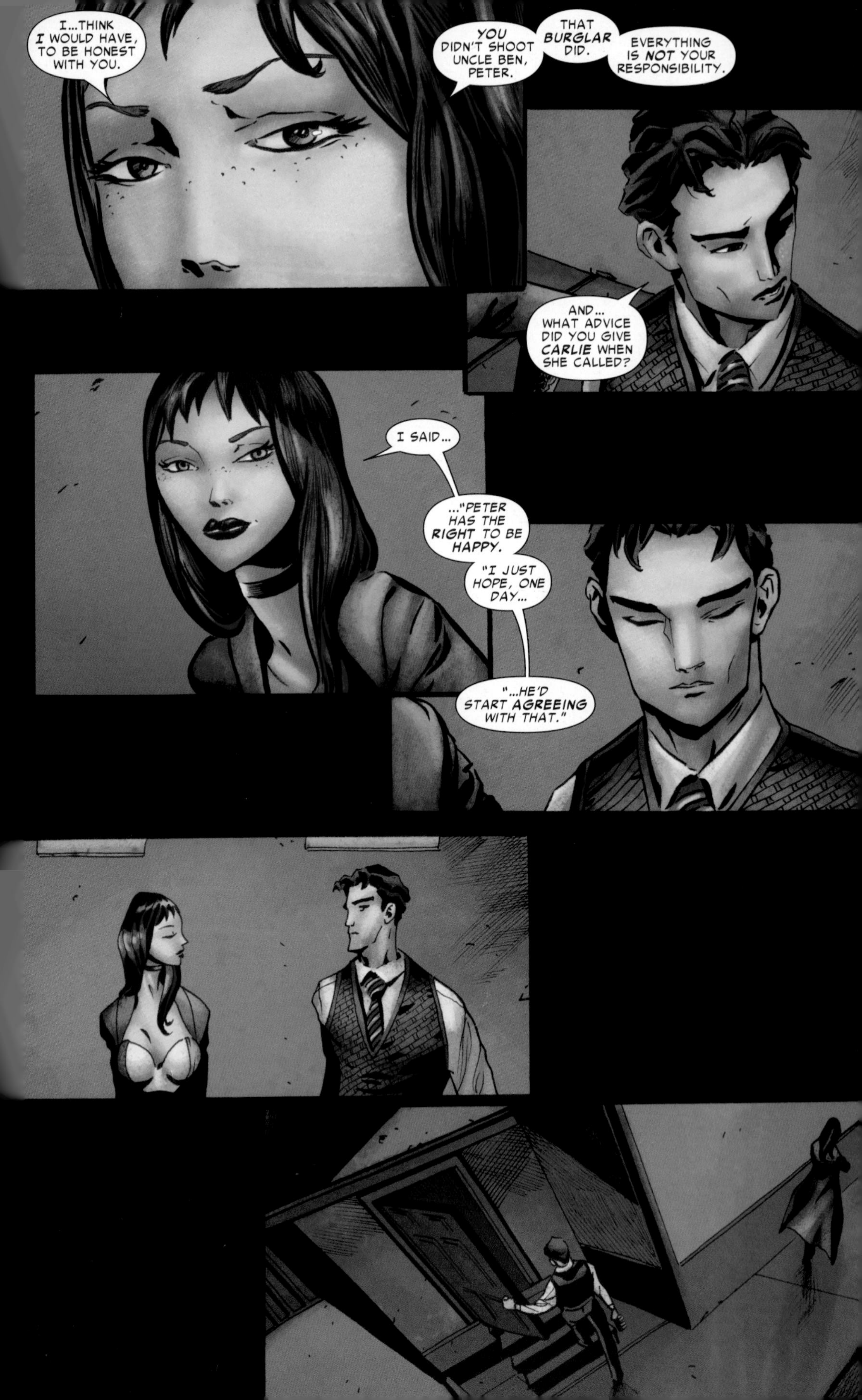
I...THINK I WOULD HAVE, TO BE HONEST WITH YOU.
YOU DIDN'T SHOOT UNCLE BEN, PETER.
THAT BURGLAR DID.
EVERYTHING IS NOT YOUR RESPONSIBILITY.
AND... WHAT ADVICE DID YOU GIVE CARLIE WHEN SHE CALLED?
I SAID...
..."PETER HAS THE RIGHT TO BE HAPPY.
"I JUST HOPE, ONE DAY...
"...HE'D START AGREEING WITH THAT."

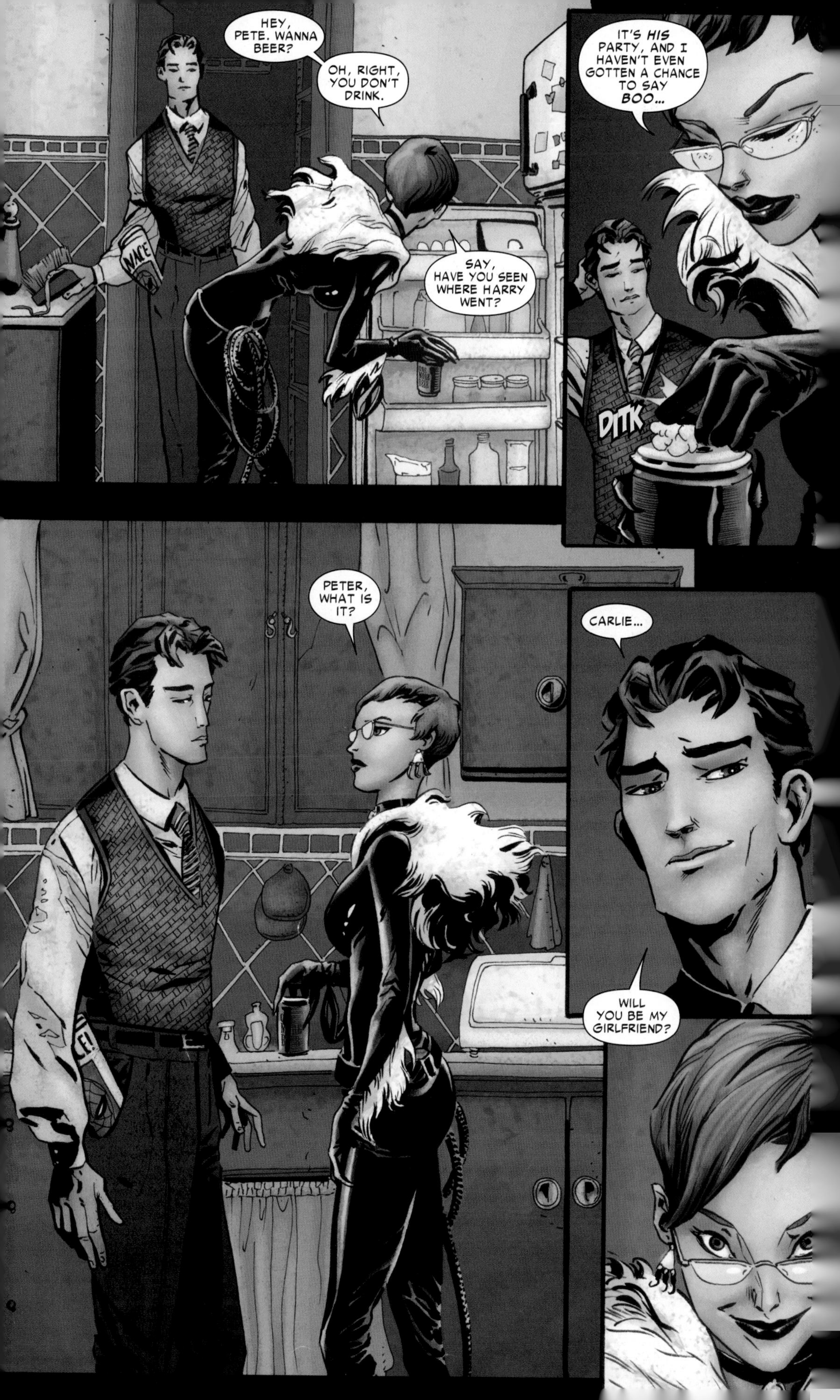
HEY, PETE. WANNA BEER?
OH, RIGHT, YOU DON'T DRINK.
SAY, HAVE YOU SEEN WHERE HARRY WENT?
IT'S HIS PARTY, AND I HAVEN'T EVEN GOTTEN A CHANCE TO SAY BOO...
DITK
PETER, WHAT IS IT?
CARLIE...
WILL YOU BE MY GIRLFRIEND?

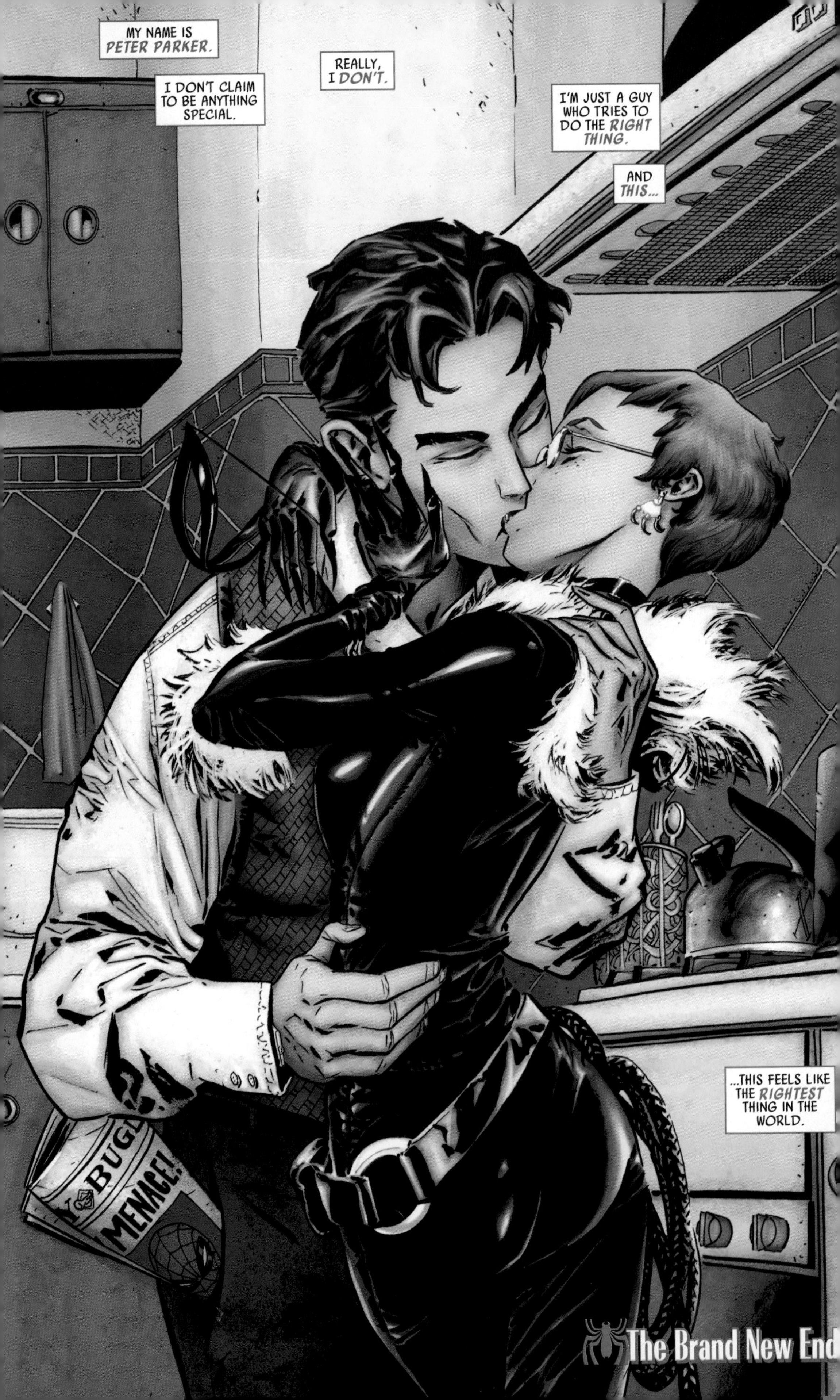
MY NAME IS PETER PARKER.
I DON'T CLAIM TO BE ANYTHING SPECIAL.
REALLY, I DON'T.
I'M JUST A GUY WHO TRIES TO DO THE RIGHT THING.
AND THIS...
...THIS FEELS LIKE THE RIGHTEST THING IN THE WORLD.
BUGL
MENACE!
The Brand New End

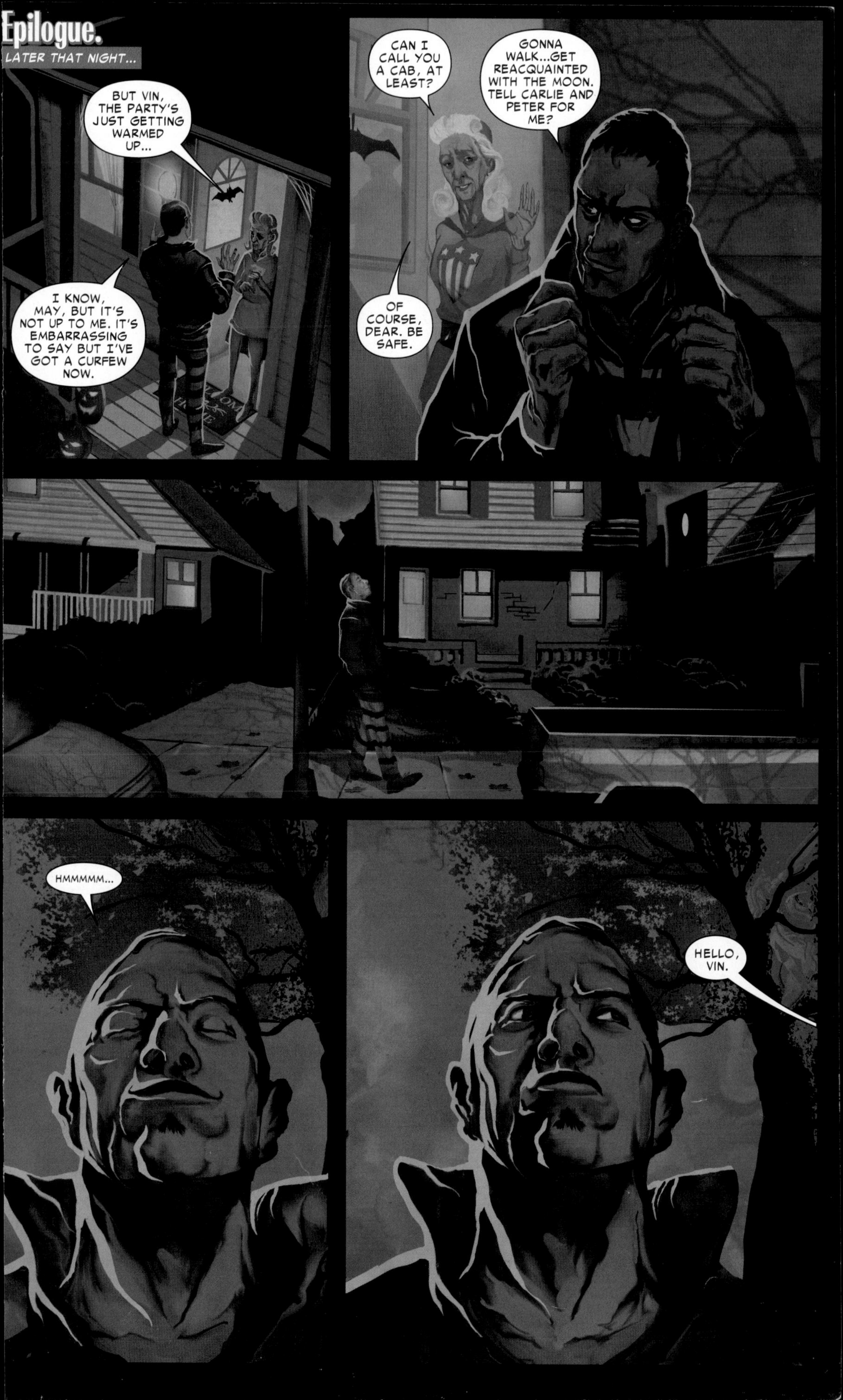
Epilogue.
LATER THAT NIGHT...
BUT VIN, THE PARTY'S JUST GETTING WARMED UP...
I KNOW, MAY, BUT IT'S NOT UP TO ME. IT'S EMBARRASSING TO SAY BUT I'VE GOT A CURFEW NOW.
CAN I CALL YOU A CAB, AT LEAST?
GONNA WALK...GET REACQUAINTED WITH THE MOON. TELL CARLIE AND PETER FOR ME?
OF COURSE, DEAR. BE SAFE.
HMMMMM...
HELLO, VIN.

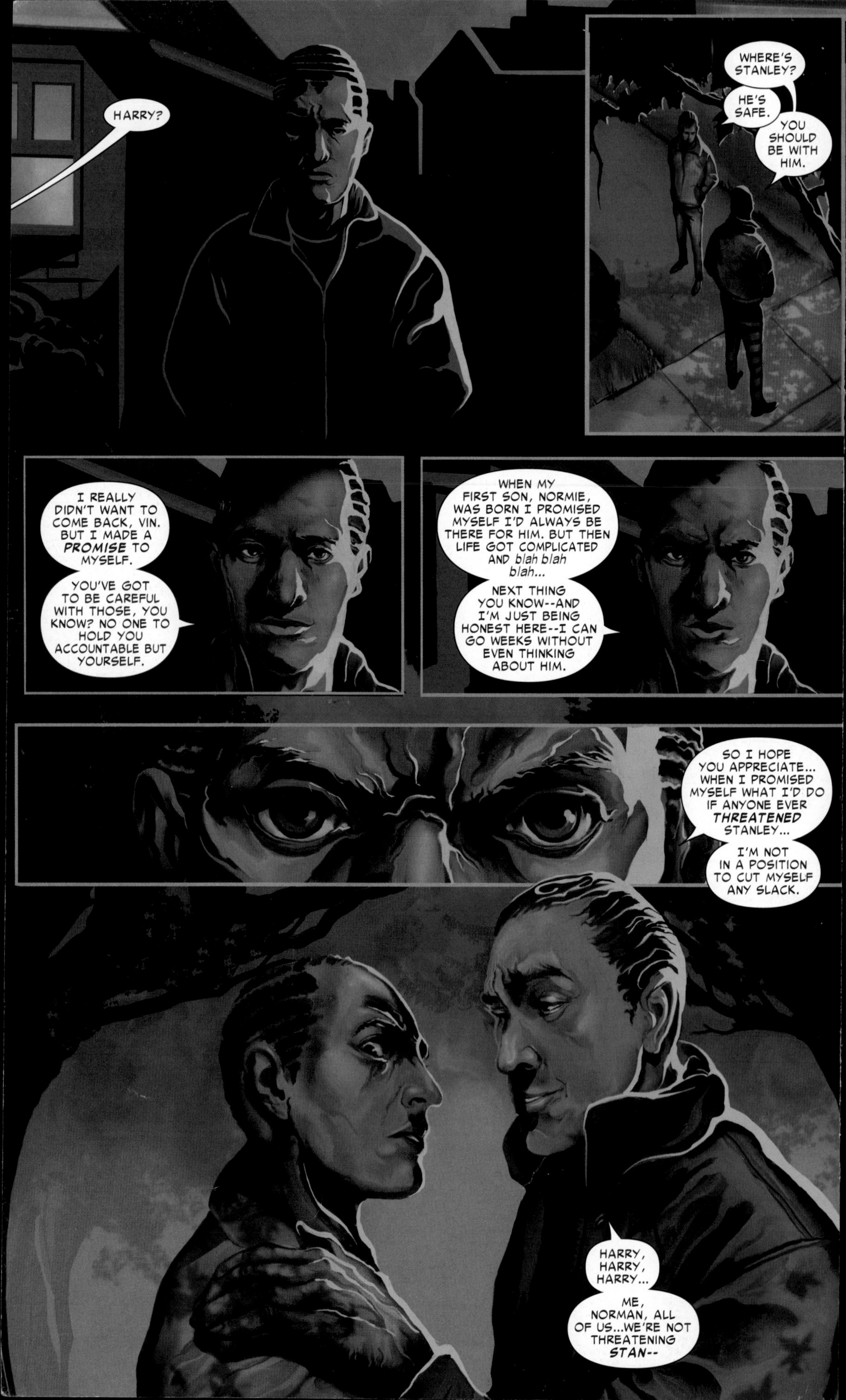
HARRY?
WHERE'S STANLEY?
HE'S SAFE.
YOU SHOULD BE WITH HIM.
I REALLY DIDN'T WANT TO COME BACK, VIN. BUT I MADE A PROMISE TO MYSELF.
YOU'VE GOT TO BE CAREFUL WITH THOSE, YOU KNOW? NO ONE TO HOLD YOU ACCOUNTABLE BUT YOURSELF.
WHEN MY FIRST SON, NORMIE, WAS BORN I PROMISED MYSELF I'D ALWAYS BE THERE FOR HIM. BUT THEN LIFE GOT COMPLICATED AND *blah blah blah*...
NEXT THING YOU KNOW--AND I'M JUST BEING HONEST HERE--I CAN GO WEEKS WITHOUT EVEN THINKING ABOUT HIM.
SO I HOPE YOU APPRECIATE... WHEN I PROMISED MYSELF WHAT I'D DO IF ANYONE EVER **THREATENED** STANLEY...
I'M NOT IN A POSITION TO CUT MYSELF ANY SLACK.
HARRY, HARRY, HARRY...
ME, NORMAN, ALL OF US...WE'RE NOT THREATENING **STAN--**

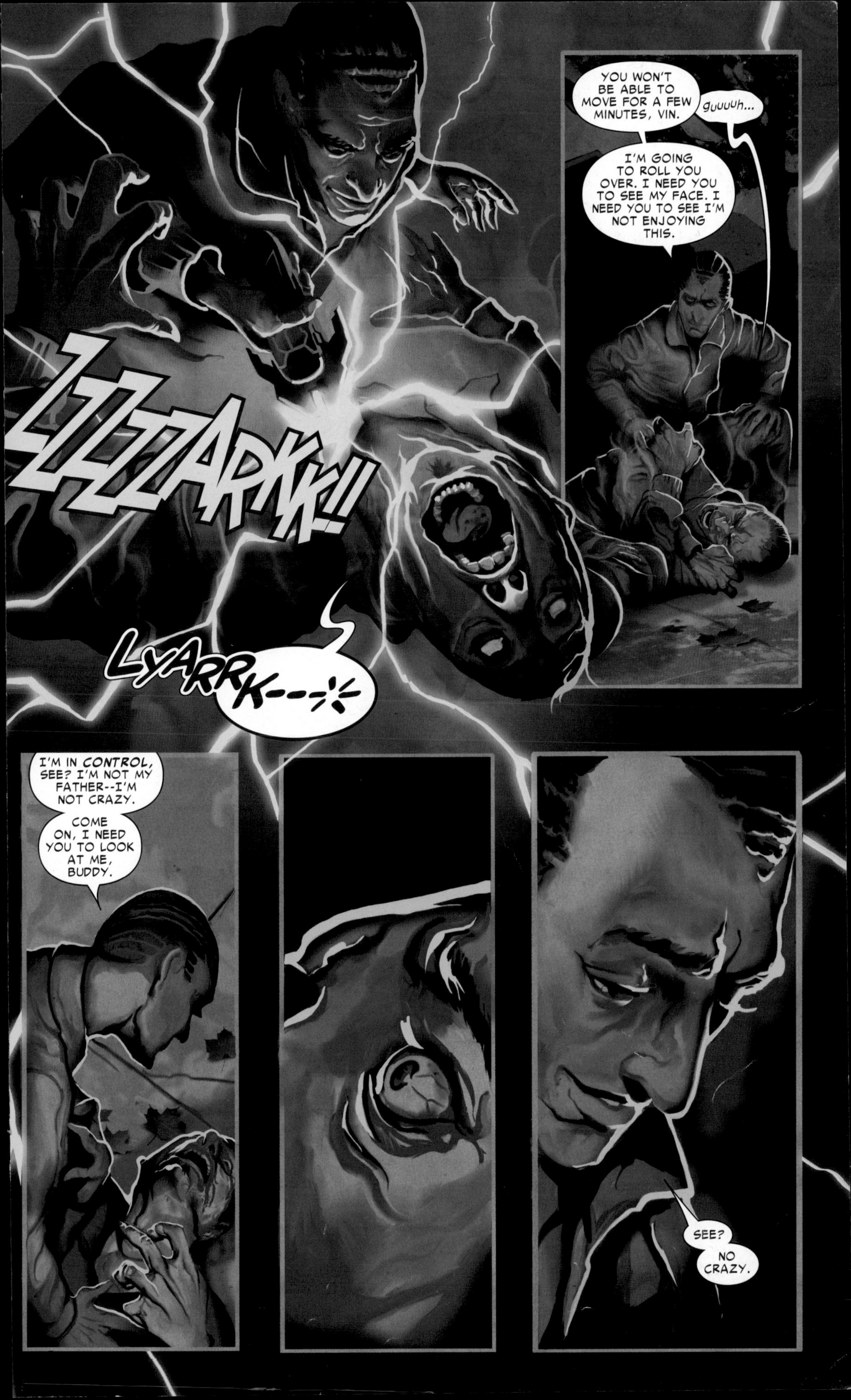
ZZZZZARKK!!
LYARRK---!
YOU WON'T BE ABLE TO MOVE FOR A FEW MINUTES, VIN.
guuuuh...
I'M GOING TO ROLL YOU OVER. I NEED YOU TO SEE MY FACE. I NEED YOU TO SEE I'M NOT ENJOYING THIS.
I'M IN CONTROL, SEE? I'M NOT MY FATHER--I'M NOT CRAZY.
COME ON, I NEED YOU TO LOOK AT ME, BUDDY.
SEE?
NO CRAZY.

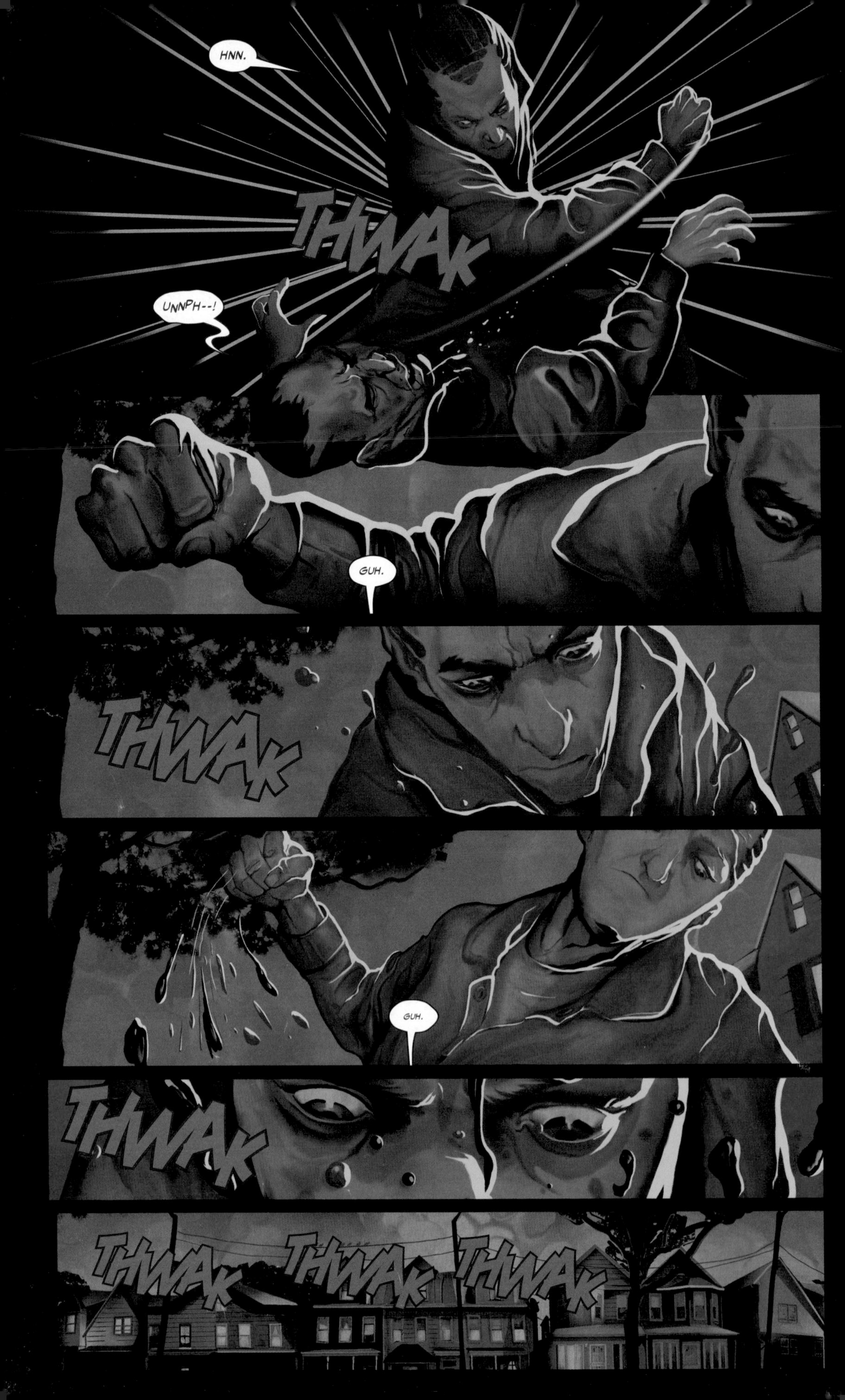
HNN.
THWAK
UNNPH--!
GUH.
THWAK
GUH.
THWAK
THWAK THWAK THWAK

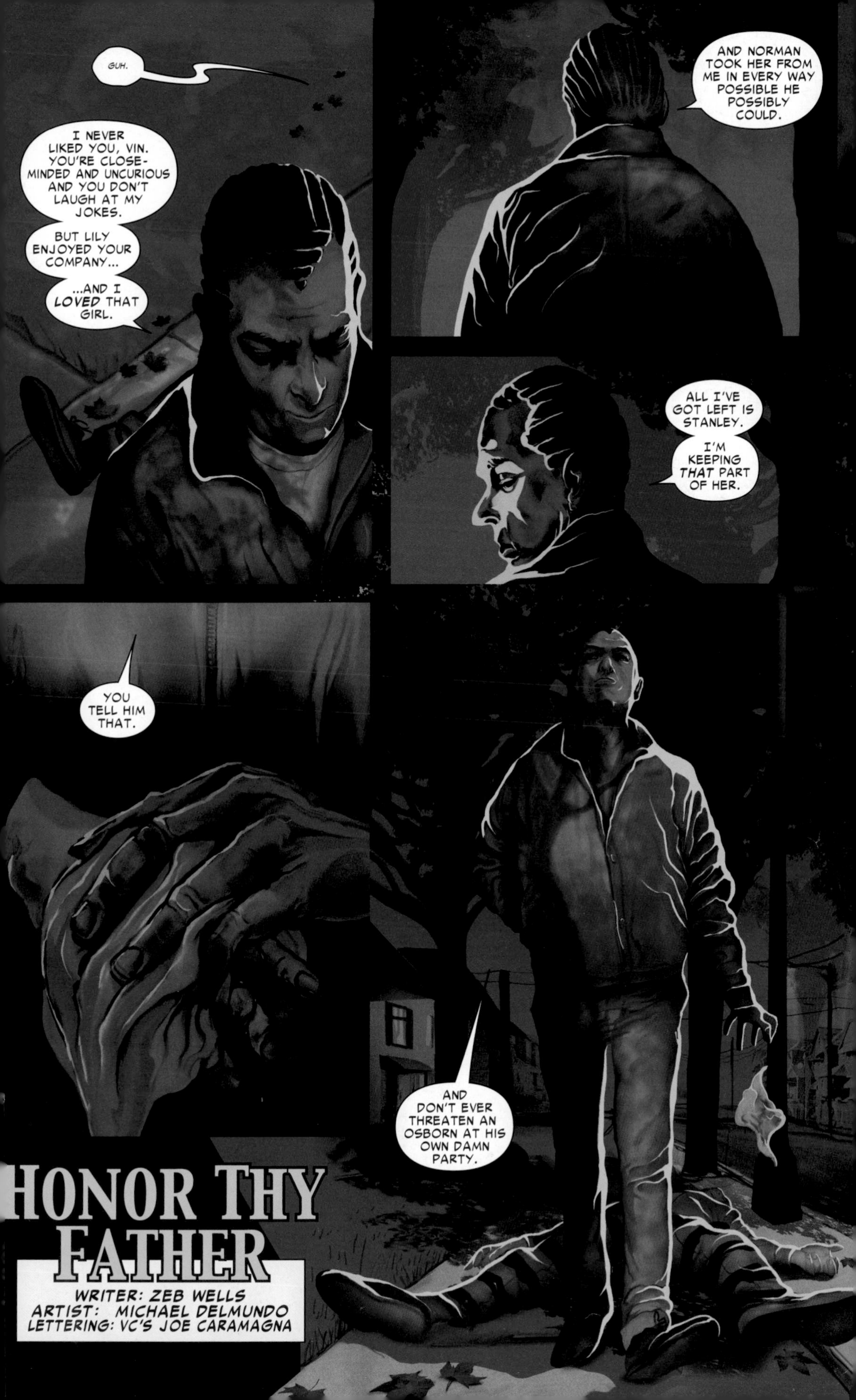
GUH.
I NEVER LIKED YOU, VIN. YOU'RE CLOSE-MINDED AND UNCURIOUS AND YOU DON'T LAUGH AT MY JOKES.
BUT LILY ENJOYED YOUR COMPANY...
...AND I *LOVED* THAT GIRL.
AND NORMAN TOOK HER FROM ME IN EVERY WAY POSSIBLE HE POSSIBLY COULD.
ALL I'VE GOT LEFT IS STANLEY.
I'M KEEPING *THAT* PART OF HER.
YOU TELL HIM THAT.
AND DON'T EVER THREATEN AN OSBORN AT HIS OWN DAMN PARTY.
HONOR THY FATHER
WRITER: ZEB WELLS
ARTIST: MICHAEL DELMUNDO
LETTERING: VC'S JOE CARAMAGNA

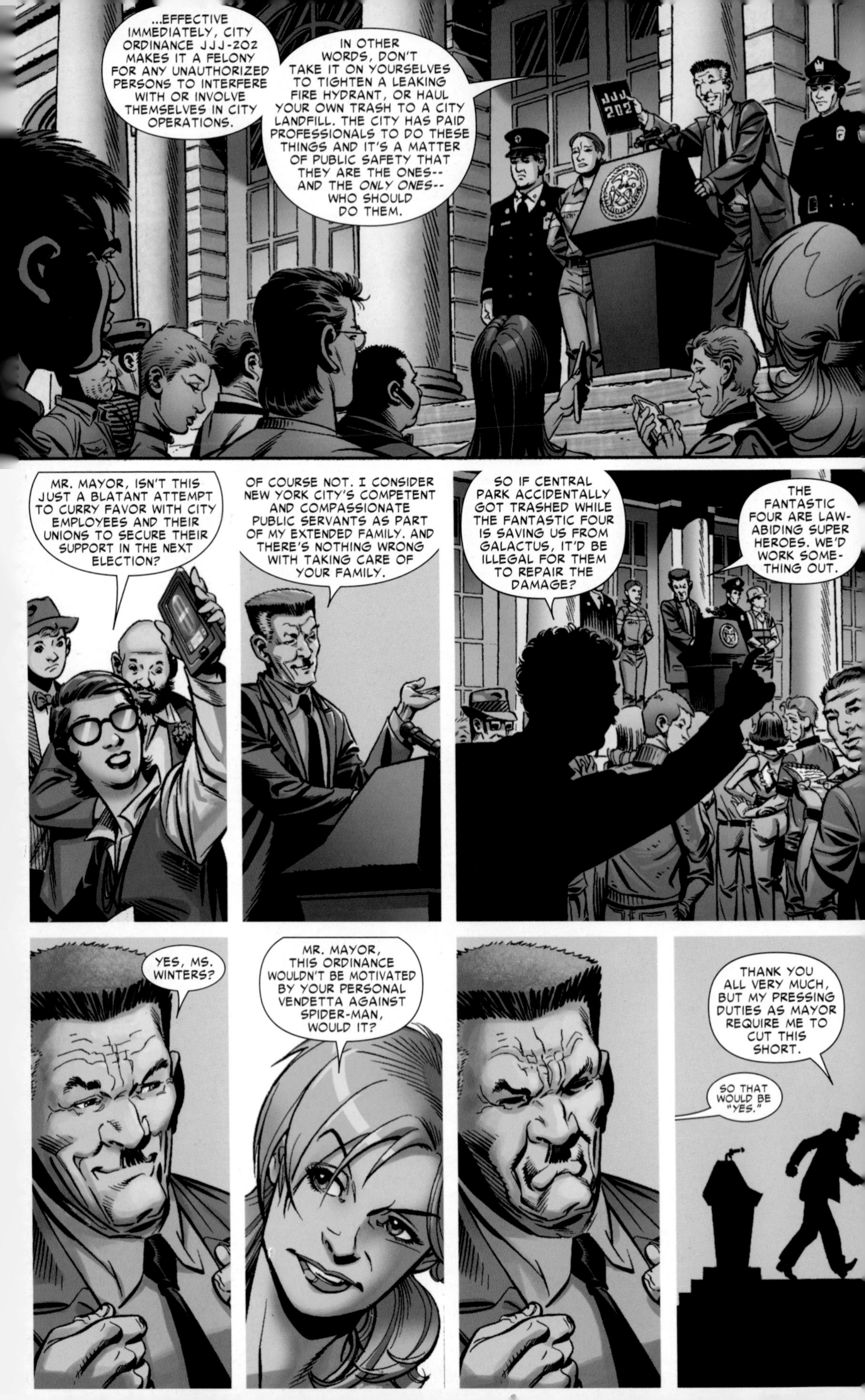
...EFFECTIVE IMMEDIATELY, CITY ORDINANCE JJJ-202 MAKES IT A FELONY FOR ANY UNAUTHORIZED PERSONS TO INTERFERE WITH OR INVOLVE THEMSELVES IN CITY OPERATIONS.
IN OTHER WORDS, DON'T TAKE IT ON YOURSELVES TO TIGHTEN A LEAKING FIRE HYDRANT, OR HAUL YOUR OWN TRASH TO A CITY LANDFILL. THE CITY HAS PAID PROFESSIONALS TO DO THESE THINGS AND IT'S A MATTER OF PUBLIC SAFETY THAT THEY ARE THE ONES-- AND THE *ONLY ONES*-- WHO SHOULD DO THEM.
JJJ 202
MR. MAYOR, ISN'T THIS JUST A BLATANT ATTEMPT TO CURRY FAVOR WITH CITY EMPLOYEES AND THEIR UNIONS TO SECURE THEIR SUPPORT IN THE NEXT ELECTION?
OF COURSE NOT. I CONSIDER NEW YORK CITY'S COMPETENT AND COMPASSIONATE PUBLIC SERVANTS AS PART OF MY EXTENDED FAMILY. AND THERE'S NOTHING WRONG WITH TAKING CARE OF YOUR FAMILY.
SO IF CENTRAL PARK ACCIDENTALLY GOT TRASHED WHILE THE FANTASTIC FOUR IS SAVING US FROM GALACTUS, IT'D BE ILLEGAL FOR THEM TO REPAIR THE DAMAGE?
THE FANTASTIC FOUR ARE LAW-ABIDING SUPER HEROES. WE'D WORK SOMETHING OUT.
YES, MS. WINTERS?
MR. MAYOR, THIS ORDINANCE WOULDN'T BE MOTIVATED BY YOUR PERSONAL VENDETTA AGAINST SPIDER-MAN, WOULD IT?
THANK YOU ALL VERY MUCH, BUT MY PRESSING DUTIES AS MAYOR REQUIRE ME TO CUT THIS SHORT.
SO THAT WOULD BE "YES."

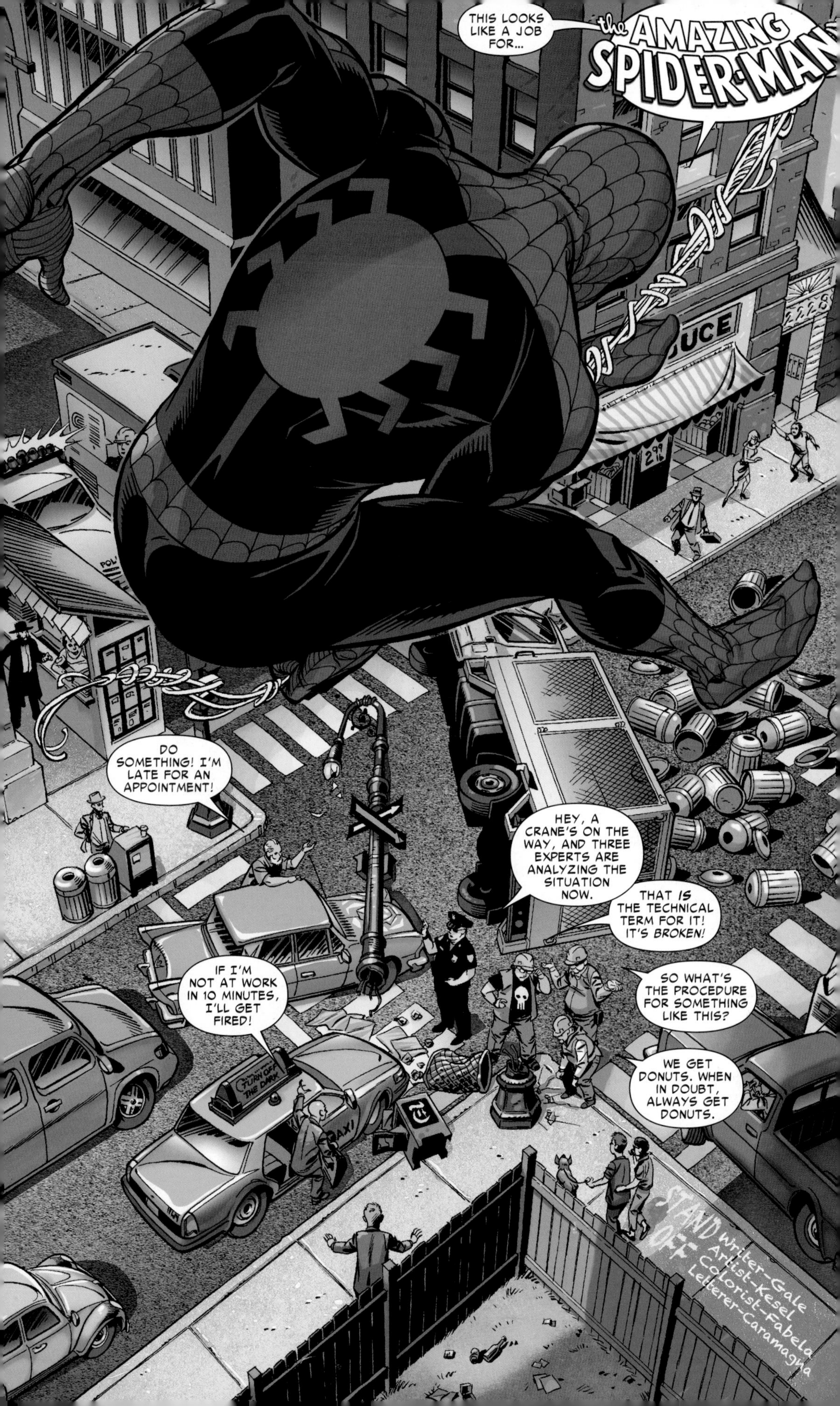

THIS LOOKS LIKE A JOB FOR...
the AMAZING SPIDER-MAN
DO SOMETHING! I'M LATE FOR AN APPOINTMENT!
HEY, A CRANE'S ON THE WAY, AND THREE EXPERTS ARE ANALYZING THE SITUATION NOW.
THAT IS THE TECHNICAL TERM FOR IT! IT'S BROKEN!
IF I'M NOT AT WORK IN 10 MINUTES, I'LL GET FIRED!
SO WHAT'S THE PROCEDURE FOR SOMETHING LIKE THIS?
WE GET DONUTS. WHEN IN DOUBT, ALWAYS GET DONUTS.
TURN OFF THE DARK
TAXI
STAND OFF
Writer-Gale
Artist-Kesel
Colorist-Fabela
Letterer-Caramagna

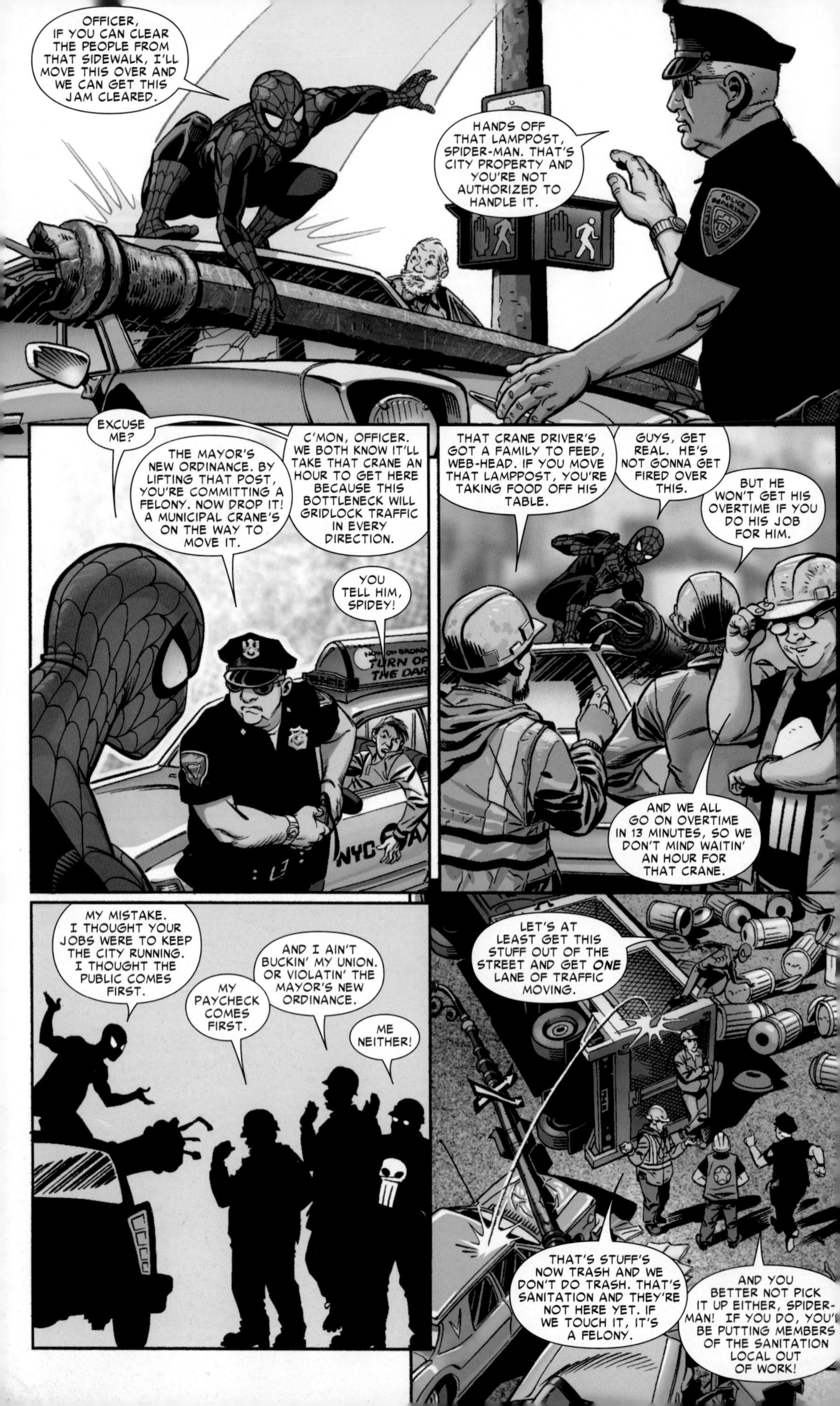
OFFICER, IF YOU CAN CLEAR THE PEOPLE FROM THAT SIDEWALK, I'LL MOVE THIS OVER AND WE CAN GET THIS JAM CLEARED.
HANDS OFF THAT LAMPPOST, SPIDER-MAN. THAT'S CITY PROPERTY AND YOU'RE NOT AUTHORIZED TO HANDLE IT.
EXCUSE ME?
THE MAYOR'S NEW ORDINANCE. BY LIFTING THAT POST, YOU'RE COMMITTING A FELONY. NOW DROP IT! A MUNICIPAL CRANE'S ON THE WAY TO MOVE IT.
C'MON, OFFICER. WE BOTH KNOW IT'LL TAKE THAT CRANE AN HOUR TO GET HERE BECAUSE THIS BOTTLENECK WILL GRIDLOCK TRAFFIC IN EVERY DIRECTION.
YOU TELL HIM, SPIDEY!
THAT CRANE DRIVER'S GOT A FAMILY TO FEED, WEB-HEAD. IF YOU MOVE THAT LAMPPOST, YOU'RE TAKING FOOD OFF HIS TABLE.
GUYS, GET REAL. HE'S NOT GONNA GET FIRED OVER THIS.
BUT HE WON'T GET HIS OVERTIME IF YOU DO HIS JOB FOR HIM.
AND WE ALL GO ON OVERTIME IN 13 MINUTES, SO WE DON'T MIND WAITIN' AN HOUR FOR THAT CRANE.
MY MISTAKE. I THOUGHT YOUR JOBS WERE TO KEEP THE CITY RUNNING. I THOUGHT THE PUBLIC COMES FIRST.
MY PAYCHECK COMES FIRST.
AND I AIN'T BUCKIN' MY UNION. OR VIOLATIN' THE MAYOR'S NEW ORDINANCE.
ME NEITHER!
LET'S AT LEAST GET THIS STUFF OUT OF THE STREET AND GET ONE LANE OF TRAFFIC MOVING.
THAT'S STUFF'S NOW TRASH AND WE DON'T DO TRASH. THAT'S SANITATION AND THEY'RE NOT HERE YET. IF WE TOUCH IT, IT'S A FELONY.
AND YOU BETTER NOT PICK IT UP EITHER, SPIDER-MAN! IF YOU DO, YOU'LL BE PUTTING MEMBERS OF THE SANITATION LOCAL OUT OF WORK!

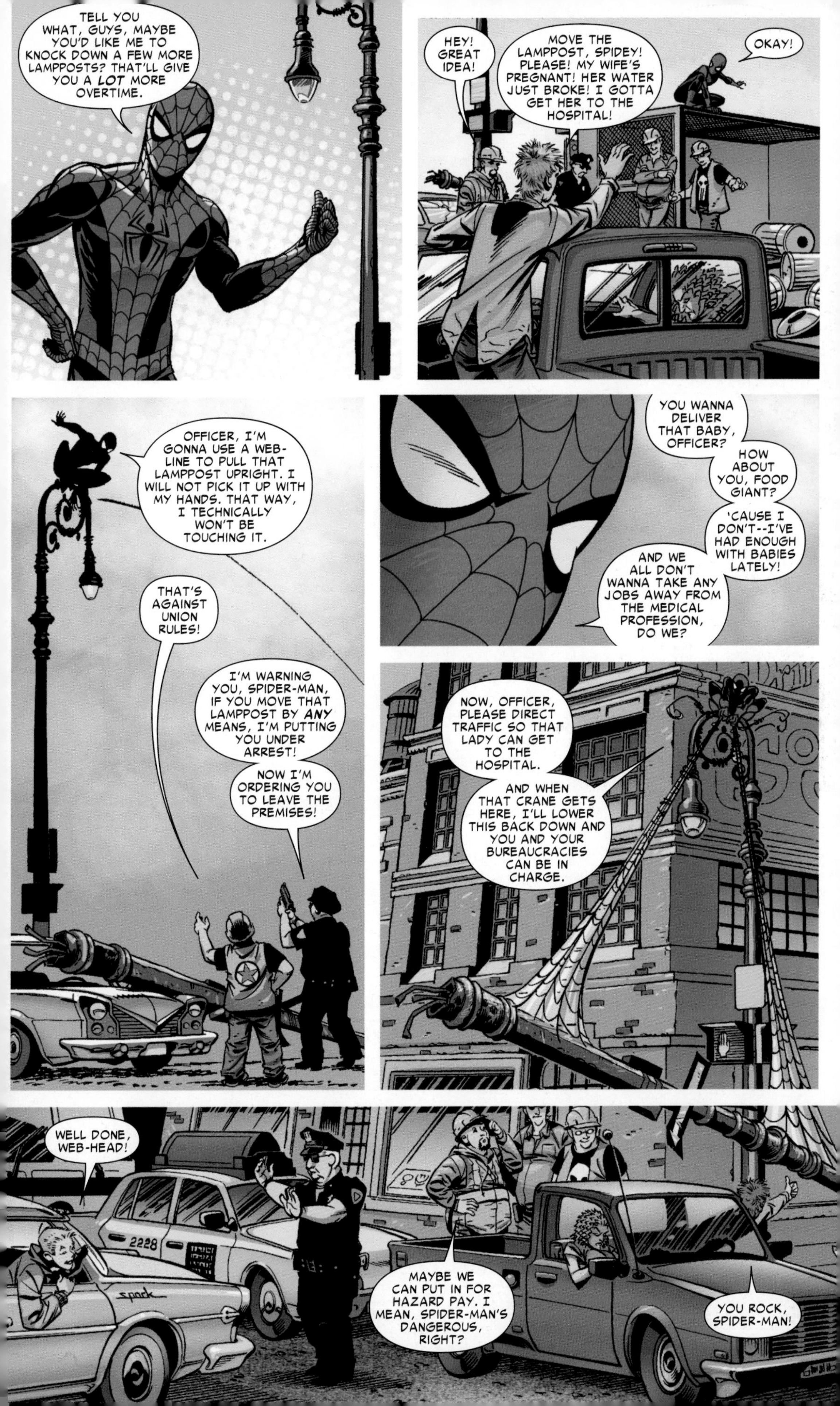
TELL YOU WHAT, GUYS, MAYBE YOU'D LIKE ME TO KNOCK DOWN A FEW MORE LAMPPOSTS? THAT'LL GIVE YOU A *LOT* MORE OVERTIME.
HEY! GREAT IDEA!
MOVE THE LAMPPOST, SPIDEY! PLEASE! MY WIFE'S PREGNANT! HER WATER JUST BROKE! I GOTTA GET HER TO THE HOSPITAL!
OKAY!
OFFICER, I'M GONNA USE A WEB-LINE TO PULL THAT LAMPPOST UPRIGHT. I WILL NOT PICK IT UP WITH MY HANDS. THAT WAY, I TECHNICALLY WON'T BE TOUCHING IT.
THAT'S AGAINST UNION RULES!
I'M WARNING YOU, SPIDER-MAN, IF YOU MOVE THAT LAMPPOST BY *ANY* MEANS, I'M PUTTING YOU UNDER ARREST!
NOW I'M ORDERING YOU TO LEAVE THE PREMISES!
YOU WANNA DELIVER THAT BABY, OFFICER?
HOW ABOUT YOU, FOOD GIANT?
'CAUSE I DON'T--I'VE HAD ENOUGH WITH BABIES LATELY!
AND WE ALL DON'T WANNA TAKE ANY JOBS AWAY FROM THE MEDICAL PROFESSION, DO WE?
NOW, OFFICER, PLEASE DIRECT TRAFFIC SO THAT LADY CAN GET TO THE HOSPITAL.
AND WHEN THAT CRANE GETS HERE, I'LL LOWER THIS BACK DOWN AND YOU AND YOUR BUREAUCRACIES CAN BE IN CHARGE.
WELL DONE, WEB-HEAD!
2228
MAYBE WE CAN PUT IN FOR HAZARD PAY. I MEAN, SPIDER-MAN'S DANGEROUS, RIGHT?
YOU ROCK, SPIDER-MAN!

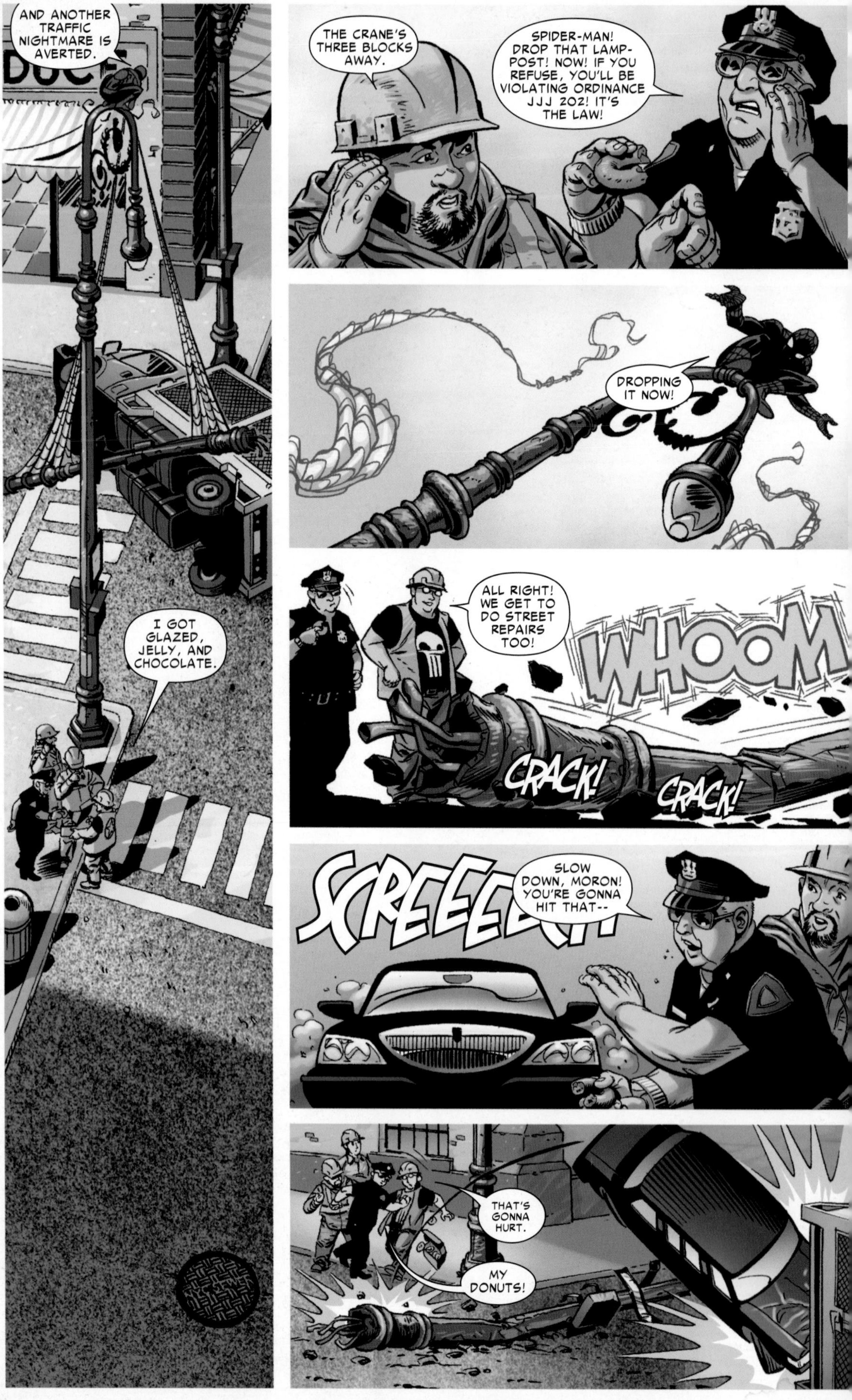
AND ANOTHER TRAFFIC NIGHTMARE IS AVERTED.
I GOT GLAZED, JELLY, AND CHOCOLATE.
THE CRANE'S THREE BLOCKS AWAY.
SPIDER-MAN! DROP THAT LAMP-POST! NOW! IF YOU REFUSE, YOU'LL BE VIOLATING ORDINANCE JJJ 202! IT'S THE LAW!
DROPPING IT NOW!
ALL RIGHT! WE GET TO DO STREET REPAIRS TOO!
WHOOM
CRACK!
CRACK!
SCREEEEECH
SLOW DOWN, MORON! YOU'RE GONNA HIT THAT--
THAT'S GONNA HURT.
MY DONUTS!

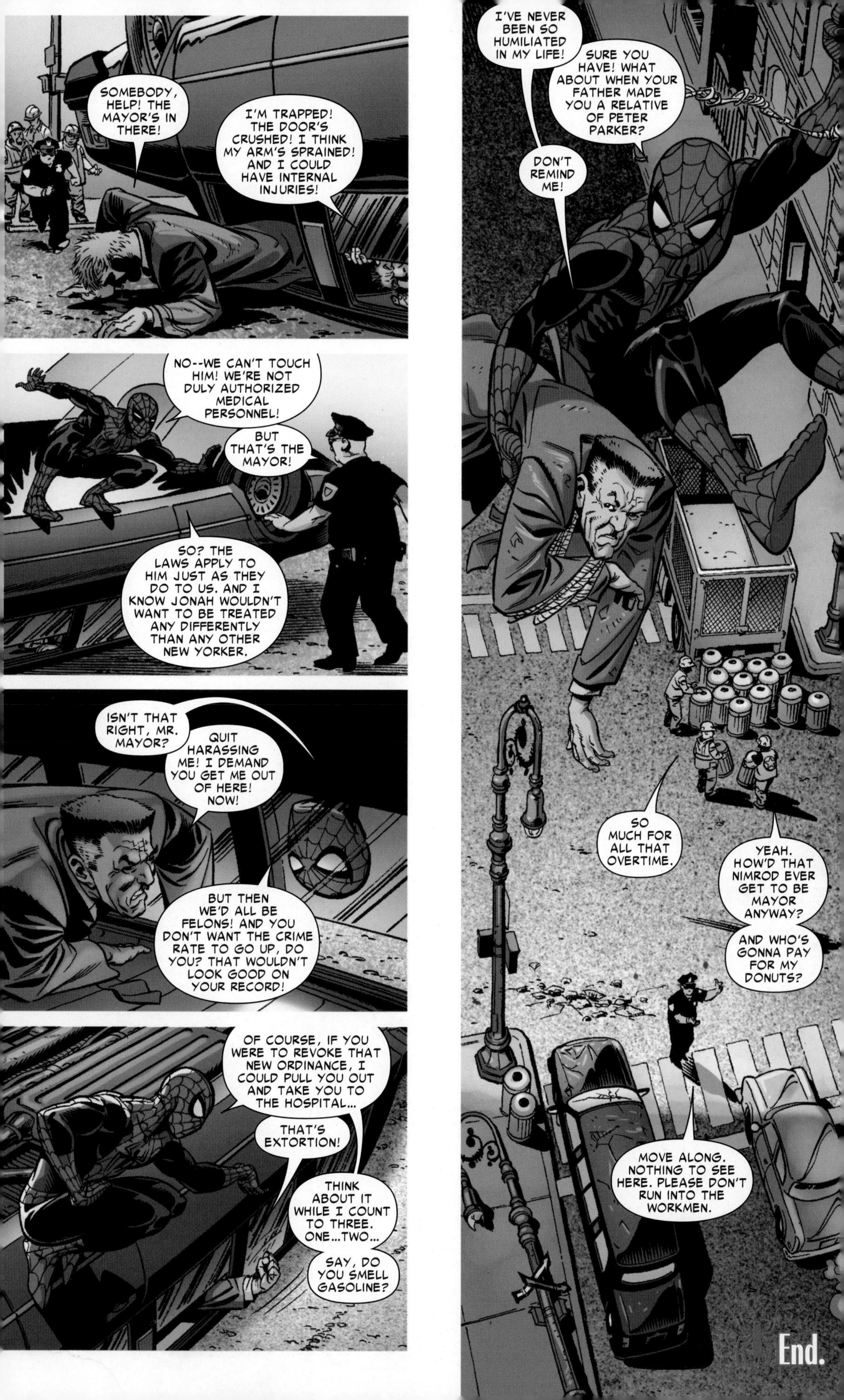
SOMEBODY, HELP! THE MAYOR'S IN THERE!
I'M TRAPPED! THE DOOR'S CRUSHED! I THINK MY ARM'S SPRAINED! AND I COULD HAVE INTERNAL INJURIES!
NO--WE CAN'T TOUCH HIM! WE'RE NOT DULY AUTHORIZED MEDICAL PERSONNEL!
BUT THAT'S THE MAYOR!
SO? THE LAWS APPLY TO HIM JUST AS THEY DO TO US. AND I KNOW JONAH WOULDN'T WANT TO BE TREATED ANY DIFFERENTLY THAN ANY OTHER NEW YORKER.
ISN'T THAT RIGHT, MR. MAYOR?
QUIT HARASSING ME! I DEMAND YOU GET ME OUT OF HERE! NOW!
BUT THEN WE'D ALL BE FELONS! AND YOU DON'T WANT THE CRIME RATE TO GO UP, DO YOU? THAT WOULDN'T LOOK GOOD ON YOUR RECORD!
OF COURSE, IF YOU WERE TO REVOKE THAT NEW ORDINANCE, I COULD PULL YOU OUT AND TAKE YOU TO THE HOSPITAL...
THAT'S EXTORTION!
THINK ABOUT IT WHILE I COUNT TO THREE. ONE...TWO...
SAY, DO YOU SMELL GASOLINE?
I'VE NEVER BEEN SO HUMILIATED IN MY LIFE!
SURE YOU HAVE! WHAT ABOUT WHEN YOUR FATHER MADE YOU A RELATIVE OF PETER PARKER?
DON'T REMIND ME!
SO MUCH FOR ALL THAT OVERTIME.
YEAH. HOW'D THAT NIMROD EVER GET TO BE MAYOR ANYWAY?
AND WHO'S GONNA PAY FOR MY DONUTS?
MOVE ALONG. NOTHING TO SEE HERE. PLEASE DON'T RUN INTO THE WORKMEN.
End.

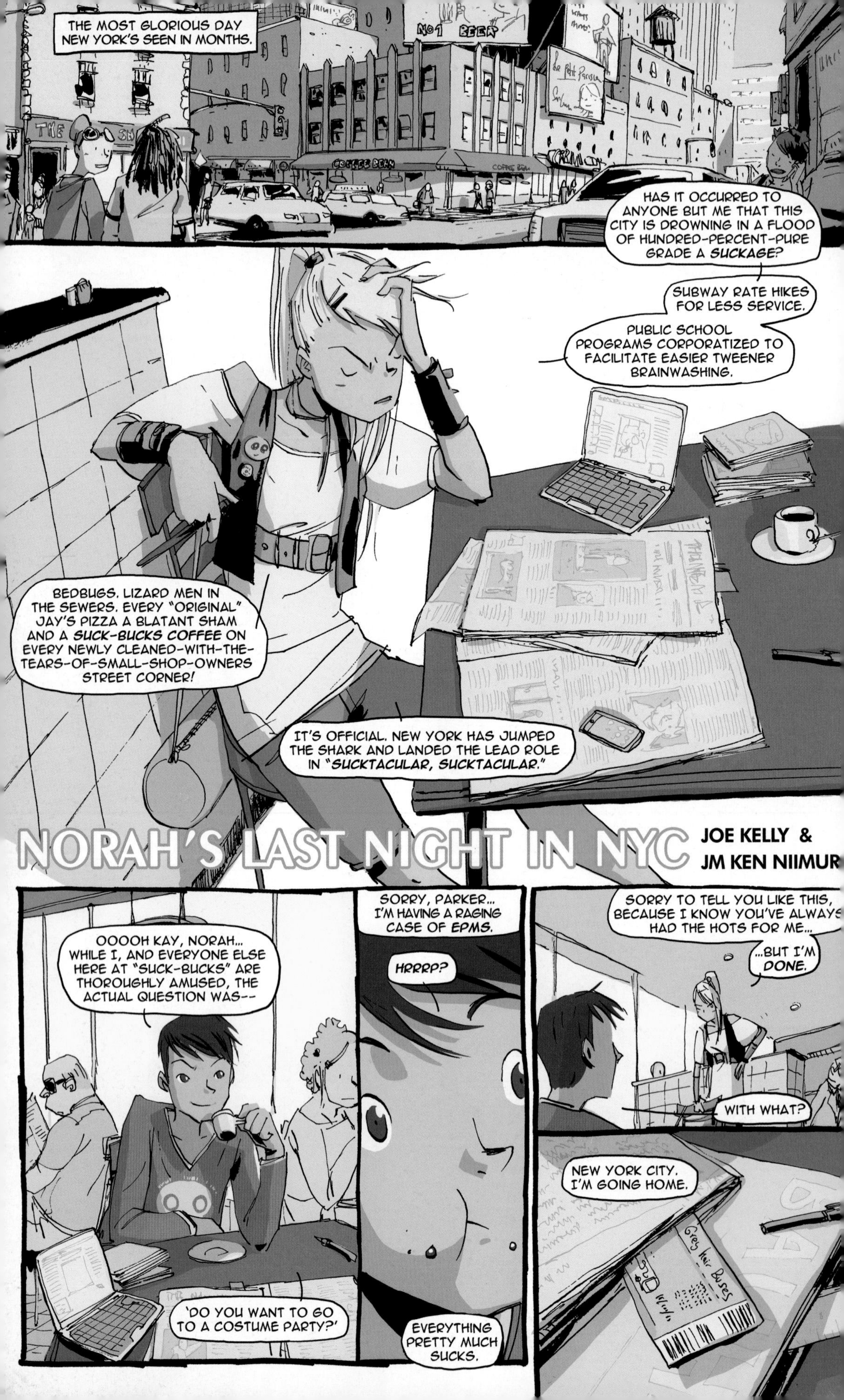
THE MOST GLORIOUS DAY NEW YORK'S SEEN IN MONTHS.
NO1 BEER
COFFEE BEAN
HAS IT OCCURRED TO ANYONE BUT ME THAT THIS CITY IS DROWNING IN A FLOOD OF HUNDRED-PERCENT-PURE GRADE A SUCKAGE?
SUBWAY RATE HIKES FOR LESS SERVICE.
PUBLIC SCHOOL PROGRAMS CORPORATIZED TO FACILITATE EASIER TWEENER BRAINWASHING.
BEDBUGS. LIZARD MEN IN THE SEWERS. EVERY "ORIGINAL" JAY'S PIZZA A BLATANT SHAM AND A SUCK-BUCKS COFFEE ON EVERY NEWLY CLEANED-WITH-THE-TEARS-OF-SMALL-SHOP-OWNERS STREET CORNER!
IT'S OFFICIAL. NEW YORK HAS JUMPED THE SHARK AND LANDED THE LEAD ROLE IN "SUCKTACULAR, SUCKTACULAR."
NORAH'S LAST NIGHT IN NYC
JOE KELLY &
JM KEN NIIMUR
OOOOH KAY, NORAH... WHILE I, AND EVERYONE ELSE HERE AT "SUCK-BUCKS" ARE THOROUGHLY AMUSED, THE ACTUAL QUESTION WAS--
'DO YOU WANT TO GO TO A COSTUME PARTY?'
SORRY, PARKER... I'M HAVING A RAGING CASE OF EPMS.
HRRRP?
EVERYTHING PRETTY MUCH SUCKS.
SORRY TO TELL YOU LIKE THIS, BECAUSE I KNOW YOU'VE ALWAYS HAD THE HOTS FOR ME...
...BUT I'M DONE.
WITH WHAT?
NEW YORK CITY. I'M GOING HOME.
Grey hair Buses

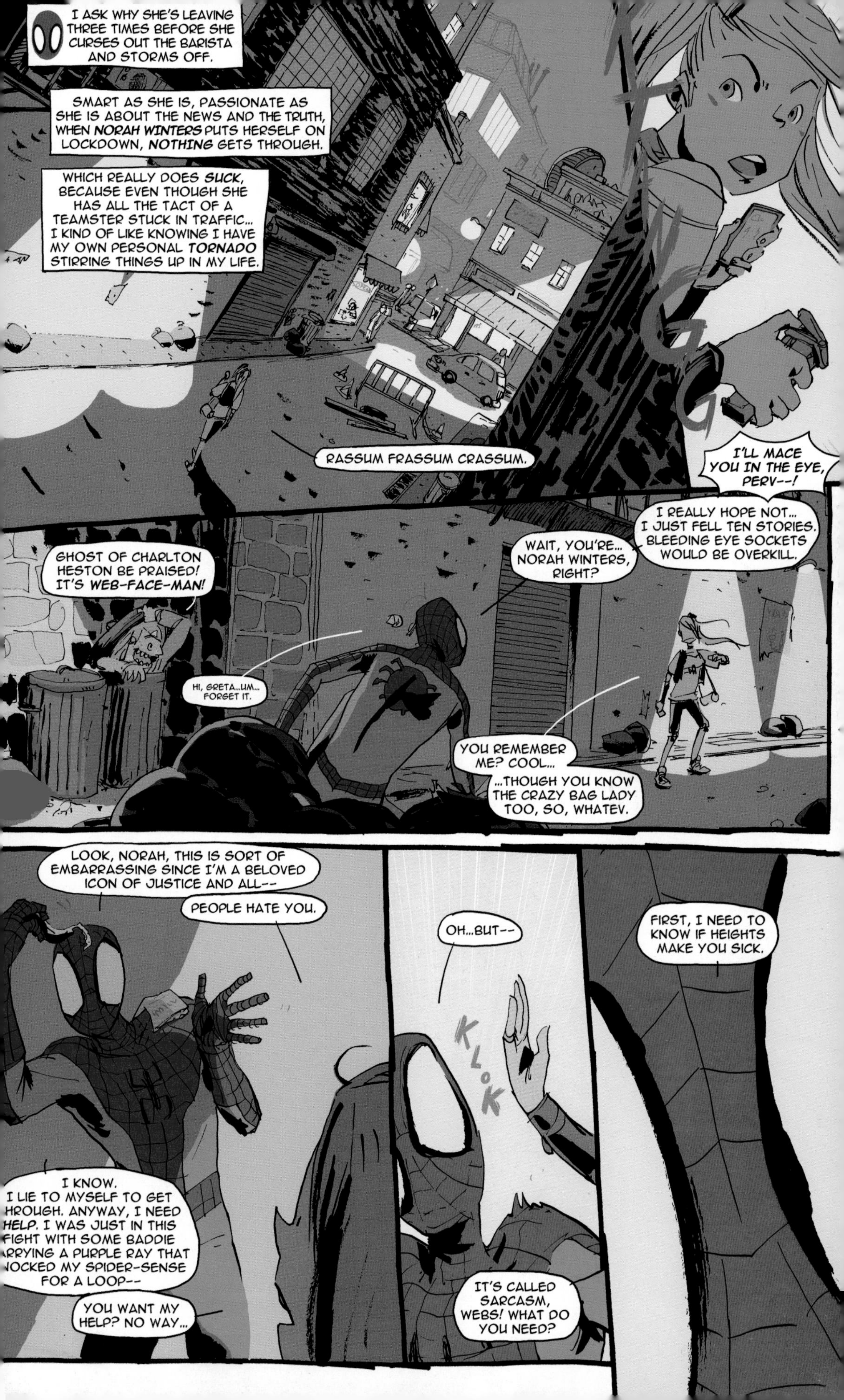

I ASK WHY SHE'S LEAVING THREE TIMES BEFORE SHE CURSES OUT THE BARISTA AND STORMS OFF.
SMART AS SHE IS, PASSIONATE AS SHE IS ABOUT THE NEWS AND THE TRUTH, WHEN NORAH WINTERS PUTS HERSELF ON LOCKDOWN, NOTHING GETS THROUGH.
WHICH REALLY DOES SUCK, BECAUSE EVEN THOUGH SHE HAS ALL THE TACT OF A TEAMSTER STUCK IN TRAFFIC... I KIND OF LIKE KNOWING I HAVE MY OWN PERSONAL TORNADO STIRRING THINGS UP IN MY LIFE.
RASSUM FRASSUM CRASSUM.
I'LL MACE YOU IN THE EYE, PERV--!
GHOST OF CHARLTON HESTON BE PRAISED! IT'S WEB-FACE-MAN!
HI, GRETA...UM... FORGET IT.
WAIT, YOU'RE... NORAH WINTERS, RIGHT?
I REALLY HOPE NOT... I JUST FELL TEN STORIES. BLEEDING EYE SOCKETS WOULD BE OVERKILL.
YOU REMEMBER ME? COOL...
...THOUGH YOU KNOW THE CRAZY BAG LADY TOO, SO, WHATEV.
LOOK, NORAH, THIS IS SORT OF EMBARRASSING SINCE I'M A BELOVED ICON OF JUSTICE AND ALL--
PEOPLE HATE YOU.
I KNOW. I LIE TO MYSELF TO GET HROUGH. ANYWAY, I NEED HELP. I WAS JUST IN THIS FIGHT WITH SOME BADDIE ARRYING A PURPLE RAY THAT NOCKED MY SPIDER-SENSE FOR A LOOP--
YOU WANT MY HELP? NO WAY...
OH...BUT--
KLOK
IT'S CALLED SARCASM, WEBS! WHAT DO YOU NEED?
FIRST, I NEED TO KNOW IF HEIGHTS MAKE YOU SICK.

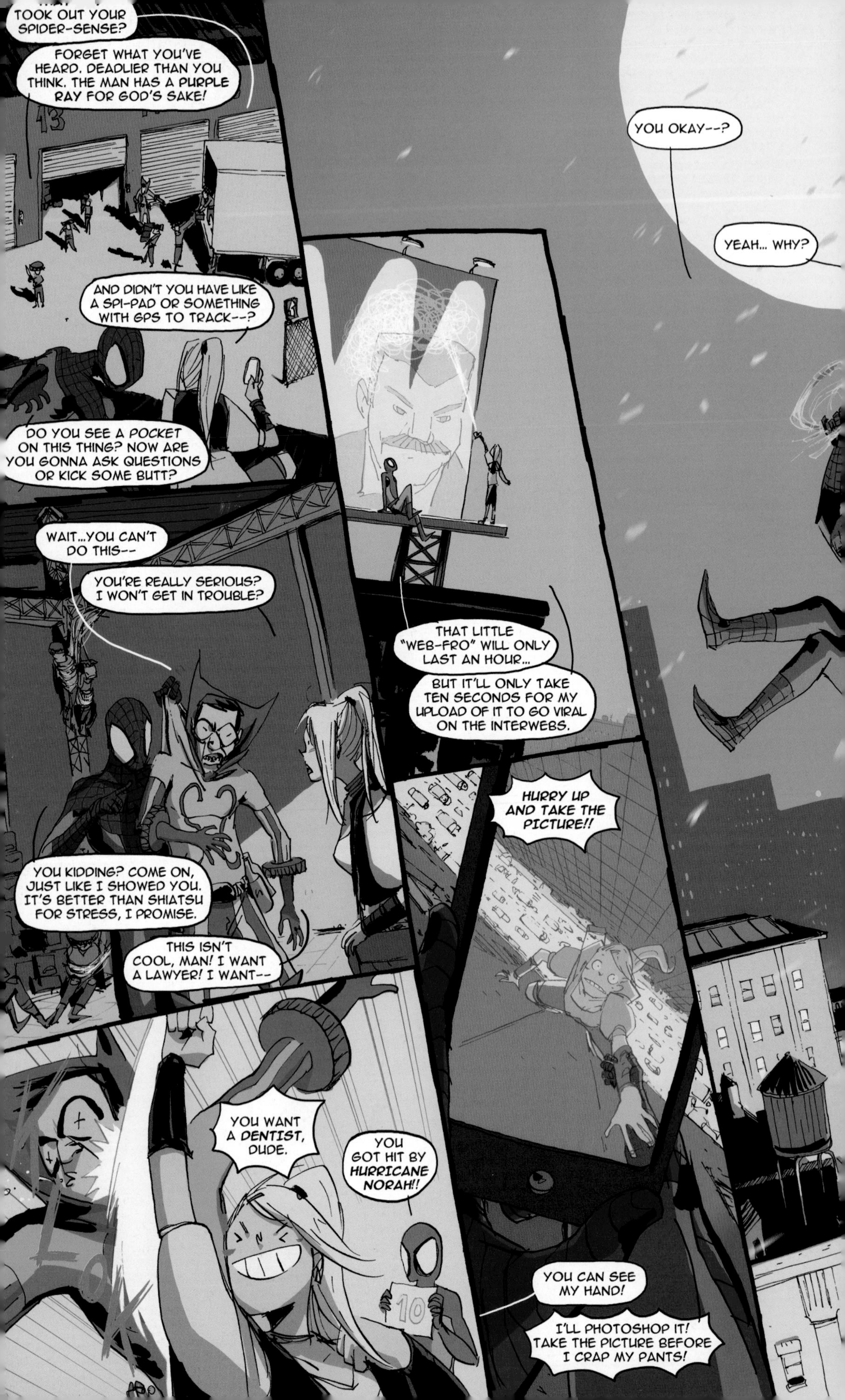
TOOK OUT YOUR SPIDER-SENSE?
FORGET WHAT YOU'VE HEARD. DEADLIER THAN YOU THINK. THE MAN HAS A PURPLE RAY FOR GOD'S SAKE!
AND DIDN'T YOU HAVE LIKE A SPI-PAD OR SOMETHING WITH GPS TO TRACK--?
DO YOU SEE A POCKET ON THIS THING? NOW ARE YOU GONNA ASK QUESTIONS OR KICK SOME BUTT?
WAIT...YOU CAN'T DO THIS--
YOU'RE REALLY SERIOUS? I WON'T GET IN TROUBLE?
YOU KIDDING? COME ON, JUST LIKE I SHOWED YOU. IT'S BETTER THAN SHIATSU FOR STRESS, I PROMISE.
THIS ISN'T COOL, MAN! I WANT A LAWYER! I WANT--
YOU WANT A DENTIST, DUDE.
YOU GOT HIT BY HURRICANE NORAH!!
10
THAT LITTLE "WEB-FRO" WILL ONLY LAST AN HOUR...
BUT IT'LL ONLY TAKE TEN SECONDS FOR MY UPLOAD OF IT TO GO VIRAL ON THE INTERWEBS.
HURRY UP AND TAKE THE PICTURE!!
YOU CAN SEE MY HAND!
I'LL PHOTOSHOP IT! TAKE THE PICTURE BEFORE I CRAP MY PANTS!
YOU OKAY--?
YEAH... WHY?

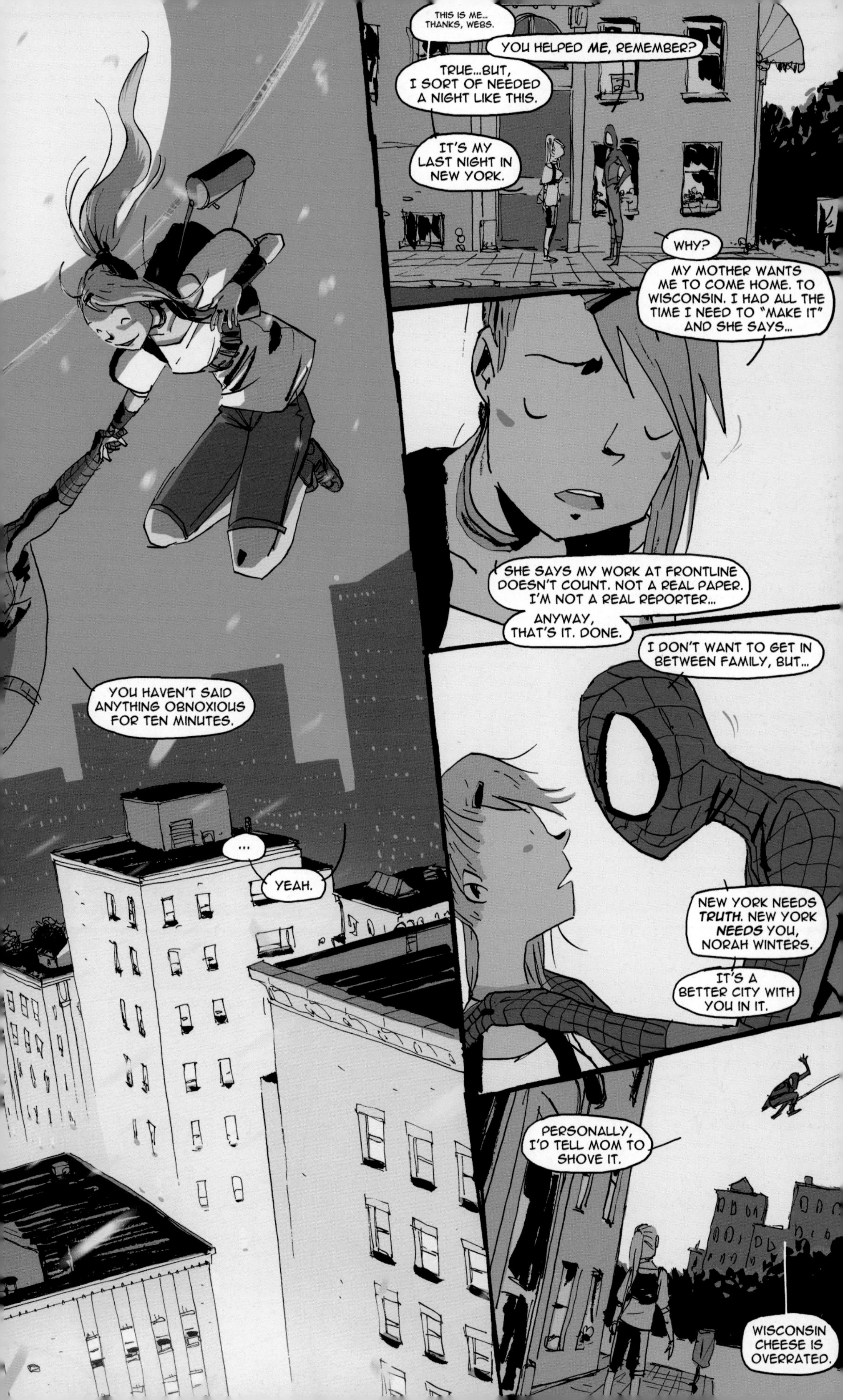
YOU HAVEN'T SAID ANYTHING OBNOXIOUS FOR TEN MINUTES.
...
YEAH.
THIS IS ME... THANKS, WEBS.
YOU HELPED ME, REMEMBER?
TRUE...BUT, I SORT OF NEEDED A NIGHT LIKE THIS.
IT'S MY LAST NIGHT IN NEW YORK.
WHY?
MY MOTHER WANTS ME TO COME HOME. TO WISCONSIN. I HAD ALL THE TIME I NEED TO "MAKE IT" AND SHE SAYS...
SHE SAYS MY WORK AT FRONTLINE DOESN'T COUNT. NOT A REAL PAPER. I'M NOT A REAL REPORTER...
ANYWAY, THAT'S IT. DONE.
I DON'T WANT TO GET IN BETWEEN FAMILY, BUT...
NEW YORK NEEDS TRUTH. NEW YORK NEEDS YOU, NORAH WINTERS.
IT'S A BETTER CITY WITH YOU IN IT.
PERSONALLY, I'D TELL MOM TO SHOVE IT.
WISCONSIN CHEESE IS OVERRATED.

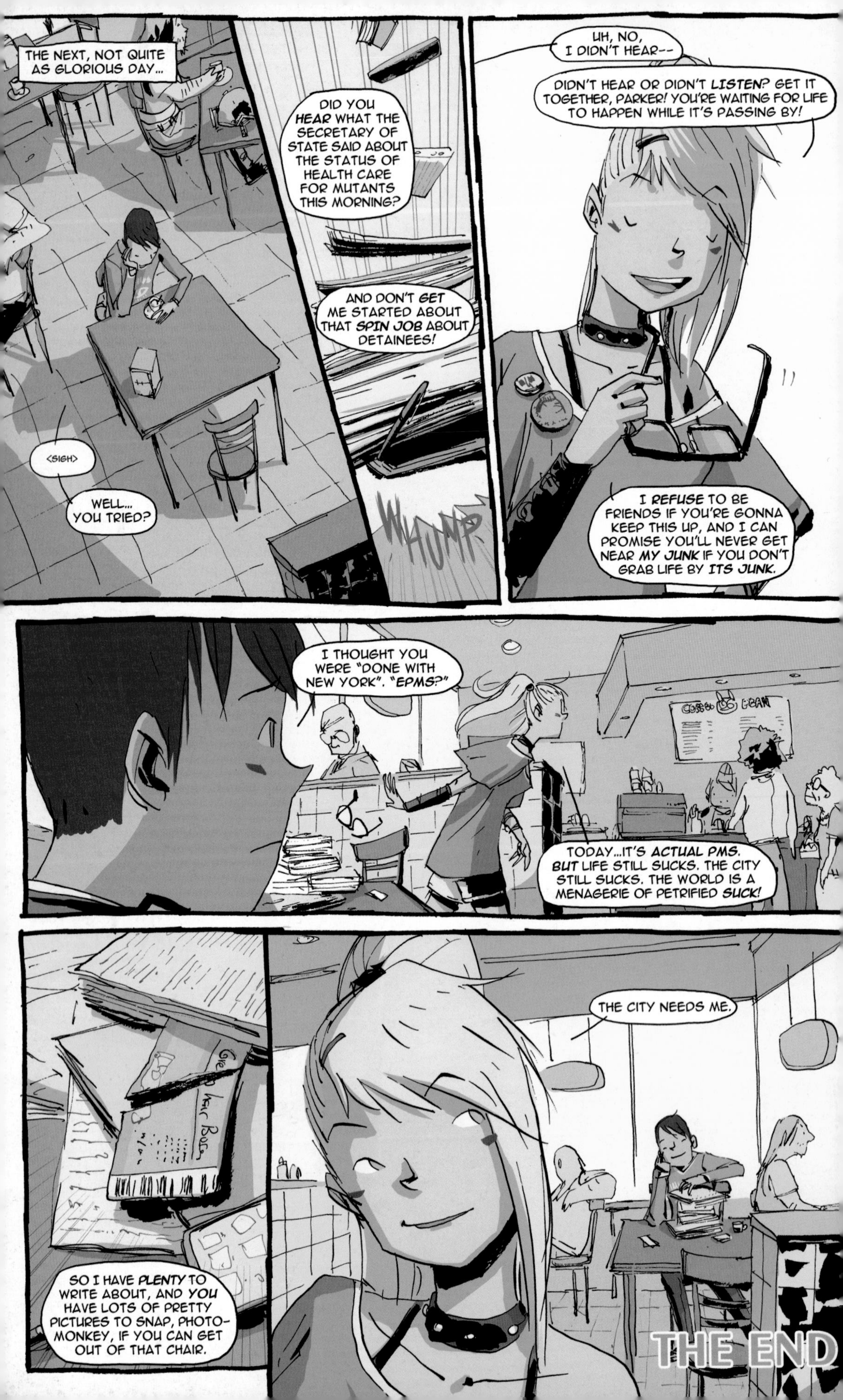

THE NEXT, NOT QUITE AS GLORIOUS DAY...
DID YOU HEAR WHAT THE SECRETARY OF STATE SAID ABOUT THE STATUS OF HEALTH CARE FOR MUTANTS THIS MORNING?
AND DON'T GET ME STARTED ABOUT THAT SPIN JOB ABOUT DETAINEES!
<SIGH>
WELL... YOU TRIED?
WHUMP
UH, NO, I DIDN'T HEAR--
DIDN'T HEAR OR DIDN'T LISTEN? GET IT TOGETHER, PARKER! YOU'RE WAITING FOR LIFE TO HAPPEN WHILE IT'S PASSING BY!
I REFUSE TO BE FRIENDS IF YOU'RE GONNA KEEP THIS UP, AND I CAN PROMISE YOU'LL NEVER GET NEAR MY JUNK IF YOU DON'T GRAB LIFE BY ITS JUNK.
I THOUGHT YOU WERE "DONE WITH NEW YORK". "EPMS?"
TODAY...IT'S ACTUAL PMS. BUT LIFE STILL SUCKS. THE CITY STILL SUCKS. THE WORLD IS A MENAGERIE OF PETRIFIED SUCK!
SO I HAVE PLENTY TO WRITE ABOUT, AND YOU HAVE LOTS OF PRETTY PICTURES TO SNAP, PHOTO-MONKEY, IF YOU CAN GET OUT OF THAT CHAIR.
THE CITY NEEDS ME.
THE END

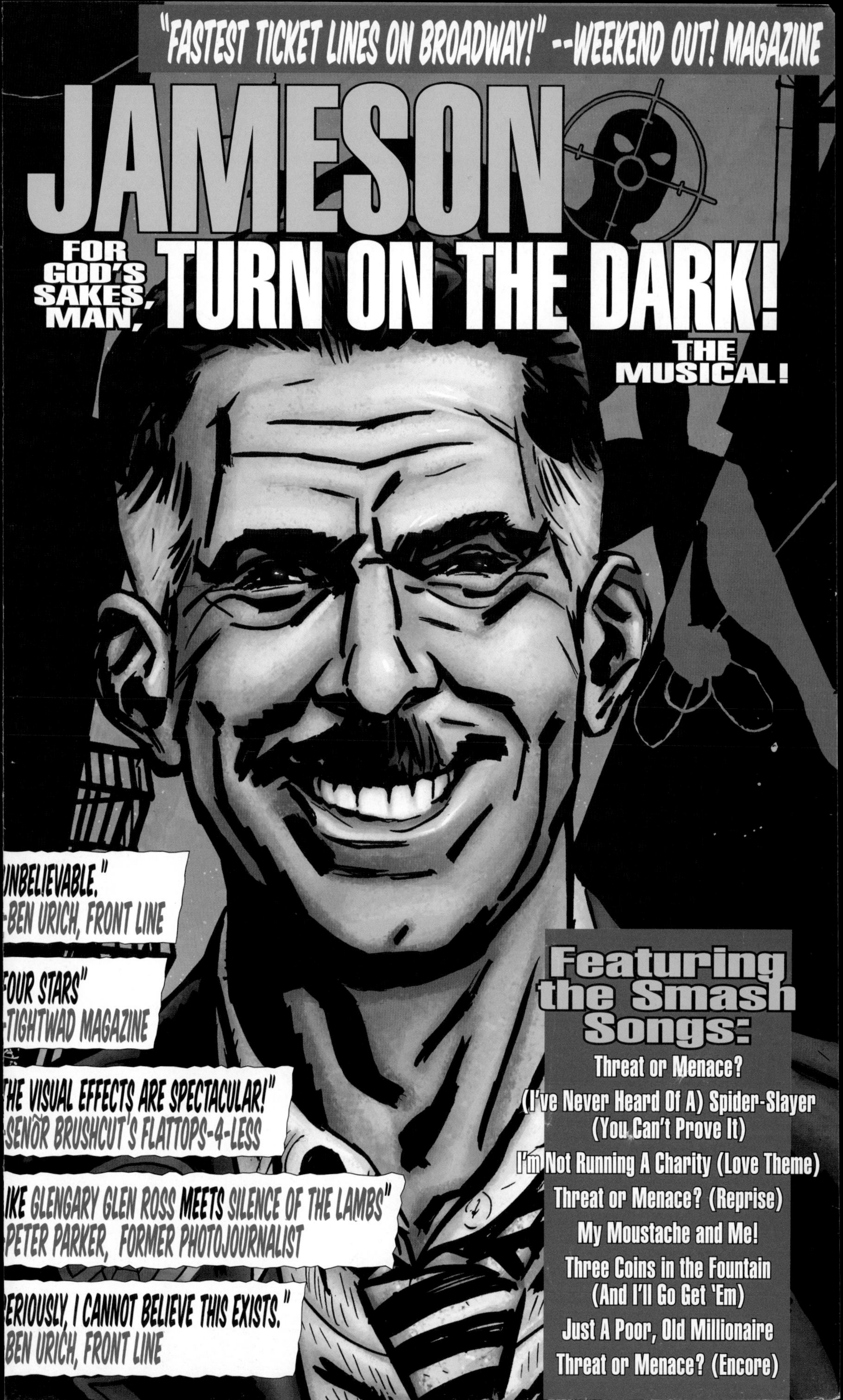
"FASTEST TICKET LINES ON BROADWAY!" --WEEKEND OUT! MAGAZINE
JAMESON
FOR GOD'S SAKES, MAN, TURN ON THE DARK!
THE MUSICAL!
UNBELIEVABLE."
-BEN URICH, FRONT LINE
FOUR STARS"
-TIGHTWAD MAGAZINE
THE VISUAL EFFECTS ARE SPECTACULAR!"
-SENÕR BRUSHCUT'S FLATTOPS-4-LESS
IKE GLENGARY GLEN ROSS MEETS SILENCE OF THE LAMBS"
PETER PARKER, FORMER PHOTOJOURNALIST
ERIOUSLY, I CANNOT BELIEVE THIS EXISTS."
BEN URICH, FRONT LINE
Featuring the Smash Songs:
Threat or Menace?
(I've Never Heard Of A) Spider-Slayer (You Can't Prove It)
I'm Not Running A Charity (Love Theme)
Threat or Menace? (Reprise)
My Moustache and Me!
Three Coins in the Fountain (And I'll Go Get 'Em)
Just A Poor, Old Millionaire
Threat or Menace? (Encore)

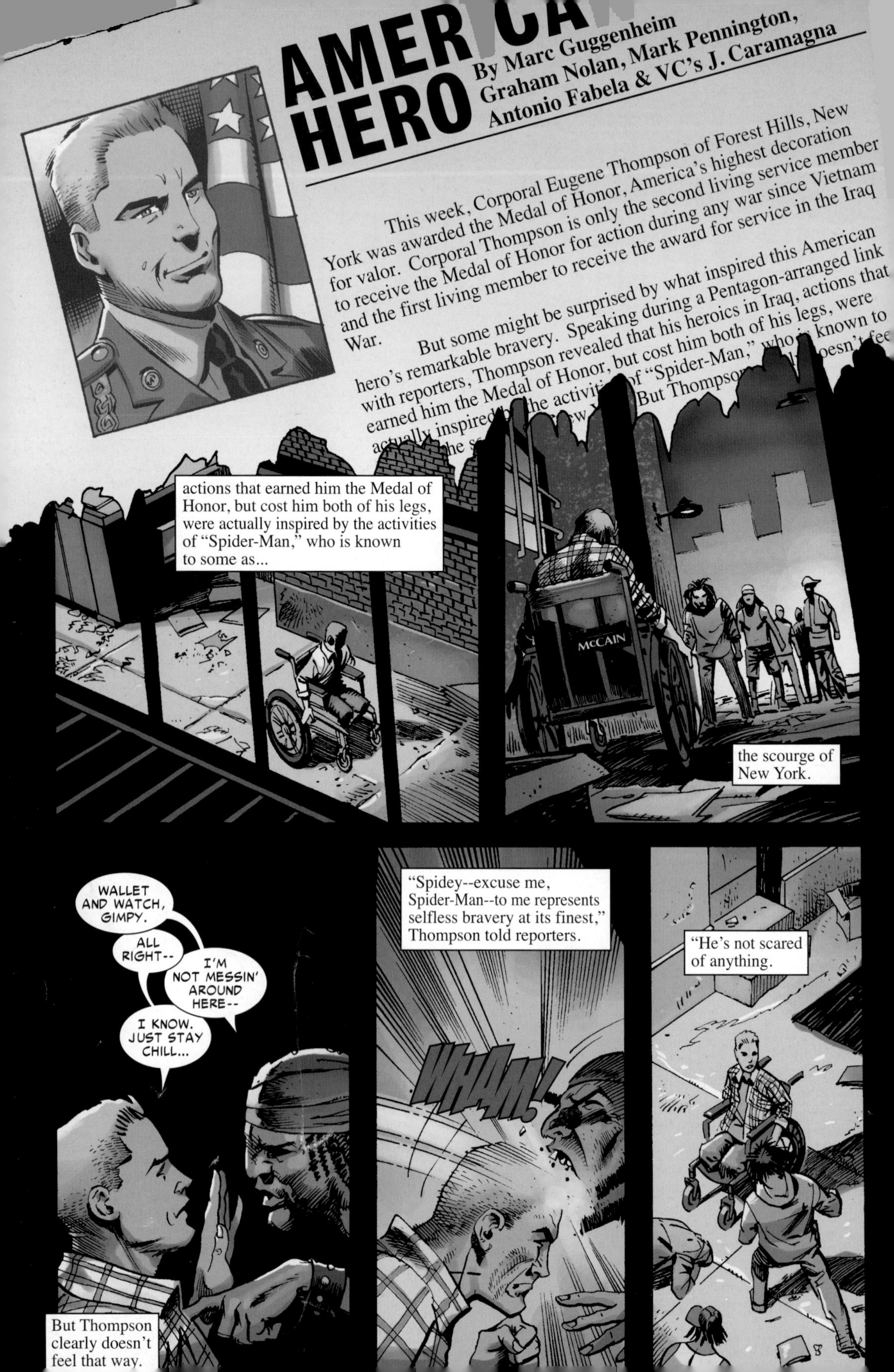

AMER CA HERO
By Marc Guggenheim
Graham Nolan, Mark Pennington,
Antonio Fabela & VC's J. Caramagna
This week, Corporal Eugene Thompson of Forest Hills, New York was awarded the Medal of Honor, America's highest decoration for valor. Corporal Thompson is only the second living service member to receive the Medal of Honor for action during any war since Vietnam and the first living member to receive the award for service in the Iraq War.
But some might be surprised by what inspired this American hero's remarkable bravery. Speaking during a Pentagon-arranged link with reporters, Thompson revealed that his heroics in Iraq, actions that earned him the Medal of Honor, but cost him both of his legs, were
actions that earned him the Medal of Honor, but cost him both of his legs, were actually inspired by the activities of "Spider-Man," who is known to some as...
McCAIN
the scourge of New York.
WALLET AND WATCH, GIMPY.
ALL RIGHT--
I'M NOT MESSIN' AROUND HERE--
I KNOW. JUST STAY CHILL...
But Thompson clearly doesn't feel that way.
"Spidey--excuse me, Spider-Man--to me represents selfless bravery at its finest," Thompson told reporters.
WHAM!
"He's not scared of anything.

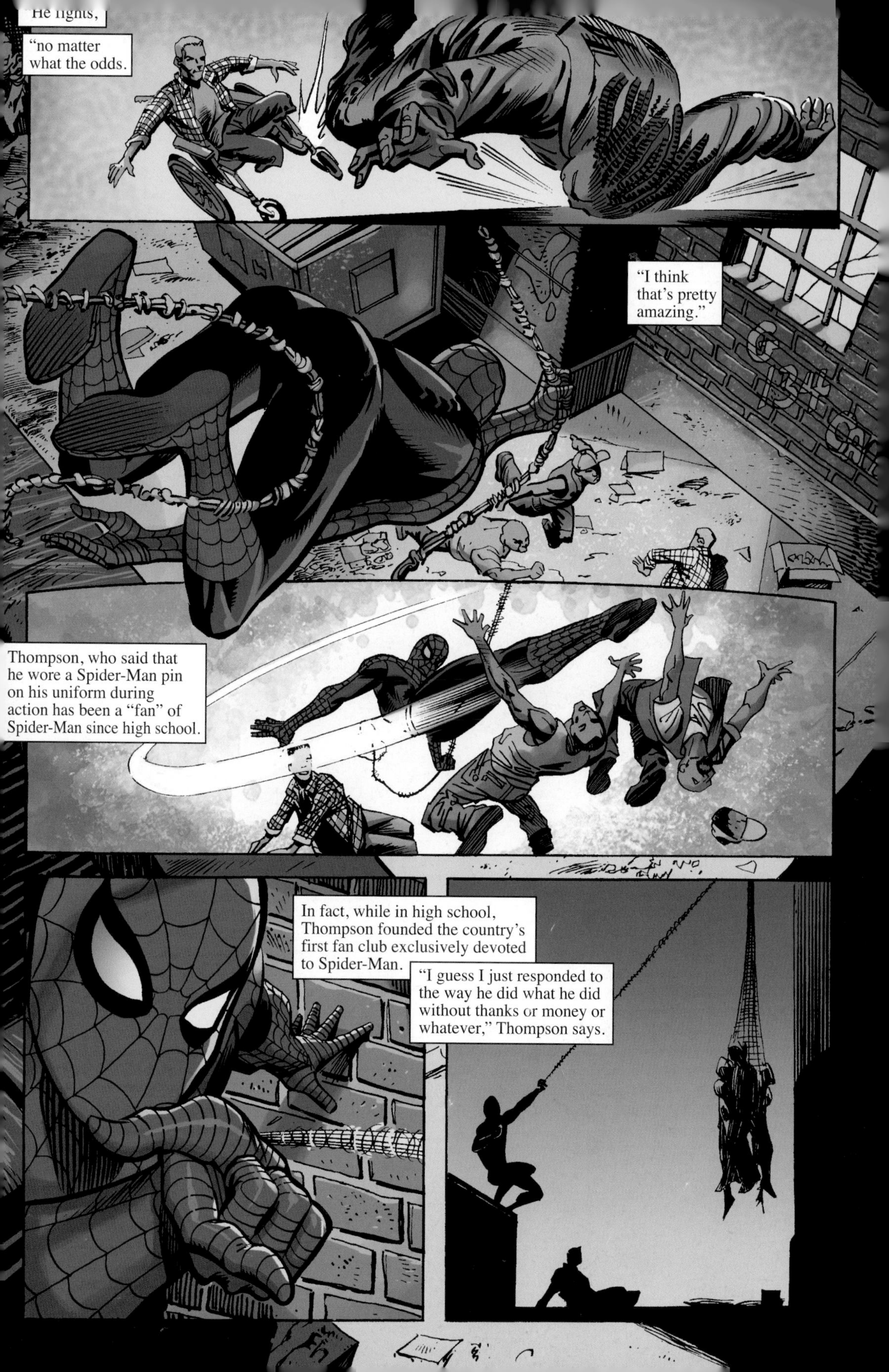
"He fights,
"no matter what the odds.
"I think that's pretty amazing."
Thompson, who said that he wore a Spider-Man pin on his uniform during action has been a "fan" of Spider-Man since high school.
In fact, while in high school, Thompson founded the country's first fan club exclusively devoted to Spider-Man.
"I guess I just responded to the way he did what he did without thanks or money or whatever," Thompson says.

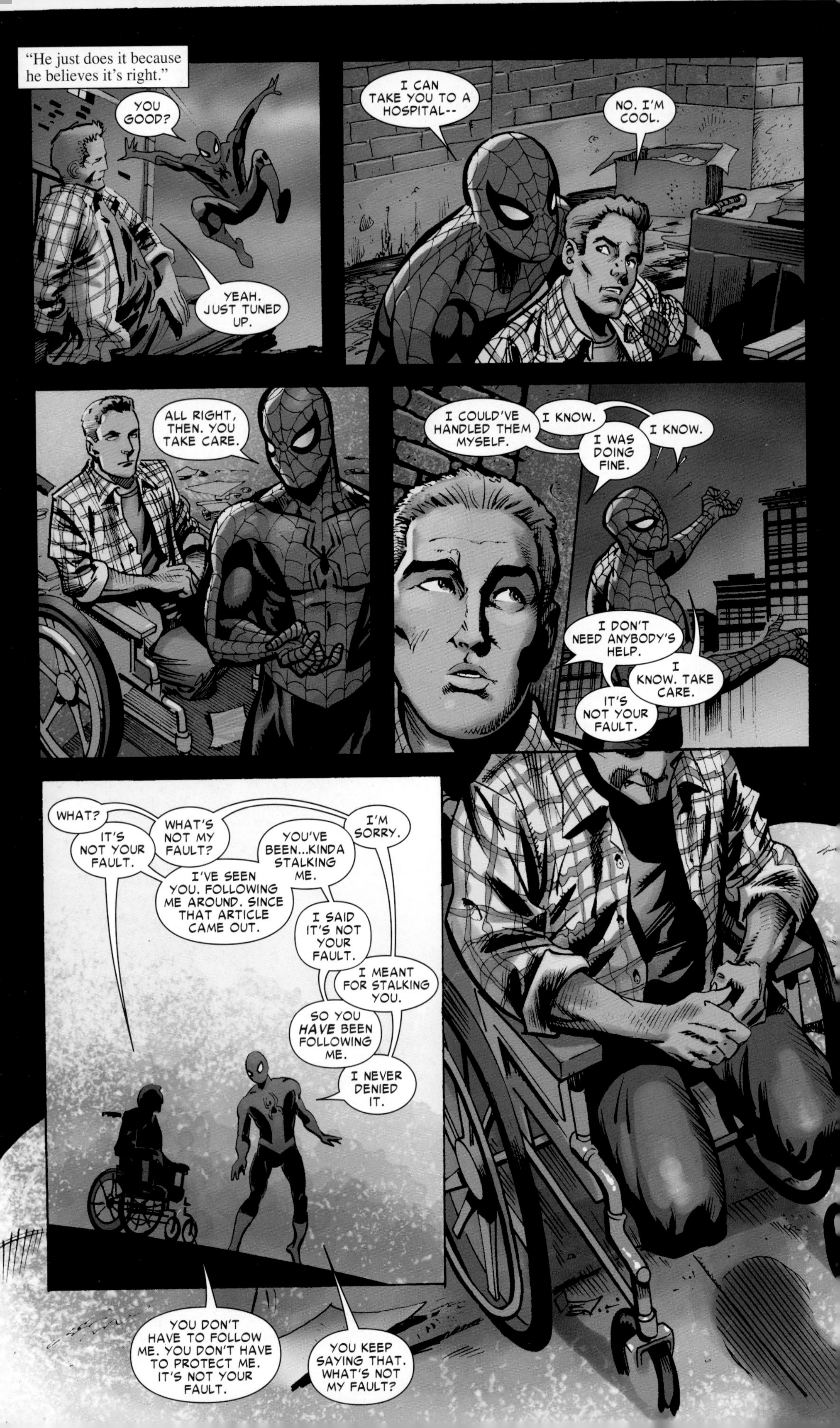
"He just does it because he believes it's right."
YOU GOOD?
YEAH. JUST TUNED UP.
I CAN TAKE YOU TO A HOSPITAL--
NO. I'M COOL.
ALL RIGHT, THEN. YOU TAKE CARE.
I COULD'VE HANDLED THEM MYSELF.
I KNOW.
I WAS DOING FINE.
I KNOW.
I DON'T NEED ANYBODY'S HELP.
I KNOW. TAKE CARE.
IT'S NOT YOUR FAULT.
WHAT?
IT'S NOT YOUR FAULT.
WHAT'S NOT MY FAULT?
YOU'VE BEEN...KINDA STALKING ME.
I'M SORRY.
I'VE SEEN YOU. FOLLOWING ME AROUND. SINCE THAT ARTICLE CAME OUT.
I SAID IT'S NOT YOUR FAULT.
I MEANT FOR STALKING YOU.
SO YOU *HAVE* BEEN FOLLOWING ME.
I NEVER DENIED IT.
YOU DON'T HAVE TO FOLLOW ME. YOU DON'T HAVE TO PROTECT ME. IT'S NOT YOUR FAULT.
YOU KEEP SAYING THAT. WHAT'S NOT MY FAULT?

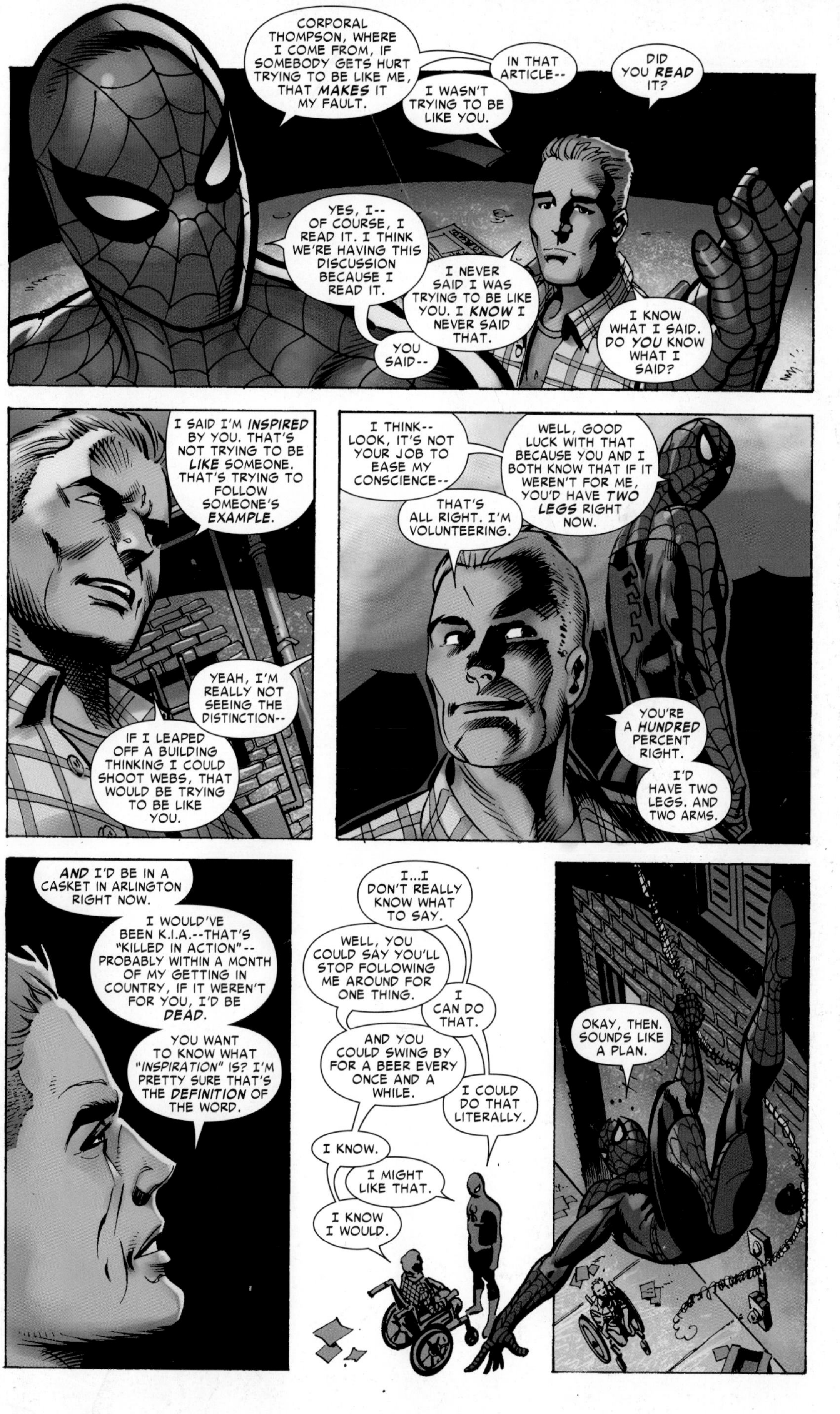
CORPORAL THOMPSON, WHERE I COME FROM, IF SOMEBODY GETS HURT TRYING TO BE LIKE ME, THAT MAKES IT MY FAULT.
IN THAT ARTICLE--
I WASN'T TRYING TO BE LIKE YOU.
DID YOU READ IT?
YES, I-- OF COURSE, I READ IT. I THINK WE'RE HAVING THIS DISCUSSION BECAUSE I READ IT.
I NEVER SAID I WAS TRYING TO BE LIKE YOU. I KNOW I NEVER SAID THAT.
YOU SAID--
I KNOW WHAT I SAID. DO YOU KNOW WHAT I SAID?
I SAID I'M INSPIRED BY YOU. THAT'S NOT TRYING TO BE LIKE SOMEONE. THAT'S TRYING TO FOLLOW SOMEONE'S EXAMPLE.
YEAH, I'M REALLY NOT SEEING THE DISTINCTION--
IF I LEAPED OFF A BUILDING THINKING I COULD SHOOT WEBS, THAT WOULD BE TRYING TO BE LIKE YOU.
I THINK-- LOOK, IT'S NOT YOUR JOB TO EASE MY CONSCIENCE--
THAT'S ALL RIGHT. I'M VOLUNTEERING.
WELL, GOOD LUCK WITH THAT BECAUSE YOU AND I BOTH KNOW THAT IF IT WEREN'T FOR ME, YOU'D HAVE TWO LEGS RIGHT NOW.
YOU'RE A HUNDRED PERCENT RIGHT.
I'D HAVE TWO LEGS. AND TWO ARMS.
AND I'D BE IN A CASKET IN ARLINGTON RIGHT NOW.
I WOULD'VE BEEN K.I.A.--THAT'S "KILLED IN ACTION"--PROBABLY WITHIN A MONTH OF MY GETTING IN COUNTRY, IF IT WEREN'T FOR YOU, I'D BE DEAD.
YOU WANT TO KNOW WHAT "INSPIRATION" IS? I'M PRETTY SURE THAT'S THE DEFINITION OF THE WORD.
I...I DON'T REALLY KNOW WHAT TO SAY.
WELL, YOU COULD SAY YOU'LL STOP FOLLOWING ME AROUND FOR ONE THING.
I CAN DO THAT.
AND YOU COULD SWING BY FOR A BEER EVERY ONCE AND A WHILE.
I COULD DO THAT LITERALLY.
I KNOW.
I MIGHT LIKE THAT.
I KNOW I WOULD.
OKAY, THEN. SOUNDS LIKE A PLAN.

CORPORAL THOMPSON.

FLASH--

... FLASH.

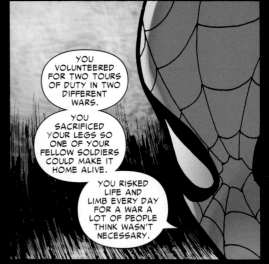

YOU VOLUNTEERED FOR TWO TOURS OF DUTY IN TWO DIFFERENT WARS.

YOU SACRIFICED YOUR LEGS SO ONE OF YOUR FELLOW SOLDIERS COULD MAKE IT HOME ALIVE.

YOU RISKED LIFE AND LIMB EVERY DAY FOR A WAR A LOT OF PEOPLE THINK WASN'T NECESSARY.

I KINDA KNOW ALL THAT. WHAT'S YOUR POINT?

THIS INSPIRATION THING?

IT WORKS BOTH WAYS.

After passage of the Superhuman Registration Act, Araña registered and received training under Ms. Marvel and Wonder Man, much to her father's dismay.

Battling the Doomsday Man with Ms. Marvel, Araña's carapace was violently torn from her body.

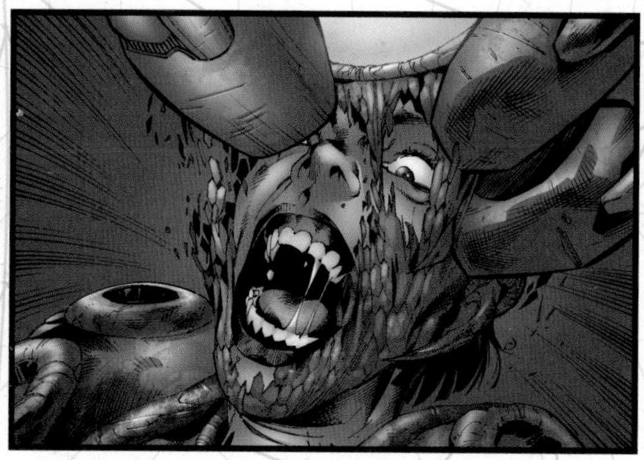

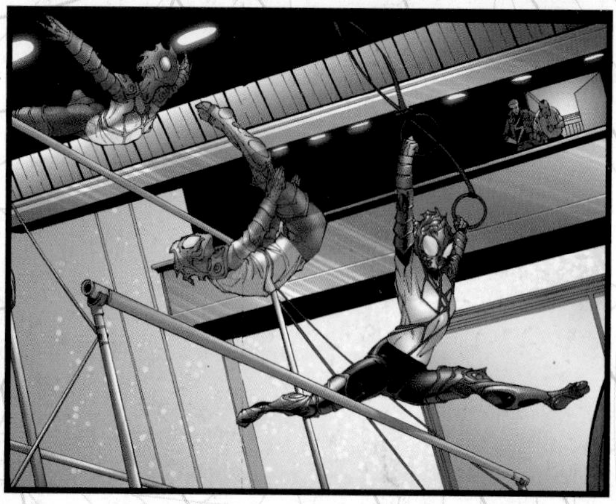

Despite this, Araña remained a hero and became friends with Nomad (Rikki Barnes); the two heroines worked together to expose the nefarious clandestine Secret Empire and shared their true identities with each other.

Kidnapped by the Kravinoff family – making human sacrifices to resurrect the family patriarch, Kraven the Hunter – Araña was rescued by Spider-Man. In the aftermath, Julia Carpenter gave Anya her Spider-Woman costume, while Julia became the new Madame Web.

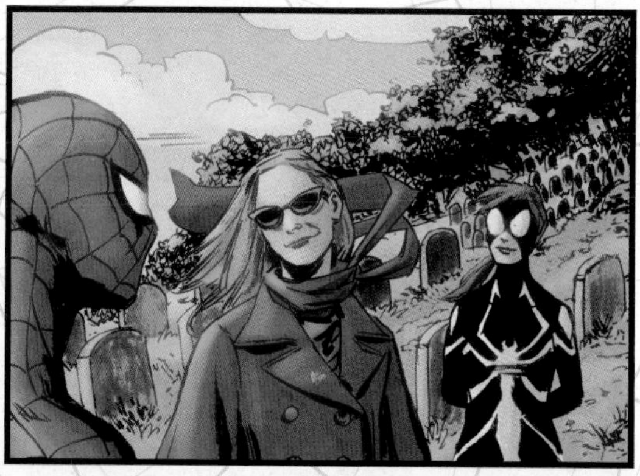

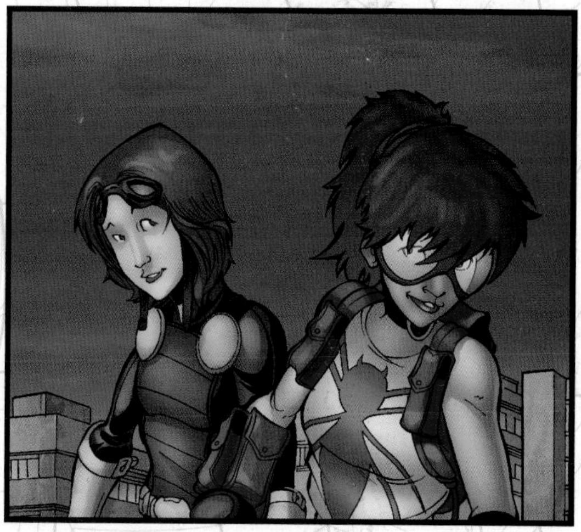

Araña and Nomad joined forces with Gravity, Firestar and Toro – forming the Young Allies and defending New York from the chaotic gang of alleged super-villain offspring, the Bastards of Evil.

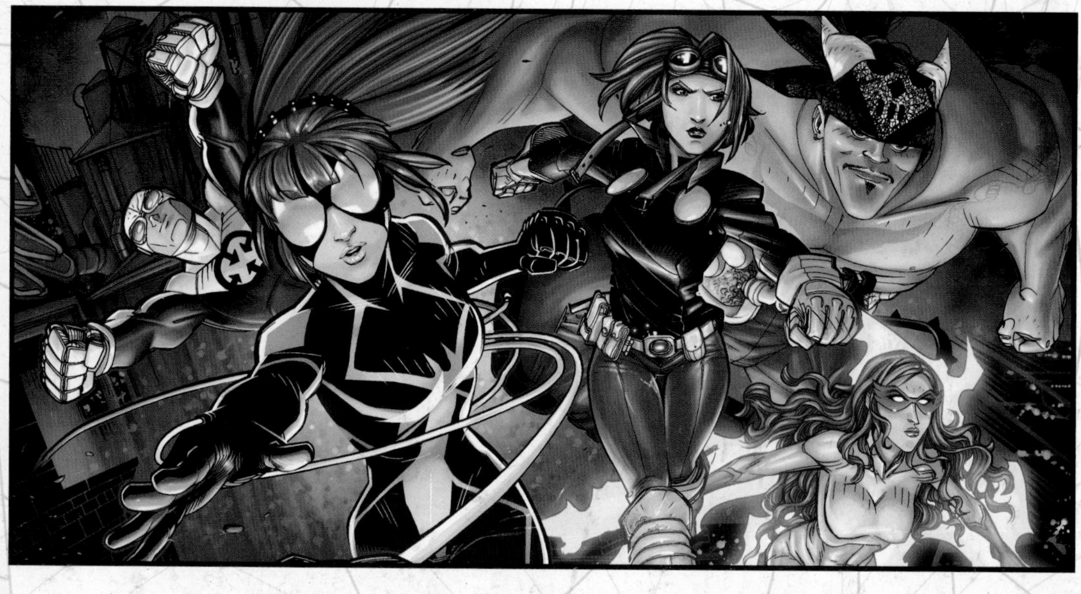

EXTREMIST

REAL NAME: Tyler Smithson
ALIASES: None
IDENTITY: Known to authorities
OCCUPATION: Terrorist
CITIZENSHIP: USA

PLACE OF BIRTH: Unrevealed
KNOWN RELATIVES: Unidentified mother (deceased)
GROUP AFFILIATION: None
EDUCATION: Unrevealed
FIRST APPEARANCE: Web of Spider-Man #8 (2010)

AS CHILD

Art by Javier Rodriguez with Pat Olliffe & Nick Dragotta (bottom inset)

HISTORY: Suffering from a rare form of Munchausen syndrome, a psychological disorder that made her falsely believe her son was a mutant, Tyler Smithson's mother repeatedly tried to enroll him in the Xavier Institute. Tyler developed a rigid sense of morality, seeing things in purely black-and-white terms; he saw super heroes as good and all who opposed them as evil agents of "the gray." When his mother was killed in a clash between warring crimelords Mr. Negative and the Hood (Parker Robbins), Tyler used the settlement money awarded to him to hire underworld surgeon Doc Tramma to give him superhuman abilities, including the power to see auras. Desiring to see only truth, Tyler gouged out his eyes and dubbed himself "the Extremist," swearing to destroy enemies of super heroes, starting by murdering TV pundit Mark Branden. He next targeted Peter Parker for posting unflattering pictures of Spider-Man online; Parker escaped his invisible attacker via his spider-sense, During the ensuing battle with Parker's alter ego, Spider-Man, Tyler was disappointed sensing the web-slinger's "flawed" aura. He next attacked New York City Mayor J. Jonah Jameson, hoping to lure Spider-Man to him and destroy him before he could tarnish his own image. After a pitched battle through City Hall, Spider-Man showed Tyler his own "gray" aura, distracting him long enough to be wounded by the building's laser defenses.

HEIGHT: 7'4" **WEIGHT:** 210 lbs. **EYES:** None (formerly blue) **HAIR:** None (formerly brown)

ABILITIES/ACCESSORIES: Smithson can fly, teleport, and become intangible; he can also make other people or objects intangible. He can also make himself visible to a selected individual, but invisible to all others. He carries a pistol that channels his energies into destructive blasts. He has limited telepathy and can perceive Kirlian auras despite being eyeless.

INTELLIGENCE: 2 **STRENGTH:** 3 **SPEED:** 2/7 (Teleportation) **DURABILITY:** 2
ENERGY PROJECTION: 5 **FIGHTING SKILLS:** 2

MICHELE GONZALES

REAL NAME: Michele Gonzales
ALIASES: "Satan," "Sheller"
IDENTITY: No dual identity
OCCUPATION: Criminal defense attorney; former public defender
CITIZENSHIP: USA
PLACE OF BIRTH: Hunts Point, New York City, New York

KNOWN RELATIVES: David Gonzales (father), Vincent Gonzales (brother)
GROUP AFFILIATION: None
EDUCATION: BS in political science, JD in law
FIRST APPEARANCE: (Partial) Amazing Spider-Man #592 (2009); (full) Amazing Spider-Man #594 (2009)

Art by Marco Checchetto

HISTORY: After working in Chicago as a criminal defense attorney, Michele Gonzales returned home to New York City, residing in her brother Vin's apartment and acting as his attorney for his involvement framing Spider-Man (Peter Parker) for murders. When Michele finally met her absentee roommate, Peter Parker, after two months, she caught him in the nude. Despite the awkward start, Michele volunteered to be Peter's date for his Aunt May's wedding, where Peter's ex-fiancée, Mary Jane, unexpectedly arrived. Anxious, Peter became intoxicated from a little champagne. Seeing her date's low alcohol tolerance, Michele substituted his subsequent drinks with soda. That night, Peter and Michele slept together, but the following morning Michele was furious that Peter remorsefully barely remembered their passionate night. After temporarily kicking Peter out of the apartment, she continued to torment him. The Chameleon (Dmitri Smerdyakov) abducted and impersonated Peter for a couple of days. When Michele requested "Peter" find a new apartment, the Chameleon seduced her, leading Michele to mistakenly believe Peter and she were a couple. The real Peter returned and explained the impersonation, but the disbelieving Michele responded to Pete's romantic disinterest with a punch to his face. Things remained tumultuous, especially in light of Peter's unemployment, until one of Michele's clients, Lucas, sought her help. Though Michele always believed in Lucas' innocence, she caught him working for the Hood. Lucas strangled Michele until Peter saved her, softening Michele's animosity towards her roommate.

HEIGHT: 5'6" **WEIGHT:** 140 lbs. **EYES:** Brown **HAIR:** Black

ABILITIES/ACCESSORIES: Cunning and skillfully manipulative, Michele Gonzales has some knowledge of Tae Bo kickboxing and claims to know the Thai martial art Muay Thai.

INTELLIGENCE: 3 **STRENGTH:** 2 **SPEED:** 2 **DURABILITY:** 2
ENERGY PROJECTION: 1 **FIGHTING SKILLS:** 3

HISTORY: Pregnant scientist Sara Ehret was working on a cure for Parkinson's disease via gene therapy when she accidentally scratched herself with a syringe containing a virus designated "Lot 777." She immediately lapsed into a coma while the virus altered her DNA. After four months, she made a full recovery and gave birth without incident; due to her accident, however, the lab lost its funding, and her employer, Dr. Philip Alex Hayes, turned to crime as the masked drug lord the Rose to keep it running. Shortly afterward, Sara, her husband, Scott, and her infant daughter, Maddie, were imperiled by falling debris, dislodged by a criminal battling Spider-Man (Peter Parker); Sara grabbed the debris before it could hit them. Realizing she had super-powers, she adopted the costumed identity Jackpot, patterning her super-hero persona and appearance after her favorite soap opera actress, Mary Jane Watson, and registered with the Initiative. After a brief stint adventuring, during which she helped Spider-Man rescue bystanders from the villainous Overdrive, she was recognized in costume by her friend Alana Jobson. Tired of super-heroics, Sara sold her Jackpot identity to Alana, who falsely claimed she had powers of her own. After battling the terrorist Menace (Lily Hollister), teaming with fellow Initiative hero Blue Shield (Joseph Cartelli) to help hunt down the unregistered Spider-Man, and helping to repulse the Skrull invasion of Earth, Alana died when the drugs she used to give herself super-powers reacted negatively with the villain Blindspot (Nick Chernin)'s neurotoxin. Spider-Man confronted Sara, angry she had abdicated her responsibility. Feeling responsible for Alana's death, Sara readopted her Jackpot identity and resumed her vigilante activities.

During a battle with the mobster Hammerhead, her loose-fitting costume became a liability; shortly afterward, she switched to a more form-fitting outfit. She generally tried to avoid superhuman opponents, but ran afoul of the super villain Boomerang (Fred Myers) while investigating a drug smuggling operation (which, unbeknownst to her, was run by Hayes). Myers got the better of her, but she escaped by shooting him with her grappling-hook pistol; Hayes later found her fingerprints on the grappling hook and discovered her secret identity. After teaming with Spider-Man to battle one of Hayes' drug dealers, the White Rabbit (Lorina Dodson), she enlisted Reed Richard's aid to determine the Rose's drugs were derived from the Corruptor (Jackson Day)'s psychoactive sweat glands. Before she could investigate further, Boomerang, disguised as a Chinese food delivery man, murdered Scott in front of her and Madeline; grievously wounding Myers, Sara escaped and teamed with Spider-Man to hunt down the Rose, then battled Myers again, nearly killing him before Spider-Man convinced her to stop. Her identity compromised, the authorities relocated Sara and her daughter to Sherman Oaks, California; to honor her late friend and protect herself, Sara changed her name to Alana Jobson. She was called back to New York to testify against Boomerang; learning Myers had been targeted by Chinatown crimelord Mr. Negative ("Martin Li") to prevent him from testifying against one of his affiliate syndicates, Eastern Wind, she donned her costume again to learn more. After battling the Shocker (Herman Schultz), she discovered an assassination attempt was imminent; at Ryker's Island, she learned Negative's agent Black Dragon had seemingly killed Myers, but she tracked him to Negative's hideout, where Myers was being held prisoner. Fighting her way through Negative and his Inner Demon henchmen to rescue Myers, Jackpot turned him back over to the authorities. Myers testified against Eastern Wind and the charges against him were dropped, leaving Scott's murder unpunished.

HEIGHT: 5'10"
WEIGHT: 140 lbs.
EYES: Green
HAIR: Black (dyed red)

ABILITIES/ACCESSORIES: Jackpot has superhuman strength (lifting 1 ton), durability, and endurance. She carries a grappling-hook launcher. Ehret is also a skilled biologist.

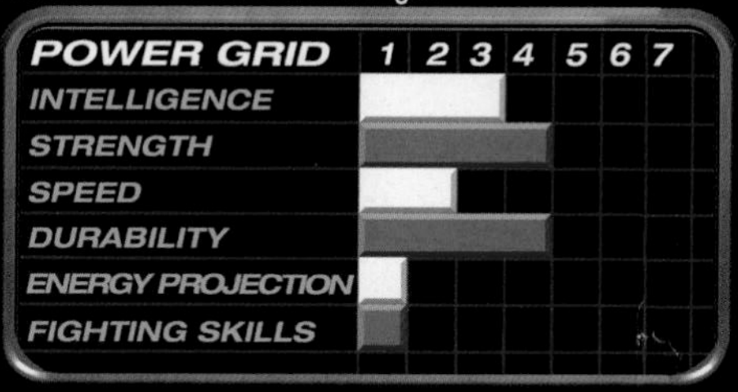
POWER GRID
1 2 3 4 5 6 7
INTELLIGENCE
STRENGTH
SPEED
DURABILITY
ENERGY PROJECTION
FIGHTING SKILLS

REAL NAME: Alana Jobson (legally changed from Sara Ehret)
ALIASES: None
IDENTITY: Known to authorities; Ehret identity publicly known
OCCUPATION: Unrevealed; former biologist, government super-agent
CITIZENSHIP: USA, with a criminal record
PLACE OF BIRTH: Port Washington, New York
KNOWN RELATIVES: Madeline "Maddie" Ehret/Sydney Jobson (daughter), Scott Ehret (husband, deceased)
GROUP AFFILIATION: Formerly Initiative
EDUCATION: BS in biology, PhD in molecular genetics
FIRST APPEARANCE: Free Comic Book Day 2007 (Spider-Man) #1 (2007)

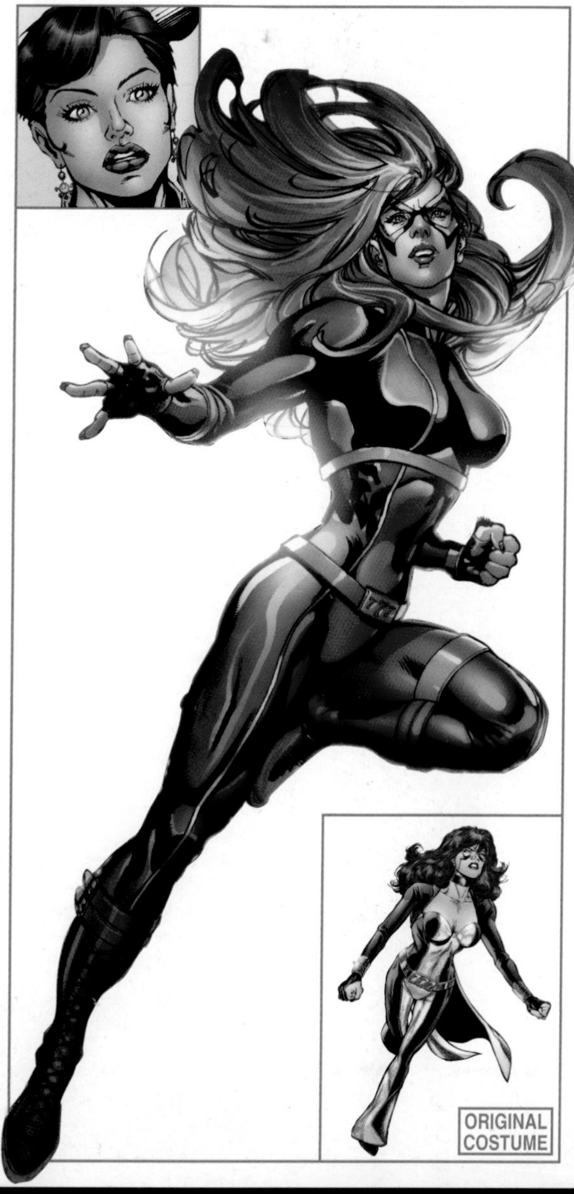

ORIGINAL COSTUME

J. JONAH JAMESON SR.

REAL NAME: John Jonah "Jay" Jameson Sr.
ALIASES: Unrevealed pseudonym
IDENTITY: No dual identity
OCCUPATION: Retiree; former writer, soldier
CITIZENSHIP: USA; former citizen of an unidentified foreign country
PLACE OF BIRTH: Lower Manhattan, New York
KNOWN RELATIVES: May Parker-Jameson (wife), unidentified first wife (deceased), J. Jonah Jameson Jr. (son), Marla Madison-Jameson (daughter-in-law), John Jameson (Man-Wolf, grandson), David Jameson (brother), Betty Burnoll Jameson, April and Jan Reilly (sisters-in-law), Peter Parker (Spider-Man, nephew-in-law), extended Reilly family
GROUP AFFILIATION: Formerly US Army
EDUCATION: High school graduate
FIRST APPEARANCE: Amazing Spider-Man #578 (2009)

Art by Barry Kitson

HISTORY: As a young man, J. Jonah Jameson Sr. went AWOL from the army to tend to his ailing pregnant wife. His wife died shortly after the birth of their son, J. Jonah Jr., and Jay was dishonorably discharged for deserting the army. Unable to raise the boy on his own, he left Jonah with his stern brother, David, and David's wife, Betty. Jay lived abroad, becoming a very successful author under a pen name. Jay returned to New York City as a retiree, approximately a year prior to his son becoming mayor. While Jay was a member of a jury traveling by subway, his train was derailed under the East River by the Shocker (Herman Schultz), who was hired by mobsters to protect one of their bosses on trial. Spider-Man (Peter Parker), also aboard the train, rescued Jay and the jury from drowning. Later, a chance encounter with reporter Betty Brant left Jay with a recommendation to meet Peter's aunt, the widow May Parker. May and Jay dated for several weeks, fell in love, and quickly became engaged. Jay surprised May at their rehearsal dinner in Boston, reuniting her with her sister and family. On May and Jay's wedding day, a dying Dr. Octopus (Otto Octavius) attempted to take over New York City's networks and public facilities. Jay was held captive until Spider-Man rescued him and regained control of the city. The couple enjoyed a honeymoon around the world.

HEIGHT: 5'8"	WEIGHT: 152 lbs.	EYES: Brown	HAIR: White

ABILITIES/ACCESSORIES: J. Jonah Jameson Sr. is a highly skilled professional writer and an amateur genealogist.

INTELLIGENCE: 3 STRENGTH: 1 SPEED: 1 DURABILITY: 1
ENERGY PROJECTION: 1 FIGHTING SKILLS: 1

SASHA KRAVINOFF

REAL NAME: Aleksandra "Sasha" Kravinoff (nee Nikolaevna)
ALIASES: Aleksandra Kravenova, "Angel"
IDENTITY: No dual identity
OCCUPATION: Hunter
CITIZENSHIP: Russia
PLACE OF BIRTH: Unrevealed
KNOWN RELATIVES: Sergei Kravinoff (Kraven the Hunter, husband), Vladimir Kravinoff (Grim Hunter, son, deceased), Anastasia Tatiana Kravinoff (Kraven, daughter), Mikhail Aleksei Nikolaevich (father, deceased), Aleksandra Nikolaevna (mother, deceased), Dimitri Smerdyakov (Chameleon, brother-in-law)
GROUP AFFILIATION: None
EDUCATION: Unrevealed
FIRST APPEARANCE: Amazing Spider-Man #594 (2009)

HISTORY: The daughter of Grand Duke Mikhail, Sasha Nikolaevna was part of the Russian aristocracy before the Bolshevik Revolution. Living in exile outside Paris, France, her father encouraged her to seduce men for fortune, including the renowned hunter Sergei Kravinoff. Tired of her father's manipulations, she killed him and eventually married Sergei. Learning the secrets of mystical jungle potions, Sergei enhanced his strength

Art by Barry Kitson with Phillipe Briones (inset)

and longevity, which he shared with Sasha to maintain her youth. Many years later, the couple had two children, Vlad and Ana, while Sergei had at least two other children, Alyosha and Ned, outside his marriage. Several years after Sergei committed suicide, Sasha schemed to resurrect her husband. After sending Ana to compile information about Spider-Man (Peter Parker), she gathered many of the wall-crawler's top foes and orchestrated a barrage of attacks to weaken her enemy. Additionally, she kidnapped Spider-Man's "family," including Madame Web (Cassandra Webb), whom she drugged and exploited her precognitive powers, and Spider-Woman (Mattie Franklin), whom she ritually sacrificed to resurrect Vlad, albeit as a lion-man. Capturing Arachne (Julia Carpenter) and Araña (Ana Corazon), Sasha lured Spider-Man into the upstate New York Kravinoff mansion. Spider-Man's clone Kaine switched places with his "brother," and Sasha sacrificed Kaine, resurrecting Sergei from the dead. Spider-Man furiously defeated each of the Kravinoffs, ripping Sasha's face with his hand's adhesive powers, but stopped himself before slaying Sergei. The Kravinoff's fled to the Savage Land, where Sergei, ungrateful for his resurrection, killed Sasha with his bare hands and slew Vlad, leaving Ana and Alyosha to hunt each other.

HEIGHT: 5'7"	WEIGHT: 136 lbs.	EYES: Blue	HAIR: Black

ABILITIES/ACCESSORIES: Sasha Kravinoff had superhuman longevity via mystical jungle potions. She had limited knowledge of the occult and was a skilled hunter and strategist.

INTELLIGENCE: 3 STRENGTH: 2 SPEED: 2 DURABILITY: 2
ENERGY PROJECTION: 1 FIGHTING SKILLS: 4

REDEEMER

REAL NAME: Shep Gunderson
ALIASES: None
IDENTITY: Known to authorities
OCCUPATION: Psychiatrist
CITIZENSHIP: USA, with a criminal record
PLACE OF BIRTH: Omaha, Nebraska
KNOWN RELATIVES: None
GROUP AFFILIATION: None
EDUCATION: MD in psychiatry from Creighton College of Medicine
FIRST APPEARANCE: The Sinister Spider-Man #1 (2009)

HISTORY: A psychiatrist at the Brooklyn Psychiatric Hospital, Dr. Shep Gunderson formed a therapy group with several super villains who "Spider-Man" (actually the deranged Mac Gargan, impersonating Spider-Man as part of Norman Osborn's Avengers) had recently dismembered. The group included the neo-Nazi General Wolfram (Claude Cramer), the hyper-evolved pachyderm Hippo (Mrs. Fluffy Lumpkins), the sonic-powered Eleven (Jenni Pate), and the madness-inducing Dementoid (Richard Earle Amtower IV); they were also joined by the allegedly omnipotent Dr. Everything (Jonathan N. York). Donning a skull-themed mask, Gunderson dubbed himself "the Redeemer" to better relate to his patients. Convinced by his patients Spider-Man needed to be rehabilitated, Gunderson outfitted his charges with prosthetic limbs and lured Gargan to a warehouse with a fake nuclear bomb threat; once Gargan arrived, Gunderson demanded he apologize to his victims and enter anger management therapy. Gargan instead devoured Eleven and all of Gunderson's limbs and handed Dr. Everything over to the police. Still wishing to save New York from Gargan, Gunderson and his remaining allies Dementoid and Wolfram (whom Gunderson enlisted to carry his limbless torso in a papoose) sent photos of Gargan (who had been fomenting a gang war to discredit New York City Mayor J. Jonah Jameson) consorting with gangsters to Jameson, who handed them over to Osborn; seeing Gargan as a liability, Osborn sent his agents Bullseye (Lester) and Daken to kill him. Gunderson also presented the photos to the two warring gangs, uniting them against Gargan. They converged on Gargan at New York's Big Apple Festival; Gargan fought and defeated Osborn's agents, the gangs, and Dementoid, while Wolfram fled, leaving Gunderson helpless. Enraged, Gunderson confessed to Gargan in front of the chief of police, who took him away.

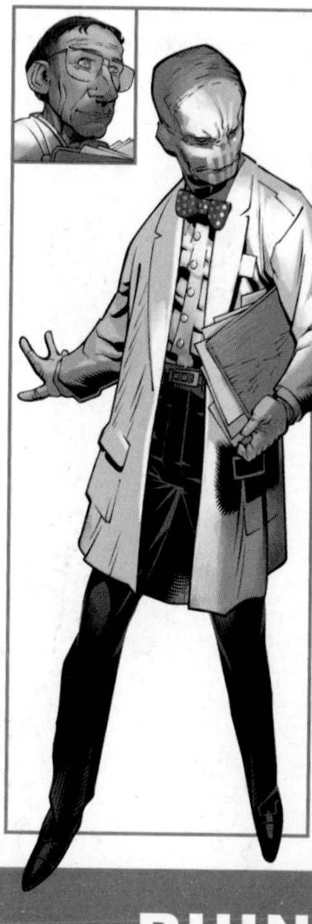
Art by Chris Bachalo

HEIGHT: 3'2" (formerly 5'4") **WEIGHT:** 105 lbs. (formerly 136 lbs.) **EYES:** Blue **HAIR:** Brown

ABILITIES/ACCESSORIES: Gunderson is an adequate psychiatrist. A quadruple amputee, his mobility is severely limited.

INTELLIGENCE: 3 **STRENGTH:** 1 **SPEED:** 1 **DURABILITY:** 2
ENERGY PROJECTION: 1 **FIGHTING SKILLS:** 1

RHINO

REAL NAME: Unrevealed
ALIASES: None
IDENTITY: Secret
OCCUPATION: Mercenary
CITIZENSHIP: Unrevealed
PLACE OF BIRTH: Unrevealed
KNOWN RELATIVES: None
GROUP AFFILIATION: Employed by unidentified gangsters
EDUCATION: Unrevealed
FIRST APPEARANCE: Amazing Spider-Man #617 (2010)

HISTORY: After giving an unidentified mercenary an armored Rhino-themed costume, Dr. Tramma, an underworld scientist and supplier of high-tech gadgetry to super villains, sold the new Rhino to a cadre of gangsters. Before joining the mobsters, the Rhino responded to a challenge from Sasha Kravinoff, widow of Kraven the Hunter (Sergei Kravinoff), to "ascend" into his new role by defeating the previous Rhino, Aleksei Sytsevich. At the Empire City Casino, the new Rhino challenged Aleksei to fight, smashing him with a racehorse, but Aleksei, now a married security guard, refused to retaliate. Ignoring Spider-Man (Peter Parker)'s interference, the Rhino departed once Aleksei surrendered. Seeing no honor in defeating Aleksei without combat, the Rhino was encouraged by Sasha, his "angel," to be patient, hone his skills and confront Aleksei again. Sasha's true motivation in developing the Rhino was to augment Spider-Man's enemies, wear down the hero, capture him, and sacrifice him to resurrect Sergei. At a naturalization ceremony attended by Aleksei's wife, Oksana, the Rhino attacked, but Aleksei told him to leave and meet him at midnight to fight. Instead, Aleksei and Oksana attempted to enter the Witness Protection Program. However, while en route to their secret destination, the Rhino destroyed their police transport, killing Oksana. While Spider-Man pleaded with him to stop, Aleksei retrieved his Rhino costume, battled the new Rhino, and apparently killed his successor.

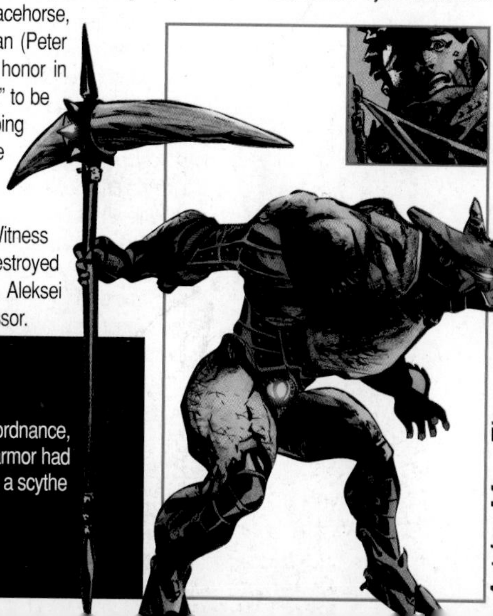
Art by Max Fiumara

HEIGHT: 7'4"; (armored) 7'10" **EYES:** Brown
WEIGHT: 456 lbs.; (armored) 1060 lbs. **HAIR:** Brown

ABILITIES/ACCESSORIES: When armored, the Rhino could withstand heavy ordnance, lift 90 tons, and charge at 125 mph via back-mounted propulsion generators. The armor had limited self-repair mechanisms and could burn debris off the eye-pieces. He wielded a scythe with a sharpened stone chine.

INTELLIGENCE: 2 **STRENGTH:** 6 **SPEED:** 3 **DURABILITY:** 5
ENERGY PROJECTION: 1 **FIGHTING SKILLS:** 3

VULTURE

REAL NAME: James "Jimmy" Natale
ALIASES: Jimmy the Fixer
IDENTITY: Known to authorities
OCCUPATION: Scavenger; former professional criminal
CITIZENSHIP: USA, with a criminal record

PLACE OF BIRTH: Unrevealed
KNOWN RELATIVES: None
GROUP AFFILIATION: Formerly Maggia
EDUCATION: Unrevealed
FIRST APPEARANCE: (Partial) Amazing Spider-Man #592 (2009); (full) Amazing Spider-Man #593 (2009)

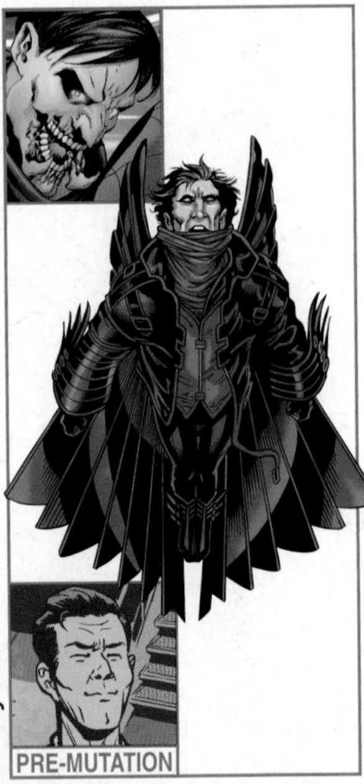
PRE-MUTATION
Art by Mike McKone with Paul Azaceta (bottom inset)

HISTORY: A "fixer" for several of New York City's low-level Maggia gangsters, Jimmy Natale excelled at cleaning crime scenes and disposing of bodies. Overwhelmed by the large amount of cleanup, Natale contacted Dr. Charles Goss, who had acquired the mutagenic equipment used by Farley and Harlan Stillwell, creators of the Scorpion (Mac Gargan) and Fly (Rick Deacon), to create a new Vulture to eliminate careless weaker criminals. Natale's bosses decided to use Jimmy as the test subject; Goss mutated him, destroying most of his memories in the process. Escaping before he could be deployed and remembering his betrayal, Natale began killing and eating wounded criminals. Spider-Man (Peter Parker) found Natale devouring a victim, and despite Natale's acid vomit blinding him, Spider-Man drove Natale off. After learning of Natale's origins from previous Vulture, Adrian Toomes, Spider-Man lured Natale into a battle, leading to Yankee Stadium. Spotting his enemy Norman Osborn in the stands, an enraged Spider-Man broke both of Natale's arms before police arrived to arrest the Vulture, but Electro (Max Dillon) freed Natale at the behest of Sasha Kravinoff, Kraven the Hunter (Sergei Kravinoff)'s widow, who sought to sow chaos in Spider-Man's life. One of Natale's old bosses lied telling Natale Mayor J. Jonah Jameson was responsible for his mutation.. Natale attacked Jameson, but when Spider-Man told him the truth about his transformation, Natale flew off to kill his former friends. Later, he was one of the many super villains Dr. Octopus (Otto Octavius) dispatched to find the pregnant Menace (Lily Hollister).

HEIGHT: 6' **WEIGHT:** 210 lbs. **EYES:** Red iris, yellow sclera **HAIR:** Brown

ABILITIES/ACCESSORIES: Natale has superhuman strength (lifting 1 ton) and durability and can fly; his wings, bonded to his torso, are razor-sharp. He can vomit a powerful acid. Before his mutation, Natale was a skilled criminal.

INTELLIGENCE: 2 **STRENGTH:** 4 **SPEED:** 2 **DURABILITY:** 4
ENERGY PROJECTION: 1 **FIGHTING SKILLS:** 2

NORAH WINTERS

REAL NAME: Norah Winters
ALIASES: "Bunny," "Nor'Easter"
IDENTITY: No dual identity
OCCUPATION: News reporter
CITIZENSHIP: USA

PLACE OF BIRTH: Racine, Wisconsin
KNOWN RELATIVES: Unidentified mother
GROUP AFFILIATION: Front Line newspaper
EDUCATION: BA in journalism
FIRST APPEARANCE: Amazing Spider-Man #575 (2008)

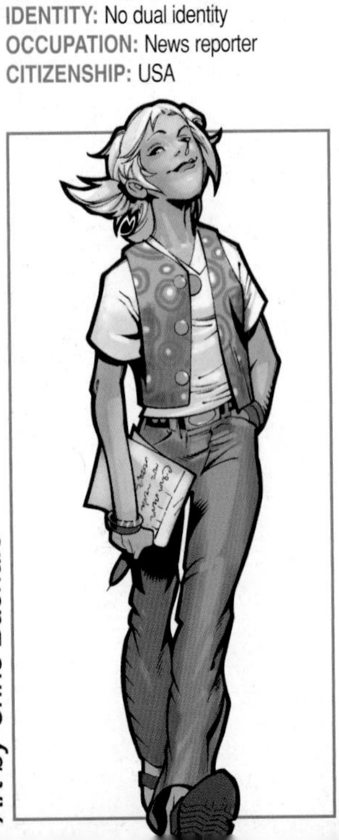
Art by Chris Bachalo

HISTORY: Front Line reporter Norah Winters earned a reputation covering community events, but she aspired for more exciting and dangerous news stories. Aided by photographer Peter Parker, who she alternately beguiles and aggravates, she broke her first big story writing an exposé of mobster Hammerhead (Joseph)'s gang recruitment activity among Bronx youth. Later, Norah began dating editor Joe Robertson's son, Randy, though she continued to flirt with Peter. Using her feminine wiles, Norah infiltrated Avengers Tower as a tour guide to obtain information on Norman Osborn, then-leader of US security forces. Though she discovered Osborn's American Son program was using human test subjects, she suppressed the story after Osborn intimidated her. Shortly thereafter, Norah and forensic detective Carlie Cooper were captured by Dr. Octopus (Otto Octavius), who was attempting to mentally control New York City's entire infrastructure; Spider-Man (Parker) and the Human Torch (Johnny Storm) rescued them. Norah accepted safer stories for a time and nearly resigned, but after witnessing a new Rhino violently challenge the retired former Rhino (Aleksei Sytsevich), she admitted to Peter his adventures as a photographer inspired her to embrace her dangerous career once again. She passed an Avengers Tower map to Peter, which enabled him, as Spider-Man, to acquire video footage of Osborn's inhuman experimentations. Parker uploaded the footage to the Internet to discredit Osborn. Later, Norah reported on the deaths of the new Rhino and Aleksei's wife.

HEIGHT: 5'8 **WEIGHT:** 118 lbs. **EYES:** Blue **HAIR:** Blonde

ABILITIES/ACCESSORIES: Norah Winters is a highly energetic and charismatic news reporter.

INTELLIGENCE: 3 **STRENGTH:** 2 **SPEED:** 2 **DURABILITY:** 2
ENERGY PROJECTION: 1 **FIGHTING SKILLS:** 2

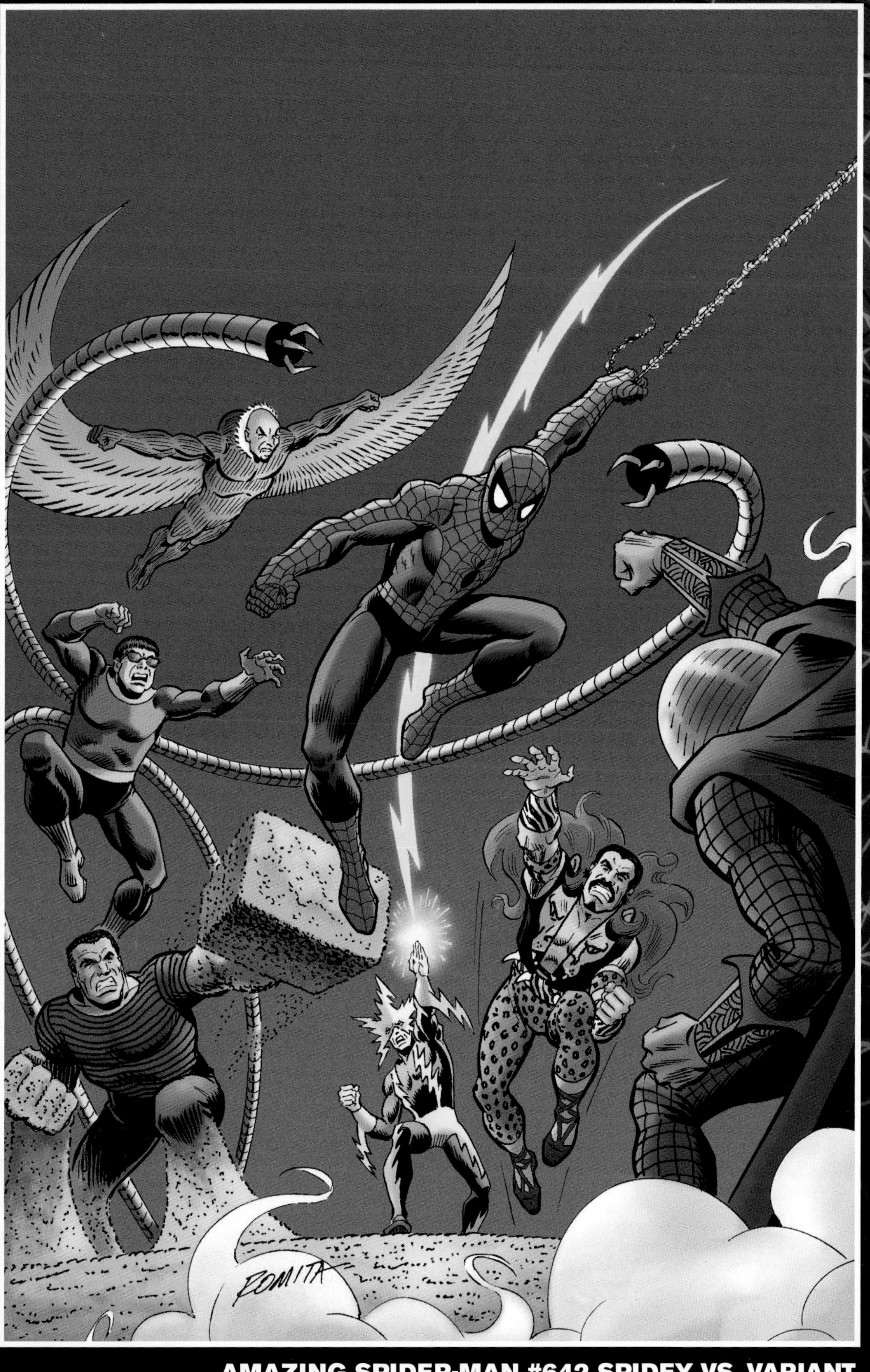
ROMITA

AMAZING SPIDER-MAN #642 SPIDEY VS. VARIANT
COVER BY JOHN ROMITA & LAURA MARTIN

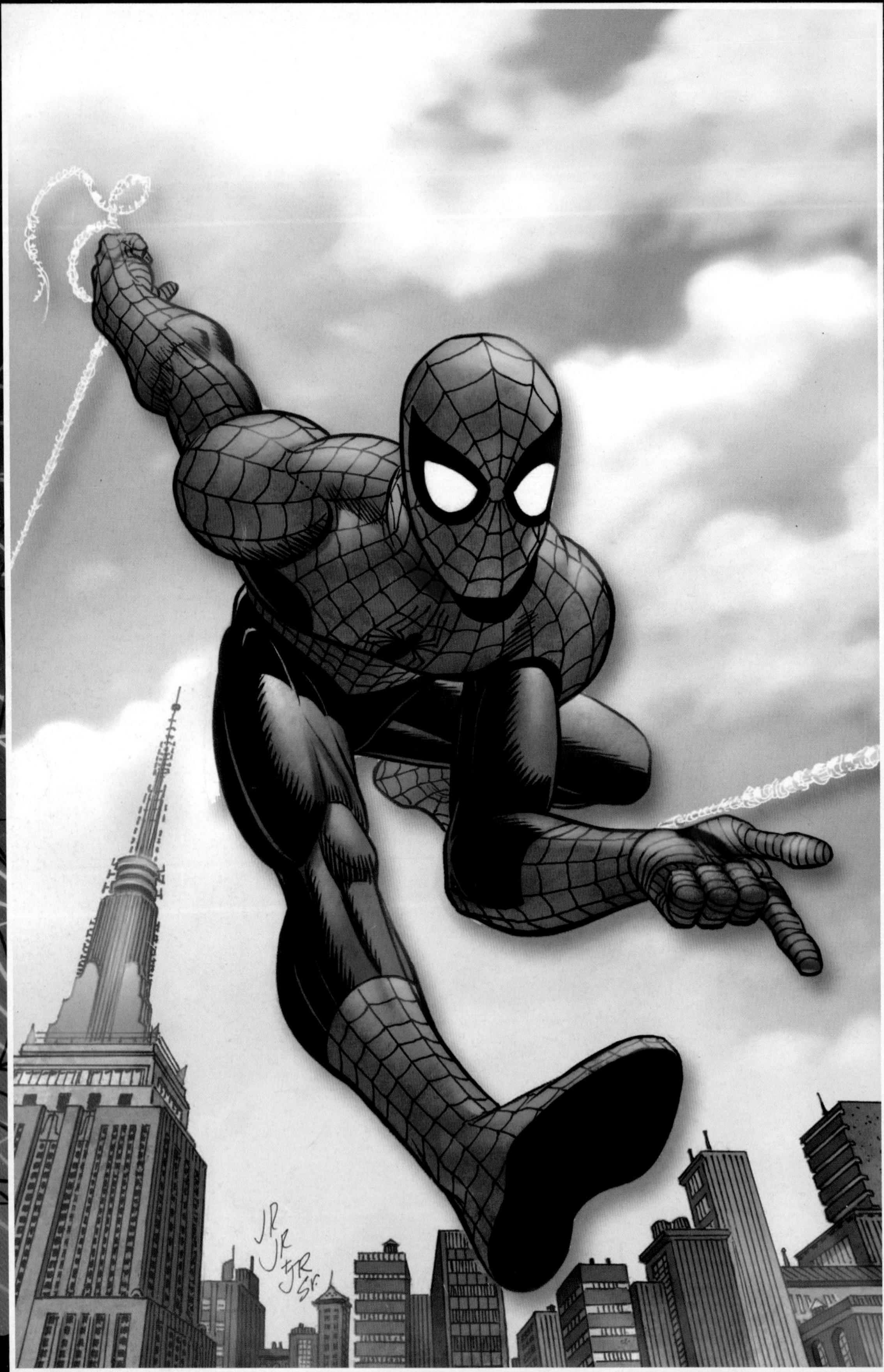

AMAZING SPIDER-MAN #642 NEW YORK COMIC CON VARIANT
COVER BY JOHN ROMITA, JOHN ROMITA JR. & SONIA OBACK

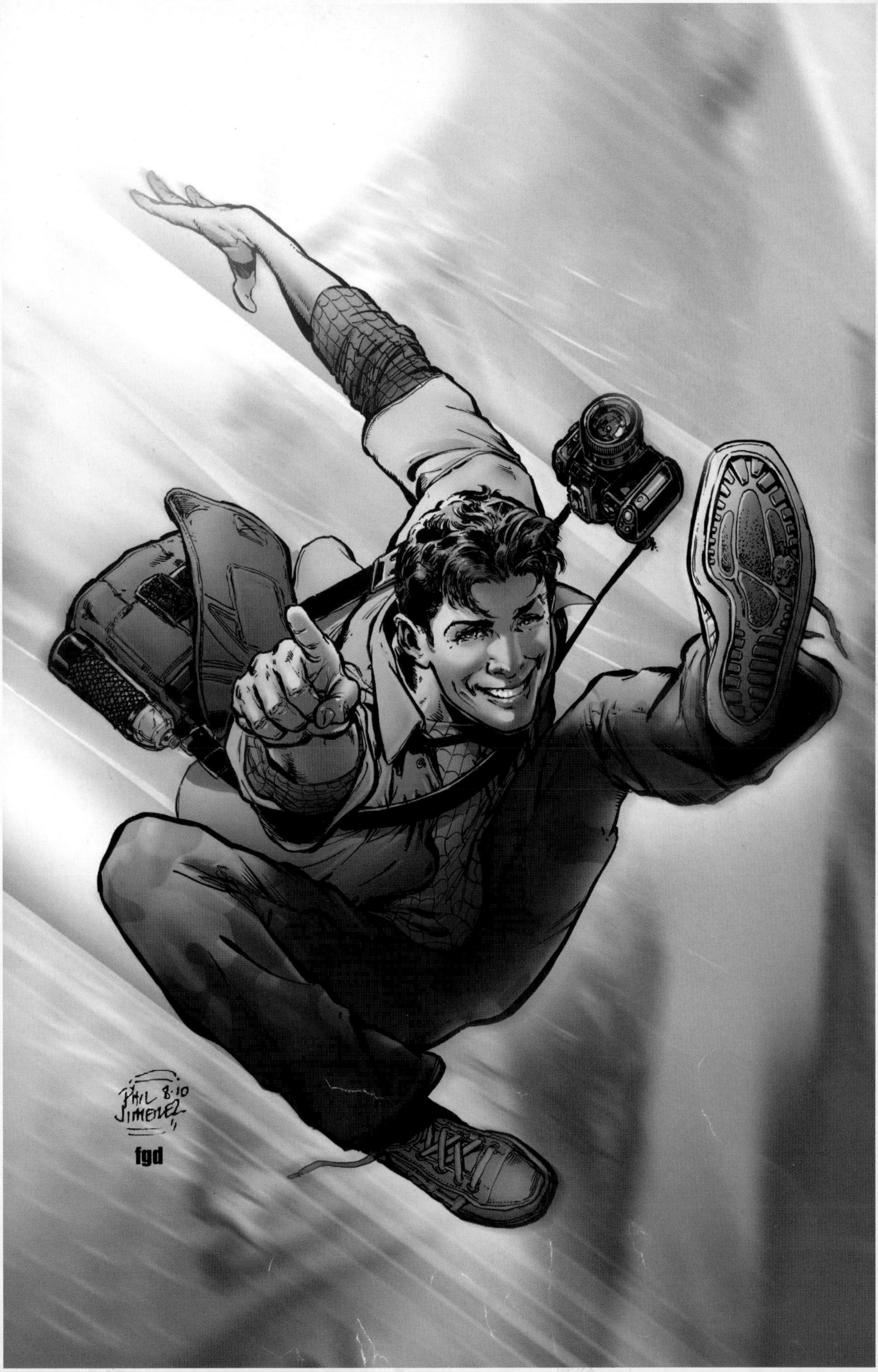
PHIL 8·10
JIMENEZ
fgd

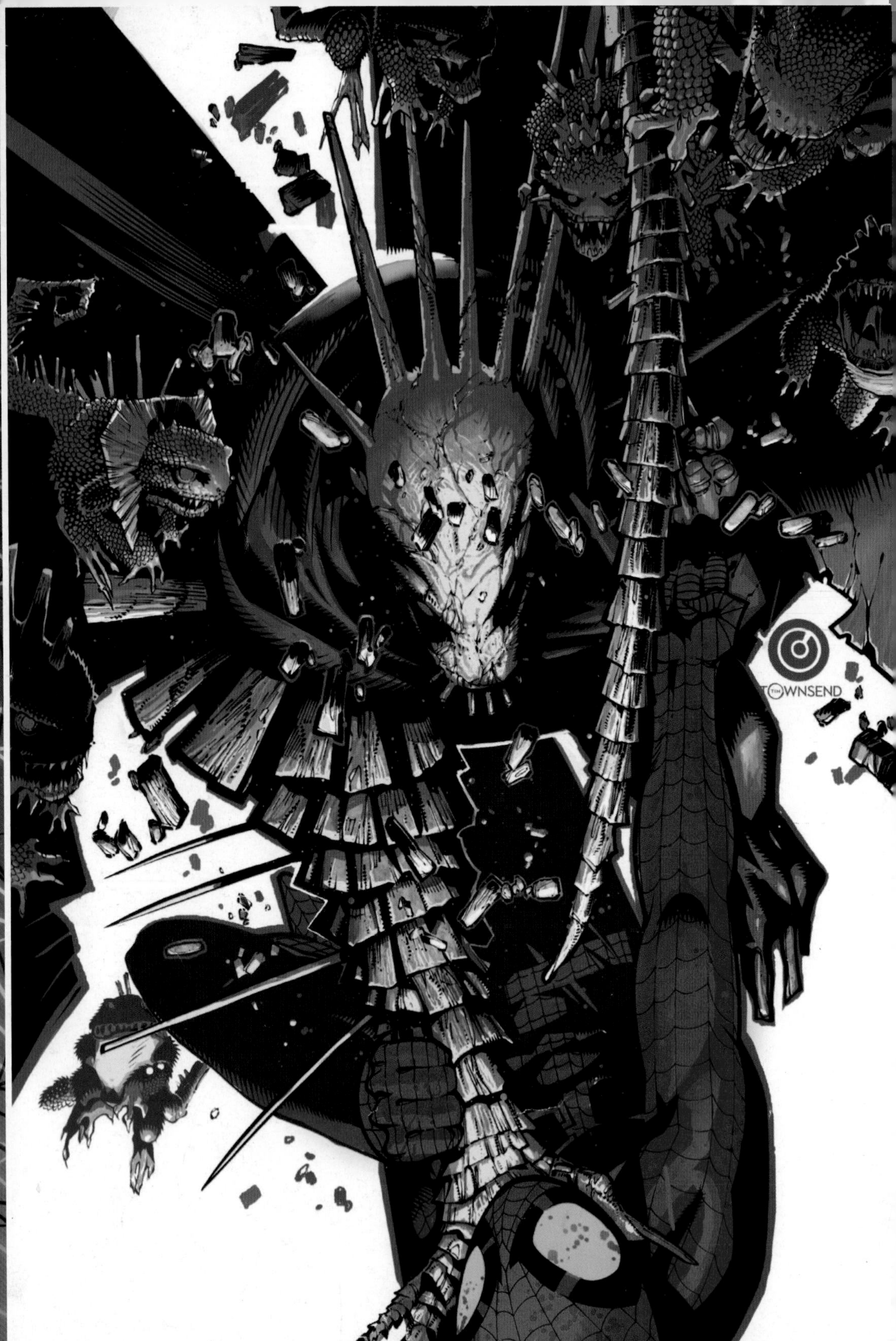
TIM TOWNSEND

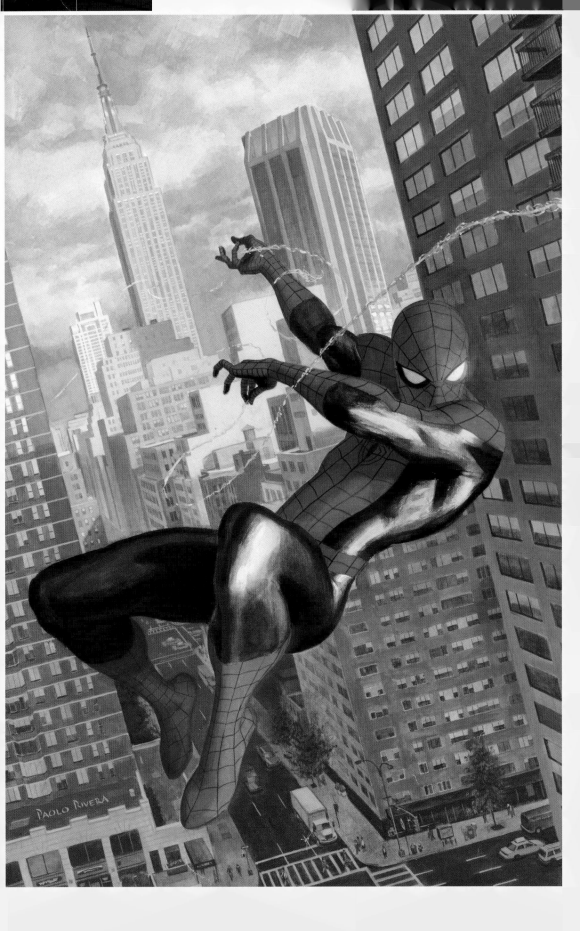

PAOLO RIVERA

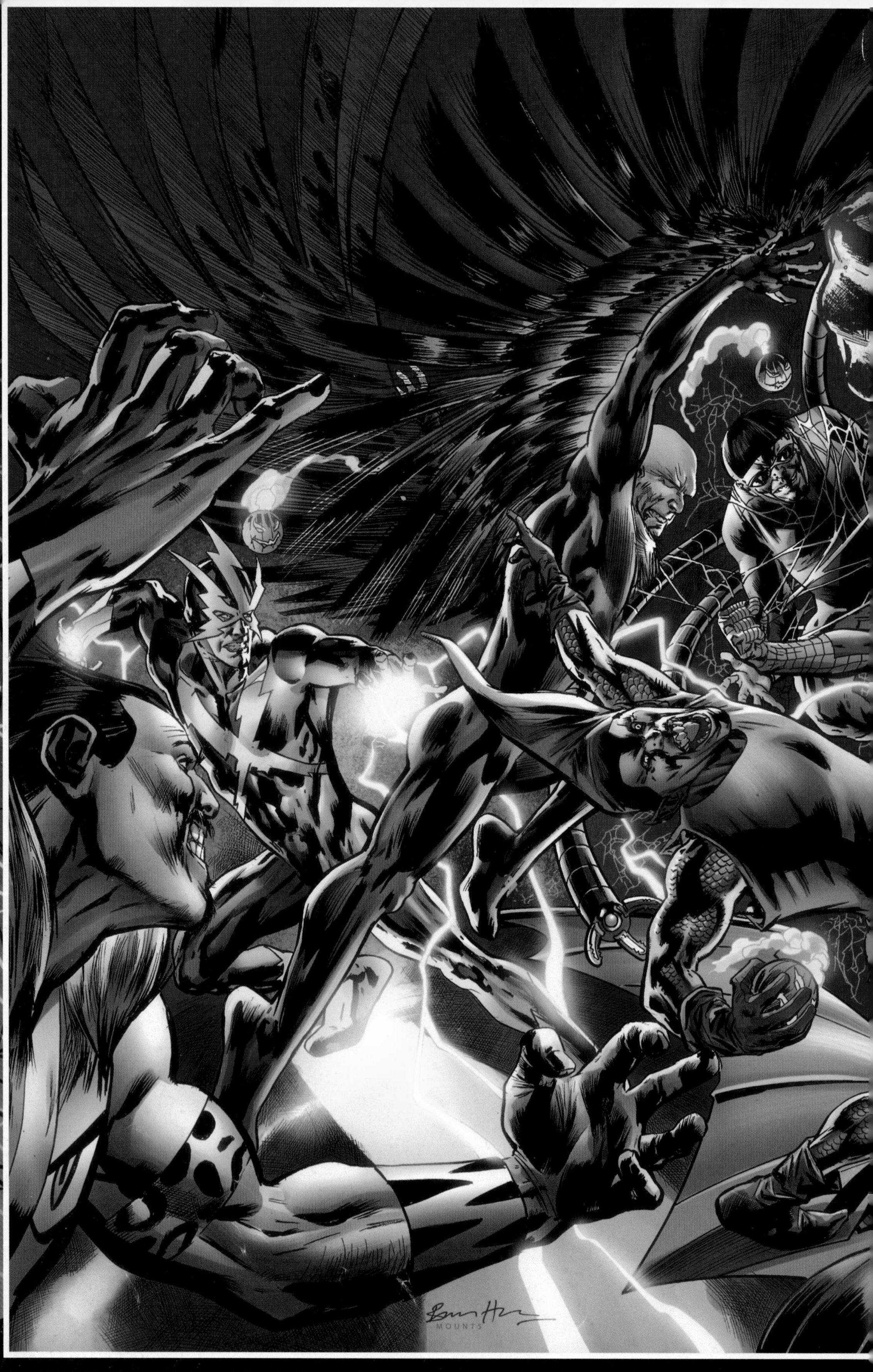

AMAZING SPIDER-MAN #645 SPIDEY VS. VARIANT

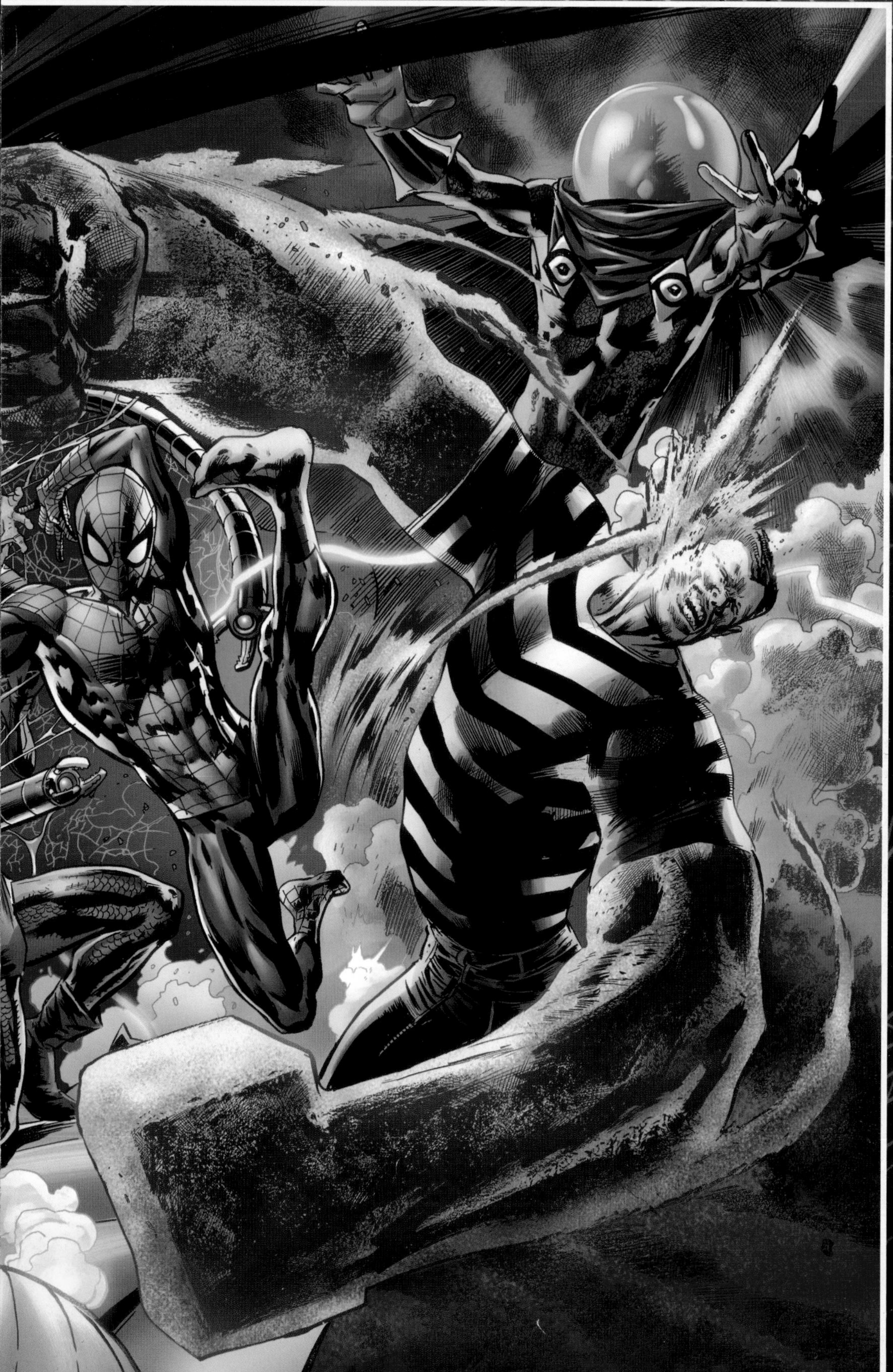

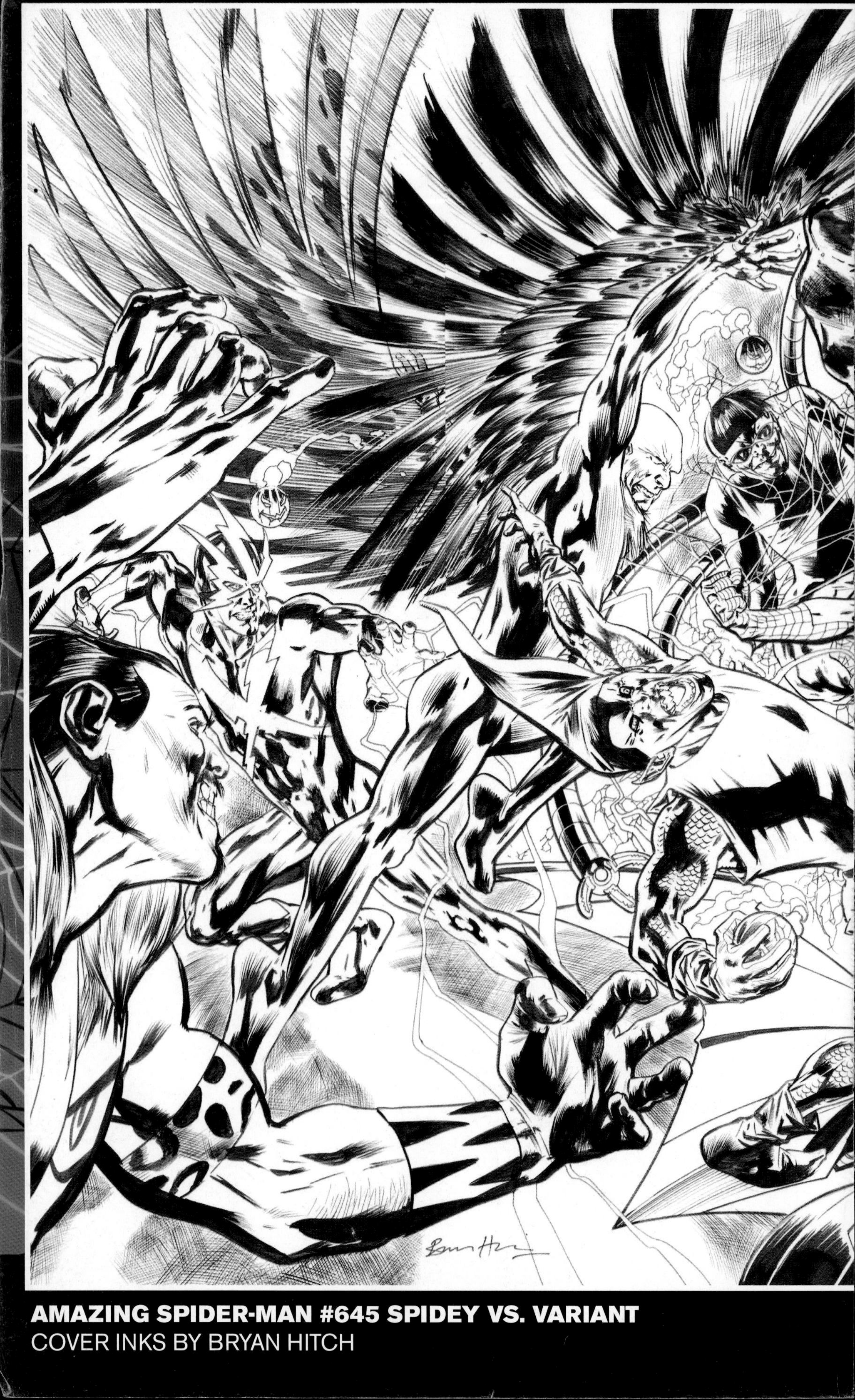

AMAZING SPIDER-MAN #645 SPIDEY VS. VARIANT
COVER INKS BY BRYAN HITCH

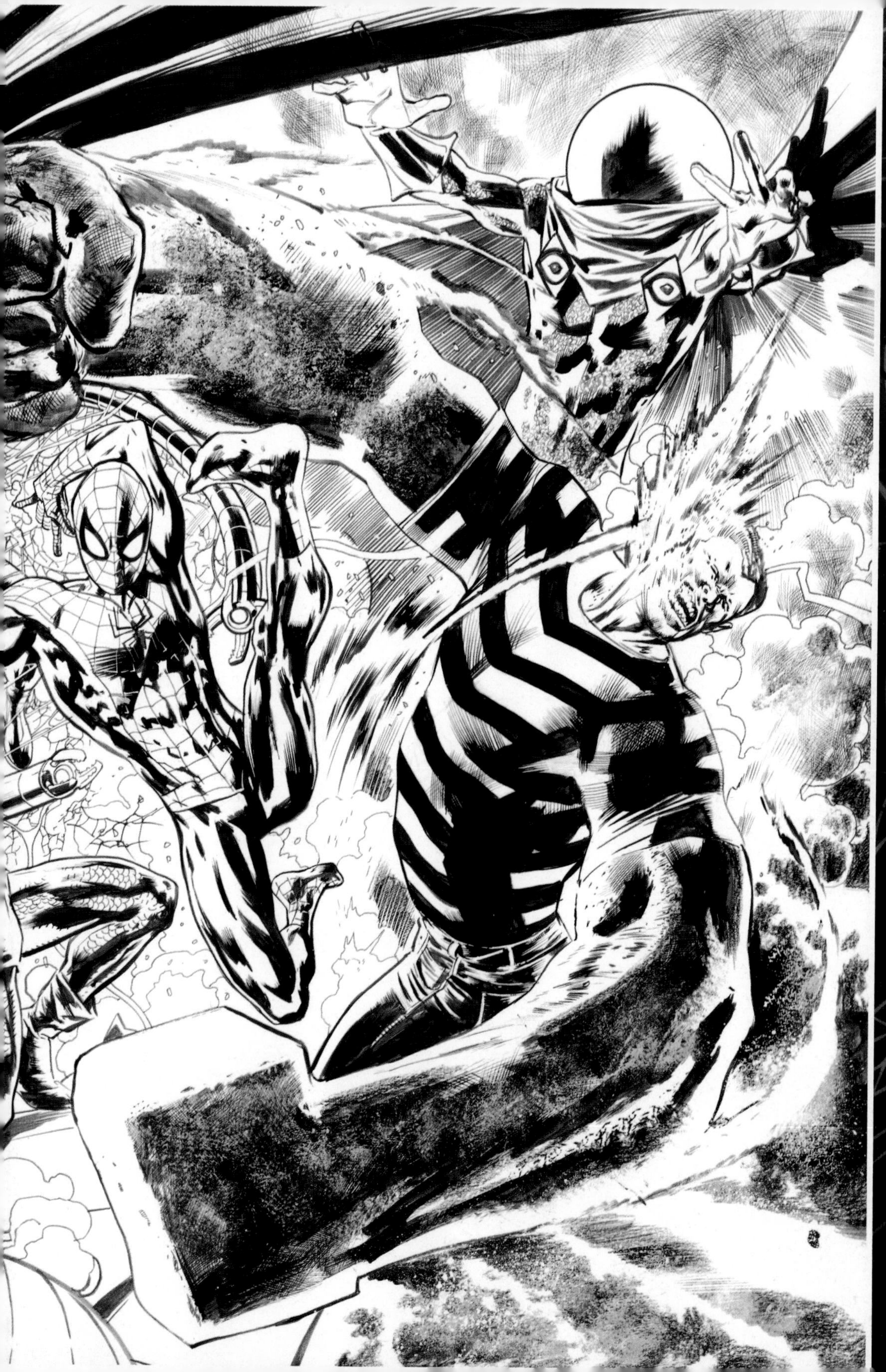

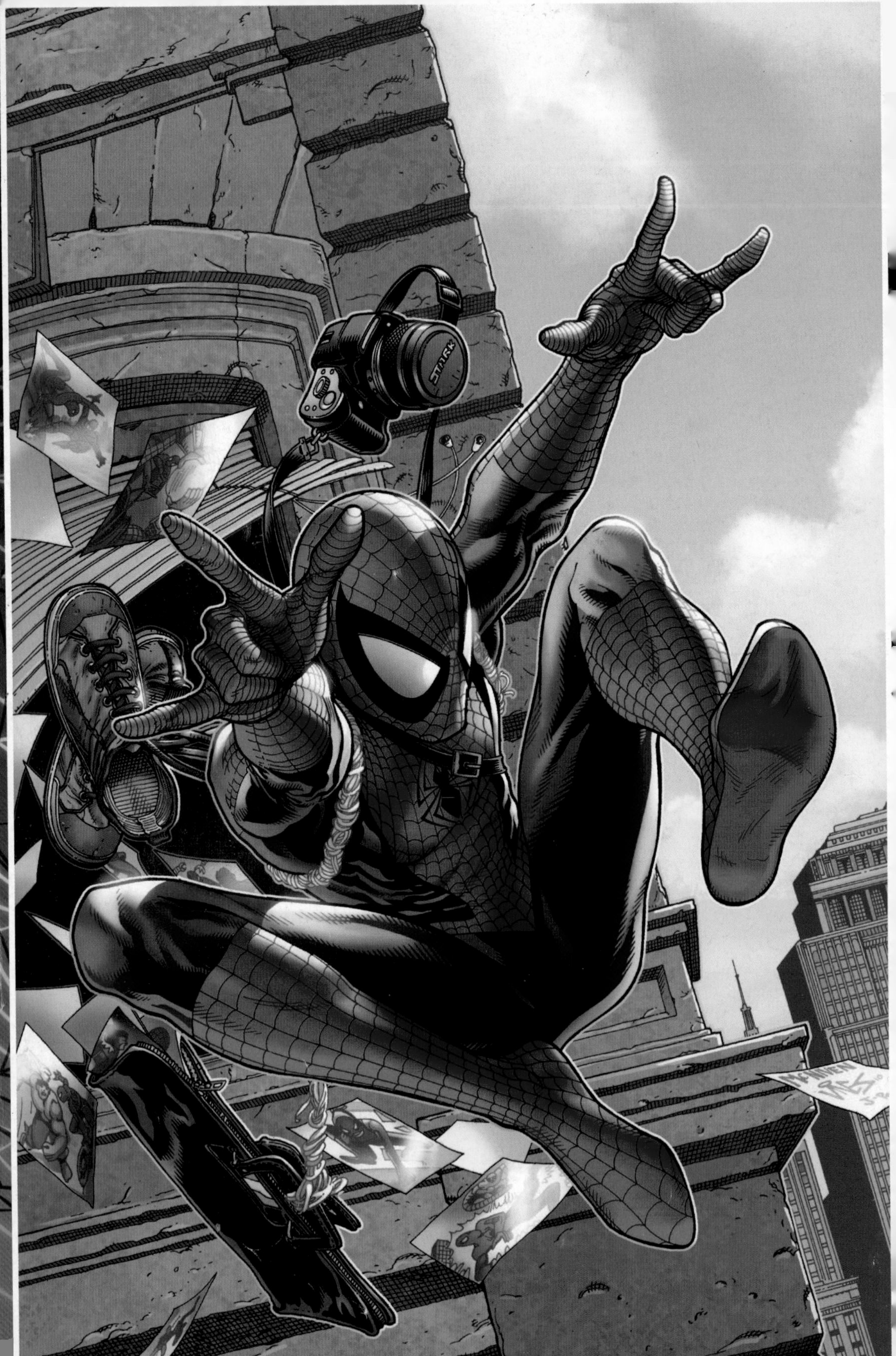
STARK
McNIVEN

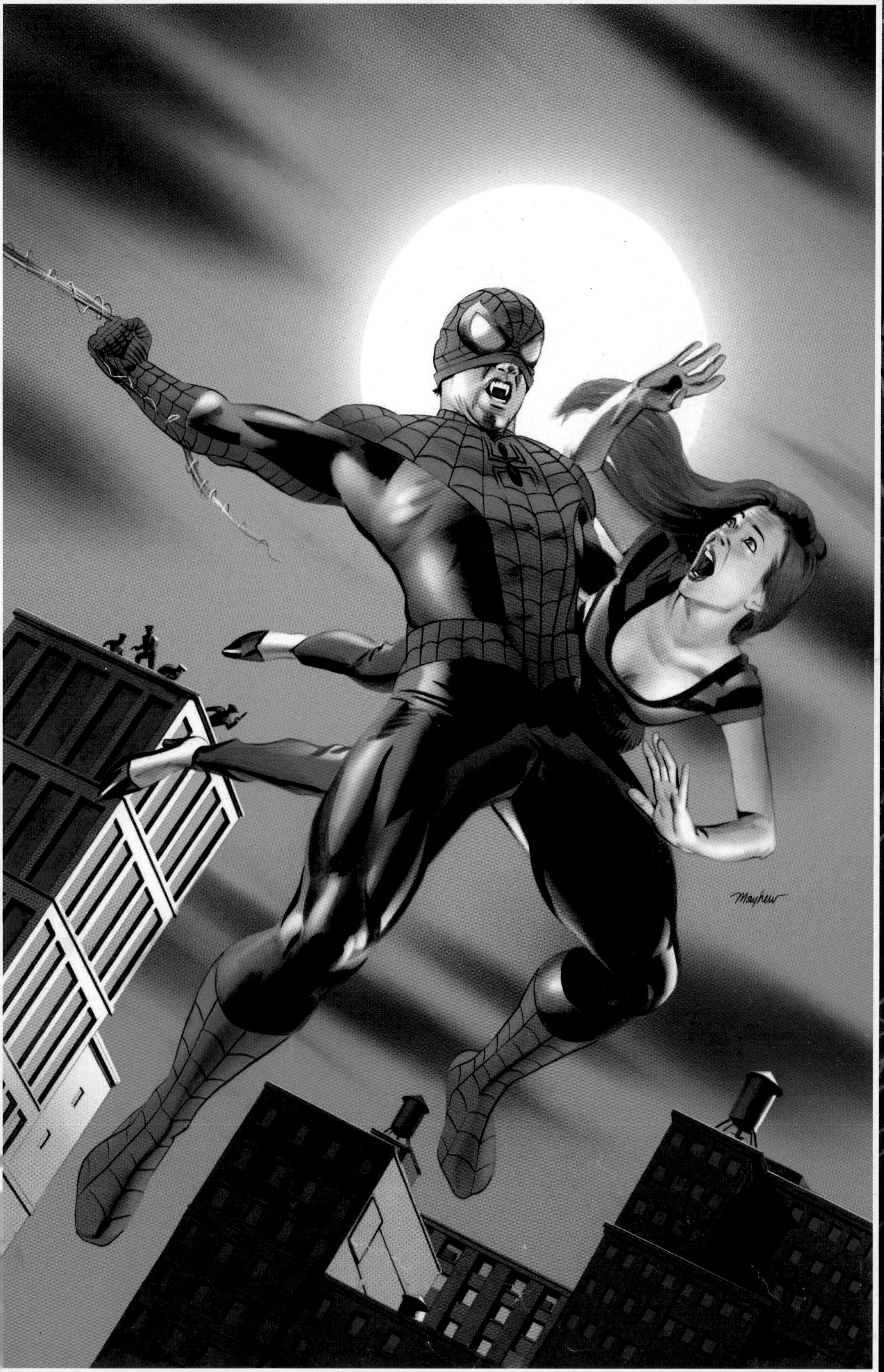
mayhew

AMAZING SPIDER-MAN #646 VAMPIRE VARIANT
COVER BY MIKE MAYHEW

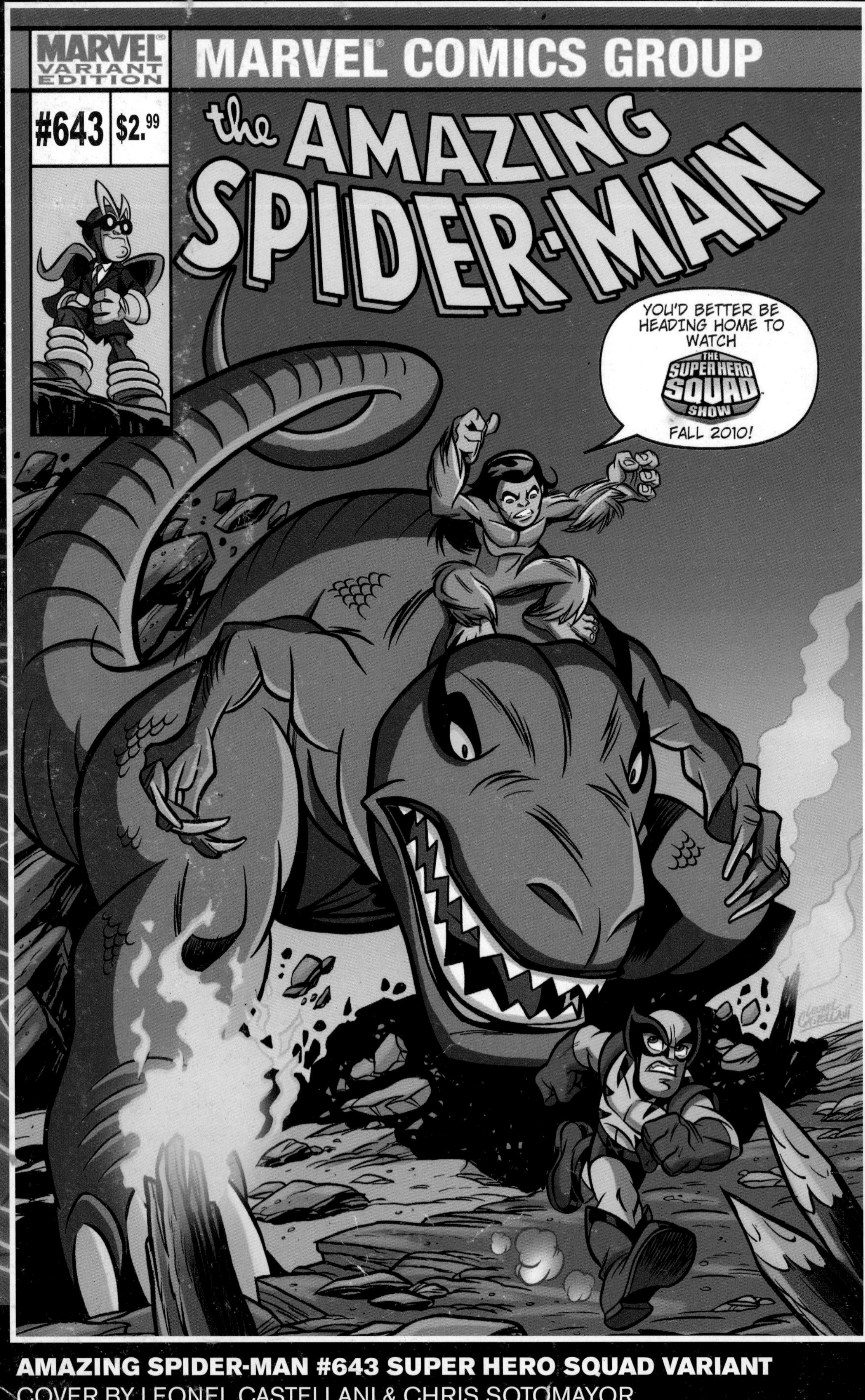
MARVEL VARIANT EDITION
MARVEL COMICS GROUP
#643
$2.99
the AMAZING SPIDER-MAN
YOU'D BETTER BE HEADING HOME TO WATCH THE SUPER HERO SQUAD SHOW FALL 2010!
LEONEL CASTELLANI

AMAZING SPIDER-MAN #643 SUPER HERO SQUAD VARIANT
COVER BY LEONEL CASTELLANI & CHRIS SOTOMAYOR